Coming to Narrative

Writing Lives
Ethnographic Narratives
Series Editors
Arthur P. Bochner & Carolyn Ellis
University of South Florida

Writing Lives: Ethnographic Narratives publishes narrative representations of qualitative research projects. The series editors seek manuscripts that blur the boundaries between humanities and social sciences. We encourage novel and evocative forms of expressing concrete lived experience, including autoethnographic, literary, poetic, artistic, visual, performative, critical, multivoiced, conversational, and coconstructed representations. We are interested in ethnographic narratives that depict local stories; employ literary modes of scene setting, dialogue, character development, and unfolding action; and include the author's critical reflections on the research and writing process, such as research ethics, alternative modes of inquiry and representation, reflexivity, and evocative storytelling. Proposals and manuscripts should be directed to abochner@usf.edu

Volumes in this Series

Coming to Narrative

A Personal History of Paradigm Change in the Human Sciences

Arthur P. Bochner

Routledge
Taylor & Francis Group

LONDON AND NEW YORK

First published 2014 by Left Coast Press, Inc.

Published 2016 by Routledge
2 Park Square, Milton Park, Abingdon, Oxon OX14 4RN
711 Third Avenue, New York, NY 10017, USA

Routledge is an imprint of the Taylor & Francis Group, an informa business

Library of Congress Cataloging-in-Publication Data:

Bochner, Arthur P.
    Coming to narrative : A personal history of paradigm change in the human sciences / Arthur P. Bochner.
        pages cm.—(Writing lives ; 14)
    Summary: "Reflecting on a 50 year university career, Distinguished Professor Arthur Bochner, for-mer President of the National Communication Association, discloses a lived history, both academic and personal, that has paralleled many of the paradigm shifts in the human sciences inspired by the turn toward narrative. He shows how the human sciences—especially in his own areas of interper-sonal, family, and communication theory—have evolved from sciences directed toward prediction and control to interpretive ones focused on the search for meaning through qualitative, narrative, and ethnographic modes of inquiry. He outlines the theoretical contributions of such luminaries as Bate-son, Laing, Goffman, Henry, Gergen, and Richardson in this transformation. Using diverse forms of narration, Bochner seamlessly layers theory and story, interweaving his professional and personal life with the social and historical contexts in which they developed"—Provided by publisher. Includes bibliographical references and index.
        ISBN 978-1-59874-037-0 (hardback)—ISBN 978-1-59874-038-7 (paperback)—
        ISBN 978-1-61132-775-5 (institutional ebook)—ISBN 978-1-61132-767-0 (consumer ebook)
        1. Bochner, Arthur P.   2. Social sciences—Study and teaching (Higher)—United States—History.   3. College teachers—United States—Biography.   I. Title.
    H62.5.U5B63   2014
    300.92—dc23
    [B]   2014000363

ISBN 978-1-59874-037-0 hardcover
ISBN 978-1-59874-038-7 paperback

Cover Designed by Karen Scott-Hoy

Contents

For Carolyn Ellis,
rose of my heart

Acknowledgments

Living a university life for the past fifty-one years brought me into contact with many creative and resourceful professors, colleagues, and students who supported, encouraged, and shaped my teaching, research, and writing. My rhetoric professor at Syracuse University, Dan Smith, showed me the pleasure that could be realized from close readings of texts and taught me the importance of editing. "There is no such thing as good writing," he insisted, "only good re-writing." David Kettler, my office mate at Syracuse, introduced me to Carl Rogers, Abraham Maslow, and Rollo May and expressed steadfast confidence in my potential as a scholar and teacher. My mentor at Bowling Green, Raymond Tucker, was an inspirational teacher and unpretentious scholar who taught me to cherish life as a professor. His enthusiasm and passion in the classroom was contagious, and he displayed a humble spirit and intellectual humility that is all too rare in the academic world.

As an assistant professor, I was fortunate to strike up friendships with Gerald R. Miller and Mark Knapp, pioneers in the field of interpersonal communication. Later on, in the first handbook in communication and rhetorical studies, John Waite Bowers, Sam Becker, and Carroll Arnold gave me wide latitude to synthesize and integrate significant ideas on interpersonal relations across the human sciences. I began a series of intense dialogues with Dwight Conquergood shortly after arriving at USF in 1984. Dwight inspired my turn toward ethnography and exemplified the good that could come from the ethical, political, and dialogic commitments of performative and critical ethnography. I hope my experimentation with genre-bending modes of expressing lived experience can serve to perpetuate the memory of his enduring contributions to communication and performance studies.

At Bowling Green, Vince DiSalvo and Ed Mabry provided companionship and spirited conversation about social science research. Another of my cohorts in graduate school, Janet Yerby, became my coauthor and good friend. She was a constant source of empathy, love, and emotional support during the darkest days of Brenda's illness.

At Temple University, Herb Simons mentored me through the faculty ranks, treating me like a loving brother and showing unwavering support and respect for my ideas and work ethic. I deeply value the memories of our many evenings of long and loving intellectual banter in which we played at work and worked at play, sharpening our aptitude for irony, paradox, and dialectic. I prize our lifelong friendship. I met Eric Eisenberg at Michigan State and recruited him to Temple, where we became friends and colleagues. The quickest study I know, Eric is an unremitting jammer who combines good humor with unparalleled administrative skill. He and Lorie Roscoe are part of our extended family. During the golden days at Temple, I was blessed with great students. I want to acknowledge the stimulation and validation provided by my doctoral students at Temple—Linda Eagle, Mary Anne Fitzpatrick, Carol Gifford, George Gum, Dorothy Krueger,Ken Leibowitz, Dory Segal, and Teri Thompson; and especially Bill Rawlins, one of the great storytellers and teachers in my field. Bill taught me the meanings (and dialectics) of friendship in and out of the classroom. You rock, Bill.

I wrote the majority of this book over seven summers at our cabin in Franklin, North Carolina. Our neighbors, Doug and Ardie Stanley, took a special interest in my project (as well as my flower garden). Doug passed away two summers ago. I miss him immensely. At USF, my chair over most of the last years, Ken Cissna, provided institutional and moral support for my project as well as companionship at USF basketball games. Charles Guignon, Daryl Fasching, and Jim Paul became interdisciplinary narrative colleagues who greatly enhanced my understanding of narrative identity, narrative ethics, and narrative methodologies. Charles read early drafts of several chapters and expressed appreciation for my experimentation with genre-bending forms of expression. Thank you, Charles, for keeping our conversation going. I also benefited from conversations and correspondence with Michael Bamberg, Rita Charon, Douglas Flemons, Mark Freeman, Ken Gergen, Ruthellen Josselson, Michal Krumer-Nevo, Maya Lavie-Ajayi, Amia Lieblich, and Richard Zaner at different stages in the formation of this project. I also want to express my gratitude to colleagues at the annual Qualitative Congress for their companionship and support of my work as well as for promoting and embodying the life of storytelling. In particular, I thank Tony Adams, Keith Berry, Shirley Drew, Stacy Holman Jones, Ron Pelias, Chris Poulos, Judith Preissle, Pat Sikes, and Sophie Tomas for taking risks and championing the cause of personal narrative and autoethnography.

The USF Communication Department has been my university home for the past thirty years, providing a safe haven and fertile environment in which to teach unorthodox courses and engage in unconventional writing. I am grateful for the opportunities I was given at USF to live the dream of developing a genuinely qualitative PhD program. My life has been enriched beyond words by the gifted and caring students who have studied here. I want to express my gratitude to the students in the twelve seminars on Narrative Inquiry that I have offered since 1990 and, in particular, to Christine Kiesinger, Tim Simpson, Deborah Austin, Lisa Tillmann, Zhong Wang, Matthew Brooks, Elissa Foster, Cara Mackey, Tony Adams, Andrew Herrmann, Dionel Cotanda, and Rachel Binns Terrill. The stories you wrote in those courses deepened and expanded my understanding and appreciation for narrative, as did your probing and evocative dissertations. I thank Nathan Hodges and Toni Powell-Young for their diligent attention to the details of bibliography, Tony Adams for his precise work on the index, and Nick Riggs for keeping me up to date on the ever-expanding narrative literature.

As drafts of the chapters of this book began to take shape, I called on colleagues across the field for feedback and advice. Tom Frentz read a first draft of two chapters in 2007 and invited me to Arkansas to give a colloquium on the project. Thank you, Tom, for your friendship, superb editing skills, and enthusiasm for writing candidly about university life. Bill Rawlins, Joyce Hocker, Tony Adams, and Chaim Noy made valuable comments on early chapters. In the last weeks of his life, Bud Goodall insisted on reading as much of the manuscript as I was willing to send. Bud identified with the stories, reminiscing about the early days of our academic lives and rekindling my motivation to complete the project. Norman Denzin read a first draft of the whole book and provided the emotional affirmation I needed to press on. Thank you, Norman, for your critical intelligence, kindness, relentless pursuit of social justice, and the high standard you set for a democratic community of scholars.

Karen Scott-Hoy went through several chapters and came up with a clever idea for the cover. Thank you, Karen, for the aesthetic touch you brought to this project.

Laurel Richardson provided wise counsel through the entire writing process and especially when the project was nearing completion. I am grateful to Laurel for urging me to keep writing about the hard stuff. Every writer needs a friend and reader like Laurel.

Lisa Tillmann served as an editor par excellence, pointing out the redundancies and exhorting me to keep the story moving. This is a better book as a result of Lisa's care and resolve for uncluttered writing.

David Epston graciously took time away from training for his bicycle tour to help me polish the prose to "its utmost lustre." Thank you, David, for your caring and perceptive comments and for championing the cause of literary and embodied writing in the human sciences.

Mitch Allen is my dream publisher. How did I get so lucky? Mitch took a chance on Carolyn and me seventeen years ago, and I repaid him by taking seven years to finish this book. Throughout all the lulls in my writing, Mitch remained fervent in his belief in me and in this project. When I finally delivered a draft, his response was so confirming that I asked for an additional three months to improve the product. I love you, Mitch.

I also want to acknowledge the significant contribution of the team at Left Coast Press and Straight Creek Bookmakers, especially Jason Potter and Josephine Mariea. I am grateful for their careful attention to detail, staunch support of the project, and tenacious labor in bringing the book into its final form.

Carolyn Ellis lived through the entire seven years with me. There are survivors, darling! You are my muse, my most ardent supporter, and loving critic. You showed me how to bring together my heart and my head. Thank you, Carolyn, for your tender, generous, and loving support of this project, for so willingly accepting a place for this project in our life, for your conscientious feedback on every draft, and for being such a great dog mommy. You catch every nuance in my expressions and make me feel understood. It's so much fun to grow older with you. Now you can come out from under my desk, Zen, and off your bed, Buddha, where you've waited patiently for me to finish (with only an occasional bark). It's time to play and run in the woods.

Credits

The author expresses his thanks to the following for permission to reproduce lyrics.

Lyrics excerpted "Born To Run" and "Backstreets" by Bruce Springsteen. Copyright © 1975 Bruce Springsteen, renewed © 2003 Bruce Springsteen (ASCAP). Reprinted by permission. International copyright secured. All rights reserved.

Lyrics excerpted from BRAIN DAMAGE & ECLIPSE
Words and Music by Roger Waters
TRO-© Copyright 1973 (Renewed) Hampshire House Publishing Corp., New York, NY. Used by Permission

Lyrics excerpted from SPEAK TO ME
Music by Nicholas Mason
TRO-© Copyright 1973 (Renewed) Hampshire House Publishing Corp., New York, NY. Used by Permission

Lyrics excerpted from TIME
Words and Music by Roger Waters, Nicholas Mason, David Gilmour, and Rick Wright
TRO-© Copyright 1973 (Renewed) Hampshire House Publishing Corp., New York, NY. Used by Permission

American Pie
Words and Music by Don McLean
Copyright © 1971, 1972 BENNY BIRD CO., INC.
Copyright Renewed
All Rights Controlled and Administered by SONGS OF UNIVERSAL, INC.
All Rights Reserved   Used by Permission
Reprinted by Permission of Hal Leonard Corporation

Preface
On the Road to Meaning

> The elusive pleasure to be found in writing is in following the
> drift, inkling your way toward meaning.
> *Patricia Hampl (1999, p. 222)*

August 2013

We are nearing an end to another summer in the mountains of Western North Carolina. The burning bushes that border our property are showing the first signs of their slow transformation to the tantalizing red hues of fall. The dogwoods, sourwoods, and maples have started turning already. It unnerves me to see the trees and plants changing so early this year. I feel anxiety rolling through me as I anticipate trading the tranquility of a mellow summer in the mountains for the frenetic tempo of university life in Tampa, Florida.

Each morning my partner, Carolyn, and I pour a cup of freshly brewed coffee into one of our favorite, one-of-a-kind ceramic cups. We signal that "it's time" to our two dogs, Buddha and Zen, open the cabin door, and begin our ritual stroll through the flower garden. The dogs dart down and around the mountainside, following their own ritualized exploration of the smells and sounds of nature. From a short distance away, we watch them sprint across various paths we've shaped through our property as they bark at nothing in particular except perhaps the joy of Being and freedom of play. On some mornings, Carolyn and I attend to plants in need of special care—pruning, weeding, staking, trimming, and/or feeding; on other mornings we land on the old wooden swing near the foot of our long, steep driveway. Sitting close to each other, we breathe in the cool mountain air. We sink into a relaxed posture, keeping one eye on the dogs, the other on a panoramic view of nearby and far-away mountains, and feel a stillness we rarely experience in our everyday lives as professors.

The grandeur of these tranquil mountains reminds us of our cosmic insignificance, of the sweetness, mystery, and beauty of this world, and how fragile, incomplete, and powerless a person can feel in the midst of it all. Turning toward Carolyn, I recognize the wistful look on her face. We've talked about these moments before, how these aged mountains evoke memories of friends and family we've lost and prompt awareness of the uncertain future we ourselves face. There is no escaping the essential human paradox of living "out of nature and hopelessly in it" (Becker, 1973, p. 26). We take care not to allow the gravitas of this existential dualism to paralyze us, reminding each other that "the secret of sanity is to exaggerate the good of the world" (Henry, 1971, p. 438).

11

Eventually we pull ourselves away from the hypnotic trance these mountains induce and return to the cabin. Each of us prepares and carries a bowl of cereal topped with fresh blueberries and shelled black walnuts out to the deck, where we eat our breakfast against a backdrop of trills, warbles, and whistles of bluebirds, yellow finches, and hummingbirds. I can't say why we ever leave this scene, but somehow we do manage to drag ourselves away to our work stations, as we kiddingly call the regions of the cabin in which we write. Old habits are hard to break.

Today I carry my second cup of coffee up the stairs and across the landing to the sacred space of my home office. It's a wide, open room with an L-shaped desk nestled in the corner of a rectangular loft that sits above our kitchen. To the south I can view the tree-lined mountain ridge of Flowers Gap hanging over Cowee Mountain. To the north, out the window next to my desk, I look down upon our flower garden. In early spring I keep watch on a dozen multicolored rhododendron bushes in full bloom, dotting a landscape of beds of just-awakened but not yet budding crocosmia, bearded-irises, and day lilies. By June, the garden takes the form of a deep, flamed invitation to the hummingbirds and butterflies, and they lustily feed on the sweet nectar of the cardinal plants, crocosmia, bee balm, and gladiolas throughout the summer months.

Most of the flower beds have died back now. They foretell our imminent departure, acting as though they know we'll be leaving soon. I think of them as performers in need of an audience. Peering out the window, my attention is drawn to the tall crepe myrtle that is just starting to throw its bright red flower buds. I recall how tiny it was when I planted it in 2007, the same summer I started writing this book.

At the time, I thought I had a good plan. My goal was to produce a unique text on narrative inquiry. I wanted to make sense of the rapid development of narrative research that blossomed in the 1980s and grew stronger in the 1990s. By early in this century, narrative had achieved the status of a genre of inquiry, taking root in the consciousness of qualitative and interpretive researchers across the human sciences. As Denzin and Lincoln (2000, p. 3) observed, "now, at the beginning of the 21st century, the narrative turn has been taken." By 2007 this turn toward narrative and storytelling research had swept across the human sciences, producing a host of new fields dedicated to narrative inquiry and narrative practices: narrative anthropology (Behar, 1996; Jackson, 1989, 1995, 2002; Myerhoff, 1978; D. Rose, 1993; Turner and Schechner, 1988), narrative gerontology (Kenyon, Clark, and De Vries, 2001), narrative medicine (Charon, 2006; Charon and Montello, 2002), narrative psychiatry (Coles, 1989; Schafer, 1981a, 1981b, 1994; Spence, 1982), narrative psychology (Freeman, 1993; Lieblich and Josselson, 1997; McAdams, 1993, 1997; Sarbin, 1986), narrative sociology (Richardson, 1990; Loseke, 1992; Maines, 1993; G. Becker, 1997), narrative therapy (White and Epston, 1990; Parry and Doan, 1994; Lieblich, McAdams, and Josselson, 2004), narrative ethnography (J. Bruner, 1987; Van Maanen, 1988; D. Rose, 1993), narrative pedagogy (Witherell and Noddings, 1991), history as narrative

(H. White, 1981, 1987), narrative and the law (J. B. White, 1985; Bellow and Minow, 1998; Brooks and Gewirtz, 1998), and wounded storytelling (Kleinman, 1989; Couser, 1997; Frank, 1991, 1995). I wanted to produce a book that would unify and draw connections among the diverse perspectives on narrative scattered across the human sciences. I had in mind something akin to what Ernest Becker (1973, p. x) once called "a throbbing, vital center," a synthesis that would merge competing viewpoints into a larger, inclusive framework, one that could bring a sense of community and common purpose to narrative inquiry. The fragmentation of narrative knowledges and the insularity of the many disciplines producing it gives the impression that narrative inquiry lacks a unifying vision or even a sense of solidarity among its practitioners. I wanted to try to open up lines of communication that could harmonize what was fast becoming a vexing corpus of isolated, divergent, and compartmentalized knowledge.

I realize how audacious such a project must sound. But I didn't think of it that way. My attention had been fixed on narrative for nearly twenty years, and I felt primed to take on the challenge. So I sat down in this very chair, at this very desk, in front of the computer that now sits to my right as a backup in case my new laptop gives out, and I began. Across the desk, I scattered reprints of three handbook chapters and a theoretical essay on narrative and interpretive social science that I had published between 1985 and 2002 (Bochner, 1985, 1994, 2002b; Bochner and Waugh, 1995), syllabi and course notes from doctoral seminars on narrative inquiry that I had offered every two years since 1991, and a pile of folders containing copies of groundbreaking essays on narrative across the human sciences (e.g., E. Bruner, 1986; J. Bruner, 1987; Crites, 1971, 1986; Freeman, 1998; H. White, 1980). At the foot of my desk, I stacked most of my extensive library of texts (e.g., Polkinghorne, 1988; Rosenwald and Ochberg, 1992; Sarbin, 1986) and scholarly books on narrative, including the pioneering monographs by Behar (1996), J. Bruner (1986, 1990), Carr (1986), Coles (1989), Denzin (1996), Kerby (1991), MacIntyre (1984), Ricoeur (1984–1988), Sacks (1987), and Taylor (1989), as well as other important philosophical volumes related to the crisis of representation and deconstruction of the correspondence theory of knowledge that helped inspire the narrative turn (Clifford and Marcus, 1986; Foucault, 1970b; Gadamer, 1975; Lyotard, 1984; Rorty, 1979, 1982a, 1989).

Getting Going

"Start with a story," I tell my students when they're struggling to introduce an essay or begin a lecture. I decided to follow my own advice. After all, shouldn't a book on narrative begin with a story? Narrative can be a dense, cerebral, and complicated topic, and I didn't want to lose readers straightaway by immersing them in a pool of murky and obscure terminology. Better to let them dunk their toes before they dive in. My aim was to gently invite readers to go on a voyage with me, one in which we would be discovering and making something together.

If this book was to have value, it would need to create a spirit of dialogue and connection between the reader and me. I figured that the best way to do this was to allow my readers to know something about me before they committed to the journey. Putting myself in the place of the other, I asked this: If I were a reader, what would I want to know about the author, my guide? I realized I would want to know the source of his inspiration, why this project matters to him.

What inspired my turn toward narrative? How did I move from facts and graphs toward meanings and stories? Starting to write the story of how I came to narrative, I worked under the assumption that I knew the answer and only needed to tell it. After a series of false starts, however, I learned that this was not the case. The question I had posed was more complicated than I originally thought. How does one get to the bottom of things, the time and place where something began, the source of the initial kick, and how it evolved from there? Every time I thought I had located the starting point, I recalled a meaningful event that had preceded it. I felt as though I were in the middle of an infinite regress. The apparent certainty with which I had begun turned swiftly into a muddle of confusion and uncertainty.

Did my turn toward narrative begin when I read Walter Fisher's monograph "Narration as a Human Communication Paradigm" (1984)? Or was it initially inspired by MacIntyre's *After Virtue* (1984), Sarbin's *Narrative Psychology* (1986), or Coles's *The Call of Stories* (1989)? The more that I contemplated the question, the less certain I became. The books and articles surrounding me as I worked made matters worse. Remembering my first reading of each of them transported me back in time. It was as though I were opening a scrapbook or old photo album and discovering that each clipping and snapshot elicited vivid memories from the past. The books and monographs were embedded in a larger context of lived experiences that was returning to my consciousness in flashes of memory, signaling something larger and more important. I realized that when I initially stumbled onto the early "classics" associated with narrative inquiry other events were going on in my life—personal and emotional experiences as well as professional and academic ones.

Suddenly it dawned on me that I may have been attributing too much significance to academic literature and not enough to my own personal experience—stories passed down by my family of origin; immersion in working-class and Jewish culture; socializing coaching of teachers and mentors; unexpected heartbreaks and disappointments; uplifting connections to students, friends, and colleagues; the thrills and letdowns of an academic life (career); twists of fate and chance; history and destiny. These flashes of memory momentarily dazed me, but when I regained my composure I realized I had been on the wrong track, looking in the wrong places. My awakening to narrative had a longer history, a context of personal and academic lived experiences that had readied me to turn toward narrative. I needed to let go of the intellectualized, academic voices in my head and pay more attention to the bigger picture that these episodic memories were

14

bringing into focus. Before I knew what was happening, the book I had started to write—the one I had planned—had morphed into a different book, a more personal, embodied, and autoethnographic one.

Now I had a book project in search of a subject—well, not exactly. I would be the subject. I had just completed my thirty-fifth year as a professor. Most of my working life had been spent in the classroom, the research laboratory, and the field. From the time I was five years old until now—more than sixty years—I've lived a life (primarily) in school. I've occupied both sides of the desk, initially as a student, then as a teacher, a professor, and a writer. Over the course of this life, teachers, mentors, and other professors whom I admired shaped my values and meanings. I took my turn too, affecting the lives of numerous students through mentoring, teaching, and publishing my work; and lifelong connections to some of these students continued to shape and influence me. I held an administrative post as chair of a department for eight years, chaired major divisions and interest groups in national and international academic organizations, served as an associate editor of numerous refereed journals in several different fields, and was elected president of the largest professional organization in the discipline of communication. I've written and edited books and journals; published articles, monographs, and chapters; delivered keynotes; and received teaching, service, and research awards.

So what? What did this life mean? What did it feel like? What did I learn from it? How has it changed over the years? How have I changed over the course of time and by means of these experiences? What might other academics—students, professors, administrators—take away and use from entering stories of my experiences?

These questions fascinated and intimidated me. I had no models to follow. There was little literature to review. The risk of failure was abundant. Still, I felt that a close examination of my life as a communication student and professor, conveyed via the warmth of storytelling, would be worthwhile if it could reveal hidden assumptions of an academic life, express some of the joys and disappointments of "a life in school" (Frentz, 2008; Tompkins, 1996), show connections between the personal and the academic, gain greater respect and appreciation for history and context, and open a conversation about what can make such a life a good and satisfying one.

These weren't entirely new concerns for me. For many years, I'd listened to students in my department's Introduction to Graduate Studies in Communication course raise these and other related questions. They've wanted to know what makes a professor's life meaningful; how they can turn what they most care about—their passions—into research projects that matter; how to maintain their enthusiasm and optimism in the face of the pressures and stresses of publishing and the indignities of the "job market"; whether professing is a job, a career, or a way of life; and what kind of personal life they can expect to live as a professor—will it be worth the struggle?

Thinking about these issues, I was reminded of an evocative little book writ-ten by the anthropologist Dan Rose, *Living the Ethnographic Life* (1990). As I reached to retrieve it from my bookcase, I imagined various ways that I could inhabit the memories swirling through my mind and treat them as though they were the "objects" of an ethnographic research project. Of course, I didn't begin my life in the academic world as an outsider. I was not a stranger intending to live for a time in an exotic or unfamiliar culture, and I didn't simply go native and never return. But there is a sense in which one's "career" as a graduate student or a newcomer to a departmental faculty is an ethnographic adventure akin to join-ing a conversation that preceded entry and will continue after that person leaves the scene, a venture into sense making for which one lacks suitable preparation. If one didn't begin with an ethnographic sensibility, couldn't he still apply an ethnographic eye retrospectively?

That must be why Rose's book came to mind. Rose (1990) bemoans the failure of academics to recognize themselves as living within a subculture that resides inside university life—a social system within a system. He believes that we academics lack an adequate understanding of our own subculture and its embodiment within the larger culture of university life as well as the culture of "disciplinary" or professional life. Insofar as "we do not talk about this in pro-foundly self-critical ways" (p. 17), Rose observes, our lack of awareness is both disturbing and ironic. Though we are taught to be analytical and critical, we rarely turn our critical acumen on ourselves—our disciplinary, institutional, and ritual practices; the received traditions we inherit; our modes of socialization, rules of conduct, methodological dictates; and conventions of writing and publishing (Bochner, 2012; Pelias, 2004).

As I re-embarked on this project, I knew that I wanted to use narrative inquiry to address the deficits Rose (1990) identified. I also wanted to cross disciplinary boundaries and different "ways of knowing" by producing a text that blended and bent various genres of representation, including performative modes of writing, edifying storytelling, essays, layered accounts, reviews of literature, and fictional dialogues. I would use genres of autoethnographic representation as a critical lens through which to view my own academic subculture, tracking my experiences over time retrospectively and consciously interrogating them (Ellis and Bochner, 2000; Bochner, 2012). I would tell stories taken from life—my life—and subject them to contemplation. What happened or appeared to have happened—can we ever "know" what really happened?—would be the raw material, but what I make of it or what it comes to mean to you, my readers, would matter most.

Blanding In/Stepping Out

As I started writing the stories in this book, I was reminded that this wasn't the first time I'd thought of writing about my experiences as a university professor. In the early 1990s, I came across several of David Lodge's novels (1975, 1984,

1988) in which he portrayed the characters roaming the halls of universities as lively, prickly, and funny, and revealed how entertaining it can be to hang around academics (if you don't take them as seriously as they sometimes take themselves). Taking a comedic view of university life, Lodge inserted an assortment of professorial characters into hilarious yet believable messes that rang true. Over the course of my academic life, I'd encountered many of these characters: the wishy-washy; the thin skinned; the pushy, vain, and egotistical; the overly ambitious; as well as those merely going through the motions. Taking advantage of the freedom and flexibility of fiction, Lodge gave a sympathetic and heartwarming portrait of university life, poking fun at our flawed human nature without ignoring the humiliations that an academic life can provoke. It was these books, which I read more than fifteen years earlier, that first planted in my mind the idea of writing an academic autobiography.

When I returned to the faculty in 1992 after spending eight of the previous ten years as chair of my department, I began to draft a manuscript based on notes I had taken over the previous decade. My working title was *Tales Out of School: Confessions of a Department Chair.* As the manuscript began to take shape, however, I got cold feet and stopped abruptly. What I was writing felt too close to the bone, too risky, likely to do more harm than good. Still, something deep inside kept hounding me: It's not time yet, but don't forget about it. Let it simmer awhile, I thought.

In 1996 I began to write "Narrative and the Divided Self" (Bochner, 1997), a genre-bending tale that folded the story of my father's sudden death into a narrative depiction of the epidemic of "institutional depression" proliferating in universities. Longing to include a review of first-person accounts written by seasoned professors in the human sciences, I searched for personal narratives that focused on academic life and quickly located two edited volumes of academic autobiography (Berger, 1992; Lee, 1993). In Berger's (1992) collection, twenty prominent and well-connected scholars were invited to tell how they became sociologists and to provide students with "a sense of the *presence* of the theorist in the text" (p. xiv); whereas in Lee's (1993), thirteen narrative psychologists (but only two women) presented consciously reflexive tales centered on how their careers had evolved as well as how writing their autobiographies had affected them. On the whole, both of these works fall within the boundaries of "collaborative autobiography," a genre of life writing that "offers the opportunity to tell aspects of a personal story under carefully controlled conditions in which not too much damage can be done" (Popkin, 2001, p. 798) and that spreads "an all too visible safety-net for its participants" (p. 799).

In his review of Berger's volume, Tilly (1993) grumbled about the contributors' muted passion, uncritical commentary, toned-down accounts of conflict, and reluctance to express disapproval of disciplinary practices. Amused by the uniformity and standardization of their accounts, he bemoaned how these sociologists "seem to have blanded in" as though they were seized by a compulsion for modesty and propriety on the order of "Don't stick out your neck; cover your ass" (p. 504).

The inhibitions reflected in the accounts of these renowned, mainstream sociologists, mostly males, were not representative of academics, particularly women, living at the margins of their disciplines. As I continued my search, I came across first-person accounts of five women academics who refused to mute their anger or hide the messiness of their academic lives (Gornick, 1996; Heilbrun, 1997; Krieger, 1996, 1997; Richardson, 1997; Tompkins, 1996). Their stories testified to a deep despair, rage, loneliness, and unhappiness in their institutional lives. Three of them ended up retiring early; two never held a permanent faculty position. The riskiness of this kind of institutional self-criticism could hardly be more apparent.

In *Fields of Play,* Laurel Richardson (1997) composed an academic autoethnography that exposes insidious departmental politics in which vulnerable faculty members attempting to innovate or adopt unconventional research and writing practices can be "buried" or "eaten-alive" (p. 186). For her, a "field" can be an open, inviting, and nurturing region, but it also can become a combat zone, a war theater, or an obstacle course that polices boundaries, obstructs change, and shuts out nonconformists by attempting to impose a single standard for assessing the forms and practices of legitimate social research. Richardson's pain and rage is palpable as she paints a menacing and revolting picture of how life is lived in some large, elite sociology departments, where university administrators seek "to eliminate all obstacles to those whose will to power has met with success" (p. 212).

Echoing Richardson's complaints about the cutthroat competiveness that typifies many university departments, Jane Tompkins (1996) described the workplace in universities as "a kind of war zone" in which faculty members build up resentments and antagonisms that never get discussed because nobody is doing any social and emotional housekeeping. She also portrayed university life as a life lived in prolonged isolation. "Nobody has to talk to anybody, because none of what college teachers do *depends* upon anybody else," writes Tompkins (1996, p. 186). Instead of striving for the ideal of an academic community grounded in a continuing conversation, the university had turned into a battleground of belligerent careerists protecting turf, seeking notoriety, and competing for limited resources. Tompkins called attention to the effects these practices have on students. In the absence of community and harmony among faculty, how can students help but learn what our institutions of higher education are modeling: competiveness, hierarchy, and isolation (p. 194)?

At the age of forty-six, having spent more than forty years in school, either as a student or a professor, Tompkins (1996) concluded that "school is no longer the place for me." Though she pointed to the university's disregard for the inner lives of students as her chief concern, Tompkins left little doubt that she is one of those (former) students whose real-life concerns have been neglected. Reading between the lines, I found almost everything that Tompkins says about how universities are failing students—by ignoring skills that are needed to cope with things that will be coming up in their lives; by showing indifference to their emotional, physical, and spiritual lives; by implicitly teaching them not to feel or respond from the source of their own experience; by servicing the intellect at the expense of the heart and the imagination; and by training them for a career without considering how that training contributes to the development of an integrated person, that is, to living a full life—can be extended to how universities are failing their faculties. In other words, the university is not a nurturing environment; it pays little or no attention to how its workers—the faculty and staff—feel or to the reality of their private lives and the skills they need to negotiate the connections between academic and personal life.

Obviously, not everyone sees the academic world the way Laurel Richardson and Jane Tompkins do. Many professors have no interest in establishing an emotional bond with students. Many others believe that their work is to exercise the intellect, not the heart, the spirit, or students' emotions. Only a few feel prepared to bring feelings and personal experiences into the classroom. Given the pain and suffering she was feeling, Tompkins's early retirement is hardly a surprise. I imagine that she awakened one day and said she'd had enough, concluded that "you can't beat the establishment. They're too ensconced." She likely didn't possess the lunacy or belligerence of Howard Beale in *Network,* sticking his neck out the open window and screaming, "I'm mad as hell and I'm not going to take it anymore!" So she wrote her book and walked away quietly.

Staying On

I wasn't wired to walk away. That's not a choice that appealed to me, though I don't begrudge the decision Tompkins made. In an earlier book, *West of Everything,* she drew on the words of Amy, the just-married bride played by Grace Kelly in *High Noon,* to express her contempt for the kind of symbolically violent "academic lynchings" that she had witnessed at academic conferences (Tompkins, 1992). "I don't care who's right or who's wrong," Amy pleads. "There's got to be a better way for people to live." Amy wants to leave town because she can't bear the thought of Kane, her partner, being lynched and her becoming a widow. But Kane, the former town marshal, decides to stay and fight against all odds because he believed it was the right thing to do, and he knew the outlaws would come after them. Running away wouldn't change anything. At the sound of the first shot Amy changes her mind. She realizes that she can't so easily walk away from what she loves.

Neither could I. Tompkins's (1996) concern for the inner lives of students; her determination to show that teachers, scholars, and students think *and* feel *and* have bodies; her resolve to insert the reality of private life into instruction and research; and her appreciation of the importance of embedding lived history in a narrative in order to show "what it was like for us to be alive and going through the world" (p. xv) resonated with me. As a full professor with tenure, I thought the right thing to do was to stay and take up the intellectual, ethical, and emotional challenge Richardson (1997) put forward, to rethink and restructure the human sciences and the universities in which they are housed—to try to make them more human. This approach—staying and trying to change things—appears to be uncommon. Tompkins left, as did Richardson and Rose. The university was no longer a significant source of affirmation and meaning in their lives.

Over the course of my academic life, I've heard the sounds of insinuations, innuendos, and invective of which Tompkins speaks, and I've felt the hurt borne of some of the kinds of exclusion and discrimination that wounded Richardson. Still, I resist the temptation to demonize the university, which is, after all, an abstraction. We are the university, or at least a major part of it. Take away all the professors (and students), and there is no university. Their power requires our submission in order to work. I can tell you stories about how discouraging, upsetting, and hurtful my life as a professor has been. But I can also tell you stories about how engaging, nifty, amusing, and uplifting it has been. Indeed, my own views are much closer, though not identical, to those of Geertz (1995), who described his life as an anthropologist as an indefinite and unsettling quest but "an excellent way, interesting, dismaying, useful, and amusing, to expend a life" (p. 168).

An Autoethnographic Experiment

In 2007, during my year as president of the National Communication Association (NCA), I experimented with an autoethnographic approach, attempting to foster a critical dialogue centered on various institutional practices within the discipline of communication as well as the influence of the growing corporatization of universities on our teaching and research. I used the space allocated to me in *Spectra*, the official NCA newsletter, to compose op-ed columns on various institutional practices that rarely get discussed openly. My intent was to invite conversation and controversy about the everyday, often institutionalized, practices of communication professors. In "Things That Boggle My Mind," I lamented the degradation of standards of civility in the classroom due largely to the rapid development of technologies of distance and the absence of rules for their use. In "Resisting Institutional Depression," I pondered the causes of burnout and sadness etched on the faces of so many midlife academics and the demoralization and demonization that arise as a result of the divide between administration and faculty. "The Case Against the Anonymous Culture of Peer Review" was my attempt to show that the double-blind system of peer review in academic journals is a socially constructed idea that doesn't necessarily achieve its intent of quality control due to reviewer fatigue, possible corruptions and delays in process, and the ironic absence of empirical validation of its practices.

I never imagined that I would touch a nerve in so many readers. These predominantly first-person accounts produced dozens of responses over e-mail and many requests to be reprinted in college and university newspapers. Some people in my field asked for permission to include various segments in memos to deans and other academic administrators. One was even reprinted in a refereed journal (Bochner, 2008). This was the most serious fun I'd experienced as a writer over the course of my academic life. The fruit of academic self-examination was ripe for the picking.

Encouraged by these affirming responses, I decided to trust my perception that I had tapped into feelings and consciousness that were deeply submerged in the lived experiences of academics, both relative newcomers and seasoned veterans. I saw an urgent need for reflexive self-criticism of the discipline of communication, the functioning of the human sciences, and the life we call "academic." During the summer of 2007, before I knew precisely which way this project was heading, I composed first drafts of three stories of formative experiences in early periods of my life without imposing a set agenda on the direction in which they were pointing. A few months later, I delivered portions of two of these stories as a public lecture at the University of Arkansas, used parts of another in a graduate seminar, and sent copies of the stories to a few colleagues and friends, inviting feedback and critical commentary. I also read over the drafts repeatedly, trying to figure out precisely what I was doing: In what genre was I working? Was this memoir, autobiography, autoethnography, ethnography, critical theory, or what? Did it matter what I called it? I was setting scenes, creating dialogue, and emplotting stories. Was this social science, nonfiction, or fiction? Did it matter if I was straddling the lines of these categorical imperatives? Could I maintain a meaningful and believable storyline through a longer series of episodes? Who was my audience? Where was this project heading?

This time, I followed Patricia Hampl's (1999) advice. In *I Could Tell You Stories*, her poetic account of the challenges and dilemmas of writing about one's own memories, she draws attention to how writers ought to use first drafts to help them find the subject of what they are writing, "what it wants to be about" (p. 29). Following her counsel, I listened closely to what the drafts themselves were telling me as well as what my friends, colleagues, and students were saying. I discovered that Hampl also was right when she said, "the heart ... is the boss" of this show (1999, p. 29). I was writing about things I really cared about, things that were close to the bone of my humanity, emotional feelings as well as ideas, and I wanted to touch not only readers' minds but also their hearts.

In Cahoots

When I write a research monograph, an essay, or a story, I imagine an ideal reader. In writing this book, I visualized different ideal readers at different times. After all, this book was written over a period of seven years. That initial ideal reader is seven years older now, and so am I.

One of my ideal readers is an inspired and thoughtful graduate student who is drawn to qualitative research, narrative inquiry, and storytelling. This reader is curious about the qualitative revolution in the human sciences or already attracted to it and wants to better understand the historical context in which it emerged. As a graduate student, this reader is coming under the influence of mentors and getting introduced to various ideas, methods, theories, and perspectives on the field. This can be both an exciting and confusing experience. There is little agreement on the precise nature of the discipline, exactly where it came from, or where it's going (Bochner and Eisenberg, 1985; Craig, 1999; Deetz, 1994; Delia, 1987). How does a student make a choice among epistemologies, theories, and methods and between ontological assumptions about work in the human sciences? Will one have to make iron-clad commitments to intellectual or methodological doctrines? This student also may be asking, "Where do I belong in this discipline?" and "How do I make myself fit into this world we call academic?"

Of course, the challenges of formulating an academic identity are not limited to graduate students. These questions continue over the course of an academic life—before and after tenure and in the lives of "contingent" faculty as well. Each of us is tugged in different directions; we have split allegiances, divided selves, different callings. Is it ever too late to change? Thus, another ideal reader is a person on the faculty who may be struggling to maintain passion about research and teaching: Does my work still have meaning? Or am I an alienated worker? Am I just going through the motions? How can I get my mojo back? Am I called by obligation or inspiration?

A third ideal reader is a person intrigued by genre-bending. This person understands the academic persona as a kind of performance, and life in a department or discipline as a drama. Yearning to play their parts differently—off script—and disturbed by pressures to conform to the received traditions of the discipline, this reader is open to the charming possibilities of representing research in new, genre-bending forms that can move the discipline away from purely academic discourses toward creative writing and spiritually edifying storytelling, which can dissolve or bridge boundaries between humanities and social sciences. These genre-bending enthusiasts are unafraid of breaking away from the familiar and may see themselves as writers rather than reporters. They care about how life gets expressed and communicated and want to read and tell stories with emotional urgency.

A fourth ideal reader is a person who came to an academic discipline with an agenda, a political ideology, an important cause, and ethical and moral commitments. To be useful and respectable, the human sciences must come to grips with social and moral problems, work on behalf of social justice, embrace a democratic epistemology, and strengthen our capacity to care (Frankfurt, 1988). This reader can appreciate one of the ideas central to this book: that our work in the human sciences, our teaching and research, is a way of dealing with our lives, our times, and our culture.

A fifth ideal reader is a lived-experience junkie. This reader recognizes that life is saturated with predicaments and contingencies—losses, traumas, illnesses, disappointments, deaths—twists of fate and chance, and drawn to stories that show what it feels like to be alive. We can't build a human science on a foundation of prediction and control because to do so would make it necessary to ignore too much of life. This reader wants to be taken into the raw materials of life, replete with naked emotions; to view lived experiences from different angles; to witness people troubled and trying to make sense of the fixes in which they've found themselves; to witness happenings and the feeling truths they spawn. The writer has to prove trustworthy and brave to this reader, willing to write things they may not want to write—embarrassments, fears, secrets, shames. Lured more by questions than by answers, this reader is wary of excessively smooth, neat, and well-ordered narratives. Life is messy, riddled with gaps, contradictions, and discontinuities. Our stories about life necessarily are incomplete and open to revision (Ellis, 2009). Dealing with life is more important than explaining it.

Actual readers need not conform to any of these ideals. As Coles (1989) observed, "Every reader's response to a writer's call can have its own startling, suggestive power" (p. xix). And that's what I'm hoping for: that you and I—reader and writer—will be "in cahoots" (p. 64), that you will allow yourself to get close to the story, and that my story will animate yours.

CHAPTER ONE

Drifting Toward
an Academic Life

Narrative Legacies

> I don't seek to tell the best story. I seek to tell a story that once was.
> I seek to fill a place that once had meaning with meaning again.
> *Bonnie Rough, "Writing Lost Stories" (2007)*

"I'm Ray Tucker. I'll be your PhD advisor, at least temporarily," the professor says, motioning me into his office. "Come in and sit down here next to my desk."

He's wearing a gray suit and narrow, maroon tie, and his slick black hair is combed straight back off his forehead from ear to ear. Immediately I'm conscious of my ratty-looking jeans and T-shirt. My long, unkempt hair covers my forehead in the front and crawls down my neck in the back. I sit, crossing my legs tightly to prevent them from shaking.

"I'm honored to meet you," I say. "I thought I'd stop by to introduce myself while I'm in town."

"I'm glad you did, so we can get acquainted and get you ready for your first term."

He has a broad, handsome face, a grin both inviting and natural. I appreciate his effort to relax me, but it doesn't soften my edginess. His strong voice resonates with self-confidence, and when he speaks he looks directly into my eyes as if he's trying to look through me. I think about what one of my graduate student cohorts at Syracuse had told me: "Tucker's the professor you'll want to study with at Bowling Green. His dissertation at Northwestern was directed by Donald Campbell, who wrote the definitive book on experimental design. He's one of the top empiricists in the field." He also warned that "Tucker has no tolerance for bullshit. He's a quick study and very demanding."

"What course will you be teaching in the fall?" I ask.

"I'm offering Communication Theory," he responds. "I've just finished a sabbatical at Harvard, where I was introduced to cybernetics and systems theory [Bertalanffy, 1969; J. Miller, 1978; Weiner, 1954]. I want my class to dig into these areas."

I've never heard of systems theory or cybernetics. I don't want to expose my ignorance, but I better say something. "That sounds interesting," I mumble, hoping he doesn't ask me precisely what I think is interesting about these topics.

"So you think you may want to take my course?"

"Yes, I do." I say, assuming *no* is not an option.

"I'm glad to hear that, Art, but a little surprised too," he says, flickering an inviting smile my way. "I saw where you had coached the debate team at Syracuse University, and I know that department is strong in rhetoric and public address." His comment makes me aware that he's already checked into my background. I worry what that could mean: *Doesn't he want me to take his class?* His cheerful grin contradicts the challenge implied by his words. *Maybe I should follow his lead, be frank and direct*

"I did take mostly rhetoric and public address courses at Syracuse," I admit, "and I did well in those courses, but I'm thinking of going in a different direction for my PhD."

"Why?"

"Frankly, I'm tired of studying dead orators, which is mostly what we did in rhetoric and public address courses. Rhetorical criticism was challenging, but I never felt as though I cared enough about the speakers or the issues. They seemed important to my professors, but they didn't speak to my life." *I'm startled by my own words. I've just dismissed the vast majority of what I had studied during my master's degree.*

"You mean public address didn't touch you where you live?"

"That's right, it didn't," I acknowledge, wondering precisely what he means.

"Well, if it's any consolation, I felt the same way when I was in graduate school. At Northwestern, they made me take a number of courses that weren't meaningful to me. I recall complaining to my advisor about it."

"What did he say?"

"He told me to find something that mattered to me and devote myself to it. That's what got me through the highs and lows of my PhD program. So I give the same advice to my students. I tell them to find something they're passionate about." He pauses and then looks me in the eyes again. "How about you, Art? What do you really care about?"

So much for casual conversation. No beating round the bush for Ray Tucker. Our first conversation, and he wants to know what really matters to me. The question he posed would haunt me for a long time: What did I care about? Why was I here? How did I get to this place at this time?

Narrative Inheritance

My father emigrated from Eastern Europe in 1920, one of more than two million Jews who came to America in the first quarter of the twentieth century (see Cohen and Soyer, 2008; Howe, 1976). When he arrived with his father and two

26

brothers at Ellis Island, Dad was eleven years old, penniless, and spoke no English. His father—my grandfather—went to work as a huckster, peddling fruits and vegetables by horse and buggy. Already poor in "the old country," my father's family confronted new forms of cultural and social impoverishment. Stigmatized by the Yiddish jargon he spoke, the odd clothing he wore, and the dirty home environment in which he lived, my father internalized deep-seated feelings of inferiority and social awkwardness that he never overcame.

A childhood of deprivation, humiliation, and discrimination took its toll. I recall stories my father told about being easily deceived and tricked by classmates. "'Greenhorn, greenhorn,' they would tease, and in the winter they'd throw snowballs and make fun of me," he told me. "Greenhorn" was used derogatorily to refer to immigrants who couldn't speak English (Cohen and Soyer, 2008). "We were considered ignorant, uncultured, and gullible."

There was more than a grain of truth to one of my father's favorite little jingles: "When I was young and in my prime I wasn't worth a single dime." At school he felt like an outsider; at home he was pressured to grow up fast and help support a family of seven riddled in poverty. "When I turned sixteen, my father insisted that I get a job and bring some money into the family," he told me. "I dropped out of high school after tenth grade and started working full time. I learned quickly that companies like Heinz and Westinghouse wouldn't hire Jews. I had to lie on applications in order to pass as gentile at work. I lost my job at Westinghouse because I called in sick over the High Holy Days. When I came back, they fired me for no other reason but being Jewish."

I was born in July 1945, about the same time that news began to spread about what the Allies were finding in the European countryside: wagons full of corpses in Dachau; half-dead and sick survivors in the small camp at Buchenwald; hundreds of dead bodies lined up in front of the ruined buildings at Nordhausen; open mass graves at Bergen-Belsen (Brink, 2000; Caplan, 2009). The extent of the Nazis' extermination camps, their solution to "the Jewish problem," boggled the mind. It took a person's breath away even to imagine such sadistic and cold-blooded acts of brutality and evil.

Though he rarely spoke in detail about his childhood or about the Holocaust, my father taught us that hatred and persecution of Jews was common and widespread. As the son of working-class, Jewish parents, growing up in the aftermath of the Holocaust, I heard countless stories of unbearable suffering, poverty, and sacrifice. As a youngster, these stories baffled me. I felt terrible about how much suffering the people of my father's generation and the Jews in the Holocaust had endured, and I had no doubt that Jewish people had been persecuted for centuries. Nevertheless, the schools I attended were populated mainly by Jewish children, and we lived in a predominantly Jewish neighborhood that was protected for the most part from any explicit exposure to anti-Semitism. Ironically, as one of the poorest families in the neighborhood and one of the few headed by a father who worked with his hands—my father was a self-employed sign painter—we felt singled out and looked down upon not only by Gentiles but also by the wealthier Jewish people who surrounded us. In retrospect, I see now that "greenhorns" like my father were doubly persecuted. They were not only ostracized by a mainstream culture that felt threatened by a scale of poverty never seen before in America but also by the middle-class, assimilated Jews who saw the impoverished Jewish immigrants as an embarrassment and worried that these uncultured immigrants would inspire a new wave of anti-Semitism (Baum, Hyman, and Michel, 1976).

I grew up not knowing where I belonged. A child is supposed to feel at home in his family, but I didn't. Quite often, my parents spoke Yiddish around the house, whereas the three of us—my brother, sister, and I—never learned more than a few Yiddish expressions. Early on, my parents tried to instill in us a moral and religious Jewish sensibility. For ten years, I attended Hebrew School four days a week (after regular school hours) and Sunday school on the weekends. There I learned to read Hebrew fluently and gained thorough exposure to Jewish traditions and history. But the progressive reforms taking hold in the secular world of the Jewish community in which we lived did not reinforce what I was taught at the Hebrew Institute about being a Jew. Many of the Jews in Squirrel Hill, where we resided, were only marginally Jewish. They didn't go to synagogue on Saturdays, adhere to Jewish dietary restrictions, or insist on a traditional Jewish education for their children. While my parents clung stubbornly to the traditions and doctrines in which they had been raised, the majority of Jewish people in my neighborhood aligned with new forms of Jewish identity that made it easier for them to move freely and inconspicuously within the non-Jewish culture in which they were immersed. They still professed to being Jewish, but theirs was a low-profile Judaism. Eventually, my parents yielded to the pressure, abandoning any attachment to the restrictive doctrines of Orthodox Judaism.

I was comfortable identifying myself as Jewish, yet I felt alienated and different from most of the other low-profile Jewish children at Taylor Allderdice High School. They wore nicer clothes, lived in bigger and more attractive homes, and got driven to and from school in expensive new cars. At school, I felt different from the other kids—poorer, less at ease with myself, more Jewish. At home, I also felt out of sync—my parents belonged to a different time and culture. My brother was five years older, and my twin sister and I too often felt more like rivals than friends. I didn't want to be like the other kids at school, but I didn't want to be like my parents or siblings, either.

My father passed down the despair of growing up poor, insecure, and out of place. His life revolved around work—hard, tiring, exhausting work. Ironically, working was the one pleasure he'd encountered in life. He showed little interest in recreation, leisure, or play. After all, he had witnessed the consequences of anti-Semitism and endured the Great Depression. These weren't abstract concepts; they were lived experiences etched on his body and submerged in his unconscious. In order to survive, he shut himself off from the risk of exposure to outside influences. If he felt an obligation to his children, it was to prepare us for the harsh realities of life. When he made himself available to us, which wasn't often, he would tell stories about the hardships endured in the "old country" and the deplorable conditions in which he and other Jewish immigrants began their lives in America.

By the time I was a senior in high school, I had heard the same family stories over and over again, and the tragic lessons of these stories had taken shape within me, however unconsciously. The moral of these stories was to be prepared to face discrimination, injustice, and suffering. Life was a problem and a struggle, not a mystery or adventure. I should expect to suffer, to fall, to face setbacks and make sacrifices. Work is what gives meaning to life. After you fall, you can rise again through hard, honest work and self-sacrifice.

I admired my father's ability, integrity, and self-discipline, but I didn't want to live a life anything like his. I felt terrible about the scars he carried from his childhood and respectful of the life he had toiled to make for himself and for us. As I grew older, I realized it was important not to forget that these events had occurred and the pain and suffering my parents' generation had endured. Fortunately, I never had to face the loneliness, isolation, and estrangement that my father must have felt at every turn. But unfortunately, this difference drove a wedge between us. There simply was no way to transform my parents' memories into my experiences. The world I was growing up in was not the same world my parents had encountered and remembered, the one that had shaped their meanings and values. My parents, especially my father, seemed to be in a perpetual state of high anxiety, just trying to get by, waiting for the next shoe to drop. They experienced little joy and showed only marginal commitment to anything other than hard work, sacrifice, and a few remaining Jewish traditions. My father often referred to himself as someone who "worked like a slave." Unwittingly, he equated work with coercion and sacrifice, and he made a clear distinction between work and play even while showing a loving attachment and commitment to his work. "You can't play today—you have to work," he would say. In fact, I can't recall ever seeing him in a playful or kibitzing state.

I didn't want to be a slave to work. As a kid, I loved to play and hated to work. I enjoyed a good belly laugh and took great pleasure at using my wit to make other people laugh. Was there any work that could also be play, fun, or enjoyable? Would work always feel like a form of slavery and coercion, or could one love work as much as play? Could work be play? Must work always be riddled with contradictions? What choices were open to me?

An Audacious Project on the Urge for Meaning

One day, shortly after the start of my senior year in high school, I was browsing books in the library and picked a copy of Albert Camus's *The Myth of Sisyphus* (1955) from the shelf. Turning to the first page, I read,

> There is only one great philosophical question, suicide. Deciding whether life is worth living is to answer the fundamental question of philosophy.

Those first two sentences startled me. What makes life worth living? If this was the question fundamental to philosophy, then I wanted to be a philosopher. I felt as though Camus had seen through me, uncovering the deepest feelings and fears rumbling beneath the surface of my consciousness. Would I always feel like an outsider, unlike my parents but also different from the kids in my neighborhood with whom I grew up? In high school, I felt pressure to conform, but I never felt at ease with other kids, and my feeble attempts to fit in often ended in humiliation or shame. The social world of high school felt meaningless and alienating. I didn't like or respect most of the other kids, so why was I trying to be like them? I didn't want to spend the rest of my life feeling so far apart from what surrounded me, but I didn't know what to do to feel more immersed and authentic. What made a person's life meaningful and worth living?

I decided to write my senior thesis on Camus, an audacious choice for a seventeen-year-old, but one I eagerly embraced. When I thought about Sisyphus perpetually rolling a rock up a hill, I began to understand my father's attachment and commitment to work in a new light. For the first time, I could appreciate the satisfaction he drew from his work. My father chose to throw himself passionately into his work in order to resist alienation, fear, and meaninglessness. Even if there was no rhyme or reason to the course of his life, he still could do something meaningful. He could work hard every day, do his best—paint beautiful signs— and exceed his clients' expectations. He could keep the ball rolling up the hill.

"One must imagine Sisyphus happy," wrote Camus (1955), because he continues to struggle to achieve new heights. This is what "fills one's heart," a human being deciding to rise above the pointless struggles of life by accepting rather than denying his plight. "Life may be tragic and absurd," I wrote in my thesis, "but it need not be faced with pessimism or misery, not if one gains awareness that life has value in its own right. Sisyphus understands the futility of his situation, yet still expresses an intense passion for life, which makes it possible to imagine him happy. He recognizes that the only real thing is human experience."

For Camus, all that was real—all that could be known—was what one could feel in his heart or touch in the world. There is no truth beyond experience. Every attempt at cosmic explanation is a threat to freedom. Sisyphus accepts the absurdity of his fate without reservations, acknowledging that the experience of living is all that can give life meaning, not some leap of faith designed to relieve him of the burdens of his own life. Sisyphus finds meaning in "the struggle itself." He is not heroic but ordinary, a mythic figure representing the fate everyone must endure. His struggle—the one we all face—is a defiant battle against meaninglessness. We cannot know why we are here or what cosmic meaning the universe possesses. Fortunately, we don't need answers to these questions to make our lives meaningful. It is what we create ourselves, what we experience and do, that gives meaning to our lives. As George Cotlin (2005, p. 228) observed in *Existential America*, "In this world, all that defines us as human, all that connects us to humanity or to the human condition, is our willingness, no matter the odds,

30

to stand up for something. Only by such a commitment do we push away the absurd, if only for a moment. And only by such a commitment do we escape the imposition of alienation and find human solidarity."

Camus gave me a framework for thinking about the connection between death and life. My only prior exposure to ideas about death and dying had come through my Hebrew education. I didn't know what to believe. In Sunday school, my teachers taught that good Jews were God-fearing and that a Judgment Day would come, implying that the soul survives death. Beyond these lessons, though, I had only the vaguest notion of an afterlife or transcendent experience. Until I read Camus, I hadn't thought seriously about death. I knew that the Orthodox Jews in our synagogue prayed energetically, pleading for forgiveness for their sins. But the ritual of Jewish repentance involved praying to be entered in The Book of Life. The whole point seemed to be to live as long as you could. Was death God's way of punishing those who refused to repent? Was faith simply a way of hedging one's bets in the face of uncertainty about an afterlife? Without the certainty of death, would religious faith even exist?

The specter of death haunts the characters in Camus's novels. They approach death not as an abstraction that draws attention to faith or an afterlife but rather as concretely particular to each person, a source of personal suffering that concentrates one's attention on how to make the most of life *now*, in the moment one is living. These characters learn that there is no verifiable meaning beyond life, no explanation for the death and suffering endemic to the human condition. Humans are endowed with an urge for meaning, but the world does not provide it. In *The Stranger* (Camus, 1946), Meursault struggles toward an openness to "the benign indifference of the universe" by purging himself of the illusions of a future life even in the face of his own impending death. In *The Plague* (1947), Dr. Rieux teaches that the healer's work is never done because there is no final victory to be won over senseless evil, disease, and terror. One can only work to keep memory alive and struggle to be a healer. The world outside the self is silent. Thus, each of us lives without the comfort of verifiable meanings. We must come to grips with the chaos, uncertainty, and brutality of life—evil, hatred, violence, disease, war, discrimination—without the expectation of a grand narrative of eternal truth(s).

The Cultural Context of the Sixties

"Philosophy isn't practical," my father insisted as I packed to go away to college. "What can you do with philosophy?"

"I'll look into other possibilities," I promised, realizing I had no answer to his question. I had a lot of growing up to do, and the kind of philosophy to which I'd been attracted appealed to the troubling questions one would expect to be circulating through an eighteen-year-old kid. I was trying to figure out what mattered to me, what could give my life meaning, and what I was meant to be or do. College seemed the ideal place to ask these questions. I wasn't thinking about

31

a career or a place to work for the rest of my life; I wanted to be able to relate to other people and grasp on to a purpose that could sustain me.

I left for college in August 1963 with no notion that the winds of change were about to gust through American life like a tornado blowing across a Kansas farm. When I arrived on campus, "My Boyfriend's Back" was near the top of the record charts, and I looked forward to the weekend shindigs where we worked up a frenzy dancing uninhibitedly to "Louie, Louie." When I graduated in January 1968, I was getting high and listening to Jimmy Hendrix's electrifying blues/rock jams or, in mellower moods, the soothing psychedelic songs of the Moody Blues. In 1963, the Beatles burst on the scene with three hit songs, "She Loves You," "I Want to Hold Your Hand," and "I Saw Her Standing There"; by 1968, they had recorded "Revolution," "Day Tripper," and "Lucy in the Sky with Diamonds."

In November 1963, less than three months after I began my college education at California State College in Pennsylvania, President Kennedy was assassinated. At the time, John Kennedy personified my generation. As the youngest man ever elected president, he became an icon of youthful passion, enthusiasm, and zest for life. His campaign promise to carve out a "New Frontier" led to the development of the Peace Corps and the Alliance for Progress, programs that encouraged young people to commit themselves to voluntary, nonmilitaristic foreign service aimed at promoting world peace and friendship through greater cross-cultural understanding between Americans and people of other countries. The Kennedy administration was the first in my lifetime to consider the need for civil rights legislation imperative. The Democratic Party marketed Kennedy as "a profile in courage," and in his public life he came across as dashingly handsome, masculine, articulate, poised, intellectual, and brave. Kennedy represented the zeitgeist of his time. Retrospectively, he appears to have formed a seamless bond with the culture of the sixties—sex, drugs, rock 'n' roll, and a rebellious voice of idealism and cultural change (Perret, 2001). Like much of the youth culture he came to represent, though, Kennedy was a romantic ruled by adolescent cravings he couldn't—or didn't want to—control.

In August 1963, the same month I left for college, two hundred thousand black and white demonstrators, led by Dr. Martin Luther King, marched on Washington in a nonviolent protest that called attention to racial inequalities; the suffering of black Americans victimized by white violence, especially mob beatings; and the burning of homes and churches in the South. Two months after I graduated, in April 1968, Dr. King was assassinated in Memphis. Sixty-two days later, Robert Kennedy was murdered during a press conference held to celebrate his victory in a primary election in California. This frightening succession of assassinations was accompanied by a burgeoning skepticism about the efficacy of American institutions and their leaders that formed a gorge between generations, referred to as "the generation gap." Notable scenes remain etched in the memories of those of us who lived through and witnessed the turbulence of the 1960s: the chaos of urban riots, the fear and anger on the faces of protestors beaten back by masked police spraying fogs of tear gas; the defiant seizure and control of campus buildings by students issuing clarion calls for change in curricula and the educational process; the flowering of a counterculture of "hippies" representing the ideals of peace, love, and creative energy but also embodying an orgy of permissiveness, free sex, and mind-expanding, psychedelic drugs that symbolized a rebellion against "establishment" values, a refusal to obey authority, and a desire for self-exploration and self-expression; and the televising of America's first unpopular war that brought to our living rooms, if not to our lives, haunting images of killing fields and atrocities of violent combat in Vietnam, Laos, and Cambodia while protestors pleaded to "give peace a chance."

Feeling Alive

Prior to leaving home for college, I had never spent any significant time away from my parents. One summer, my parents shipped me off for two weeks to a summer camp. On several other occasions, I stayed overnight at the home of one of my cousins. That was it. You could say that my parents sheltered and protected me, though I doubt whether my confinement was due to a master plan. Obviously, my parents were not worldly or cosmopolitan. I can remember only one vacation that we took together as a family, and rarely did we venture beyond a fifteen-to-twenty-mile radius from our residence. Mostly we just stayed home—day and night. Ours was the middle house in a row of five connected two-story homes. On most days, including Saturdays and Sundays, my father worked in his shop, which was located in the basement of our little 950-square-foot home. Privacy didn't exist in such a small place, where the five of us seemed always to be bumping into each other or getting in each other's way. I felt as though I were living in a closet, a place without elbow room, a suffocating space in which I couldn't breathe my own air.

Going away to college felt like being let out of jail. But it also felt hazardous, as though I were walking alone in the woods on an unfamiliar trail without a map. Which way do I go? Where am I headed? What danger lurks? For the first time nobody was watching—no shadows hovering over me, nobody asking me to account for my whereabouts. I was responsible for myself.

Freedom came with constraints. I was paying my own way, and that meant rising at six in the morning to serve breakfast in the college dining room, work that earned me 70 cents an hour. I had saved enough money to pay tuition, room, and board, but I had no funds left to buy books, school supplies, or clothes; or to have fun on the weekends, which, in the context of the sixties and my adolescent urges, seemed every bit as important as the other stuff. So I took a job as a waiter and a dishwasher—breakfast, lunch, and dinner—on time and overtime, though the long hours meant missing some classes and being half asleep in the ones I did attend.

I floated aimlessly from one major to another—biology, English, speech education—barely escaping dismissal due to bad grades. Truth be told, I wasn't ready for all the freedom. I'd never had so much fun, so many friends, and so little monitoring. I was getting an education, but it wasn't in the liberal arts or sciences; it was an education on feeling alive; developing an awareness of myself; exploring my desires, sensations, and sexuality; and figuring out what I valued. Though work as a waiter and dishwasher meant longer days and less sleep, I felt more energetic and full of life than ever. After a while, it dawned on me that now I was responsible for how my life was going and how it would go in the future. This realization was not all that comforting insofar as it shattered the illusion that I could go on blaming my parents for whatever went wrong in my life. I was supporting myself; making my own decisions; choosing where to go, with whom, and when; deciding what was important to study, think about, or value. Certainly there were things I couldn't control, would never control, but at least I could choose a direction to take.

Psychology 101: Scientists as Storytellers

The seeds of my academic destiny were planted in my consciousness for the first time in two courses I took during my sophomore year. The first, Psychology 101: Introduction to Psychology, was taught by an unconventional and eccentric professor, Dr. John Brammer. Standing about six-foot-four, Brammer towered over the class. His face was longer than it was wide, and his protruding angular jaw seemed to be dragging his skinny, narrow nose downward. He would constantly brush back his floppy, light brown hair with his extensive, thin fingers to keep it out of his eyes. A smile seemed to be permanently etched on his face, and when he got excited his green eyes would widen, his arms would flail wildly, and his voice would reach a fever pitch. On most days, he wore a blue or black turtleneck sweater, faded jeans, and tennis shoes. His presence compelled attention. When he entered the classroom, you could hear a pin drop.

Brammer referred to himself as an "antipsychologist." It wasn't that he didn't love his subject matter; indeed, he described psychology, especially the human mind, as full of wonder, mystery, and surprise. But he was a student of the history of psychology, and that history showed, according to Brammer, that darker, egotistical motives had driven psychologists to move in the wrong direction. Brammer's passion for his subject was evident every day of class, but so was his distaste for psychology as a discipline. "Professionalization is ruining psychology," he grumbled. "Psychologists worry too much about their careers and status in the field and pay too little attention to what psychology really ought to be about."

Most of the course focused on two famous psychologists, Wilhelm Wundt and Sigmund Freud. Brammer identified Wundt as the founding father of psychology, the person who made psychology a science by establishing an experimental laboratory for studies of sensations and perceptions. He pointed out, however, that Wundt did not conform to the orthodox vision of psychology as a science of *behavior*; instead, he considered *experience* to be the essential subject matter of psychology.

"Who is in a better position to observe an experience than the person having the experience?" Brammer asked, driving home the thesis of several of his lectures. "Psychology needs to respect personal experience and the significance of subjectivity. Wundt pioneered introspection as a research method for accessing mental processes. Though introspection was applied in hundreds of studies supervised by Wundt, or conducted at his laboratory, the scientific merit of introspection as an objective method of inquiry eventually became controversial and contentious."

Brammer insisted that psychology made a big mistake when it turned away from the centrality of experience and the method of introspection, allowing behavior and behaviorism to trump human experience and meanings. "It was very political!" Brammer shouted, pounding his fist on the podium. "You see, psychology wanted to establish itself as a unique and independent *scientific* discipline and to distinguish itself from philosophy, physiology, and biology. That was the reason the early behaviorists, such as John B. Watson, pleaded for psychologists to reject all subjective methods, especially the method of introspection. They wanted psychology to become a purely objective experimental science akin to the natural sciences (Watson, 1913). Their goal was to enable psychology to achieve a place at the trough by gaining status and credibility as a science. Watson's manifesto urged psychologists to rid themselves of the baggage of consciousness and take up residence as an objective science of behavior."

I could see from the pained expression on his face that Brammer was agitated by what had happened to his beloved discipline of psychology. He left no doubt that he admired Wundt and despised Watson. But why he was making such a big deal of this controversy puzzled me. Nevertheless, the way he told the story kept me on the edge of my chair. I wanted Wundt to win the day, though I realized that he was already dead when Watson came on the scene.

Brammer convinced me that psychological processes were rife with subjectivity. Psychology wasn't psychology if it limited itself only to observable behavior and never took an interest in the inner life of an individual. When I considered my own psychological processes, I dwelled on my thoughts, motives, and inner feelings. Why would psychologists want to purge themselves of the very things that made psychology significant and interesting? Did they really believe that consciousness didn't exist, that it was an illusion?

Brammer explained the whole vexing controversy as a case of academic politics. "Consciousness exists," he exclaimed, "and nobody can reasonably deny that the mind is active, aware, and creative. The problem was the murkiness of consciousness. If psychology was to become a true science, it would have to clean consciousness out of the cupboard."

I felt disappointed when Brammer informed our class that the behaviorists had triumphed over the introspectionists. But I was glad to see that he refused to let the issue rest there. Instead, he predicted that Wundt's reputation would someday rise from the ashes of behaviorism's condemnation of subjective processes. "You see," said Brammer, lowering his voice respectfully but widening his eyes for emphasis, "Wundt was way ahead of his time. He saw that psychology would never be able to explain the phenomena of religion, social practices, or language if it operated independently of the other human sciences and refused to move beyond the individual. Wundt understood that cultural influences sometimes exceed psychological ones. Thus, late in his life he turned to folk psychology, devoting the last twenty years of his work to the study of religion, myth, and folklore, phenomena which he classified as higher mental processes. Expressing sympathy for ethnographic inquiry and the methods of folklore research, Wundt [1954] argued in *Volkerpsycholgie* that the influence of culture would have to be taken into account if psychology was to produce a full and unified account of human psychological processes" (Cole, 1990; Moll, 1992).

Toward the middle of the semester, Dr. Brammer introduced our class to his favorite psychologist, Sigmund Freud. "Dr. Freud was a genius," beamed Brammer, leaving no doubt about his reverence for the man. "He was a rigorous scientist and a masterful storyteller, an archaeologist of the mind and a poet of the unconscious."

Brammer took us through a number of Freud's famous cases, quoting liberally from texts he brought to class and working himself into a frenzied exhortation on Freud's brilliance. I found it difficult to follow all the new terms that Brammer introduced to us, but the idea of the unconscious excited and fascinated me. Freud saw each person as a civilization in her own right. If you dig deeply into your past, you will eventually find buried treasures—at least I wanted to think of them as treasures. Brammer kept insisting they were demons that needed to be exorcised, disturbing memories and experiences never forgotten but locked away. Even if they were demons, however, when brought into the waking mind they would lose their control over your life.

I thought of my father and his past. What demons were buried in the cave of his unconscious? How were these memories controlling him? Is that why he was prone to sudden fits of rage? What about me? What secrets lurked in the recesses of my unconscious? The notion that psychoanalysis could reveal secrets about you that you didn't know yourself intimidated me. Still, I also found the idea irresistible.

Some of the students in the class argued with Dr. Brammer. They weren't convinced that Freud's insistence on the importance of repressed sexuality was on target, and they adamantly alleged that some accidents are just accidents, nothing more. Brammer listened patiently and continued to defend the premise that there are no accidents. "Slips of the tongue, jokes, dreams, myths—all of these have hidden and purposeful meanings," he asserted. "We learn about ourselves by treating these things as pieces of a puzzle we are trying to solve. It's not easy, and it takes time. When you analyze a dream you place it in a new context, which becomes a point of departure for making sense of the fragments. You try on different interpretations, go deeper and deeper, until what was hidden in the symbols reveals itself. Of course, there is always another interpretation, another possibility. There is no final truth one can achieve. It's like buried ruins examined by an archaeologist: the civilization was there; now it's gone. All you can do is try to reconstruct it. You assemble the evidence—rebuild the structure—until it takes form and makes sense. But you never really know for sure that it's true."

The material we read on Freud didn't grab me. The textbook was tedious, and I didn't see why we had to memorize such obscure terminology. But when I came to class and Brammer began reciting one of Freud's cases, his passion and enthusiasm as well as the psychological mysteries that each case unraveled mesmerized me. The cases resuscitated the abstract concepts, breathing life into Freud's mysterious theoretical ideas. As I listened to the stories, I found myself drifting off into thoughts about the past, my connection to my parents, my own sexuality and erotic desires, and mystifying dreams that disturbed or puzzled me.

At night, Brammer's words circulated through me. I could see him standing erect, thrashing his arms about, and repeating the Freudian mantra over and over: "We are all entangled in the past, we just don't know it. Most of us keep repeating ourselves as we journey through life. We keep ending up at the place we're trying to escape from." What did this mean? Is life a game in which one keeps circling back to where one started? Freud seemed to be saying that digging up and talking about the past is the best way to discover what one wants and, thus, to have any hope of a promising future.

Several students in the course were psychology majors who took a dim view of Freud's stature as a psychologist. During one memorable class session, Brammer boldly referred to Freud as the greatest psychologist who ever lived. "I don't understand how you can say that," came a disbelieving male voice from the back of the room who turned out to be one of the psychology majors. "Freud may have been a physician, but he was no scientist," the student continued. "I mean, as far as I can see, Freud's method was storytelling, his interpretations were subjective, and each case had a uniqueness that defied any attempt one could make to replicate it. You can't test Freud's concepts. I mean, really, you can't observe the unconscious directly. Every dream is open to many interpretations, and the number of cases on which he based his theory is not only incredibly small but most of his patients were screwed up women who had suffered horrendous trauma. You can't generalize these cases."

A hushed silence fell over the class as we awaited Dr. Brammer's reply. Had Freud been knocked off the pedestal on which Brammer had placed him? Would Brammer take this student's remark as an insult? Would he exert the power of his position? Slowly the professor walked down the aisle until he stood only a couple of feet from the skeptical student. "Fred—that's your name, right?" Brammer began.

"Yes."

"I'm really glad you raised those points, Fred. They are valid issues." Several of us sighed in relief, glad this was not going to be a deadly showdown.

"Thank you."

"But they're only valid if you think of psychology in a certain way, as a certain sort of science, like the physical sciences. Psychological concepts aren't like mass, velocity, and temperature," Brammer said, raising his eyebrows and taking a seat in an empty chair in the row in front of Fred. Apparently, he was just getting warmed up. Turning back to face the class, he continued. "But I'm really not interested in debating measurability, sampling, or generalizability. In fact, I'm willing to concede those points. Earlier in the semester I said that Freud was rigorous, eloquent, and evocative. Today I called him 'our greatest psychologist.' But you disagree, Fred, and you're not alone. Not everyone considers Freud's work rigorous. But if you consider the whole story of Freud's intellectual adventure—the numerous cases that he and his followers put into circulation; the concepts and vocabulary that he created, refined, and elaborated; the sheer volume of works he produced; the attention his ideas attracted from the intellectual and scholarly community of his time; and his love of truth, then I think I am on safe grounds to say, yes, he was the greatest psychologist we have known." Brammer paused momentarily then turned around to face Fred.

"But if I understand you, Fred, you just don't want to think of Freud as a scientist, and if you're not a scientist, then you can't be a great psychologist. Right?"

Fred nodded his approval meekly, and Brammer continued. "Here is where you and I disagree, though I don't want to be disagreeable about it," Brammer chuckled; then turned and winked at the class. "The way I see it, a scientist is a person who tells stories that aspire to truth. Some people, like Fred here, consider Freud to have failed as a scientist. That's an arguable point. Even if Freud failed as a scientist, which I don't think he did, there is still the question of his lasting influence and contributions to understanding human nature. Freud was empirical: he observed, he took detailed notes, he developed his theories from his cases; then he looked at new cases for verification. But Fred here, he doesn't want to think of Freud as a psychologist because Freud doesn't fit his definition of a rigorous scientist. The difference between Fred and me boils down to this question: What is the goal of psychological inquiry? Fred thinks that psychology seeks to make predictions about human behavior through rigorous research, and that is enough. I want psychology to pursue broader goals, to provide insights into human nature and consciousness by introducing new ways of talking about these things that can help us better understand the workings of the human mind. I consider Freud a great psychologist because he left a lasting impression on the twentieth century. He gave us a vocabulary that became part of the vernacular and a discipline that made an imprint on our consciousness and our culture. Even today, we talk about Freudian slips, egomaniacs, displaced anger, and libidinal drives."

Fred wasn't shaken by Brammer's reply, nor was he convinced. He went on to say that what really bothered him was Freud's references to Greek myths and his use of examples from fiction. Fred's persistence and his command of unfamiliar psychological jargon impressed me. But at the end of the day, what stood out was Brammer's assertion that a scientist was a storyteller. Perhaps Freud's influence and power rested less on his data or observations and more on his gift as a storyteller. Was there anything wrong with that?

Philosophy 380: Who Do You Take Yourself to Be?

"This is a course about the being we ourselves are—we human beings," said the man behind the lectern. "My name is David Levine, and the course is Philosophy 380: Existentialism," he continued. "I'll be your instructor and tour guide through the museum of dread, alienation, and nothingness that showcases existentialism. You may find the journey mentally and emotionally draining, but if you are in good shape and prepared each day for the trip, you should find the voyage beneficial, even life affirming. I suspect that at one time or another many of you have been inclined to ask yourselves: Who am I? Why am I here? What am I meant to be? These are questions that objective sciences, like the physical or psychological sciences, can't answer. Some of the philosophers we will read—Kierkegaard, Nietzsche, Sartre, and Camus, to name a few—offer answers to these questions or different ways to think about them. You may recall from reading Shakespeare's *Hamlet* in high school the advice given by Polonius to his son, Laertes: 'This above all: To thine own self be true.' In this course, we will ask what he meant. What does it mean to be true to yourself? Is being true to yourself something valuable in its own right, or is it only a means to an end? Polonius seemed to think that if you were true to yourself, you couldn't be false to anyone else. What do you think?"

Levine took a piece of chalk from his pocket and wrote **EXISTENTIAL** on the blackboard. "You will notice that the root of the word existential is *exist*. The question of existence, of Being, is the core issue of existentialism. What does it mean to be? In several important respects, existentialism is antiphilosophy, at least insofar as it offers an alternative to nineteenth-century philosophy, which wanted to define philosophy as a science and to treat human beings as no different from any other objects in the world.

"But it's not just *that* we exist but *how* we exist that really matters. Existentialists like to say 'one must become an issue for oneself.' This expression focuses attention on what I will call the self-referential quality of human existence. You cannot separate yourself from what you take yourself to be. But I don't want to get ahead of myself or give you too much to chew on too soon, so let me give each of you a copy of the syllabus for the course, and we can go over the assignments."

Too much to chew on, indeed! Who am I? Am I true to myself? Do I take myself as an issue for myself? Nothingness! Dread! Alienation! My jaw wasn't sore, but my head certainly was spinning. On the syllabus, Levine mentioned that the course would focus on "individual freedom and social responsibility," on "despair and affirmation," and on "creativity and conformity." Was I ready for this? Brammer's course had introduced me to the dark side of human experience through Freud's brilliant but depraved attachment to human misery. Reading Freud (1961), however, left me despondent about the human condition. Had I unconsciously signed up for

Existentialism because I wanted to dwell in the darkness without feeling so pessimistic? Flashing back to my high school thesis, I recalled that Camus imagined Sisyphus happy because he accepted the absurdity and suffering of life and, thus, rose above it. Could existentialism offer the optimism I seemed to need to cope with the awareness of human limitations Freud and Brammer had taught me?

Short and slim, Dr. Levine's physical appearance was the antithesis of Brammer's. He wore the same brown tweed sports coat every day with an open-collar shirt, khaki slacks, and brown loafers, and he brought a pipe to class, which he chewed on constantly but never smoked. The hacking, chronic cough that sometimes interrupted his lectures suggested he found ample time to smoke outside of class. His thick-rimmed eyeglasses, pale complexion, and short, cropped hair reminded me of Wally Cox who played Mr. Peepers, a shy and mild-mannered science teacher, on one of my favorite TV shows of the early fifties. Often prone to long and deliberate pauses, Levine spoke softly and deliberately in a monotone, often staring off into space and rarely making eye contact with students. He wasn't energetic like Brammer, but he had an impressive vocabulary, and his calm and quiet manner eventually made me feel more comfortable in his presence than in the company of any professor I'd known.

Levine referred to himself as "an old-school professor." "Don't rely on the books about the books," he advised. "Read the books. Then ask questions, make comments, and use the terms advanced by these philosophers to think about your own life." At times, I felt lost and frustrated, trying to make sense of terms such as Cartesian dualism, nihilism, Dasein, cohistoricizing, facticity, transcendence, and contemplative intuition. I had no idea what Sartre meant by his paradoxical observation that "Existence is what it is not and is not what it is," though I surmised from the thrill it gave Levine each time he said it that this was the key to unlocking the mysteries of existentialism. These philosophers seemed to be speaking in code, and unlike Freud, they rarely illustrated their abstractions with concrete examples or detailed cases. Fortunately, Levine seemed less interested in vocabulary than in what he called "the big picture." But the picture he drew in class—the big picture—looked pretty gloomy to me and belied his optimistic and relaxed demeanor.

"The universe is indifferent; neither kind nor cruel," Levine quietly announced at the end of the second class session. "It provides no answer to the question, Why am I?" he continued. "Our mundane, everyday life is acutely unfulfilling, our existence groundless and absurd, and our world meaningless and incoherent. We dwell in a condition of nothingness. Death proves the absurdity of life and the inevitability of nothingness. We have to accept that we live in the midst of nothingness." The bell rang, and class was over.

"See you on Monday," Levine said cheerfully as he gathered his notes and walked swiftly out the door without looking back. Most of my cohorts looked stunned. So was I. Hadn't Levine promised us a life-affirming class? Hadn't he just said that we humans are unfulfilled, groundless, and immersed in nothingness?

What's the point? I didn't know whether to cry, shoot myself, or just blow off the lecture as the ravings of a madman. But Levine didn't look or act like a lunatic—how could he be so calm about the tragic plight of humanity?

On Monday, Levine began class by asking how we reacted to his statement at the end of class. "What did you think about over the weekend?" he queried. "And how did you feel?"

For a minute or two, we sat in frozen silence, nobody wanting to speak. "Come on," Levine pleaded with the class. "I know you had to feel something." A female in the front row was the first to speak. "I felt betrayed and abandoned," she said, her voice cracking to get the words out. "And alone," another girl interrupted.

"That's enlightening, isn't it?" Levine beamed uncharacteristically.

"I'd say it was frightening, not enlightening," the same girl countered. "I struggled all weekend to try to make sense of what you said. If the world is meaningless and nothing matters, why am I in school? What am I doing getting an education, reading these books? I want to get good grades and have a promising future, you know, make something of my life. But you make it all seem like an illusion. I felt as if you were stripping away the very things that give my life meaning."

"I think you're on to something important," Levine said. "You seem to be contrasting what you feel is meaningful about your life, what you're doing here—studying hard, working toward a bright future, committing yourself to certain values—with my claim that the universe is indifferent about what you choose to do. Do you see that?"

"I think so, but I'm not sure I get the point."

"Does anybody see how her statement fits with what I referred to as groundlessness?"

Levine was beginning to make sense to me, so I raised my hand and he called on me. "I think you're trying to say that we choose our own meanings, or at least we should," I said. "She's creating her own meanings and values by how she's acting, what she's doing, and the choices she's making. It's her choice and her responsibility to make the choice."

"That's right," Levine exclaimed, showing unusual passion and making me feel like I'd said something smart. "What is distinctive about human life and human beings is our capacity to give our lives enduring meanings. The world may be meaningless, but that only makes it imperative that we find or create meanings that can sustain us. Our meanings arise from our struggles and by means of the commitments and decisions we make about how to live. And it's not just the words we speak; it's also the actions we take that define us."

"I object to your methods of teaching us this lesson," a guy in the front of the class interrupted, and then stopped himself cold as though afraid of Levine's reaction.

"Continue, please," Levine requested. "I want to hear what you have to say."

"You asked how we felt. Well, I felt miserable when I left here Friday. I was nervous and anxious all weekend. For the first time in my life, I thought about

41

my own death, the experience of nothingness, and the unknown associated with death. Last night I had a dream in which I saw myself as an old man. I looked sick and alone. I kept searching for my watch, but I couldn't find it. Then I heard myself mutter, 'There's no time left and I'm not finished.' I woke up in a cold sweat. I felt terrified."

Levine was chewing hard on his pipe, appearing deep in thought about what to say next. After a long pause, he put his pipe on the desk, took a piece of chalk from his pocket, turned away from the class, and wrote on the blackboard:

EVERYBODY LIVES WITH ANXIETY.

"Does anyone disagree with the statement on the board?" he asked. Nobody spoke.

"Think about it for a minute. Would your life be better if you never felt anxious? Kierkegaard referred to the spiritual experience of anxiety, evident in that student's dream, as a kind of fear and dread, what he termed angst and other philosophers call existential angst. I expected many of you to feel anxious and to be in touch with your anxiety—to learn from it. I did not intend to terrify you, but I was aware that my comments might heighten your anxiety and make you aware of the choices you have to make about how to live and what gives meaning to your life."

Levine walked over to the guy in the front row and touched his shoulder. "We should be grateful to this young man who shared his dream so courageously. The dream poses a serious existential question: Should we wait until we are near death to contemplate the significant questions associated with being and living? The watch expresses his concern over time—how much time does one have in a lifetime? And the ideal of finishing is central to any meaningful interpretation of this dream. When we think of a life, often we think of beginnings and endings. We can tell the story of how our life began and how it is going now, but what about how it will end? What is a meaningful end to a life? What will it take to pronounce your life good or meaningful? These are universal concerns of existence—not just his, but yours and mine too."

"Perhaps we're all too anxious about being anxious," Levine grinned. Some of us laughed nervously, not knowing where he was heading. "Seriously," he continued, "anxiety tells me something matters; so does fear and dread. Nothing is certain in life but death, and the uncertainty of the aftermath of death need be no more threatening than any other sort of uncertainty. To exist—there's that word again—and to be truly aware of your existence is to be confronted with anxiety, uncertainty, and the question of meaning. Existentialists believe that you have to accept death to enjoy life. Life contains death within it. This is what Paul Tillich [1952] meant when he said that 'non-being is part of one's being.' He thought of anxiety as the existential awareness of your non-being, that your life can end at any time. Tillich thought it was necessary to experience your own mortality concretely—that is, to make it part of your being in order to live a meaningful life.

'The courage to be,' according to Tillich, was a commitment to live a meaningful life in the absence of any known or certain purpose. Similarly, Martin Heidegger [1962] talked about ontological anxiety—the anxiety of being—as a necessary condition of existence. He saw the realization of one's own death as a road to a higher plane of being. Another existentialist, Victor Frankl, who survived a concentration camp, said that human life cannot be complete without suffering and death. He believed that how one deals with suffering, the choices one makes under duress, is a measure of freedom that can give one's life meaning or rob it of purpose [1959]. In the presence of death and in the midst of immense suffering in the camps, still there were choices to be made every day, decisions that either renounced or reinforced a sense of one's dignity and worth.

"In this little exercise, I tried to put you in touch with your own existence. Perhaps what some of you have called terrifying is nothing more than experiencing the angst of existence itself. When you face the possibility of nothingness, you confront the question of your own being and becoming. If I am not any-thing, then I must make some-thing of myself. You see that you have been tossed into the world without knowing why or what for, and the world is silent; it doesn't tell you what it means to be you. You are forced to construct and define your own meanings and values. What makes you who you are is what you make of yourself."

Several of my classmates replied that, on the contrary, they would rather live without anxiety. One woman spoke defiantly about having her whole life ahead of her and not wanting to think about depressing topics like death and suffering. Another mentioned her faith and how it was her religion and belief in God that gave meaning and ultimate purpose to her life, implying that somehow this refuted Levine's claim that we construct our own meanings. I thought she was missing the point, that her faith was a choice she had made or one to which she had conformed, but I chose not to speak. Levine listened intently but quietly to the comments, giving everyone who wanted to speak a chance. I interpreted many of the comments as the sort of resistance to change that Brammer had tuned us into in his course. As the class period came to an end, Levine cleared his throat and said, "I want to continue this train of thought over the next few sessions. On Wednesday and Friday, we'll be viewing *The Seventh Seal,* a film directed by Ingmar Bergman [1960] that takes up some of the themes we've been conversing about today."

It was not difficult to figure out why Levine had chosen this film. You couldn't watch *The Seventh Seal* and not think about the ghostly presence of death that hovers over life, about uncertainty, and the question, What makes life meaningful? The centerpiece of the film is a dialogue between the knight, Antonious Block, and Death. Block convinces Death to spare his life, challenging him to a game of chess with the knight's life at stake. During their conversation, Block refers to the emptiness in his heart as "like a mirror in front of my face." He feels isolated and indifferent toward other people. He tells Death that he wants to die but not before God reveals himself, implying that he wants to believe but can't. "I want knowledge, not faith, not suppositions … I want God to talk to me."

"But he is silent," Death replies "… maybe there is no one."

"Then life is an atrocious horror. Nobody can live waiting to die and knowing that everything is nothing … within our fears we make up an image and call this image God."

Toward the end of the film, Death announces, "When next we meet, the hour will strike for you and your friends."

"And you will reveal your secrets?" asks the knight.

"I have no secrets," replies Death.

"So you have nothing?"

"Nothing."

Levine asked us to write our reactions to *The Seventh Seal* in our notebooks and come to class prepared to discuss what we learned from the film. In my notebook, I wrote that I didn't understand the title of the film, but I did recognize how the film illustrated the existential themes and questions we had been discussing in class. "The knight seemed to be searching for definitive and ultimate answers to the meaning of life," I read aloud from my notebook when we returned to class the following week. "The knight expected Death to shed light on the meaning of life and the existence of God, but Death was silent and so was God. If there are no secrets or ultimate answers—only silence, or what Dr. Levine called 'indifference'—then maybe we are wasting our time obsessing over ultimate purposes and what God may want from us. We expect that when we die, we will know why we have lived. But Bergman suggests that may not be the case. The only certainties are that we will die and that we are alive now. I think he's saying that living is what gives life meaning, doing something meaningful and valuable with your life."

"That's a good start, Art," Levine acknowledged. "Now I want us to go a little deeper and be a bit more detailed. Can anyone help Art with the title of the film?"

"I can," says Michelle, a female sitting next to me. "It's taken from a passage in the New Testament, in Revelations. If I remember correctly, the passage appeared twice in the film: that when the Seventh Seal was broken there was silence in Heaven for about half an hour. I think the title symbolizes the silence of God in the world, and the film reveals the persistence of that silence regarding ultimate purposes or the meaning of life. Bergman's film helped me better understand what you mean by nothingness and the importance of self-created meanings."

"Go on," Levine encouraged.

"Well, in the beginning of the film, the knight tells us that he is searching for a single act that will give his life meaning, but then he moves away from his own acts and toward the distraction of what God may want. He is troubled by doubt and uncertainty, and he seems to think that concrete evidence of God's existence would restore his faith and give his life meaning."

"Does he ever find that life-defining act of meaning?" asks Levine.

"I'm not sure," says Michelle. "But I think that helping Jof and Mia escape, you know, the two players, gave significance to the end of his life."

"Yes," interrupts an excited male voice from the back of the room. "That's what clinched the existential point of the film for me. The knight can die knowing that his action saved them. It's what we do more than the faith we have that gives meaning and purpose to our lives. Maybe that's why the arrival of death is depicted as a dance and not as some grim, sorrowful ending."

"I'm delighted and impressed with these responses," Levine says. "Some people think Bergman is obscure, but this is a transparent film. Knowing that life will end ought to make us more secure. It can free us simply to live and be responsible for our own choices and decisions—not have to look outside ourselves. Life offers us simple pleasures. Take, for example, the scene in which they share the wild strawberries and milk. In this film, the squire, Jons, also is a significant character. Like the knight, he has experienced the fruitlessness of the Crusades and the annihilating threat of the Black Plague. In comparison to the heaviness of Block, however, Jons exudes a lightness, offering an alternative philosophy of life. He chooses to enjoy his daily existence, living meaningfully by being in the moment, ignoring the question of what will happen in the end."

As Levine continues, my mind drifts toward another one of my father's expressions. "Nobody gets out of this life alive," he would say in jest, often to stifle some distressing news about a friend's illness or death. Levine's course made this little jingle into a profound philosophical stance on the question of how to live. "Embrace living," Levine liked to say, "and remember that the choices you make become acts of self-creation." On several occasions, he warned us about the perils of conformity. "Remember what Sartre shows in the play we read, *No Exit.* The image other people have of you is not who you are or have to be. Resist the temptation to play the parts other people want you to play. You don't have to conform, and if you do, you are abrogating your responsibility to make your own choices and decisions. It's the actions you take and the commitments you make that give a sense of direction and a point to your life."

One day near the end of the course, Dr. Levine asked to see me in his office after class. He told me that he had wanted to give me an A in the course, but my test scores came up short. "I don't think you take yourself seriously," he gently observed. "You have a sharp mind. Perhaps you don't realize how talented you are. I'm disappointed that your work outside of class didn't measure up to your performance in class. If you made a commitment to apply yourself, oh, you could be quite a student. Perhaps other things are more important to you. I don't know. You're the one who has to decide what really matters to you."

I didn't know how to take what Levine was saying to me. I had struggled with some of the more difficult readings in the course. Admittedly, I gave up instead of challenging myself—and I hadn't studied for the exams. He had me pegged. I couldn't fool Levine, but perhaps I was fooling myself. What would it mean to take myself seriously, to make a genuine commitment? What did I want? What did I really care about? This was the only meeting I ever had with Levine, but it was one I never forgot.

One Thing Leads to Another

In January 1968, I graduated with a bachelor's degree and took a position as an English and speech teacher at East High School in Auburn, New York. As a condition of my employment, I agreed to direct the senior play and to start a debate club. I didn't realize that I would have to submit the play I chose for approval by the school board and that debate topics also would be screened.

Midway through the semester, I assigned *Inherit the Wind* (Lawrence and Lee, 1955) to my ninth–grade honors English class. To enliven my lesson plan and instill a greater understanding of the issues at stake in the Scopes trial, I decided to hold a debate in class on the proposition: "Genesis 1:1 is literally true." Several of the students in the class had joined the new debate club, and interest in the debate over Genesis 1:1 ran at a fever pitch. Unfortunately, the high school principal, without notifying me, chose the day of the debate to visit my classroom for the purpose of evaluating my teaching.

At the start of class, I asked the students to shift their seats from one side of the classroom to the other as their convictions about the proposition changed during the debate. I also encouraged them to question and challenge evidence as it was presented. The debate was heated, and the students were well prepared, animated, and fervent about the arguments they made. They cheered and clapped when they thought their side made a winning point, and a few of them heckled and hissed as well. During the time between speeches, the students in the audience tried to coach the debaters on one side or the other, sometimes interrupting or preempting each other in a disorderly but well-intentioned fashion. I thought it was the best class session of the semester—fun, energetic, and edifying.

At the end of the school day, I retrieved a memo from the principal in my mailbox: "Mr. Bochner: Your job is to control the classroom. The commotion and chaos in your classroom bordered on pandemonium. This is unacceptable! Consider yourself on notice. Also, stop wearing those turtleneck sweaters, and please, please, get a haircut."

Her message stunned me. Why hadn't Miss Parsons commented on the students' high level of motivation and excitement or on what they had learned? I had no idea what it meant to be on notice, but I did grasp the significance of the school dress code. Still, I drew the line at haircuts. Levine's words echoed in my eardrums: "The image other people have of you is not who you are."

Miss Parsons and I were on different wave lengths, but we weren't the only ones. Most of the other teachers were decades older than me and frowned on my interactive teaching methods. At first, I would eat my lunch in the smoke-filled teachers' lounge, where groups of male teachers played cribbage and gossiped. Most of them seemed burned out, unimaginative, and apathetic. There was no fire in their bellies. They were tedious, grouchy, and humorless. Occasionally, I would close my eyes and imagine myself sitting in this room twenty years from now. The images frightened me. I didn't want to end up as a dispirited old teacher, sitting at a cribbage table, talking that way. I couldn't see myself in that story. But what options did I have?

The concerns with which I was preoccupied shifted suddenly in spring 1968. Shortly after I arrived in Auburn, New York, the Viet Cong launched the Tet Offensive, attacking cities in South Vietnam and making it clear the United States was not winning the war. Then in April, Martin Luther King was assassinated; and less than two months later, Bobby Kennedy was shot and killed at the Ambassador Hotel in Los Angeles, triggering riots around the country. Everybody was in a state of shock. We were trying to comprehend something that made no sense, had no reasonable explanation, and could not be excused. A potentially toxic blow had been delivered to our collective psyche and national self-image. The bullets that killed Martin Luther King and Bobby Kennedy had wounded the nation.

The day after the Kennedy assassination, I phoned the high school principal and volunteered to deliver a eulogy. She arranged for an assembly of the entire school—several hundred students and dozens of teachers and staff. I put everything I had into that short speech. I spoke from my gut and from the source of my grief, expressing a sorrow that many people, whose hearts were aching, also shared. When I finished, I felt as though I had finally accomplished something in my first term as a teacher.

As it turned out, my experience that day was an epiphany—a moment at which I was turning away from one path toward another, however uncertain I may have been at the time. High school teaching likely was not my calling, but something about being in the middle of a healing moment of connection among people suffering deep loss and grief—teetering on the edge of an abyss of sorrow and anger—felt deeply satisfying and energizing.

A Fateful Summer Course

As summer approached, the generation gap was widening, and prospects for the immediate future looked grim. With no options apparent, I signed a contract to return to East High School the following year. When I opened my contract, I found attached a letter informing me that I would receive a $300 raise if I completed a graduate course in my field prior to the fall. Syracuse University was only twenty-two miles from Auburn, an easy commute, so I enrolled in a course entitled Great Speakers, with Professor Dan Smith, chair of the department and an authority on British public address. As luck or fate would have it, I had nothing else going on that summer, so I threw myself wholeheartedly into writing the course term paper. On the last day of class, Dr. Smith returned the papers. I was thrilled to receive an A, but humbled by all the red ink Smith used to edit and rewrite my sentences. As I stood to leave, he stopped me abruptly. "You put a lot of thought and effort into that paper. You should be proud," he said. "Have you thought about going full time to graduate school?"

"No, I haven't. I teach high school in Auburn," I replied.

"I know. You mentioned that on the first day of class. You also said you had been a college debater and started a debate club at the high school in Auburn."

"That's right."

"Well, I'm looking for someone to coach the debate team here. We would give you an assistantship to support your work on your master's degree, and your tuition would be waived. It isn't a lot of money, three thousand dollars, but it's enough to live on. We also would want you to teach a section of our public speaking course."

I did the math quickly in my head. My annual salary as a high school teacher was going to be $4,200 next year. I'd be making less money, but Syracuse was an expensive, private university, and I'd come away with a master's degree. Dr. Smith must have seen the glow covering my face and the excitement growing in my eyes. "If you're interested, here's what you need to do. Go over to the campus Testing Center and tell them you want to take the Miller's Analogy test. Then come back next Friday. I'll prepare some paperwork for you to sign and take over to the Admissions Office. In the meantime you'll need to get me your undergraduate transcripts."

Walking across campus to turn in my paperwork, I danced on cloud nine. The graduate assistantship was a novel concept that I had to get straight in my mind: *They're going to pay me to read books and get a graduate degree, and I'll get to teach and work with college kids and take courses from graduate professors.* I felt as though I were walking on air. Levine entered my head again. No fooling around this time, Levine, I thought. I'm not going to blow this opportunity. I'm committed.

No Backing

"You did what?" my father moaned into the phone.

"I resigned my position at East High School," I repeated. "I'm going back to school to get a master's degree."

"But you just got out of school a few months ago, and they're paying you good money at the high school. I think you should hold on to your job. Go see your boss and tell him you made a mistake. He may still take you back," he pleaded.

"My boss is a woman, Dad. Besides, I don't want to go back. I want to go to graduate school."

"What will you do with a master's degree?"

"I don't know. Teach, I suppose."

"You're already teaching."

"Dad, please, I don't want to argue with you. I'm not sure where graduate school is going to lead. I just know I want this."

"We're talking about your future, Arthur. Aren't you concerned about your future?"

"The way the country's going, I don't have high expectations about the future. What I know is this is where I want to be now. If I work hard and do well, I expect the future will take care of itself. Isn't that what you tried to teach me—do your best every day?"

"You're impossible. Just impossible ..."

Sensitivity Training

The School of Speech at Syracuse was housed in the oldest building on campus. Opened in 1873, the Hall of Languages stood at the top of a steep hill. Each day, I would search for parking, take the long trek up University Avenue, and climb three flights up to an office I shared with three other graduate students. The winters were long and cold in Syracuse, where snow fell practically each day. To get a decent parking space I would shower and leave my apartment as early as possible. My long, thick, shoulder-length hair would still be wet when I parked and began the hike up the hill. By the time I got to my office my hair would be immersed in icicles, which melted gradually throughout the morning. I had to keep a towel at my desk to dry my hair. My advisor, Paul McKee, recommended that I keep a pee can there as well, as the only bathroom was on the first floor. I opted instead to make numerous "relief" trips up and down the creaky old wooden stairs each day.

The graduate program at Syracuse centered on public address, argumentation, and rhetorical criticism. In addition to the thesis requirement, I took courses in classical rhetoric, medieval and modern rhetoric, rhetorical criticism, historical research methods, British public address, argumentation and debate, and communication education. I also enrolled in a course on the philosophy of language offered in the Newhouse School of Communications that focused on Wittgenstein and Ryle, as well as a class in organizational communication offered by Charles Kelly, the newest member of the speech faculty. Dr. Kelly had teamed with another member of the faculty, Joe Maraglia, to form a Center for Organizational Communication, which offered consulting services to local businesses and organizations. Both Kelly and Maraglia had been mentored by Charles Redding at Purdue University. By the late sixties, Redding had established a reputation as one of the leading social scientists in communication. In some circles he was deemed "the father of organizational communication." At Syracuse, however, the curriculum was organized around rhetoric and public address. Ordinarily, graduate students were not exposed either to social theory or to behavioral science methodology. Thus, Kelly and Maraglia had only a marginal presence in the graduate program.

"I want to invite you to a special presentation on the cutting edge of organizational communication," Kelly announced in our seminar one day toward the end of the semester. "As you know, Dr. Maraglia has been away on leave this year. He's just returned from the National Training Laboratory in Bethel, Maine, and has agreed to give an informal presentation on his experiences there tomorrow afternoon at 2 in this room. He told me this morning that his life had been profoundly changed by his experiences, and I'm looking forward to hearing what happened there. You're all invited."

I wasn't convinced that the "cutting edge" of organizational communication was where I wanted to hang out. Dr. Kelly was a low-key, soft-spoken instructor who gave the appearance of someone not all that interested in teaching, and the focus of the course—improving organizational and business practices by analyzing or auditing internal communications—did not resonate with my own personal values and interests. I suspected that organizational communication was largely uncritical and manipulative, representing the interests of the corporation over those of the employees, and I worried about the moral sensibility underlying this burgeoning new area of the field. Nevertheless, the department was buzzing with intrigue about Maraglia's life-changing experiences, so I thought I better find out what all the noise was about.

"Sensitivity training changed my life," Maraglia stated matter-of-factly. "I'm not the same person I was a month ago. I've lost a lot of my defensiveness and found new feelings of love, joy, and inner peace. It wasn't easy getting to this place. I am grateful for the truthfulness and honesty of the people with whom I shared this experience, the people in my group. I never really knew how other people saw me. Maybe I really didn't want to. But sensitivity training forced me to get feedback. I had to listen to how other members of my group perceived me. Let me tell you, that was not easy to hear, at least not at first.

"Sensitivity training seeks to expand your consciousness and help you become more aware of how other people perceive you. Emotionally, I had to hit bottom, to travel to the cellar of my soul, in order to wake up. Our trainer kept saying we all have pain in need of healing, and we can't get to the other side of the tunnel, where the light is, unless we are willing to move through the darkness. He asked us whether we hungered for greater awareness in our lives. I know now that's what I want—greater awareness—because the more aware I am, the freer I am, and the more open I become to try out new things. I'd given so much of my energy to my career and my work that at the end of the day I had nothing left for the people I care about. It never dawned on me that life is supposed to be an adventure. 'What do you mean by adventure?' you might ask. Well, to me adventure means exploring new dimensions of myself and my life without any certainty about where they will lead. I didn't know how I'd feel when I got back here. Would this experience, these feelings of joy and ecstasy, transfer to my life away from Bethel, my everyday life? But what I found was how filled with love and acceptance I'd become. I fell in love with my wife all over again, and our love continues to unfold and deepen. We've committed ourselves to treat each other with unconditional positive regard. I have no illusions. I know there will be roadblocks as I move forward, but I'm committed to making positive changes in my life and to be a source of happiness and healing in other people's lives. So that's my story in a nutshell. I'd be happy to answer questions and listen to any comments you may have."

Around the seminar table, we all sat in stunned silence. How do you respond to such a personal and emotional statement? This was not the sort of academic lecture I'd grown accustomed to at Syracuse. I'd never heard a professor bare his soul in public. It was appealing and at the same time intimidating. Admittedly, some of Maraglia's euphoria seemed a bit far-fetched to me. I had my doubts that one's life could be so quickly transformed. My cynical side wondered what drug he'd been smoking. Yet the ease with which he communicated his personal and private feelings also had a hypnotic effect on me. In my transfixed state, I relaxed my argumentative impulses and let myself imagine what it might be like to be overcome with joy and love and to experience life as an adventure, treating loved ones with unconditional positive regard. If sensitivity training was even half as good as Maraglia claimed, then I wanted to experience it. What harm could it do?

During the discussion period, Dr. Maraglia highlighted his new academic interest in "the human potential movement," an existential approach to personal growth rooted in Abraham Maslow's (1968) hierarchy of human needs, which idealizes self-actualization. He also recommended Carl Rogers's *On Becoming a Person* (1961). Maraglia pointed out that Rogers had grounded his development of "client-centered therapy" on the ideal of unconditional positive regard mentioned in his talk. Apparently, Rogers disagreed with Freud's premise that humans are motivated by dark and repressed urges. Instead, he saw a positive, actualizing drive that makes humans strive to make the most of their lives. "Get a copy of Rogers's book," Maraglia advised as he gathered his notes and stood to leave. "It'll make you think differently about yourself and about your work in the field as well."

I took Maraglia's advice and purchased a copy. I also purchased Maslow's *Toward a Psychology of Being* (1968) and Rollo May's *Man's Search for Himself* (1953). These books spoke to me in a deeper and more personal way than anything I had studied in rhetoric and public address. The humanistic psychologists concentrated on subjective experience—our inner lives, feelings, and thoughts—but they also brought to light the importance of how humans interact with others and deal with social relationships. They introduced me to terms and ideals that had obvious relevance to human speech but had never come up in my graduate studies, concepts such as compassion, empathy, spontaneity, identity, and relatedness. I couldn't help wondering why the topics they emphasized—human suffering and healing, spiritual experience, the "will to meaning" (Frankl, 1969)—had been left out of my formal education. Maraglia was right about one thing: These writers had planted new ideas in my head about the kind of work I might want to do in my own field. These books also stirred something deep inside me. I was beginning to long for something different from what rhetoric and public address had offered me. Wasn't the human potential movement and humanistic psychology relevant to human speech?

Still, I had an MA thesis to write on "The History of Academic Debate at Syracuse University" (Bochner, 1969). I had to finish on time to secure my spot in the doctoral program to which I had been accepted at Bowling Green University. For the time being, my obligations were more urgent than my inspiration, so I throttled my excitement about the writings of humanistic psychologists. But their ideas had taken up residence in my soul and would accompany me to Bowling Green.

"I've been reading a lot of humanistic psychology—Rogers, Maslow, and May," I say, pausing momentarily to gauge Tucker's reaction. I don't want him to think I'm a kook and have to exit with my tail between my legs.

"Uh, huh," he nods. He isn't giving any cues.

"They really touch a chord in me. They're working with ideas that can make a difference in people's lives. I want to make a positive contribution, to help other people live better lives. That's what I care about. The humanistic psychologists emphasize healing, loving, and doing meaningful work. I haven't figured out how their ideas translate to our field, but I'd like to try to make some connections between humanistic psychology and what we do in the field of speech."

"That's a great idea, and very ambitious," Tucker says approvingly. "You've given me an idea. Since you plan to enroll in the communication theory course, you could start us off the first night. Prepare a talk on the humanistic psychologists— say, a half-hour—and then take some questions. I'll pass out the syllabus and talk about the reading and paper assignments. Then I'll turn the session over to you. That'll be a good start to the semester and to your doctoral work."

CHAPTER TWO

Graduate Student Socialization

On Becoming a Divided Self

> The amount of "room" to move a person feels that he has is related both to *the room he gives himself and the room he is given by others.*
> R. D. Laing (1961, p. 135)

Not wanting to be late the first night of Dr. Tucker's class, I dash down the corridor in South Hall carrying all the books I can hold in two hands without dropping any. If I didn't know what I was talking about, at least I would look prepared. I sneak quietly into the room and take the first empty seat I see. When I glance up I notice that most of the seats—twenty-five or so—are occupied.

"You look like you've been busy," says the woman in the seat next to me, glancing at the books now stacked high on my desk. Turning toward her, I notice her straw-colored hair, cut short and boyish. She's wearing jeans and a loose, blue T-shirt with a peace emblem pinned on it. Nibbling on a bagel, she appears casual and rebellious. Probably a hippie, I think to myself.

"Yeah, Dr. Tucker asked me to give a presentation on humanistic psychology," I say, rearranging the books that threatened to topple.

"On the first night of class—are you serious?" she asks, raising her eyebrows in disbelief. "You must be one of his students."

"No, I'd like to be, but I just met him last month. I have no idea what he expects. Do you know anything about him?"

"Not much. I heard he used to be a debate coach, but now he's into behavioral science and statistics. He teaches all the methods and research design classes. By the way, my name is Barb."

"I'm Art Bochner. I just arrived yesterday from Syracuse, where I did my master's. How about you?"

"I've been teaching in Texas but got a leave for two years to work on my Ph..."
The background buzz of conversation among other students ceases suddenly. I look up and see Tucker, wearing a dark blue suit, walk across the front of the classroom. He looks shorter than I remembered.

Interrupting the silence, he begins, "My name is Ray Tucker and this course is Communication Theory." He rests his hands on either side of the lectern and sweeps his eyes across the class, seeming to take in every face along the way. "Have any of you had a course in communication theory before?"

A couple of hands go up, and Tucker nods to a skinny guy in the second row. "What was the focus of your course?" Tucker asks.

"We began by examining models of communication process. Later on, we concentrated on theories of attitude change."

"Do you recall what models you covered?"

"Uhmm, let's see, uh, Berlo's model was one [1960]. We used his textbook, *The Process of Communication*." Tucker jogs to the blackboard and writes, "S-M-C-R," then whirls around to face the class. "Is that the model, uh—what's your name?"

"Scott," he says quietly. "Yeah, that's it—source, message, channel, receiver. And I remember another one—Lasswell's model [1927, 1949]. Let me think, yeah, Lasswell's was similar to Berlo's, but he added the effect of the message."

Tucker turns toward the board again and writes, "*Who* says *what* to *whom* through what *channel* with what *effect*?" "That's good, Scott, very good. These are two of the most cited models in the literature. And you're right; they're nearly identical. *Who* is the source. *What* is the message. *To whom* refers to the receiver, the target of the message. The *channel* can be audio, video, person-to-person, telephone, or whatever mode is used to deliver the message; and the *effect* is an assessment of whether the message is successful—did the message work? Lasswell's research focuses on mass communications and advertising. Obviously, it's important for advertisers to be able to predict the effects their messages will have on consumers. Lasswell's model is helpful because it defines the variables that can influence the effect of a message. In sociology and mass communications, they call this *effects research*."

Looking around, I notice other students writing down everything Tucker says. I open my notebook and copy what he's written on the blackboard.

"Oh, I just remembered another one," Scott interrupts excitedly. "Shannon and Weaver's information theory [1963]. As I recall, their model was a little different from the others. They were very concerned about something they called *noise*. And weren't they the ones who used the term *destination* instead of *receiver*?"

"Yes! Excellent! You're on fire, Scott," Tucker chuckles, and the class roars with laughter. Although he's talked only to Scott, Tucker seems to be building rapport with the whole class. As a relatively new teacher, I marvel at how effectively he uses supportive responses to encourage participation.

"Shannon and Weaver worked for Bell Labs," Tucker continues, "a telephone and telegraph company. Think about the work of a telephone company. If you're sending a message over a wire, you want the message to get to its destination, right? So noise becomes very important to you. Everything that can distort or interfere with the message becomes noise. You know how sometimes you hear static on the radio or when someone's talking to you on the telephone and you get interference on the line. You're not getting a clear signal. That's noise."

Tucker walks slowly back to the lectern and clears his throat. "Here's the point I want to make." Tucker pauses and we lift our pens, ready to write. "These three models are commonly assumed to be the foundation of communication theory. But they're not. Don't get me wrong—these models are useful. They specify what's involved in making and delivering a message and what can distort a message before it reaches its destination. But," he pauses again and waits until all eyes look up. "These aren't models of *human* communication. You see, Shannon and Weaver [1963] are concerned only with whether the message gets to its destination without distortion. They don't care how the receiver responds to the message. In fact, there aren't any people in their model. So you see, they think of communication as a technical problem. They don't even use the term *communication*—they call it *information*, a mathematical theory of information.

"Now Lasswell, he's a different case entirely. He doesn't care about how the receiver hears the message. For him, everything rides on message construction. Communication is primarily about producing an effective message, one that will achieve its purpose—you know, sell products.

"So what do we have here? In both cases, problems of communication are reduced largely to constructing and transmitting messages. Nothing comes back from the other end. There's no feedback; everything flows one way. But that's not the case in human communication, where the other person looms large. Human communication involves interaction and transaction. So if we want to model human communication, we have to move beyond merely constructing and transmitting messages. The question is, How should we conceptualize human communication? What does communication do?

Tucker pauses and scans the faces in the room again, locking in on mine. "You, Art Bochner, do you have an opinion on this?"

Though impressed and flattered that he remembered my name, I feel my knees trembling and my face getting flushed. Every face in the room is turned toward mine.

"Meaning," I spit out. "I'd say we have to move to processes of meaning making."

"Meaning? What's meaning got to do with anything?" Tucker challenges as if I'm way off the mark.

"I'm not sure," I begin tentatively, hedging my bets. I think about what I'd read in preparation for my talk tonight. Now seems as good a time as any to try out what I'd been learning. "I think communication creates meaning and value. We need to understand how people create and negotiate meanings. These models don't deal with meaning."

"That's very interesting, Art. Did the rest of you get that?" Tucker asks the class, implying that what I said was worth writing in their notebooks. I feel a glow coming over me. "Communication is the means by which we create meaning and value. Indeed, indeed, it is!" he exclaims, underscoring the point.

"Should we let the cat out of the bag, Art?" he winks at me in full view of the class. I'm not sure what he means, but I nod anyway. I'm embarrassed that other students might think I'm some sort of favorite son, but at the same time I love getting the sort of attention my father never gave me. "Art's been doing some homework that I assigned him this summer when he stopped by to introduce himself. He agreed to give a brief presentation tonight on some of the humanistic psychologists he's been reading. Come on up to the front, Art."

I weave my way through the rows of occupied seats and walk awkwardly to the front, carrying my stack of books. I place the books on the table behind the lectern and take the note cards I'd prepared out of my pocket. Aware that my hands are quivering, I squeeze the edges of the lectern tightly and begin.

"The idea that meaning is central to communication theory provides a good segue into my presentation, because humanistic psychology starts at just about the same place." I pause for a few seconds to retrieve a page of notes I'd scribbled on a yellow pad.

"The pioneers of humanistic psychology [Maslow, 1968; May, 1953, 1967; Rogers, 1961] felt that a good deal of psychology was not applicable to human beings because it didn't center on what is unique about a person. Even when psychologists do focus on human beings, they tend to ignore or dismiss crucial aspects of what makes us human, namely our self-awareness, emotionality, and subjectivity. Humanistic psychologists believe this is a mistake. They want to apply psychology to the full range of human experience, including subjective thoughts and feelings, empathy, authenticity, intimacy, death and dying—everything involved with finding meaning in life.

"Humanistic psychology began as a reaction to the excesses of behaviorism and the negativity of psychoanalysis. For behaviorists, the only real things are those we can observe directly and publicly, objects and behaviors that can be verified by multiple observers. Everything else is considered a black box [Skinner, 1953]. In behaviorism, a human being is not much different from a rat. It's no wonder, then, that so many psychologists confine their research not to people but to rats, mice, monkeys, or dogs. Humanistic psychologists reject the premise that research on animals can provide a bridge to human experience. They also question whether the physical and natural sciences are an appropriate model for the development of psychology as a science.

"Psychoanalysis is another story entirely. To their credit, Freud and his followers took subjective experience seriously and recognized the healing potential of a relationship between an analyst and a patient. But psychoanalysis maintains a dim view of human nature, often depicting human beings as powerless pawns shaped by cultural forces outside their awareness and driven by dark, submerged desires. Freud's pessimistic image of civilization's disquieting influence on individuals encouraged the view that individuals would inevitably succumb to neurosis. One of my undergraduate professors thought Freud was far and away the greatest psychologist who ever lived. No doubt, Freud's influence on psychology has been profound and important, but it has not been entirely positive. Freud made psychology a science of abnormality and dysfunction. Humanistic psychologists reject the notion that psychology should focus on neurotic and dysfunctional individuals. Instead, they want to study optimal functioning, what Carl Rogers

[1961] called *the fully functioning individual* and Abraham Maslow [1968] referred to as *self-actualization.*"

I put down the yellow pad and look directly at my cohort, collecting my thoughts. "One of the terms I kept running across in my reading was *third-force psychology*, a term applied extensively by Abraham Maslow [1968] to underscore humanistic psychology's rebellious intent to counter the influence of psychology's other forces, behaviorism and psychoanalysis. Third-force psychology assumes that people are basically good and that psychology should be aimed at facilitating human potential. That's why some people refer to it as the human potential movement. They think that human beings have the potential to live happy, creative, and joyful lives.

"I was initially introduced to humanistic psychology by a professor at Syracuse University who had participated in an encounter group at the National Training Laboratory in Bethel, Maine [Eadie, 2009]. He told us that the task of an encounter group is to analyze itself. That's why encounter groups are sometimes called self-analytic groups. Apparently, the people who go to encounter groups are not neurotic or dysfunctional. They're functioning effectively—like you and me." I hear some students giggling and realize that the thought of graduate students being classified as functioning effectively was pretty funny, even absurd, to most graduate students, who tend to see themselves as severely stressed, unconventional, even abnormal. I bite my lip to keep from losing my composure.

"But there's a difference between functioning effectively and functioning fully," I continue. "These individuals feel secure and effective, but they don't feel as if they've reached their full potential. They don't want merely to survive; they want to thrive. Encounter groups offer an experience that can make it possible for them to open up. My professor told how his group created a trusting environment in which group members felt sufficiently safe to provide honest feedback about how they perceived each other.

"You may be wondering why humanistic psychology appeals to me." I pause momentarily, grabbing and twirling the long strand of hair hanging over my right ear as I contemplate what to disclose about my past. "I wrote my high school thesis on Albert Camus, the French existentialist, and later took an undergraduate course on existentialism. These were two of my most memorable educational experiences. They helped me figure out what I valued and who I could become—you know, the choices that might be open to me. Now I see humanistic psychology in the same vein. I think Maslow [1962] titled his book *Toward a Psychology of Being* because existentialism focuses on the question of what it means to be human. Maslow's psychology is an existential psychology, a psychology of being, becoming, and living. Preparing this presentation, I later discovered that some humanistic psychologists refer to themselves as existential psychologists. One of them, Rollo May [1961], links humanistic psychology to existential traditions. He emphasizes freedom, choice, and responsibility, similar to philosophers such as Sartre and Camus.

"In my graduate work, I want to find a way to connect humanistic psychology to what we do in our field, and frankly I haven't figured out how to achieve that goal. But when Dr. Tucker was critiquing communication models, it dawned on me that I may have been thinking too much about speech and not enough about communication. If meaning making is central to human communication, and humanistic psychology encourages us to focus on human values and meanings, what Victor Frankl [1959] called 'man's search for meaning,' then I may have found a link to our field. If we have time for discussion—do we Dr. Tucker?"

"Yes, after our break," he replies, looking at his watch. I take the cue.

"Okay, yeah, after the break. I'm eager to hear everyone's reactions and suggestions."

During the break, Tucker tells me that he needs time to distribute the syllabus and go over the course assignments. "Take about fifteen minutes to field questions and comments; then we have to move on," he says. "You did a fine job. We'll build on the foundation you laid."

On the whole, the class responded positively to my presentation. Several students asked me to recommend specific books, and I indicated that I'd prepare a complete bibliography for the next class. One woman said she'd heard encounter groups criticized as touchy-feely and that she questioned their academic merit. "I think it's accurate to say that encounter groups focus on feelings," I reply, "but that doesn't necessarily make them anti-intellectual, if that's what you're implying. I've heard people say something like that before, but I don't buy it. A human being is not just a thinking animal. We have feelings too. We react emotionally as well as intellectually. Your question reflects the bias in our culture against expressing emotions. The humanistic psychologists want to put feeling on an equal plane with theorizing. Most of our educational experiences are cerebral. It's as if we are cut off at the head. Our bodies and emotions are left out of education and learning. The humanistic psychologists resist this norm of over-intellectualizing. They want education to be subversive, and they insist on educating the whole person. You can't do that if you don't talk about feelings and continually disregard everything below the neck." One of the other students remarked that "touchy-feely" sounded like a putdown and agreed that more attention needed to be given to feeling. But another fellow said he wouldn't be comfortable sharing his feelings with strangers, and several other students nodded in agreement.

Eventually, the discussion turned toward how humanistic psychology might relate to the field of speech. Barb said she thought the comments about expressing feelings might show the way to a connection. "You're talking about a form of speech, aren't you? In rhetoric, we talk about pathos and the importance of emotional appeals, inserting stories in your speeches that evoke emotions from an audience. Great speakers like John Kennedy and Martin Luther King did that repeatedly. But you seem to be saying that humanistic psychology encourages us to go beyond speeches and speech making, you know, to everyday communication between people where meanings and values are created. Communication is how we relate to each other, how we live our lives, build friendships, fall in love, make commitments. That's the connection I made. I don't think that's such a big step for our field to make."

"But that's not part of our field," Scott interjects. "That's psychology, not speech. We can bring psychology into our research on how people are persuaded or convinced, how their beliefs are changed, but beyond that we have to respect boundaries. We're not psychologists. Our expertise is speech making."

"That would freeze our field in the past, Scott," Barb counters, convincing me that my initial impression of her was right. She's one of only three women in the class of twenty-five, but she's not afraid to speak her mind. "Art mentioned the subversive mission of humanistic psychology," she continues. "That's what appeals to me. We ought to ask, What can we become as a field? and not confine ourselves to reproducing the past. Personally, I think speech should be about more than just analyzing texts."

Suddenly Tucker bounces out of his seat giving the impression that the dialogue between Scott and Barb had touched a nerve. He clears his throat, hesitates for a second, and then continues. "This is a good place for me to enter the conversation, but first I want to thank Art for getting us off to such a good start. He's set the bar high." I gather my papers and books quickly, take a deep breath to relax, and edge my way down the row back to my seat, eager to hear what Tucker was about to say.

"There's a method to my madness," Tucker begins. "I was hoping that Art's presentation would raise your consciousness about how other fields, such as humanistic psychology, relate to ours. I know most of you came here from speech programs and that most of those programs didn't offer communication theory or behavioral science research methods courses. But as Bob Dylan [1964] says, 'The times they are a changin.' Barb's last comment was right on target. To use the terms of humanistic psychology, it's not only about Being; it's also about becoming. Besides, quite a few of the most famous speech professors got their PhD in psychology. Have any of you heard of Charles Woolbert?" When nobody responds, he says, "Well, you should have. He had one of the most brilliant minds in our field, and his PhD degree was in psychology. My doctoral advisor at Northwestern, Donald Campbell, also is a psychologist. In a few minutes, I'm going to distribute the syllabus for the course. When I do, you'll see that the vast majority of assigned readings were published outside of our field—by psychologists, sociologists, social psychologists, linguists, anthropologists, philosophers, mathematicians, psychotherapists, and so on.

"My point is that communication theory is an interdisciplinary field. You need to get over any parochial attitudes you may have developed. When you walked through the door to this classroom tonight, you entered a new universe of communication theory that will twist and turn you in many directions. I believe communication theory and behavioral science research is the future of our field. In thirty years, you'll be looking back on this as the time of a new beginning, the start of a field of communication not confined to speech, though speech certainly is an important part of it. You'll be moving within the larger world of inquiry into human communication systems emphasizing culture, meaning, relationships, and, yes, even emotions. You're getting in on the ground floor. That's the wonderful thing about being a graduate student. You're the ones who will make the future.

"But you don't have to take my word about the changes that are coming," Tucker continues. "A few months ago, the Speech Association of America held a conference in New Orleans [Kibler and Barker, 1969] that focused on behavioral science approaches to research in our field. The participants spent a lot of time discussing communication and its connection to speech. After a lot of bickering, they proposed a new name for our discipline: speech communication. They reasoned that it was important to extend the focus of research beyond speech making and rhetorical persuasion to communication in the widest sense. I applaud this proposal, though I don't believe it goes far enough. You don't really need speech in the title, because the term *communication* encompasses speech. I'm not offering a course in speech theory here; no, I'm teaching communication theory, and there's a big difference."

Tucker pauses as if he were waiting for someone to ask him to specify the difference. Warming to the task, he takes off his suit coat, wipes his brow, loosens his tie, and rolls up his sleeves like a country preacher. I love his knack for the dramatic.

"The difference should be obvious," he declares. "Communication is not just verbal—it's visual and vocal, too. It involves not only action but also interaction. And it's not an object. It's a process—a cultural, social, and relational process. When you understand what you're studying as communication and not just speech, you introduce a whole range of new issues, and you touch on a lot of different fields of inquiry. You have to get comfortable crossing boundaries. You're going to have to read widely in many different fields. Communication doesn't belong to any of these disciplines *per se*; it lies between and among them. So if you want to be a communication theorist, you have to extend yourself beyond the literature of speech. You have to be interdisciplinary, even multidisciplinary."

Tucker's enthusiasm was contagious. I couldn't help but feel as if I were riding a wave to the future. When he finally got around to disseminating the syllabus, however, my excitement turned to fear. I didn't recognize a single author on the reading list, not one. I felt utterly unprepared and a little intimidated. But I was determined to persevere.

Tucker began the second class session by highlighting the centrality of meaning making in human communication. He lectured for the first hour on symbolic interaction, emphasizing the symbolic actions that humans use to make sense not only of the world around them but also of themselves. Citing a book by Arnold M. Rose (1962), Tucker dictated three important assumptions of symbolic interaction:

1. Human beings live in a symbolic environment as well as in a physical environment and can be stimulated to act by symbols as well as by physical stimuli.
2. Through symbols, a person gains the capacity to stimulate others in ways other than those in which he or she is stimulated.
3. Through communication of symbols, human beings can learn large numbers of meanings and values—and, hence, ways of acting—from other people (A. M. Rose, 1962, pp. 5–12).

"A symbol is something that represents or stands for something other than itself," Tucker says. "Take my wedding ring, for example. I never take my ring off—never! My wedding ring represents my bond with my wife and what my marriage means to me. It's a symbol of something other than itself. If I lost or damaged it, I would feel terrible. You might say, 'It's just a ring; get another one,' but you'd be missing the point of what this ring means to me. In the chapter I assigned for tonight, George Herbert Mead [1934] discusses a concept he calls *significant symbols.* Do you recall how he defines a significant symbol?"

Tucker nods at a fellow named Cliff, whom I met at the graduate student orientation. Cliff reads from his notebook: "A significant symbol is something that calls out in others what it calls out in the self."

"Put that in your own words, Cliff. What do you think he means?" Tucker asked.

"Well, I found Mead's prose pretty abstract, but what I think he's saying is that symbols give us the capacity for shared meaning. I can think about how I would react to something I'm about to say and imagine that you would react the same way. That's the essence of meaning, at least its social essence. If symbols didn't have this sort of significance, we wouldn't be able to predict other people's responses. Communication would be impossible."

"You've said a mouthful, Cliff," Tucker chuckles. "Let's see if we can break it down and simplify it. Incidentally, I agree with you—Mead is a tough read. But it's not his fault. You can blame his former graduate students. When he died, his students, most notably Charles Morris, put together notes of Mead's class lectures into what became *Mind, Self and Society* [1934]. If you folks ever decide to publish notes from my lectures, promise me you won't be this dull," he jokes. "But let's get back to the main idea, that when we talk to other people we are also talking to ourselves—our talk is directed back at ourselves. This appears to be an important difference between animals and humans. The noises that animals make, a dog's bark or a hen's cluck, for example, can signal something significant to other members of the same species, but these signals don't act back on the animals because they aren't reflexive."

"Is that what Mead meant by becoming an object to yourself?" a student in the front row asks.

"Good question," Tucker beams. "Here's where Mead's theory of self comes into play. We not only attribute meanings and values to objects like the ring I mentioned; we also attach them to ourselves. You say to yourself, I'm a good person, I'm a louse, I'm sympathetic, I'm cold-hearted, I'm honorable, I'm a liar, and on and on. You think well or badly of yourself. When you make these attributions, you step back from yourself and act toward yourself as you would act toward other objects. You become an object to yourself."

"Charles Cooley was one of the first sociologists to describe this process. He used the metaphor of a looking glass to help us imagine how becoming an object to yourself works. When we look in the mirror, we get an image of how we look and make judgments about what we see—'damn, I look good' or 'oh, I hate my big nose.' Here's how Cooley (1902, p. 184) put it:

> Each to each a looking glass
> Reflects the other that doth pass.

"Just as a mirror reflects back to us and we react to the image we see, the significant others in our lives also offer up an image of our meaning and value. We see how they see us, or at least we think we do. We imagine the attitudes they take toward us, and we form judgments and feelings about ourselves accordingly. We may feel pride or humiliation, esteem or degradation, self-importance or self-hatred.

"Mead extended Cooley's depiction of a social self by describing the developmental stages children pass through in developing a self. He emphasized the importance of imitation, playing roles, and participating in games, drawing connections among language competence, cognitive ability, and self-development. According to Mead, the development of self-consciousness was rooted in social interaction and dependent on the child's evolving communicative abilities to 'take the role of the other.' An infant is not born a self, but rather becomes a self socially over time. By the time the process is completed, the self has internalized the attitudes of others into a generalized view, the generalized other, a global standpoint from which you perceive yourself. In other words, the self is largely a social creation, a process through which one internalizes the reactions of others, especially significant others. All of us are vulnerable to the reactions of powerful and significant people in our lives. We all run the risk of taking on other people's attributions and attitudes as our own. If your parents repeatedly tell you that you can't do anything right, that you'll never amount to anything, eventually you may believe it. You start to see yourself as a loser."

Tucker was giving me a headache. His examples hit me close to home. That was my father he had just described. I could never please him. He always found fault with my work, never expressed any faith in my abilities, and gave me no singular attention that wasn't criticism, punishment, or denunciation. Never the apple of his eye, I functioned instead as the rotten core. It wasn't tough love he gave; it was insufferable disgust. Still, there was a sense in which his constant disapproval may have communicated that how I acted mattered to him, even though he always seemed to be there, peering over my shoulder, waiting for me to make a mistake.

Somewhere along the line, I must have been exposed to an alleviating condition. I may not have loved myself in the most self-affirming way, but I never completely internalized my father's views either. Why hadn't I accepted my father's view that I was a loser? Most likely because I was much closer to my mother, who lovingly muted the influence of my father's negativity. She thought of me as her "baby" and worked hard and deviously to protect me from his physical and mental assaults. Mother cuddled and nurtured me, smothering me with the affection she never got enough of from my Dad. In her own quiet way, she affirmed and respected me, made me believe I had talent, even when the evidence was negligible. Contradictory images clouded my looking glass. Given the presence of these oppositional reflections, I couldn't wrap my mind around Mead's notion of a generalized other. Had my mother's validation superseded my father's negativity? Is the person looking into the mirror actively affecting what he or she sees in it? What happens to a self created out of contradictory and oppositional attitudes?

Wandering through the thicket of contradictory self-images that constituted memories of my childhood, I was brought back to earth by Tucker's dramatic ending to the class. "Next week we'll look at some of the consequences of assumption number two: that I can stimulate other people in ways other than I am myself stimulated. We'll ask, Is man a manipulator? Are we all liars compelled by self-interest? What games do people play?"

Blown Away by Goffman

I pick up the receiver and recognize Barb's voice on the other end. We've quickly developed a close friendship, and we talk frequently, often late at night, about the books and articles we've been reading. "Have you done the communication theory readings for this week?" she asks.

"I just finished about an hour ago."

"Goffman's book ([1959] blew me away," she says, sounding all charged up. She talks like a hippie too, I think to myself. "I couldn't contain my excitement. I had to call and find out what you thought."

"I think the book is brilliant but also disturbing. After all the time I invested in the humanistic psychologists, to read Goffman was a real downer. He doesn't have a high opinion of human nature."

"You can say that again," Barb chuckles. "But once you get past his negativity, there's so much there. His use of metaphor is thrilling and ingenious. I've never read anything like it. He's a sociologist but writes like a novelist."

"So you think behavioral scientists should write like novelists?"

"I don't see why not. It's a whole lot more interesting than all that abstract stuff we're usually assigned to read. It's not as if his work is devoid of concepts or theory—it's saturated with theory. But he keeps your attention by dressing up concepts with anecdotes and little stories drawn from literature or from his own observations. Didn't you find the book engaging?"

"Actually, I couldn't put it down. He reminded me of this professor I had as an undergraduate, you know, the one who loved Freud so much."

"Uh-huh."

"He thought Freud's greatest gift was the stories he told, and he challenged us to think of psychological theories as stories. Brammer—that was his name—was quirky and unconventional, and after I left his class I never heard anyone associate stories or storytelling with science or theorizing again."

"I did the very first night of class," Barb reminds.

"And Goffman shows how right you were," I say, trying to cover up my omission. "He's an insightful theorist and a terrific storyteller. I may not agree with his cynical view of human nature, but I love the way Goffman uses anecdotes from everyday life."

"Yeah, the stories sucked me in immediately," she replies. "I loved the episode he took from the novel about the Englishman vacationing on the beach in Spain. I could picture that guy parading his physique across the shore, acting as if he didn't notice anyone else. I've known a lot of guys like that."

"I don't think men do it any more than women," I challenge. "Women just do it more subtly."

"You're not a woman, Art, so you don't see it," Barb says, and I think to myself that she's probably right.

Not wanting to quibble, I say, "Regardless, it was a perfect example of the concepts he was introducing, the two types of communication."

"You mean expressions given and expressions given off?" she asks.

"Yes. Every public social action seems to be a performance to Goffman. He sees through all the social games we play, like how that guy was imagining the way others would look at him as he performed his little scripted scene on the beach. He puts himself in their place, sees them seeing him, and acts accordingly to create a desirable image of himself for them to perceive."

"Very cool, indeed," Barb laughs faintly. "You could teach a whole class session around that one anecdote."

"And you'd be showing something important about communication and social order," I reply. "Don't you think?"

"I do. I'm totally turned on to Goffman. He theorizes how the social order is maintained and does so unconventionally, more like a storyteller than a social scientist." I love Barb's exuberance and gut reaction to things. She continually colors outside the lines, refusing to accept anything on faith.

"I don't know if you can call him a social scientist," I reply. "He's not applying rigorous methods, at least not any we've been learning around here. He's not collecting data, giving questionnaires, or using one of Campbell and Stanley's quasi-experimental designs" (1963).

"He's observing people in natural settings, you know, drawing observations from everyday life. What's wrong with that? It's empirical."

"Yeah, but he's as likely to refer to literary depictions as he is to real life encounters to make his points."

"So?" Barb questions.

"Well, you've heard Tucker," I remind her. "You know how he harps on rigor and the importance of controlling error and manipulating variables. Goffman doesn't do anything like that. He makes reference to his fieldwork, but he doesn't lay out any methodological procedures. He leaves them implicit. Do you think Tucker would let us get away with that?"

"No, I don't think so," she replies. "He seems to draw a line between imaginative ideas and methodological rigor. Sometimes I even feel confused about what Tucker is trying to teach us about the moral dimensions of human communication. He seems to love all the humanistic and touchy-feely stuff that shows people aspiring to become themselves, to communicate honestly—loving, empathizing, and treating other people well. On the other hand, the readings for this week show all the contradictions and difficulties we face in everyday, face-to-face communication, not only the fragility and precariousness of everyday interaction where social order can break down at any time—like Goffman shows—but also the bad things that can happen to people. Like if you're born to the wrong parents or to critical parents who may unwittingly teach you to think badly of yourself. I swear other people can really screw us up, especially the ones who play a significant role in our lives."

"That's why Sartre [1958] said, 'Hell is other people.'"

"Tucker would probably call him soft on method," Barb jokes. "Maybe it's not a question of whether people are by nature good or evil," she continues, "but rather how they deal with various unexpected life circumstances that they have to face. Fate and chance can play a huge role in a person's life."

"R. D. Laing [1965] says something like that in the book on Tucker's syllabus."

"You're way ahead of me, Art. Those readings aren't assigned for a couple more weeks."

"Well, the titles of his books caught my attention—*The Politics of Experience* [1967], *The Divided Self* [1965], and *Self and Others* [1961]—so the other night I started the chapters we were assigned, and I couldn't put them down either."

"Aren't you the good student?" Barb teases.

I interrupt with a cough and clear my throat. "I'm going to ignore that comment," I jab back. "But seriously, Laing points out how vulnerable we are as children. Given how many parents are unprepared for parenting—you know, they're anxious and neurotic and don't know what the heck they're doing—it's no wonder so many children end up disturbed, frightened, and fearful."

"Can we get back to Goffman?" she asks, as if I'm breaking line.

"Okay, okay," I apologize. "You're the one who brought up the negative effects of significant others."

"All I was trying to say is that Tucker wants us to be authentic, caring, and empathic communicators, but I think he also wants us to see that the social order requires a certain degree of control and manipulation. If you begin to think of social life as largely Machiavellian, you know, manipulative and controlling, you could easily go over to the dark side and live as if your life is one big game of impression management."

"That's certainly what the readings for this week show. Goffman [1959], Berne [1964], and Shostrom [1967] see social life as riddled with manipulation and deception."

"So much for human potential," Barb sighs. "Tucker keeps twisting my head. I can't figure out what he really thinks. He says he wants us to be rigorous behavioral scientists and to use the most advanced methods and statistical procedures, but what he shows us as exemplars of the best work on communication are people like Goffman."

"And Laing and Bateson. Wait until you get to Bateson [Bateson, 1967, 1972; Bateson, Jackson, Haley, and Weakland, 1956]. I've started reading him too. He's another theorist whose work is impossible to fit into any kind of traditional behavioral science methodologies."

"Good for you, goody two shoes," Barb says sarcastically; then laughs aloud.

"I'm just echoing *your* point, Barb. Like you, I'm turned on to communication theory but confused about how to translate what I'm reading into a research project that would fit Tucker's definition of rigorous behavioral science."

"Maybe Tucker's just trying to prepare us for the harsh realities of academia? You know, publish or perish! He seems to admire empiricists in communication such as Gerald Miller and Jim McCroskey because they're so productive."

"I'm not so sure. He admires that they publish, but he doesn't seem to feel the same way about *what* they publish. He isn't in awe of them the way he is Mead and Goffman."

"And probably Bateson and Laing to come," Barb chides sarcastically.

"Do you think he'd let someone do a dissertation like Goffman's?"

"I'm sorry to be the first to tell you this, but I don't think there are any Goffmans strolling around South Hall."

"That wasn't my question. I'm not asking whether any of us are creative or ingenious enough to become another Goffman. I'm asking whether we could model our work after his, try it out, and see where it leads? Would Tucker let us do this?"

"Well, from what I can tell so far, he'd insist that we develop hypotheses from a literature review and specify our procedures and methods step-by-step."

"Goffman doesn't do any of that."

"You're not getting my point, Art. Goffman is a genius—he doesn't have to do any of that stuff."

"It was good enough to get him a PhD at the University of Chicago, wasn't it?" I ask rhetorically. "You know, the book was from his dissertation."

"Look, I love his book, but I couldn't begin to tell you how to do a dissertation like it. He doesn't tell you his method. Sometimes the book reads like a scholarly monograph; sometimes it sounds like something you'd read in a magazine or newspaper."

"But shouldn't this option be open to us? Why do we have to restrict ourselves to experimental research?" I ask, as much to myself as to Barb.

"I guess if you're Goffman, you don't have to choose. You can merge the art of the storyteller with the theorizing and abstractions of the scholar. I hope you'll ask Tucker that question."

"I'm not ready to do that," I respond. "I'm just thinking aloud. You started this conversation full of excitement about Goffman. You don't get that excited about Campbell and Stanley [1963], do you?"

"You're so right," Barb agrees. "Goffman is a trip. He creates these elaborate analogies like "all the world's a stage," and then he uses them to illustrate through little stories how the performances of everyday life are both comedic and tragic. He formulates evocative metaphors like face-work and then weaves them through these richly textured anecdotes. I kept stopping and saying, 'This rings true … I've thought that … I've done that.' How thrilling."

"I admire him too, but for different reasons. He's opened my eyes to a different kind of scholarship and research, a different way to write and communicate what we observe as researchers and scholars. Tucker's training us to do experiments, whereas Goffman shows what you can learn from being alert to what's going on all around you. For Goffman, it's all data—every conversation, every public place, everywhere people meet. And the method seems to be in the writing, placing life into stories that exemplify concepts."

"So if that means writing like a journalist, then maybe that's what we need to do," Barb adds emphatically.

"Frankly, I think Goffman's cynical portrayal of social interaction is exaggerated. Do people manage impressions? Of course we do—some of the time. Is interaction in everyday life precarious and fragile? Yes, a lot of interaction is delicate and vulnerable to breakdown. But are we all incorrigible con artists—you know, cool, calculating, and deceiving swindlers. I'm not so sure. I don't see social life as nearly that sordid and unpleasant."

"You just have a hard time accepting a dark side to interactional life," Barb replies. "You're one of those half-full guys. I like that about you, really I do. Of course, social life is not all duplicity and despair. But there is a lot of suffering created by our so-called social order, and sometimes you need to take off the rose-colored glasses. Besides, I think you exaggerate Goffman's claims. He's largely dealing with life out there on the street, in public places. And by tuning us into deception and dishonesty, he's making us aware of the moral dimension of communication. I expected that to appeal to you."

"Okay, so you're one of those both/and rather than either/or kind of people. But sooner or later a person has to make a choice. You can't stay in the middle on everything," I sigh. "But I don't think we can settle this tonight. You've exhausted me, and I should probably go to sleep soon. But, hey, thanks for talking through this stuff with me."

Barb pauses, clears her throat, and moans in a deep, male voice, "Louie, this could be the beginning of a beautiful friendship" (Lebo, 1992).

Communication Theory Meets Lived Experience

[I had met and fallen in love with Brenda Runyon a few months before completing my master's program at Syracuse. We had married in August 1968, several weeks before I started my doctoral program.]

One evening, in mid-October, I find myself immersed in the readings Tucker assigned on antipsychiatry (Laing, 1965, 1967; Szasz, 1961). These books strike a chord because Brenda's father had been involuntarily committed to a state mental hospital more than fifteen years before. Diagnosed as paranoid-schizophrenic, my father-in-law likely will remain in this facility for the rest of his life.

R. D. Laing and Thomas Szasz are licensed psychiatrists who question the scientific and medical legitimacy of the concept of mental illness as well as the practices of mainstream psychiatry. Laing (1965, p. 17) uses the term "lived experience" to draw an important distinction between the objectified world of scientific inquiry and the world of immediate experience that defines a person's "being-in-the-world" (Heidegger, 1962). According to Laing, physicians and scientists roam a world of concepts and explanations that are largely depersonalized; they see a man or woman as "an organism" or "a system of processes" akin to a machine. When this happens, a patient's personal experience can get translated into depersonalized clinical terms familiar to the psychiatrist but outside the patient's lived reality. The patient becomes a clinical specimen, and the meanings of his or her life experiences are converted into psychiatric jargon or diagnostic categories considerably removed from the patient's experience of her own world and herself.

As an existential phenomenologist (Hegel, 1949; Heidegger, 1962), Laing argues that lived experience precedes the abstractions of scientific inquiry. He describes how the concepts, jargon, and abstractions of scientists can have the effect of depersonalizing and objectifying the very people psychiatrists are trying to understand. Laing (1965, p. 18) acknowledges that "as a psychiatrist, I run into a major difficulty at the outset: How can I go straight to the patients if the psychiatric words at my disposal keep the patient at a distance from me?" His remedy is to seek meticulous fidelity to experience in a descriptive fashion. He believes that you really can't understand a person who is different from you by relying on your own point of reference. Instead, "one has to be able to orientate oneself as a person in the other's scheme of things ... without prejudging who is right and who is wrong" (1965, p. 26).

Laing was the first scholar I'd come across who explicitly emphasizes the importance of the relationship in understanding a person's behavior and/or communication. He insists that "the study of human beings ... begins from a relationship with the other as person" (1965, p. 21). This relational perspective is the starting point for Laing's critique of psychiatry, which rests on the premise that in a psychiatric setting or interview, the behavior of the patient is a function of the behavior of the psychiatrist. The two persons—psychiatrist and patient—exist in the same behavioral field and collaborate to define the situation and their relationship to each other. The fact that the psychiatrist is trained to look for signs of disease complicates the situation, and the task essential to psychiatry is *interpretation* of the patient's behavior in the language and terminology of psychiatric symptoms. The psychiatrist's taken-for-granted preconceptions about normality and psychopathology, including the whole taxonomy of mental disorders, blur perceptions of the other as a person. Training and professional socialization make it highly unlikely, Laing claims, that the psychiatrist can grasp the patient's way of experiencing and understanding his own situation. Instead, the psychiatrist places his or her own constructions and interpretations on the behavior and communication of the patient.

Laing implies that even the most bizarre and deviant behavior might make sense and seem reasonable, or "sane," if one could grasp the context in which the behavior took place. A psychiatrist—or any observer for that matter—cannot achieve this sort of understanding by examining or observing the person in isolation, that is, outside the context in which the person behaves bizarrely. A relational orientation that would encompass a whole system or network of relationships had to replace the individualistic (or monadic) methodological tradition of looking at one person or consciousness in isolation. Thus, Laing implements a transpersonal or interpersonal approach to psychiatric therapy and research (Laing, Phillipson and Lee, 1966).

In "The Ghost of the Weed Garden," Laing (1965) tells the story of Julie, a ward of a mental hospital for nine years, from age seventeen. Julie hears voices and feels an upsetting, invisible barrier between herself and other people. Over the course of more than 180 interviews spanning more than 250 hours, Laing attempts to decode Julie's habitually obscure and secret language, emphasizing the existential predicament in which she had been immersed and showing the kind of understanding that can be reached by examining the family's experience of Julie and her experience of them as a relational system operating together. Laing (1965, p. 182) writes, "These three stages in the evolution of the idea of psychosis in members of a family occur very commonly. Good—bad—mad. It is just as important to discover the way the people in the patient's world have regarded her behavior as it is to have a history of her behavior itself."

The other antipsychiatrist I was reading, Thomas Szasz (1961), claims that mental illness is not a disease because it is not located in the body nor does it have an organic origin. Calling an illness "mental," says Szasz, confuses the mind with the brain. Mind is a concept; the brain is an organ. Besides, if we thought that mental illnesses were diseases of the brain, then we ought to call them brain diseases and send patients to neurologists instead of psychiatrists. But there are no objective diagnostic tests—neurological or otherwise—that can determine organically whether a person has a mental illness. You can't determine whether a person has depression by looking at blood tests or X-rays. You have to rely completely on the person's outward appearance, behavior and/or what other people or the person herself says about her behavior or mood. Thus, mental illness remains the province of the psychiatrist, a doctor whose expertise is confined mainly to helping people deal with "problems of living"—in other words, human relations. "I submit," writes Szasz (1960, p. 117), "that the idea of mental illness is now being put to work to obscure certain difficulties which at present may be inherent—not that they need be unmodifiable—in the social intercourse of persons. If this is true, the concept functions as a disguise; for instead of calling attention to conflicting human needs, aspirations, and values, the notion of mental illness provides an amoral and impersonal 'thing' (an 'illness') as an explanation for *problems in living.*"

Growing up in a working-class family, I understood that life could be arduous and that social relations, even among people who loved each other, were rife with conflict, argument, and even violence. When the phone stopped ringing, my father's work slowed down, meaning money became scarcer and bills mounted. My body absorbed some of my father's stress; I could feel the strain and void in my gut. Predictably, my father's volatile temper erupted more frequently at these times. Enraged by circumstances over which he had no control, Dad said hurtful things and flung his fury onto us. I never doubted my father's sanity, but on several occasions I heard my mother refer to his outbursts as "the ravings of a madman." Looking back now, I realize that I may have defined my father's quick temper and sudden violence as normal because I had nothing with which to compare it. Besides, our family needed my father; we couldn't have made it without the income he earned. When it came right down to it, his work ethic provided security and comfort. He had survived the Eastern European *shtetls* and the Great Depression, and he showed a tenacious determination to survive whatever life threw at him. Frankly, mental illness wasn't really a concept in our world, and we couldn't have afforded treatment anyway.

Szasz opened my eyes to the moral and ethical dilemmas everyday life poses. We have to figure out how to relate and treat other people and how to deal with differences between them and us—differences in values, desires, needs, and ideas, such as what is right or wrong, good or bad. People differ widely in their views about birth control, suicide, abortion, and euthanasia as well as how they regard people of different races, sexual orientations, ages, and political and religious affiliations. Indeed, each generation invents and molds new categories for classifying (and judging) people and behavior, and the new descriptions they mold introduce new choices for judging good or evil. Szasz (1961) is harshly critical of the urge to medicalize and pathologize behavior that deviates from an arbitrary standard established as normative. He wants us to consider deviant behavior not

70

as a medical issue, but as a social, ethical, or moral one. We can argue and try to reach agreement about what moral criteria should be used to judge a person's character and personal conduct, but we should not turn an ethical issue into a medical one. When we medicalize (mis)behavior, we introduce a slew of new problems: We displace personal responsibility, we justify involuntary treatment, and we license coercion.

"What people now call mental illnesses," writes Szasz (1960, p. 116), are for the most part *communications* expressing unacceptable ideas, often framed, moreover, in an unusual idiom." What constitutes an unacceptable idea or unusual idiom, one that deviates from the norm? This is the ethical dilemma the psychiatrist faces. Who gets to say what is normal and what is deviant? Whose interests are served by classifying a person as sufficiently deviant to be considered mentally ill? Who benefits?

One reason why this dilemma can be so wrenching is that someone other than the patient may get to decide whether the person himself is sick, or, in Laing's terms, either is mad (crazy) or bad (evil) (1961). It may be a spouse, a parent, or a relative, or it may be legal authorities, physicians, or society in general. What then? Social control disguised as medical treatment. Medicalization justifying coercion. Other people get to decide what is best for "the patient," though, in fact, they may be deciding what is best for themselves. They can deny the patient the right to consent to treatment, forfeiting the person's liberty and freedom. In a free society, should a person be protected from himself?

Such a Vexing Question

I close the book and sigh. Sitting quietly at my desk, I try to take in the full weight of what I've just finished reading. After a few minutes, I grab the book off the desk and walk through the narrow hall in the home we rent, looking for Brenda. I find her in our tiny living room, sitting in her favorite chair. "Do you have a few minutes to talk?" I ask, taking a seat on the corner of the couch next to her.

"Sure," she says, "I've been reading some Anne Sexton poetry [1962]. You know how I love her poems." She closes the book and looks up at me.

"I don't see how you can tolerate reading those poems. She puts so much naked suffering on the page. Her poems make me cringe."

"She writes some joyous ones too," Brenda replies. "But it's her sadness that touches me. I feel as if I'm suffering with her when I read these poems."

"That's more suffering than I can take," I say in an exasperated tone.

"That's how you are. You want to see the best in people and in life. But that's not me. I can't readily forgive or forget all the awful things I witnessed as a child. My mother's gone, and my father will be in a mental hospital the rest of his life. When I think about them, I'm filled with sorrow. I realize some people find Anne Sexton depressing, but she helps me cope with the pain. In one of her poems, she talks of powdering your sorrow, giving it a back rub, then covering it with a

71

blanket, letting it sleep awhile until it can awake transformed to the wing of roses. I'm paraphrasing her, but you get the point."

"She's saying you have to embrace your sorrow. Treat it lovingly. You don't wallow in your pain, but you don't run away from it either. You allow yourself to feel and nurture it. Give it time to heal and recover. Is that how you interpret it?" I ask.

"Something like that," she says. I never seem to get a definitive interpretation from Brenda. She writes and studies poetry intensely, and she holds a conviction that it's best to leave meanings somewhat open-ended.

"Come on, tell me more," I urge.

"I think she's saying that it really takes guts to endure the despair and pain you encounter over the course of a lifetime. But if you can muster the courage to hold it close to you for awhile, you may be able to turn what is hurtful and ugly into something beautiful like a rose. But that's enough about Sexton. What did you want to talk about?"

"Oh, that's a lovely interpretation," I say, pausing before shifting the topic. "I just finished reading this book that Dr. Tucker assigned us," I say, handing it to her.

"*The Myth of Mental Illness*," she reads. "Well, that's a catchy title, but in my family, mental illness is anything but a myth. It's a reality."

"How sure are you?" I proceed cautiously, not wanting to offend or make her defensive.

"Are you serious?" she screeches. The high pitch of her voice shows her irritation. I knew this could be difficult. I don't want her to think that I don't believe her or trust her judgment, but reading Laing and Szasz raised so many questions and doubts. Their theories hit me—hit us—where we live.

After a few moments of awkward silence in which we both wiggle and fidget in our seats, Brenda looks me in the eyes and says, "I've told you before that I remember my father throwing my sister's high chair through the kitchen window and nearly burning down our house. My mother got to the point where she was afraid of him. She didn't know what he'd do. He went through the family fortune after the war, and he squandered every opportunity to make a life for himself. You read the medical reports at the veterans' hospital. They said he had become a danger to himself and to everybody around him and that he was paranoid."

"You mean that's what the doctors said and what your mother told you. But you also have that stack of letters from your dad you've saved all these years." I clasp Brenda's hand gently, trying to show that I'm not challenging her but really trying to understand.

"Yes, and I wanted to believe him for a long time."

"You mean you believed he was sane and competent?"

"Well, the letters sounded normal. I could see he had a good mind. He wrote beautifully and told evocative stories about being a journalist during the war. He blamed everything on my mother for committing him and keeping him locked away in the hospital. He said she hated him, that everything was her fault, and that I needed to come and rescue him, get him out of jail. That's what he called it—jail. I didn't know what to think. I was only seven years old when he was committed. My mother refused to talk about him, and I didn't have any opportunity to visit him until I went away to college. That's why I chose Syracuse University, because it was so close to the veterans' hospital in Rochester. But when I went to see him there for the first time I realized he was sick and that he'd never be able to leave. He was like a child frozen in time. He wore suits from the fifties and thought Eisenhower still was president."

"What did you expect? He had a lobotomy."

"But the operation didn't seem to alter his intellectual functioning. I thought if he can write such coherent letters, he must be normal—maybe my mother is hiding something. She never allowed us to see him after he was committed, which increased my curiosity and made me doubt what she told me. But when I finally did see him I knew she had been telling the truth all along."

"What do you mean? What had she been truthful about?"

"That he couldn't care for himself; he needed to live in a hospital. You saw how modulated he was."

"Yes, I was shocked at how flat he was emotionally. He spoke in a monotone and his face showed no emotion. I got the impression that all feeling had been burned out of him. The thought crossed my mind that if someone touched the flesh on his hand with a lit cigarette, he wouldn't react. He wouldn't feel it. It frightened me to imagine what it would be like to be unable to feel pleasure or pain. I guess that's why some people equate being lobotomized with becoming a vegetable."

"So you see what I mean. He needed to be in the hospital."

"Of course, he can't leave *now*—after the lobotomy, and after fifteen years of institutionalization. But seeing him now isn't the same as seeing him *then*. You've said yourself you can't remember what he was like before he was institutionalized and lobotomized."

"I remember that he was violent and irresponsible. He put our whole family at risk."

"Lots of people are violent and irresponsible. That doesn't make them sick."

"After I read the medical reports I had no doubt any longer that he was mentally ill. The doctors said he was psychotic, and they described some of his delusions in detail." Noticing the frown on my face, Brenda stops abruptly. "Why are you looking at me like that?"

"What you're describing isn't mental illness."

"What would you call it?"

"Bad behavior."

"Is that what Dr. Szasz says?"

"Yes, that is what he says. In his view, what you've described is misbehavior or, in the case of delusions, bizarre behavior. But it's not a disease or an illness, and it's not indicative of a medical problem."

"If it's not medical, then what kind of a problem is it?"

"It's an ethical problem," I say.

"Oh come on, Art, that's absurd. I guess the next thing you'll say is my mother should have consulted a philosopher. Here, I don't want to read this book." She tosses the book onto my lap. "I don't understand why Dr. Tucker would assign such a book."

"I think you *should* read it," I say, gently handing the book back to her. "Why did Tucker assign the book? That's a good question. My guess is that Tucker sees Szasz as a communication theorist because his critique of psychiatry and mental illness is a communication theory. He's saying that what we call mental illness—the term *mental illness* itself—is a metaphor. There is no such *thing* as the mind. The mind isn't an organ like the heart or the liver; it's an abstraction, and you can't have a disease of an abstraction."

"What about the brain? That's how they treated my father's mental illness. They did surgery on his brain because that's where his mental illness was located."

"You mean that's where they assumed it was located. They couldn't prove that the source of his 'behavior problems' was his brain, which would, I agree, conform to the biological model of disease. But let's imagine for a moment that they could. Then wouldn't it make more sense, be more honest, to call it brain disease? Calling it mental illness has severe consequences for the person assigned that label. We don't normally think of a person with brain disease as 'certifiable' or 'insane,' and we don't lock them up against their will."

Brenda shakes her head. "This sounds to me like nothing more than semantics. We should call it *this* instead of calling it *that*."

"You say 'nothing more,' but I think what we call it makes a huge difference. Szasz is debunking the pretense of psychiatry. He's saying that accepting the idea of mental illness completely transforms the idea of disease. It becomes a rhetorical strategy for medicalizing personal or social problems that aren't really medical, then using a medical diagnosis to take away the person's freedom."

"The question is what do you do with someone who acts as crazy as my father did?"

"I don't want to sound harsh, but it seems to me that calling your father's behavior 'insane' or 'psychotic' was a means of justifying what turned out to be cruel and unusual punishment. Nobody examined his brain, and there was no objective evidence that he had a disease, not unless you consider bad behavior an illness, in which case, not to beat the drum again, but you've transformed the definition of disease. You're no longer insisting on an organic or biological diagnosis based on medical tests. Instead, you're willing to accept the evidence provided by how the person acts or what other people say about the person. These are value judgments, not objective, scientific tests."

"I guess that's why he says it's an ethical problem," Brenda says. She sounds exasperated. She's a brilliant, highly educated person and grasps the concepts quickly, but I feel as if this whole conversation is bringing her too close to the most terrifying memories of her childhood.

"That's the heart of his critique of psychiatry," I continue. "It's not just that psychiatrists are allowed to classify misbehavior as an illness, but they're able to do so without acknowledging that their evaluation is a judgment based on values. The value judgment and the whole realm of their own interpretation—their own participation in the diagnosis—gets disguised. You don't catch a mental illness like you do a cold or an infection. Instead of categorizing abnormal behavior as an illness, Szasz wants us to see it as part of the human struggle with the problem of how to live, something to voluntarily talk over and decide about. He believes that everyone should have the right to reject treatment. Involuntary hospitalization should not be allowed."

"It sounds as if you're defending my father. You're saying, 'Oh, he had a hard life, and he just couldn't cope, so you can understand why he became psychotic.' That's pathetic. What about all the pain he caused the people who loved him?"

"Please don't be angry at me, darling. I'm trying to understand and work my way through these ideas. Frankly, I'm not sure what I believe. We're a society that takes for granted the reality of mental illness. Szasz makes me question what I've taken for granted. I'm thinking out loud. I'm wondering, when we call somebody mad or bad, is it because we don't know how to relate to them or how to cope with them? They bother us. They're a nuisance. They're different. They're strange, and they disturb us. But if a person says he's Jesus Christ or that he talks to God, does that make the person insane? Does that mean we should lock him up or give him electric shocks without his consent?"

"I know you're not trying to hurt me, Art. But I do feel sad and a little angry about our conversation. You're working through a theory, but for me it was a living reality. I didn't have a father at home, and it took me a long time to accept that my mother had him institutionalized for what she believed was the good of our family. I think making that decision killed her; it crushed her spirit. She never forgave herself for signing those papers. That's why she never divorced my father and she never dated or went out. She worked herself to death for us; then one day she just keeled over and died—way before her time. I think she died of a broken heart. Now you seem to want me to question whether she did the right thing."

"Oh, honey, I'm so sorry. I didn't know our conversation would go in this direction. I don't mean any disrespect to your mother. I would never want to have to stand in her shoes. She was given not only the power but also the awesome responsibility to decide what was best for your father and for the family as a whole."

"What was she to do? She had three little girls to support and nurture and a husband who terrified and mystified her. She couldn't control him, and he was of no use to her."

"What was she to do? That's such a vexing question."

Between Teaching and Fathering

On the first day of class, Dr. Tucker had promised to twist and turn us in many directions. He didn't disappoint. Tucker took us to the cutting edge of scholarship on communication and social interaction in the behavioral sciences: cybernetics,

75

general systems theory, symbolic interaction, dramaturgical sociology, cultural anthropology, general semantics, humanistic and existential psychology, social psychology, interpersonal psychiatry, family therapy, and ethnomethodology. Unconstrained by disciplinary boundaries, Tucker had no tolerance for colleagues in the field who wanted to insulate communication from other social sciences. "We are making the future," he would say. "We can't be bothered by parochial and narrow-minded views of what belongs to one field or another. If an idea, a theory, or a research study contributes to our understanding of the processes by which people make meaning and value, and/or grasp other people's meanings and values—how communication works or fails to work—then we ought to take note."

By the end of my first semester, Tucker had turned me on to behavioral science. His lectures were like a symphony—he was the conductor, and we were the orchestra. Enchanting us with stories that kept us on the edge of our seats, Tucker poked fun at the preoccupying dramas of everyday life while also prodding us to take seriously the existential realities of the human condition that make it imperative we use communication effectively to bring meaning and significance to our lives. How much self-awareness is too much? What are the risks of revealing ourselves too honestly? If you want your life to mean something, how should you act? What should you do? Are we all too self-absorbed? Why do people lie, deceive, manipulate, and think they have to communicate strategically? How do we balance our need for feelings of self-worth, independence, and freedom against the desire to be part of something larger than ourselves—a relationship, community, or society? These were some of the questions we wrestled with, argued about, and fought over in class.

It had never occurred to me that I could build an academic life around questions and issues that really mattered personally to me. Tucker made me feel it was not just possible but, in fact, necessary. I had found myself on the pages of many of the books and articles he had assigned. These writers were trying to get a grip on what was happening around them and to them—perhaps even because of them. They were focused on ideas vital to understanding the big problems of life, and they were examining these conditions of human life in an imaginative and systematic way.

But there was another side to Tucker: the science side. Tucker was a tenacious and intractable empiricist. During the years I was his student, he held an unyielding commitment to empiricism and quantitative research. He had been mentored by Donald Campbell, one of the world's foremost authorities on research design and statistics. "In Campbell's courses, we learned that you have to justify any conclusions you reach in research. The best way to do that, he would say, is through valid and controlled research designs, objective measures, and statistical analysis." The power of Tucker's personality and charisma as well as the manner in which he embodied and performed his convictions about empiricism—his excitement about being on the cutting edge of complex multivariate statistical analysis—transferred this conviction to his students. He didn't just teach research design and multivariate statistics; he practiced and lived them. He had one or two research studies going at all times, and his methods courses involved running data from his studies through multiple analysis programs and reporting and interpreting the results in class. He liked to say, "If you can't measure it, then it doesn't exist," and he relished the work of creating and validating questionnaires through his favorite analytic tool, factor analysis (Cattell, 1978; Rummel, 1967).

These were the days of computer printouts and data card entries. You had to type your data onto cards, submit program cards, and read and analyze the printouts. Whenever I had an advising appointment with Tucker I would observe computer printouts on his desk and pinned to bulletin boards in his office. Moreover, he would type his notes for course lectures onto computer cards, which he would keep in his shirt pocket and then conspicuously place on the lectern. Within a short time, many graduate students, mainly Tucker's students, adopted this practice as well. It became a tie sign (Goffman, 1971) that symbolized a connection to Tucker as well as a marker for the behavioral science students. Like Tucker, we carried data decks around with us, and the desks in our offices were covered with printouts and cardboard boxes full of data cards. Our book shelves were lined with computer program manuals (as well as statistics texts), and we spent more time in the computer center than in our offices or residences.

The campus computer center was a hangout for graduate students conducting dissertation and course research projects. Students spent endless hours there tirelessly typing data entries onto cards, submitting program cards with their data, and waiting for printouts of their results. If you made a format typing error, you wouldn't get any results, only an error message that meant you had to retype and resubmit (and you'd wasted hours of valuable time). The computer center was a little social world, a hub for budding researchers to network, pick up tips and hints from cohorts in other departments to improve computer skills, and gossip and socialize in an atmosphere of collegiality and friendship. All the graduate students who were actively engaged in empirical research knew each other. For graduate students doing quantitative research, the computer center became a home away from home and office, a place to mix work and play—at least for those of us who delighted in being called "computer nerds."

Tucker became a major transference figure for me. He was not only a teacher but also a father figure. In my eyes, he embodied everything that was lacking in my own father. He paid attention to me, and he complimented, encouraged, supported, and believed in me. He propped up my sense of self-worth, making me feel not only capable but also special, even exceptional. I felt as if he constantly gave me the biggest piece of candy.

I quickly developed a consuming love and admiration for Tucker. I hung on to his every word and became slavishly devoted to the academic ideals he promoted. "Being a professor is not a job; it's not even a career," he would say. "It's a way of life that demands total commitment." He embraced the importance of producing scholarship, contributing to the accumulation of knowledge in one's field, but he also cautioned against overproduction. "You can perish by publishing," he warned, "so never put your name on something that isn't your best work." Often, he used his methods classes to critique published research. "Just because it's published doesn't make it true," he proclaimed, and he proved the point by showing us the flaws in published articles' research designs and how frequently researchers used inappropriate statistics or statistics inappropriately.

Under Tucker's spell, I uncritically accepted his version of the meaning of an academic life and the skills necessary to flourish in the academic world. The incongruities between the progressive theorists he embraced and the cutting-edge though conservative methodologies he promoted baffled me, but I realized he was delivering a superb education and believed he had my best interests at heart. I was determined to please him and validate his faith in me. If Tucker said I had to master statistics to be a behavioral scientist, then I was going to become the best statistician in my cohort and one of the best in the field. At the time, I couldn't see beyond my fixation on Tucker. It didn't matter to me how much work was involved in mastering statistics or how far removed quantification seemed from the ideas about communication and meaning making that really turned me on.

Frankly, I didn't really think about these things. I simply did what I was told. I bought lock, stock, and barrel into the ideology of quantitative research. Statistics became a game to play, one that was important to win. Methodological expertise separated the winners from the losers. And the rewards for being a winner were considerable. Tucker saw communication as infinitely complex and multivariate. If you could master the most complicated statistical procedures of the time—multivariate analysis of variance, multiple regression, canonical correlation, and structural equation modeling—you would put yourself in a position to study communication in a fashion that conformed to its complexity. Moreover, you could also play in the big leagues of academia and gain entry into the club of elite "scientists" in the field. As a methodologist, I would find it easier to design and conduct research as well as to publish it. Opportunities would knock, doors would open, the future would brighten. Though Tucker frequently reminded me that graduate school was preparing me for "a way of life" that would be all-encompassing and morally indivisible from the rest of my life, I actually understood what I was going through as preparation for a career. The prospect of a career sounded good to me. Maybe later I'd have time to think about my *calling* (Bellah, Madsen, Sullivan, Swidler, and Tipton, 1985).

CHAPTER THREE

Staging a Dissertation

Entry into a Professor's Way of Life

Like others of my generation, for me a Ph.D. in the social sciences meant that results were only meaningful if full of numbers, chi squares, and cluster diagrams and had a statistical significance of .05.... Yet I found that the noise, the outliers that blew away my 0.05 level of confidence, was where some of the interesting information lay. I felt an almost tangible beauty in the patterns, especially ones that outliers helped to foreground; surely they were part of the story.

Ellen Pader (2006, p. 161)

The Call

"Yes, he's here," Brenda says. "Who should I say is calling?" Holding her hand over the receiver she whispers, "It's the dean at Cleveland State." A smile covers Brenda's face and she starts jumping in place like a kid opening presents on Christmas morning. I feel a rush of excitement.

"Hello," I say, trying to contain my joy. Dr. Tucker told me that the dean would be the one to call if they were going to make me an offer.

"You probably know why I'm phoning, Art. You made a strong impression on the faculty in the speech department during your interview. I'm calling to offer you a tenure-track position as an assistant professor. My office will provide funds for moving expenses, and we'll start you at $11,500, contingent on finishing your dissertation. If you don't finish your degree by August 15, the salary will be reduced by a thousand dollars, and you'd start at the rank of instructor. You are going to finish, aren't you?

"Yes. I'm working on the final chapter of my dissertation. I've promised my committee a draft of the whole dissertation by early next month."

"That's what I want to hear, Art. We need you PhD in hand. You'll be the first behavioral scientist in the department, and I want you to assume a leadership role in reshaping the department's curriculum. I know that's a lot to ask from a young guy in his first academic position, but you strike me as someone up to the challenge. I held a meeting last week with the department. I told them that

Coming to Narrative, by Arthur P. Bochner, 79–100. © 2014 Left Coast Press, Inc. All rights reserved.

hiring you would be the first step in reshaping the department in the direction of behavioral science. The faculty agreed to change the name of the department to communication, and I gave my consent to search on three new faculty lines in communication research over the next two years. One of these lines will be dedicated for a senior scholar to chair the department. How does that sound to you?"

"Fantastic! My only concern was about being the lone behavioral scientist in the department and ..."

"You won't be for long, I can promise you that," he interrupts. "I'm making a big investment in this department, and I'm going to rise or fall on whether this pays off. As soon as you get here, I'll want to meet with you. I want to pick your brain about what shape the new curriculum in communication should take."

"I look forward to that. I've got some definite ideas about new courses and an interdisciplinary orientation to behavioral science," I say.

"Is that a yes, then? Can I tell the department you'll be joining them?"

"Yes."

"That's wonderful. You've made my day."

The Dissertation

I arrived in Cleveland, PhD in hand, in August 1971. A month earlier I had successfully defended my dissertation, "A Multivariate Investigation of Machiavellianism and Task Structure in Four-Man Groups" (Bochner, 1971), a study that reflected the schism of my graduate education and socialization. Seduced by Goffman's accounts of the fragile interactions of everyday life (Goffman, 1959, 1961, 1963, 1967, 1971), I had immersed myself in the scholarly and trade book literature that portrayed human beings as calculating con artists, strategic manipulators, and/or phony game players. Leaning heavily on the psychological theatrics of social interaction described by Berne (1962) and Shostrum (1968), I drew a sharp line between the pessimism and negation of the strategic school of impression management and the optimism and affirmation of humanistic psychology. Under Tucker's influence I designed an experimental study that would allow me to observe how these differences play out in small-group interaction. Tucker insisted that I needed a measuring instrument that could compare cool, detached, and task-oriented communicators who control, deceive, and manipulate other people for personal gain with spontaneous and social-emotionally motivated communicators who seek harmonious, candid, and emotionally expressive relationships. I settled on a measure of individual differences referred to as the Mach IV scale that was developed and validated by Richard Christie, a political scientist at Columbia University (Christie and Geis, 1970). Dividing subjects into groups of four, I varied the composition of each group systematically according to their scores on Mach IV. I assigned each group a task that was structured or unstructured, and I trained two observers to code the live interaction among the members of each group. I also analyzed the quality of the solutions to the task reached by each group (Bochner, 1971).

I didn't dwell on the question of whether research on the differences between calculating and spontaneous communicators could best be carried out in the environment of a controlled empirical study in which primary emphasis was placed on producing data that could be subjected to sophisticated statistical operations. I took for granted that communication phenomena could be expressed as quantities. As an empiricist, I felt obliged to formulate synthetic statements, convert these statements into verifiable operations of the variables, and develop procedures that would maximize the precision and validity of the measures as well as control any bias that could taint my results. The fact that none of the social theorists whose work I admired used numbers to represent the phenomena they were investigating didn't deter me, nor did I see their use of stories, clinical cases, and anecdotes from everyday life as a research model that I should emulate. These weren't the kinds of materials I had been trained to produce or examine. I never even considered them an option. I had taken on a blinkered view of communication research in which scientific method and quantitative analysis eclipsed all other considerations.

Tucker had drummed into my head a distinctively multivariate view of communication. "The phenomena of communication are complex, dynamic, and multivariate," he declared. "We have to get away from univariate, single-response modes of analysis and turn to more powerful and sophisticated multivariate strategies of data analysis."

I bought into empiricism not only because he spoke about it with such conviction, but also because no other option was available or known to me. "Yours will be the first dissertation in the field to use multivariate analysis of variance, least square estimates, and discriminant function analysis to assess trends and explain significant differences between experimental conditions," Tucker said in a tone reminiscent of a proud father.

Discovering a Relational Worldview

During my final year of graduate school, I cloistered myself in a library carrel. I had been assigned as a research assistant to Dr. Del Hilyard, the director of the Center for Organizational Communication. The first time I met with him, Dr. Hilyard handed me a stack of lined three-by-five note cards.

"You know where the current journals are kept in the library?" he asked.

"Yes. They're on the same floor as my carrel."

"Good. I want you to go through every journal you find there, start with A and end with Z. Study the contents of the last few issues of each journal. If you determine the journal has anything to do with communication research, write down the information on an index card, one card per journal."

"What information do you want?" I asked.

"Write the title of the journal, the name and address of the current editor, a description of the focus of the journal, and the instructions to authors for submitting manuscripts. You'll find this information inside either the front or back cover of the journal. I expect you'll end up with data for at least seventy-five journals, which should be very useful for our center."

I thought this library work would be drudgery. "What a dreary routine of busywork this is going to be," I complained to Brenda when I got home. "Hilyard doesn't know what to do with me, so he's made up this monotonous assignment to keep me out of his hair."

I couldn't have been more mistaken. Reading and codifying academic journals quickly evolved into an enlightening project, one of the highlights of my graduate education. I discovered dozens of journals connected to communication research. *Symbolic Interaction, Small Group Behavior, Journal of Applied Behavioral Science, American Behavioral Scientist, Family Process*—these were journals I had never come across until I undertook this project. Eventually, they formed the nucleus of my ongoing reading program. When I left Bowling Green, I had a detailed description of more than one hundred journals that published work relevant to communication research.

I was not surprised to discover that research on communication was spread across so many different fields. What did shock me, however, was how independently academic disciplines seemed to operate. Each discipline functioned as a little world of its own, content to be cut off and insulated from other disciplines with which it had much in common. If you were a psychologist, you paid attention to work in psychology and largely ignored research in other disciplines. In sociology, you referred to the research literature in sociology, but only rarely mentioned studies in allied or related disciplines. By reading journals in all of the behavioral sciences, I got the impression that membership in a discipline tended to be associated with a myopic and parochial attitude toward scholarship. I was energized by what I was reading in the literature of social psychology, symbolic interaction, cultural anthropology, linguistics, phenomenology, philosophy of language, and social theory, but I wondered whether I would ultimately be excluded from conversations with these materials because I was an outsider. A degree in communication would not qualify me for a seat at the table, even if I did know more sociology than many sociologists or more social psychology than many psychologists. Social science disciplines were as fenced in as gated communities. I might be able to visit, but I wouldn't be allowed to take up residence. Sadly, those confined to the inside usually can't see over the fence.

However, the library project strengthened my conviction that the study of communication offered a fascinating and important challenge that could hold my interest for a long time. At first I was astonished to discover that communication had captured the attention of scholars in so many different fields. But gradually I realized that this is what I should have expected. What is more basic to being human that the capacity for symbolic communication? Relationship is the core of humanity, and without communication there could be no meaningful connection between human beings; no capacity to share and make meanings, express desires, create art and cultures; or show emotions of love, rage, fear, and sympathy. To be human is to desire to understand other people and to be understood by them. Thus, to study communication was to try to understand understanding, its possibilities and limitations. Any science that called itself "social" would necessarily have to place communication at the center of inquiry.

Gradually working my way through these journals, I began to realize that knowledge about communication would never be confined to a single field called communication. A thousand voices clamored to be heard, each speaking in its own disciplinary vernacular. Research dealing with communication was scattered all over the place—anthropology, sociology, social psychology, psychiatry, philosophy, speech, linguistics, family therapy, history, and on and on. This discovery was both depressing and thrilling. On the one hand, how could one ever make sense of this stifling mountain of data? On the other hand, wasn't this a marvelous problem to encounter? One could never exhaust the task because there would always be something new to learn.

Each time I discovered a new journal for my list, I felt as if I'd received a birthday gift. Sometimes I'd spend the whole day reading back issues of the same journal. Other days, I'd go to the open shelves and run down volumes from the past ten years or more. I was a kid in a candy store who couldn't satisfy his sweet tooth.

One of the first journals I selected for my list was *American Behavioral Scientist*. Skimming back issues, I came across an article entitled "Some Formal Aspects of Communication," in which Paul Watzlawick and Janet Beavin (1967) attempt to develop a calculus of human communication in the form of basic axioms. "In the communicational perspective," they write, "the question whether there is such a thing as an objective reality of which some people are more clearly aware than others is of relatively little importance compared to the significance of different *views* of reality due to different punctuations" (p. 7). In other words, subjective experience is crucially important to understanding how human relationships work as well as how they change. Whether I perceive the world *accurately* is not nearly as important as what my perceptions—accurate or not—*mean* to me, what sense I make of them, and how different they may be from my partner's. For Watzlawick and Beavin (1967), the kinds of change that people seek in therapy is contingent on the therapist's capacity to alter the way they punctuate events and experiences—that is, their subjective ways of viewing events and experiences.

Watzlawick and Beavin (1967) also claim that the self-reflexive quality of communication makes it difficult if not impossible to fully understand the communication patterns between oneself and another person from within the relationship. You can't be standing inside a relationship, involved in ongoing interaction with your partner and, at the same time, occupy a position outside the relationship as a detached, uninvolved observer. "This is essentially similar to the impossibility of obtaining full visual awareness of one's own body," they write, "since the eyes, as the perceiving organs, are themselves part of the body to be perceived" (p. 7).

The distinction between events or objects in the external world (objective reality) and our perceptions of events or objects (subjective reality) reminded me of an essay by Gregory Bateson that Dr. Tucker had assigned in communication theory (Bateson, 1951). Bateson used the term "codification" to represent the perceptual processes by which we translate events or objects in the external world. External events are different from internal representations of those events, and codification expresses the way humans transform what is outside internally—that is, through the process of perceiving, categorizing, and interpreting events and objects. We think that we think in terms of *things,* but we actually think only in terms of *relationships.* "Our initial sensory data," wrote Bateson (1951, p. 169), "are always 'first derivatives,' statements about *differences* which exist among external objects or statements about changes which occur either in them or in our relationship to them.... What we perceive easily is difference and change—and difference is a relationship." Bateson pointed out that when we don't recognize an object or we're not sure what we're seeing, we usually change our relationship to what we are viewing; we move closer, touch it, or do something to change our relationship to the object, giving us a different perspective on it. Our "knowledge" is thus contingent on our positionality. When I say I know something, I necessarily implicate myself in my knowledge claim. I am the one who knows. What I know is the result of a complex system of perception, codification, and translation passing through me. Thus, the relationship between the knower and the known is of prime importance. Because what is known has to be codified, what we perceive is the product of our perceptions rather than something we might call objective reality.

The first time I read Bateson's essay, I focused mainly on his ideas about therapeutic change. According to Bateson, change was contingent on the communicative relationship between therapist and client. Thus, communication was the heart of therapy. Bateson had fascinating and fresh things to say about communication and interpersonal relationships. I was mesmerized by his notion that all messages are double messages, both response and stimulus—in his terms, "report and command"—and by the concept of metacommunication, which implied that every message was a statement about the nature of the relationship between communicators. For example, if my partner asks me to get her an aspirin and I say, "Get it yourself. You have two feet," my message is a both a response to hers and a stimulus inviting her further response. At the metacommunicative level, my message suggests that I am not necessarily compliant to my partner's requests. Collectively, the two messages—hers and mine taken as a single unit—show a couple immersed in a symmetrical struggle. If I had complied with her request—"Yes, dear, here you are, and I'll get you a glass of water too"—our exchange would be considered complementary—that is, one message fits with or complements the other.

Bateson was not so much concerned with a single unit of exchange, such as the exchanges described above, as he was with repeated patterns of interaction, however unconscious, that eventually take control of the relationship. Ironically, couples become locked into patterns of their own making but outside their awareness. Indeed, Bateson claimed that patterns of relating exert more control over the relationship than the partners themselves (Bateson, 1951, p. 208). As he expressed it, "the characteristics of ongoing process in this larger entity control both individuals in some degree."

These were complicated issues to wrap my mind around. If the relationship system controls the individual and not the other way around, then the only way to change a relationship is to change the patterns that control it. But if humans don't have the capacity to be involved in and detached from a relationship simultaneously, then there will always be a limit to our understanding of the patterns that control us. The only hope appears to be intervention from outside the relationship system.

Bateson's article was dense and difficult, the kind of theoretical essay that gives you a severe headache as you're trying to figure out precisely what the author means and how you can use it. He doesn't tell stories or present cases that clarify or exemplify his concepts. Still, I could see that he was grappling with crucial ideas about communication and relationships that were essential to understand.

I scratched the following remarks in my course notebook: "Bateson implies that the individual person is not the proper unit of analysis in the study of communication; it's the relationship between persons that matters—therapist and client, husband and wife, teacher and student. The study of communication needs to center on what takes place between people—the world of the *between*. We have to get away from the individual and move toward the relationship or toward patterns of interaction between people. I don't know how you would do this methodologically, but I'm beginning to see how important it is to draw a line between psychology, which emphasizes what is inside an individual, and communication, which focuses on what takes place between people. We need methods that can incorporate multiple perspectives, multiple meanings, mutuality, collaboration, and relationality. It's *we* who are crucial; not *I*."

Compartmentalizing Empiricism

In my final year at Bowling Green, Tucker offered a seminar on philosophy of science in which he emphasized the importance of the received view of knowledge developed by logical positivist and logical empiricist philosophers of science. "In science," Tucker said, "truth is dependent on method. The goal of scientific research is to represent reality as accurately as possible. Knowledge has to be based on observations of the empirical world that eliminate or minimize the intrusions of the observer. Objectivity is achieved through systematic procedures that eliminate bias. We divide inquiry into facts and theories. Facts are represented by the observation language, which is neutral with respect to theories and uninfluenced by any theoretical preconceptions. You see, theories deal principally with statements that are to be subjected to empirical evaluation. These observational statements are tied to theoretical propositions through the application of operational definitions." (Bridgman, 1929, 1959; Hempel, 1966, Popper, 1972).

Tucker went on and on about the importance of operational definitions and how theoretical terminology had to be unambiguously tied to observations. "It is crucial that these operational definitions exhaust the meanings of the theoretical terms," he insisted.

Empiricism rested on the idea that the object of knowledge could be entirely separated from the knowing subject, the researcher. The whole point of the objectifying procedures of empiricism seemed to be to take yourself—the researcher—out of the picture. Tucker was adamant about this: "Science had to be value-free. We can't allow any bias or interference based on the researcher's beliefs or values."

But the more I learned about communication theory—especially codification and classification—the more uncertain I became about the soundness of this realist account of objective knowledge. Reading Bateson a second time, I had this uneasy feeling that empiricism was unrealistic. Observed reality would always be something different from (real) reality because human codification and valuation inevitably transform rather than copy reality. Bateson considered this transformation mathematical. Thus, an observer's representation of objective reality could be thought of as the product of an observer's *internal computations*—that is, the person's (researcher's) own system of codification and evaluation.

These might have been unsettling thoughts for a person still in the middle of collecting data for his dissertation, but I had learned to compartmentalize the self who was a scientific, quantitative researcher. Later there would be time to explore my phenomenological, philosophical, and introspective self. I stayed insulated from these thoughts largely by immersing myself in the frenetic activity of data-collecting projects and my obsessive desire to master advanced statistical procedures. There was a practical side to this as well. "Only a handful of people in our field know anything about multivariate analysis techniques," Tucker gloated during a meeting with me in his office. "Your methodological skills are bound to pay huge dividends. You'll be in demand. I guarantee it." At my first professional conferences I learned he was right. Empiricists were just starting to get a foot in the door of speech communication departments, which were only then, in the early 1970s, beginning to embrace communication as a social science discipline. Many of the job listings were for methodologists who could supervise graduate research projects, theses, and dissertations—something right up my alley.

The New Model of Family Therapy

Several weeks into my journal project, I discovered *Family Process,* a multidisciplinary journal that published work in the broad area of family studies, especially family psychotherapy. Founded in 1961 by Donald Jackson and Nathan

Ackerman, *Family Process* focused on theory and research that moved away from mentalistic, individualistic, and psychodynamic concepts and toward directly observable interactional or behavioral phenomena.

As soon as I started reading I felt at home. Many of the articles were grounded on ideas developed by Gregory Bateson and situated in the cybernetic and systems theory on which Bateson's writings on communication originated. The authors of these articles were developing a new framework for understanding and treating emotional and behavioral problems. Instead of concentrating on internal (mental) processes within a person, the new model of family therapy fixed attention on relationships between people.

Family therapy questioned the conventional understanding of a psychiatric symptom, developed by Freud and largely taken for granted in psychiatry and psychotherapy. In the Freudian worldview the individual was a closed system and the symptoms that brought a patient to therapy were rooted in the person's past, usually in the family history. In psychoanalytic or dynamic therapies the patient worked through buried memories and called up events shrouded in secrecy from a dark and distant past. The new schools of family therapy rejected this historical view and, in the process, overturned the longstanding professional taboo against including other family members in therapy sessions. When they began to invite the whole family into therapy sessions, these family therapists saw the potential for an entirely new understanding of the meaning of a symptom. Where once they had located "illness" inside the identified patient, now they realized that the whole family was complicit in what ought to be understood as "family disorder." The parents and children shared in this conjoint dysfunction; the identified patient, usually one of the children, was not so much a victim as an agent who helped sustain the family dysfunction.

Family after family appeared to perform a similar balancing act. When the identified patient got better, someone else in the family got worse. In one of the earliest articles published in *Family Process* Jay Haley (1962) described families as *homeostatic systems* in which change in one part produces reactions in another part. If the family collaborated to coproduce the dysfunction, then perhaps they could also become a source of positive change through therapeutic interventions aimed at changing the interactional dynamics among family members.

On the pages of *Family Process* therapists and family researchers told evocative stories of therapeutic sessions that revealed the underbelly of dysfunctional family life—the myths, secrets, rituals, alliances, triangles, mystifications, and collusions that often lead to bizarre and deviant behavior on the part of one of the children—and offered strategies and interventions designed to recalibrate the family homeostasis in order to produce a positive outcome. As Boszormenyi-Nagy and Framo (1965, p. xvii) summarized, "It was learned that there is always cross-complicity in what people do to each other, and that the giving, getting, and withholding is reciprocal."

Family therapy offered a new outlook on the problems individuals encounter in their family lives. Each family was a single system, a world unto itself. A symptom wasn't something that marked an individual; rather, it belonged to the family. Thus, it was the family that had to be treated; the whole family was the "patient." Moreover, bizarre behavior suddenly appeared to be adaptive and to make sense. Often, the family therapists started by asking, What does this behavior mean for different members of the family? What does it do? What function(s) does it serve?

Showdown at Home: A Strategic Intervention

What if my family had gone for family therapy? I recall how my mother used to complain that I was "a troublemaker." She and my dad wondered whether some of my misbehavior at school meant I wasn't normal. "On your report card, your teachers always check the box that says, 'lacks self-control.' Frankly, we don't know how to control you either." They used to threaten to send me away to the Yeshiva or to a military school if I didn't change. Reading *Family Process* made me think that I hadn't been the problem after all.

I remember how anxious and fearful I felt when my parents quarreled, which happened often. When they argued, my father would get a delirious look in his eyes, and he would fume about some small thing, like soup that wasn't hot enough or dirty dishes left in the sink. "If you don't stop, I'm going to leave and never come back," Mom warned on more than one occasion.

After reading literature on family systems I began to question whether my misbehavior during these episodes was a way of keeping the focus on me. I was frightened that one of Dad's explosions would blow up our whole family. I felt safer when the focus was on me, even when it meant I had to take the full brunt of my father's rage. The possibility that Mom might leave terrified me. Without Mom there to keep Dad's fury in check, I didn't know what he might do. Though she occasionally betrayed my trust, Mom was my only ally.

On one occasion, Mom left for a week until, as she demanded, Dad begged her to come back. It was one of the scariest weeks of my life, though, to my surprise, my father acted like a horse broken to harness. Humbled into submission, he retired to the safety of his workshop. I hardly heard a peep out of him all week. Looking back, I can understand now how my mother's action—walking out like that—must have frightened him. Though not a therapist, my mother had enacted a restructuring intervention. After she came back, the whole organization of our family changed. She went back to work for the first time in more than twenty-five years, and I never witnessed another verbal brawl between them.

Pragmatic Communication Theory

The writings of the family therapists put me in a trance for weeks. Their enchanting cases kept me spellbound as I turned page after page of the journal and opened a new chapter in my academic life. These family therapists showed me that communication theory didn't need to be confined to testing hypotheses in a research laboratory. Instead, communication theory could be used to make a difference in people's lives, to change their relationships with people close to them, even to alleviate pain and suffering.

On the pages of *Family Process* I was introduced to a theory of therapeutic change extrapolated from the communication theory of Bateson, which consisted largely of concepts originating in cybernetics; information theory; and principles of living systems such as feedback loops, homeostasis, boundaries, circularity, differentiation, and equifinality (see Miller, 1978). I learned that in 1952, Bateson had received a two-year grant from the Rockefeller Foundation to extend Russell and Whitehead's Theory of Logical Types (1909), a mathematical formulation of classification systems, to communication in general. Russell and Whitehead's theory emphasized the discontinuities between a class and its members that arise from different levels of abstraction—different Logical Types. Bateson theorized that discontinuities in abstraction were not confined to classification systems such as scientific taxonomies; human beings are enmeshed in classification problems as well because we have to label the messages we send to and receive from others. Communication exchanges in which classification produces unsolvable paradoxes in a form akin to those logicians posed particularly fascinated Bateson. The most famous of these is Epimenides paradox: if a person says, "I'm lying," how do you know if the person is telling the truth? If he's lying, then he's not telling the truth, but if he's telling the truth, then he's lying.

The research team Bateson assembled to investigate paradox in human communication soon discovered, however, that whether a statement was true or untrue—a question near and dear to logicians—was not so important in ordinary human communication, where one typically is concerned not with truth but with *meaning*. How one interprets and responds to the meaning of a statement seemed, on the whole, considerably more important than whether the statement was true. Thus, to understand classification in human communication, it would be necessary to develop a language that could show how humans signal their intentions about how to interpret what they mean by what they say (or do). Bateson's research team eventually arrived at the concept of "levels of communication," in which every message includes both a main message and a qualifying message—that is, a message and a meta-, or framing, message. "Once we had arrived at the idea of the framing message," said Haley (1976), a member of the team, "it became possible to see a relevance between a paradox such as 'All statements within this frame are true,' and a piece of human communication where one person indicates with a framing message how his or her subsequent message is to be received" (p. 62).

Later on, the research team saw that the concept of a message framed by another message could lead to not only confusion but also error. The idea of a framing message implied a hierarchy of messages in which it appeared that one level of a message was of a higher order than another and that messages were confined to two levels, one of which was meta to the other. But in face-to-face human communication, when we are trying to figure out, for example, whether a message is meant as playful, ironic, teasing, or intentionally hurtful, we are confronted simultaneously with verbal, visual, and vocal messages as well as with the context of our encounter. In these cases, there is no message per se, only metamessages qualifying each other in ways that could be interpreted as congruent, incongruent, or conflicting and in which a communicator's strategic ambiguity or desire for deniability can make interpretation both difficult and perilous.

When the Bateson research team renewed their grant through the Macy Foundation, they turned their attention to the study of schizophrenia from the point of view of communication, focusing on the pattern of conflicting injunctions communicated between parents and children in which the schizophrenic child is punished for expecting punishment. In the process of applying for the grant, Bateson gave the example that parents will hit a kid, and when they see him again, the kid will cringe. The parents will get angry with him because he's cringing as if he's going to be punished, when actually he has been punished already. And so he expects punishment (Sluzki and Ransom, 1977).

In the second project, the one that led to the double bind theory of schizophrenia, the Bateson team became intrigued by the metaphoric quality of schizophrenic communication. When one patient was asked, "What's your mother like?" he replied, "Skinny as a wolf, painted like a cat with a large tail like a scorpion that stings" (Haley and Richeport-Haley, 2007, p. 134). Obviously, the mother is not a wolf, a cat, or a scorpion, but these metaphors speak volumes about the relationship between mother and son from the son's point of view. The relationship level of the statement is *analogic*; it requires us not to take it literally but rather to see it as an analogy for the type of relationship existing between mother and son. The idea is that symptoms always analogize the relationship— they always signal something about the relationship. As Haley (1963) observes, "The fight a married couple have over who is to pick up whose socks does not necessarily have socks as a referent but rather what the socks have tended to mean in the context of the relationship" (p. 84).

As communication theory gradually became imported into family therapy, the analogic qualities of communication assumed increasing importance. In the context of the family, messages always carry multiple levels of meaning. For a family therapist, a symptom is a message that can be considered adaptive to the ongoing behavior of other family members. You can call it character disorder, phobia, or hyperactivity—no matter: to a family therapist it is simply communication that carries out some function within the family system. The goal is to intervene into the system in such a way that the symptomatic behavior is no longer adaptive and, hence, no longer necessary.

For several weeks, I sat in rapt attention, unable to pull myself away from *Family Process*. Sooner or later, I was going to have to put this project aside and concentrate on my dissertation, but for now, this was where I wanted to be. *Family Process* was different from any academic journal I had previously encountered. Don't get

90

me wrong: There was plenty of theory on these pages, many of the articles were data driven, and there was no lack of charts, tables, and graphs. But the authors I came to adore—Jay Haley, Salvador Minuchin, Carl Whitaker, Virginia Satir, Carl Sluzki—also were skillful and brilliant storytellers. It was the stories they told that brought theory to life and held me captive.

For example, Haley illustrates how symptomatic behavior can be understood as a means of controlling the definition of the relationship between a husband and his wife by telling the story of a patient who was married to an alcoholic wife. When he saw them together in therapy, the man said there were things he would like to control, but his wife always got her way by getting drunk. The wife indignantly disputed her husband's version, saying her drinking was involuntary and brought her only misery. Haley (1963) argues, however, that this woman obviously had won control over the definition of their relationship. "He could not go where he wanted because she might drink; he could not antagonize her or upset her because she might drink; he could not leave her alone ... because of what she might do when drunk; and he could not make any plans but had to let her initiate whatever happened." As Haley metaphorically expresses her commanding presence, "... she could bring him to heel merely by picking up a glass" (p. 17). Her drinking effectively controlled the definition of her relationship with her husband. She was able to restrict and confine his behavior while indicating that she herself was powerless.

Speaking for My Data

Returning to my dissertation, I submerged myself in a pool of computer printouts only to find that the meaning of the statistical analysis was not self-evident. Based on the research literature, I had anticipated that groups with more High Mach members would show a greater proportion of task activity; they would stay focused on the job at hand and not get carried into conversations extraneous to completing the task. Flipping through the pages of the printout for task activity, I saw a significant difference for group composition.

Yes! This is great news. Exactly what I predicted! My exuberance didn't last long. As soon as I saw the distribution of group effects, I knew I was in trouble. The differences were the reverse of what I had predicted. As Low Mach membership in the group increased, task activity increased. Now I had some explaining to do. These data were not going to speak for themselves.

Fortunately, the reading I had completed for the journal project was fresh in my mind. I kept thinking about what Jay Haley had said about the process of defining a relationship. "When two people meet for the first time and begin to establish a relationship," wrote Haley (1963, p. 1), "a wide range of behavior is potentially possible between them.... As [they] define their relationship with each other, they work out together what type of communicative behavior is to take place in this relationship." Although these were zero-history groups—strangers interacting together for the first time—they still were engaged in a process of defining their relationship. Whether the relationship is short term or long term doesn't matter. As Haley (1967) observed, "It must be emphasized that no one can avoid being involved in a struggle over the definition of his relationship with someone else.... It is impossible for a person to avoid defining, or taking control of the definition of, his relationship with another" (pp. 9–10). Goffman (1967, p. 5) had much the same process in mind when he introduced the idea of a person's "line" in face-to-face contacts: "In each of these contacts, he tends to act out what is sometimes called a line—that is, a pattern of verbal and nonverbal acts by which he expresses his view of the situation and through this his evaluation of the participants especially himself. Regardless of whether a person intends to take a line, he will find he has done so in effect. The other participants will assume that he has more or less willfully taken a stand, so that if he is to deal with their response to him he must take into consideration the impression they have possibly formed of him" (p. 5).

The tasks I had given to the groups defined a context for group interaction, but they did not define the relationships among the members, which was another important dimension of the situation in which group members found themselves. The members themselves had to work out these definitions interactively. The groups had to develop a working consensus on how they would approach the tasks and relate to each other. I had assumed that group behavior was a straightforward arithmetic sum of its individual members' beliefs about the nature of human beings and the importance of relating openly and honestly. My data showed, however, that this was not the case. Nevertheless, I still didn't want to give up the notion that Machiavellian conceptions of human nature influenced interaction among group members.

When I examined the distribution of scores within the task activity category closely I discovered a second flaw in my thinking. I had emphasized the *amount* of interaction in the overall category, task activity, thus ignoring the variety of *forms of interaction* by which individuals carry out their work on a task. Because High and Low Machs differ significantly in their orientations toward interacting with other people, the *qualitative* differences in their interaction styles may have proved more important than the quantitative ones.

Now I was on to something. I theorized that Machiavellianism could be understood not only as an individual trait but also as a feature of the group as a whole. In the process of defining their relationships, each group developed an atmosphere—a group climate—congruent with their dominant Machiavellian trait. When I examined the individual interaction scores, I found significant support for this interpretation: the Low Machs dealt with the task through socio-emotional modes of behavior, whereas the task behaviors that normally single out High Machs were displayed much less frequently by High-Mach members of Low Mach–dominated groups than by High-Mach members of High Mach–dominated groups (Bochner, 1971).

92

Defending My Dissertation

I pace back and forth in the department office, waiting for members of my dissertation committee to arrive. *Is it normal for committee members to arrive late to a dissertation defense? It's already fifteen minutes past the scheduled starting time. Did they forget? Is this a sadistic act intended to make me sweat? Tucker said this would be "a piece of cake," but I never received any feedback from the other committee members. What if Ober and Hilyard hated my dissertation? I know I'm not one of Dr. Hilyard's favorite students. I wonder whether he's going to come in loaded for bear. He never said anything about the quality of my work on the indexing project. No, I'm letting my imagination get the best of me. Calm down, Art! This is your day. You couldn't be any more prepared.*

The door opens, and Tucker walks through followed by the other members of my committee. Tucker smiles and tells me to follow them into the small conference room. As we enter the room, he says, "Give us a brief overview of your study; then we'll start the questioning." *None of my committee members acknowledge that they've shown up late. That's odd. Oh well, I guess they figured I wouldn't be going any place.*

As I prepare to deliver my opening remarks, I notice the other members of the committee have on their solemn game faces. Because the dissertation defenses in our department are closed meetings, I have no idea whether this is normal. *I sure hope this doesn't turn into one of Goffman's degradation ceremonies.*

I finish my presentation, and Tucker tells me to sit down across from the committee. "Professor Ober will begin the questioning," he says.

Students fondly refer to Ober as the department's "group guru." He teaches all the group process courses, including a fascinating course on self-analytic groups in which the whole class functions as a group and analyzes itself. There is no definite structure for the course, and he provides little direction or leadership. Some weeks, we sat in a hushed silence for what seemed like hours. When the tension or anxiety got to be too much, we would begin to talk about our reactions to silence, especially how we felt. On other occasions, members of the group would get into conflicts, and we'd end up expressing how we felt during these confrontations. Ober assigned few readings; instead, he required weekly reaction papers that required us to analyze ourselves and the group, focusing on our emotions. He insisted that we stay at the feeling level: "Avoid being too cerebral. You get enough of that in your other courses." His class implicitly critiqued the over-intellectualization of social relations. "What good is communication theory," he would ask, "if you can't use it to understand and improve your own communication, especially your capacity to understand, express, and deal with your own emotions?"

After a few warm-up questions about various details of the dissertation, Ober throws me a sharp-breaking curve ball. "So Art, tell me where you would want to score on the Mach scale. Ideally, would you rather be a High Mach or a Low Mach?"

Startled by the question, I take a deep breath and decide to let it all hang out. "When I started the study, I would have said Low Mach without blinking. As you know from our group course, I'm a relationship junkie. My ideal would be to relate to other people as unique human beings with whom I could build a harmonious relationship. You can tell by my literature review that I have little tolerance for manipulators, con artists, and deceptive communicators. But I have to admit, the more I watched these groups interact, the more respect I developed for the High Machs. They get things done. They're shrewd, cunning, and clever, and they don't waste time."

"Sounds like the ideal college professor," Tucker quips. The other committee members crack up, and for the first time, I feel at ease.

"So you'd rather be a High Mach? Is that what you're saying?" Ober asks. He's not going to let me off the hook, I think.

"Not exactly," I equivocate. "I find the Low Machs frustrating. They can't stay on topic very long, and they're overly other-directed, but they are warm and empathic. You could trust them as a friend or a colleague. The High Machs, they're on the ball, but they're also sneaky and conniving—not good attributes in someone you would want to call a friend."

"So which is it, Art? I haven't heard an answer," Ober presses.

"This is a tough call for me. I'd rather not have to choose. But if you put a gun to my head, I'd choose to be a Middle Mach, if that were an option."

"I guess I'm going to have to shoot," Ober jokes.

"Oh no, please don't shoot. I don't want my life to end before I complete my PhD," I play along.

"Seriously, Art, I thought for sure your relationship orientation would tip the scale toward the Low Machs."

"I may be a relationship junkie, but I'm also driven. I want to do something productive with my life. Low Machs see work as drudgery; they're not inspired to exert themselves. They can't be counted on to produce. But there's something missing in High Machs as well, something emotional. They stand apart, if you know what I mean. They're clinical and distant."

"Clinical, eh? That reminds me of the major finding you reported from Christie's research, that medical students scored higher on the Mach scale than any other professional school students. What did you make of that finding, Art?"

"It didn't surprise me in the least. These High Machs have self-selected a profession that fits their temperament and outlook on life and people. They're cut out for a profession that stays emotionally distant and makes heavy demands on efficiency, productivity, and staying on task."

The room grows quiet, and I sense we've come to the end of this line of questioning. Not comfortable with the silence, I continue. "To sum up, in an ideal world I'd want a little of each Mach personality type. I'd want the capacity to empathize and love, but I'd also want to make a contribution, do something of value, and get things done."

94

"You're up, Del," Tucker says, pointing to Dr. Hilyard.

"Congratulations, Art. You've produced a first-rate dissertation. The study was well conceived and well executed. The data analysis was a bit torturous for a univariate guy like me to plow through, but I really appreciated your thoughtful analysis of the results. You made a persuasive case for your interpretations. It takes courage to admit you were wrong and talent to reframe your original thinking in a manner that makes being wrong an opportunity for greater insight and imagination. You pull it off. You make being wrong not only honorable but perceptive."

"Thank you, Dr. Hilyard," I say, trying to sound grateful, though feeling uncertain whether he is complimenting or condemning my study. *I wish he'd have put a bit more emphasis on the word "perceptive."*

"I'd like to hear you elaborate on this relational definition idea you discussed in the final chapter. I wonder if you aren't introducing a problem for yourself. It seems to me that your study is grounded on the idea of individual differences and how they affect interaction between people. Am I right about that? Isn't Machiavellianism an individual difference?"

"Yes, it is," I agree. I feel my heartbeat quicken. I'm afraid Hilyard sees another flaw in my thinking.

"Then this approach you take, is it fair to say that it's psychological insofar as you're looking at how individual differences influence social interaction?"

"Yes, I think that's a reasonable way to put it."

"I do, too. But in the last chapter, things get a little muddled when you bring in this business of relationship definition, the line, and working consensus from Haley and Goffman. Their concepts are fresh and intriguing, but they appear to come from left field. Nothing in your dissertation prepared me for them. It's as if you're speaking two different languages. How do you reconcile the approach of individual differences with a relational or systems orientation? Aren't they competing perspectives?"

Bang! Hilyard had hit the nail on the head. I knew this was a problem. Privately, I'd thought long and hard about it, but I couldn't work out a way to incorporate my thoughts on this question into my dissertation. The whole question was too complex and layered. There was the issue of what constituted a "communication perspective" and how it differed from other perspectives. Was communication a discipline in its own right? If so, how do you study communication as opposed to psychology, anthropology, or sociology? Don't we need to apply methods that conform to a communication perspective? These were important questions, but I wasn't ready to address them. Nor did I want to launch into a critique of self-report data, even if I had formulated one, which I had not.

As if these concerns weren't difficult enough, I had to consider my relationship with Tucker. He had been educated largely in the tradition of social psychology. His mentor, Donald Campbell, was a psychologist. Tucker also had met and corresponded with the famous psychologist Carl Hovland (Hovland, Janis, and Kelley, 1953), and he frequently praised the work of other social psychologists such as Leon Festinger (1962), Harold Kelley (Thibaut and Kelley, 1959), Gordon Allport (1955), and Daryl Bem (1970). Tucker's dissertation was an empirical study of persuasive appeals and attitude change, a line of research that originated in social psychology. Perhaps he was passing his own indoctrination down to me, like father to son. My dissertation reflected many of his biases, though when I began, I hadn't seen them as biases. Only after studying Batesonian communication theory and reading the work of family therapists had I begun questioning the appropriateness of individual difference research to the study of communication.

"Do you follow my question, Art?" Hilyard asks, noticing that I've drifted off.

"I'm sorry. I was just trying to collect my thoughts."

"You can think out loud," Hilyard replies, encouraging me to begin.

"Okay, I'll try. As you observed, I didn't start out with a relational or systemic perspective. I simply was fascinated by the idea that the way people think about the place other people occupy in their lives makes a difference in the way they relate to them. People who think of others instrumentally will communicate differently from people who want to get to know others, you know, to form relationships with them. At the time, it didn't matter to me whether this was a psychological attribute. I was just enthralled by the idea. Then I found the book by Christie and Geis [1970] and discovered that I could measure these differences. I was excited by that prospect. Machiavellianism seemed to fit perfectly with the work on deception and manipulations that I had read in Dr. Tucker's course. To me, the communication part of the study was the direct observation of interaction. My question was, Would differences in Mach scores yield differences in communication behavior and interaction style? Do High and Low Machs relate to people differently? That's how I saw the relevance of individual differences to communication." I feel the sweat dripping down my brow. Realizing that I'm not really answering the question, I fear I'm about to be humiliated.

"But if you want to generalize about individual differences, doesn't that make you a psychologist?" Hilyard asks.

"I suppose it could, but not necessarily. My focus is on communication, on how different people relate to each other given how they generally think about people."

"You keep bringing up the word 'relate.' Is that how you understand communication, as a process of relating?"

"Yes. Yes, I do."

"Then you're really interested in relationships, not individuals, aren't you?" A grin covers Hilyard's face as if he's toying with me. I wonder if it's the game Eric Berne (1962) calls "now I've got you." Hilyard finds this amusing, but I feel as if I'm getting tied in knots. He knows I'm enchanted with the work of family therapists and by Batesonian communication theory, and he's calling me out.

"To be honest, I'm still trying to work this out," I reply.

"I don't follow. Either you're an individualist or a relationalist," Hilyard presses on. "You can't be both. They constitute different worldviews. Your study is conceived in the tradition of individualism, but when we get near the end you shift direction with all this relational talk—relationship definition, working consensus, social context. What are you trying to say?"

"You're right, Dr. Hilyard," I say. "Where I ended was not where I started, but I don't think that's a bad thing. I've been reading Gregory Bateson and the family therapists, and I'm coming around to something that might be called a relational conception of human being. When I examined my data closely I began to see that the individual differences may not have been as important as the social circumstances—in my case, the structure of the tasks and the relationships evolving among the group members."

"I think there's a better or, at least, a different way to put this, Art," Tucker interrupts. "You're saying that individual differences account for a significant proportion of the variance, but not as significant as the context, the social situation, and the relationships among members. Isn't that what you found?" Leave it to Tucker to state the matter in statistical terms, I think.

"Yes, in a manner of speaking, that's what I found, Dr. Tucker."

"Then we can leave it there," Tucker declares, signaling he's taking control of the meeting. I breathe a sigh of relief. Like a good parent, Tucker has intervened to protect me. "We're close to our ending time. I've got one final question. Look into your crystal ball, Art, and tell me where you think you'll be in three years. I don't mean physically; I mean mentally. What will your head be puzzling over? What research questions will be occupying your attention?"

I cup my hands as if I'm massaging a crystal ball, then I stare intently at an imaginary precious stone. My committee members crack up in unison. "I see myself trying to work out a new vocabulary to overcome some of the problems we discussed today," I tell them. "I want to understand some of the terminology used by psychologists in a relational way, such as *depression* or *addiction*. These terms usually are used to describe characteristics of an individual person. What we need are concepts that refer to patterns of communication and exchange between people. I also want to better understand what we mean by authenticity and, again, how we might think about authenticity relationally in terms of our connections to meaningful projects and community life."

"I guess Hilyard and Ober here have you pegged. You're a relationship guy," Tucker says. *I wonder if he's hurt that I didn't say anything about my work as a methodologist.* "Do you see anything else in your future?"

I gaze into the imaginary crystal ball again. "Yes. Yes, I see one more thing coming into focus. The fog is lifting. The object is becoming clearer and clearer. It looks like a diploma. Yes, it is a diploma made out to Dr. Arthur Bochner, Middle Mach!"

A Generation Gap

In July 1971, I celebrated my twenty-sixth birthday and packed for the move to Cleveland. Brenda and I were set to leave when Tucker demanded that I attend

97

graduation. "I won't take no for an answer," he said one day while we were chatting in his office. "You'll walk in graduation, and I'll be there to hood you. It means a lot to me, and it ought to mean a lot to you." I didn't have the heart to tell him that the pomp and circumstance of graduation was utterly unappealing to me.

I remember how lonely I felt at my high school graduation, sitting by myself, watching how joyously other kids' families were celebrating that evening. I imagined for a few seconds what it might feel like to have my parents applaud me that way. But when I looked at my parents' faces all I saw was an expression of the relief they felt that this period of their life finally had ended. Did I really have to go through this again?

Besides, I didn't need a ritual like graduation to make me feel good about completing my degree. I was proud of what I had achieved. Graduation wasn't going to augment how I felt. What could I gain by wrapping myself in a robe and parading across a stage? Doesn't that give the appearance of arrogance and pretense?

"One more thing," Tucker continued. "Make sure your parents know they're invited to dinner at our house after graduation."

"They're not coming," I replied.

"What do you mean your parents aren't coming?"

"I wasn't planning to walk in graduation, so I didn't invite them. I doubt whether they'll want to attend anyway."

"Sure they will. Here, call them," Tucker insisted, stretching the cord of his phone to reach me. "You can put me on the line. I'll invite them myself."

Tucker was my advisor and my friend, but there were things about me—my troubled relationship with my father and my liberal political values—that I had never confided in him. He could probably read my politics from the way I dressed, the long hair running down my neck, my jeans and T-shirts, and the antiwar buttons I sometimes wore. Once I caught him frowning at my "Never trust anyone over 30" T-shirt, but we'd never really discussed my attachment to counterculture causes. Tucker was straight as an arrow, formal in dress and manner, neat, religious, and devoted to his family. Though most of his students were leftist, activist hippies who marched in campus antiwar protests, participated in sit-ins, and demonstrated vigorously on behalf of the fight for equality for women and civil rights, Tucker never gave any hints about his own political convictions. Ever the neutral scientist, he must have wanted to keep it that way. We did too. Occasionally his advisees would gossip about how odd it was to have chosen a mentor who represented the "old culture" and, most likely, many of the traditional values against which we were rebelling. No matter, Tucker was generous, kind, and loyal to each of us, and we weren't about to say or do anything that would threaten our relationship with him. I wasn't going to let my opposition to institutional rituals come between us.

The graduation convocation was something I was going to have to grin and bear. Once my parents accepted Tucker's gracious invitation, I was stuck. It was too late now to disclose why I didn't want my parents to attend my graduation, and there was no way I was going to get out of it. Nor did I think that anything would be gained by telling Tucker that I thought rituals like graduation processions were empty and vain performances that posed as events to honor graduates while they actually validated the authority of cultural and institutional values such as the family, hierarchy, and corporate clout. My generation was trying to break away from the oppressive control of the patriarchal family, authoritarian schooling, and intense individualism, all of which would be celebrated at graduation.

Opportunity Gained/Opportunity Lost

"Wasn't that uplifting?" Tucker asked when we took our seats after the hooding.

"Yeah," I lied, thinking all the time how torturous it felt to sit through the dull speeches and the endless parade of graduates marching across the stage as their names were called.

Suddenly it dawned on me that I was thinking selfishly about this whole event: *This isn't my day. I've got it all wrong. This is Tucker's day. Just look at him. He's having a ball.* I felt a lot better thinking of the convocation as a gift from me to Tucker. It was the least I could do to repay him for the new life he had made possible for me, the yearning he had stirred, the confidence he had boosted, the future he had prepared for me. The feelings of alienation I felt at the beginning of the day disappeared when I saw how much Tucker was enjoying himself. For the moment I felt an intimate connection born of witnessing the expression of sheer joy and pleasure covering Tucker's face. Sitting there observing him, I wondered whether he thought of me as a son. I relished that thought. What would it feel like to have a father who was not disappointed in but rather proud of me? Tucker could be that father. All three of his children were girls. I could be the son who completed the picture. Looking across the auditorium, I spotted my father and felt ashamed of the thoughts racing through my mind.

After the convocation Tucker and I posed together for pictures, then with Brenda and my parents. Dad said he still didn't understand what it meant to be a communication professor but was glad to know that finally I was going to have a steady job. "This does mean you're through with school, doesn't it?" Dad asked.

"Yes, in a manner of speaking. I've finished my formal education. But professors have to continue to study their whole lives. It's the way of life we've chosen." Tucker grinned as I knew he would, hearing his words coming out of my mouth.

After dinner at Tucker's house, I walked my parents to their car to say goodbye. Mom hugged me tight and slipped an envelope into my pocket out of the sight of my father. "You may need this to get started," she whispered. "Your father and I want to help."

Dad opened the passenger's door, and Mom got in the car. As we walked to the driver's side Dad put his arm around me, stopped abruptly, and kissed me on the cheek. "I'm proud of the person you've become. I don't know how you did it. I didn't expect it."

There was a lot I wanted to say to Dad. I wanted to ask him whether he loved me, whether he had ever loved me. I wanted to ask him why he showed up at my PhD graduation but never took me anywhere I wanted to go when I was a kid. Why weren't you ever there for me? Didn't you know that being a father isn't simply a matter of convenience? There are obligations. There are ethical standards. You showed me your strength and resolve, but where was your tenderness, warmth, or affection? Wasn't I worth your time? I wanted to ask him why he never played with me—or with anyone. I wanted to ask him to share with me some of what he'd suffered through in the old country, to ask him why he never talked about it and what good it did to hide from it. I wanted to ask him why he spent his whole life in the basement while the rest of us were living our lives above ground. I wanted to ask him how he felt when he beat me with his belt. And right before, and after. I wanted to tell him how I had hated and feared his violent temper. A boy should feel safe in the company of his father, Dad. A boy shouldn't feel terrified, humiliated by, or ashamed of him. I even wanted to tell him how much I admired and revered his honesty, integrity, and work ethic, how grateful I was that this part of him had rubbed off on me. Who are you, Dad? Why don't I know you? Does anybody know you? I wanted to tell him how much I had needed a father.

"Thanks, Dad. I'm glad you came. Have a safe trip home." I stood and watched the car pull away. When will the right time come? Will I ever feel at peace about us?

CHAPTER FOUR

Raising Consciousness and Teaching Things That Matter

Education is simply the soul of a society as it
passes from one generation to another.

G. K. Chesterton (1924)

American Pie

"Good morning, the time is 8:35, and you're listening to WMMS-FM, Cleveland's choice in progressive rock."

Good. I'll arrive at the university in plenty of time to run off the mimeo of the syllabus for my ten o'clock class. I'm glad I don't have to rush. Late to class on my first day would not make a great impression.

I press on the gas and steer my car out of the apartment complex parking lot, past the road sign, CLEVELAND 21 MILES. On most days I've made it from home to office in twenty-five minutes, but colleagues have warned me it will take a lot longer in winter when snow storms blow off Lake Erie. I'm not looking forward to that. Entering the ramp onto I-271, I relax into my seat and turn the volume up on the radio.

"Have we got a treat for you," the DJ announces. "This next song is going to blow your mind. It's the mysterious new single 'American Pie' by Don McLean, from his album with the same name. I tell you this song is one big riddle, a real mind-twister. McLean does give a hint, though. He's dedicated the album to the memory of Buddy Holly. The song runs for eight and a half minutes, so breathe deep and take a listen."

> A long, long time ago
> I can still remember how
> that music used to make me smile
> And I knew if I had my chance
> That I could make those people dance
> and maybe they'd be happy for a while
> But February made me shiver
> With every paper I'd deliver
> Bad news on the doorstep

> I couldn't take one more step
> I can't remember if I cried
> When I read about his widowed bride
> But something touched me deep inside
> The day the music died ...

A chill runs down my spine and I decide to pull into the emergency lane and park. I don't want to split my attention between the highway and the radio. I've got to listen to this song, really listen to it.

When McLean sings, "but something touched me deep inside," I feel as though he is singing directly to me. I remember the "bad news on the doorstep." In 1959, I had been a thirteen-year-old paperboy delivering the evening edition of the *Pittsburgh Press* to my customers when I saw the headline that Buddy Holly had died in a plane crash shortly after takeoff from Clear Lake, Iowa. As their paperboy, I brought the bad news to the doorsteps of my subscribers. I rode my bike home as fast as I could peddle, the tears streaming down my face, and spent the rest of the evening playing over and over the two Buddy Holly 45s I owned.

Twelve years later, I sit in my car on the side of this road, visualizing the teen dance parties where my friends and I danced to the innocent, carefree, energetic music; the pictures of Buddy dressed in tuxedo or jacket and narrow tie, wearing his black, clunky, thick-framed glasses; and his thrilling performances with the Crickets on *American Bandstand* and *Arthur Murray Dance Studio*. I hear Buddy's rhythmic, staccato singing in that high-pitched, child-like voice of his that conveyed the intense yearning and restlessness of adolescent emotion so unsentimentally. "Peggy Sue" was my favorite Holly song. Was there ever a more lively and supple expression of male vulnerability and yearning? "I love you, Peggy Sue, with a love so rare and true"—such simple lyrics expressing so much feeling: the fear of unreciprocated romantic love, the loneliness of absence, the doubt, and the wonder.

These memories crowded my mind as I listened intently to the rest of *American Pie*, puzzling over its maze of mixed metaphors, multiple layers of meaning, and allusions to a broad spectrum of historically important pop-music characters from Elvis Presley to Bob Dylan, Janis Joplin, the Rolling Stones, and John Lennon. Though these referential riddles made the song irresistible, they had the effect of diverting my attention from the song's dark and sorrowful message. Wasn't this a song about death, not only about Buddy Holly's death but also the demise of an entire era, the Golden Age of fifties rock 'n' roll? Why had Don McLean chosen to express his mourning and lament in such a playful and lighthearted form?

As I pull back onto the highway and turn down the volume on the radio, my mind races with questions: What did "American Pie" mean? What made the song at once so inviting yet so despairing? What could I learn from McLean's method, his manner of delivering a pessimistic, derogatory message in a highly appealing way? Enchanting disenchantment—now there's something to wrap a person's mind around. But isn't this a dangerous tact, risking the possibility that listeners would only want to sing along and not reflect on the message? (See Baur, 2006.)

My first thought is that this is no ordinary pop song. "American Pie" feels like a cultural wake-up call, a farewell to American innocence and the untroubled rock 'n' roll of the early 1950s. I'm reminded of the expression "simple as pie." The associations are easy to make—simplicity with innocence, innocence with idealism, idealism with the youthful counterculture of the sixties. But we aren't teenagers anymore—we've grown up. What a struggle it is to hold onto your idealism after you've become an adult. "American Pie" strikes me as both a nostalgic yearning for the innocence of fifties rock 'n' roll and a mournful critique of the eclipse of sixties idealism. On the heels of the disorderly decade of the sixties— assassinations, war protests, civil unrest, counterculture, sexual revolution, and deception and lying at the highest levels of government—the youthful dreams of freedom, community, and unconditional love so often associated with the healing and hopeful power of music have given way to cynicism, materialism, and pessimism. Yet "American Pie" doesn't encourage me to sink into despair. Why not?

The song pulses through me all day. After distributing and discussing the course outline, I ask students in my first class if they've heard "American Pie." We have a lively discussion, but they mainly want to focus on the metaphoric references to pop stars. Following my afternoon class, I drive to Record Rendezvous and purchase the album. As soon as I get home, I make a beeline for my turntable, taking my notepad with me. I play the song again and again, jotting notes as ideas come to me. Listening closely to the upbeat piano and sing-along chorus that provide a buoyant and lighthearted atmosphere, inviting my participation, I imagine Don McLean on stage imploring the audience, "Now everybody, together. Sing along!"

Sing about the day you die! How absurd is that? He seems to be saying, "This is serious stuff, but don't take it too seriously." Is there a method to his madness?

McLean sounds as though he's enjoying himself immensely. He may be angry and disillusioned about what's happened to rock 'n' roll, but he has something he wants to teach, and he realizes he can't reach most people if he begins by alienating them. Besides, he seems to have worked through his grief and arrived at a place where looking back at the past is pleasurable, however turbulent and disappointing what he remembers may have been. His voice expresses to me the delight a person can take in an enhanced self-awareness born of critical reflection on the past (Baur, 2006; Schuck and Schuck, 2012).

The more I reflect on the song, the more fascinated I am by how Don McLean uses himself to get across his message. He's telling a story of his life and his feelings, drawing listeners in by using the first person: "I couldn't take one more step. I can't remember if I cried." This is his story, but he's also inviting us to make it ours.

Given my own life history, I identify: I'm with you, Don. We belong to the same generation and some of the emotions and concerns that course through you also flow through me. I doubt if I'm the only one who feels this connection with McLean. You're counting on that, aren't you, Don? Could there be a universal truth here, something beyond just his story or mine? When he shifts later in the song to the second person—"Do you recall what was revealed the day the music died?"—I feel as though he's addressing me directly: What did I learn? What can I discover by reviewing this history? Like a good teacher, he refuses to give the answer. Does that mean nothing was learned? Or must I go figure it out for myself? Is my generation so "lost in space" that we can't start again? Is it too late to wake up and change our lives?

Don McLean is speaking for himself, but not *only* for himself. He's representing the experiences of a whole generation. "American Pie" is his expression of what the 1960s meant to him, not only the cultural importance of those years but also their emotional significance. He's asking us to acknowledge the turbulence and corruption of the current times—in rock 'n' roll as well as in "American Pie." Ironically, McLean delivers his message through the same medium that is a target of his critique (Baur, 2006). He uses rock 'n' roll to critique rock 'n' roll. The music hasn't died!

A Counterculture Searching for Meaning

At Cleveland State, most students were the sons or daughters of white working-class parents, the first in their families to attend college. A few were trying to get deferments to avoid the military draft, but most came because college represented their best chance to achieve a higher standard of living than their parents had. Or so parents, teachers, other elders, and the media had led them to believe. Still, the state of the US economy couldn't have inspired a lot of confidence in the future. The recession that started in 1970 appeared to be deepening. None of the economic experts seemed to know how the country was going to pull out of a deteriorating recession complicated by the unprecedented combination of rising prices, high unemployment, and a sluggish economy. The economic buzzword of the day was "stagflation," the simultaneous occurrence of inflated prices and a stagnant economy. In August 1971, the same month I moved to Cleveland, the Nixon administration imposed wage and price controls. Instead of curbing inflation, however, Nixon's fiscal restraint increased unemployment and froze the job market.

But these students had more on their minds than the economy. They had lived through the tumultuous sixties, a decade born in optimism and ending in distrust. By 1971, the hope and idealism of John Kennedy had given way to the duplicity and trickery of Richard Nixon. Witnesses to more than their share of loss, betrayal, and violence, these students wanted little to do with a power structure they saw as square, corrupt, and greedy. Money and material possessions were not as important to them as freedom, sensitivity, and openness to experience. Things were changing fast. Life seemed all too short, and if they weren't careful, they could miss the pleasures and possibilities it offered.

These teenagers and young adults had a different outlook than their parents on what it meant to achieve a higher standard of living. The good life was an existence devoid of the kind of loneliness, isolation, and role playing they had witnessed in their parents' lives. Like Ben Braddock in the movie they adored, *The Graduate*, these students saw no future in "plastics." Fashioning a counterfeit self would be akin to a kind of death in life—a thankless death following a mournful life. What a waste it would be to lose one's innocence, to never achieve a state of wonder or awe in the face of the majesty and mystery of existence. Living an authentic life, open to experience, became a moral mandate, the foundation of their clash with the mainstream culture they were trying to counter. In the reality these baby boomers chose to construct, one had no choice but to resist the cultural imperative of achievement motivation, other-directness, and materialism on which the older generation's authoritarian, puritanical, and subjugating individualism had been built.

The term "counterculture" had been introduced into the public consciousness in a series of articles published in *The Nation* in 1968 by the historian Theodore Roszak. These articles formed the core of Roszak's best-selling book, *The Making of a Counterculture* (1969), in which he argued that campus protests represented a broad resistance to the burgeoning power of America's evolving "technocracy." Roszak (1969) saw the counterculture as a rebellion against the political, religious, and social imperatives of America's escalating consumer society and its infatuation with new technologies aimed at advancing the goals of efficiency, rationality, and standardization. Not wanting to become victims of social engineering and unwilling to submit to the authority of technological expertise and mechanistic organization, the counterculture expressed a defiantly nonconformist and anti-institutional attitude; embraced a politics of liberation; rejected the ideal of a life of sacrifice to a job; took a stand against multinational corporations, the military-industrial complex, and the draft; tested the limits of sexual freedom and consciousness raising; and championed the causes of women's rights, civil rights, social justice, and communitarian democracy.

Although other cultural critics of the time, such as Philip Slater (1970), saw important differences between militant activists and hippies, Roszak (1969) used counterculture as a unifying term encompassing a wide diversity of commitments spanning the politics of emancipation and social justice, spiritual rejuvenation, sexual liberation, alternative and experimental lifestyles, and grassroots and community democracy. The varieties of dissent represented in the causes to which various factions of the counterculture were pledged tended to obscure the degree to which the "mind-blown bohemians" and the radically activist student New Left shared a commitment to what Roszak (1969, p. 58) called "an extraordinary personalism," a devotion and openness to flesh and blood experience and to deep levels of self-examination.

Profoundly alienated by what they perceived as a dehumanizing social order embodied in the pale lives of their own parents, the youth culture wanted little or nothing to do with meaningless work or joyless relationships. They'd seen the consequences of being married to a job, exchanging happiness for security, and conceding one's deepest desires for the safety of conventionality. In their brief lifetimes, they'd witnessed the harsh consequences of senseless wars, racial injustice, abject poverty, and police brutality. No amount of consumption, full employment, or high productivity could compensate. This was generational warfare. The only choice was to undermine and counter the conventional society of one's parents, the generation that had so diminished the prospects for living a just, humane, and joyful life. For some members of the youth culture, this meant making a commitment to political confrontation in the hope of transforming the basic structure of industrial society's institutions; for others, it meant rejecting imprisoning cycles of production and consumption by refusing to accept conventional definitions of success and happiness, opting out of the marketplace of competitive individualism and/or by refusing to "keep up with the Joneses." For some of them, it meant leaving the comfort of their suburban middle-class families and moving to the rural countryside where they could embrace a return to nature, setting up communal living arrangements devoid of dogmatic authority structures and gender role and sexuality prescriptions; while for others it meant opting to forget the past and future and to try to live in the present—here and now—by being spontaneous, on edge, and playful or, as Timothy Leary put it, to "drop out, tune in, turn on" (Leary, 1967).

Similar to most college students of the time, the undergraduates at Cleveland State were searching for a meaningful system of values by which to interpret and organize their lives. They questioned nearly everything about their lives and about American life in general, trying to answer the existential question Roszak (1969, p. 233) posed: "What is worth living for?" Or, better yet, what is worth dying for? What is the meaning of love, work, friendship, intimacy, sexuality, family, religion, spirituality? Why is there so much violence and so little love in the world? Why is our government so secretive and unresponsive to the will of the people? Why is our country so militant and aggressive? Why aren't psychedelic drugs legal? Why can't our parents understand us, appreciate the music that turns us on, or identify with our desires and hopes? What will happen to us if we don't conform?

The Cleveland State students were not strangers to what was going on in the world. Their country had been torn apart by war, dissent, civil disobedience, police brutality, and a generation gap saturated with distrust, hostility, and a clash of lifestyles and values. They felt exposed and vulnerable, with no place to hide. The men knew they could be called up to the draft any day; the women realized they weren't occupying an even playing field. Many of them had marched in organized protests against the Vietnam War, some had participated in sit-ins at restaurants or student strikes on campus, and most were acquainted with urban violence provoked by police brutality. On their way to school each day, some students had to drive past 79th Street and Hough Avenue, where broken windows, boarded-up shops, and burned-out residential buildings remained in various states of decay and neglect in the aftermath of the 1966 Hough race riots.

On April 30, 1970, President Nixon announced in a televised address to the nation that he had authorized a major new incursion into Cambodia. The decision to invade Cambodia was widely perceived as an escalation of the war and a return to Lyndon Johnson's determination to win a military victory in Vietnam. In the speech, Nixon implied that antiwar demonstrators were responsible for destroying America's great universities, and that Americans were witnessing "mindless attacks on all the great institutions which have been created by free civilizations in the last 500 years"' (Bochin, 1970, p. 64).

War protestors met Nixon's words on a scale and with a force never witnessed before on American campuses (Katsiaficas, 1987). Within ten days, more than forty ROTC buildings had been burned or bombed; and within thirty days, "80 per cent of all universities and colleges in the United States experienced protests, and about half of the country's eight million students and 350,000 faculty actively participated in the strike"(Katsiaficas, 1999, p. 120). The protestors demanded, among other things, "that the universities end their complicity with the United States war machine by the immediate end to defense research, the Reserve Officer Training Corps (R.O.T.C.)."

On Friday, May 1, 1970, university students at Kent State, a campus culture normally energized by football, fraternities, and frivolity, staged a protest on campus. After students set fire to an ROTC shack located at the center of campus, National Guard troops were called in by Governor Rhodes, who explicitly instructed them to restore order and take control of the campus over the weekend. By Monday, however, tensions heightened again as students resisted the state of martial law and the dusk-to-dawn curfew that had been established on campus. Gathering on a hill in front of a campus building, the students shouted at the troops, who stood in a line down the hill from them. The troops yelled back to no avail; then tossed tear gas at the students to break up the crowd. The situation quickly grew chaotic until an order was given to start shooting, and the National Guard soldiers, kids themselves, turned in unison and fired at the students, killing four and injuring nine others.

The killings at Kent State sent shock waves through the country, touching off a chain reaction that emboldened and accelerated the antiwar movement. In every section of the country and in practically every walk of life, people found themselves caught in the grip of a new wave of antiwar sentiment provoked by the powerful emotional current resounding from the shots fired at Kent State and the mounting violence on the streets and campuses, where it was estimated that more than one hundred people were killed and dozens more injured by law-and-order officers or guardsmen (Katsiaficas, 1987). Extending far beyond the halls of ivy, the antiwar movement was now able to mobilize the participation of previously uninvolved groups—prisoners, war veterans, professionals, women's rights activists, and blue-collar workers (Katsiaficas, 1987)—and within weeks, public opinion turned decidedly against the war.

The shootings at Kent State University were still fresh in the minds of my students when I joined the faculty at Cleveland State. How could they forget the shocking image of that grief-stricken girl kneeling behind a fallen student gunned down by National Guardsman; her arms extended outward as though to implore "how could this be happening?"; her opened mouth and frightened eyes screaming in disbelief and horror? Appearing on the cover of *Newsweek*, this candid photograph was etched in the minds of all of us who lived through that awful week in May 1970.

Teaching Things that Matter

In the spirit of the sixties and the aftermath of the calamity of Kent State, I felt compelled to make my classroom a laboratory for conversation about things that mattered. I had just turned twenty-six. Not much older than most of my undergraduate students—younger than some—I found myself struggling with many of the same issues as they were. Caught in the grip of a free-floating anxiety, I was going through a major life transition. Already distanced from my parents, I had landed in a place in which I felt isolated from my oldest and closest friends, cohorts, and graduate school mentors.

How was I going to fit into this new academic life I was entering? Nobody had warned me that this could be difficult. Nobody had said, "You may feel lonely, disconnected, and unsure, but don't worry—that's natural. You'll get over it." I knew I was no longer in graduate school. Still, I felt more like a student than a professor. Student was what I knew best. In graduate school, I had supported student strikes in opposition to the war and on behalf of racial equality and women's rights, but my activism was not entirely positive because it exacerbated my distrust of politics and politicians and alienated me further from the values of the major cultural institutions of society. I experimented with drugs and made the most of my sexual freedom, but I had the uneasy feeling that my attraction to danger and adventure was just another form of escapism. I didn't want to go through life feeling angry, alienated, and disconnected. "I'm empty and aching and I don't know why," sang Paul Simon (1968) and Art Garfunkel, whose words perfectly captured my state of mind. Except I wasn't "looking for America"; I was searching for an intense feeling of connection to something meaningful. I yearned to be part of a community of goodness and value that would enable me to make my life of work something I could experience as play, a vocation grounded in love and trust rather than an exercise in alienated labor.

In the classroom, I had a huge and seductive advantage. Though a professor, the students saw me as one of them. I was roughly the same age, and we talked and looked alike. My long, thick hair flowed down my neck onto my shoulders, and a beard covered my face. I wore tie-dye T-shirts, hip-hugging blue jeans, and sandals with no socks. Immersed in the music of Bob Dylan, Jimmie Hendrix, Joan Baez, Judy Collins, the Doors, Isaac Hayes, Otis Redding, Janis Joplin, and the Rolling Stones, I knew the lyrics to most of the students' favorite songs. We spoke the same language, and my working-class roots gave me credibility and identification. We were on the same plane—well, pretty much. They had no in-terest in multivariate designs for research or grand theories of communication; instead, they wanted to experience and talk about life, about the failures and hopes of existence, about the generational gap in values and interests they were experiencing, and about the relevance of "higher" education to the prospect of leading a meaningful life. Truth be told, so did I.

"Relevance" was the new buzzword in higher education. At teach-ins and campus demonstrations, students clamored for a more relevant curriculum. They wanted courses that would elevate political consciousness and tackle important cultural, social, and moral issues of the day.

The students had a point. Undergraduate education had turned largely into a job-training program, as departments increasingly focused on narrow disciplinary and professional skills. The demand for relevance was an attempt to undermine and shift this focus. What I heard in the students' call for relevance was a desire for more meaningful and meaning-centered education—teaching that touched them where they live; their hearts as well as their minds. Students wanted the university to connect to them on a more personal level. At least some of their education ought to speak directly to what they worried about, coped with, and struggled to understand outside of the university. As far as I was concerned, this was a good thing—for them as well as for me. Their concern for relevance freed me to think about how I could use the communication classroom to focus on what students cared about and what might make a difference in their lives, validating my desire to make communication a moral rather than a professional subject.

Raising Consciousness

In the winter of 1970–1971, the book everybody was talking about was Charles Reich's The Greening of America. Reich argued that false consciousness, a pervasive unreality that was ruining America, had spawned the problems of lawlessness, alienation, racism, and military aggression. But it was not too late. America still could be saved. What was needed was "a revolution by consciousness" that would produce a new worldview, a new consciousness that the younger generation had already set in motion. Berated by most critics but adored by most readers, Reich's book spoke to the zeitgeist of the moment, lavishing praise on the counterculture and inviting the older generation to see reality through the lens of the new genera-tion. Within weeks of publication, the book shot to the top of the New York Times' best-seller list, and Reich, a little-known law professor, became a national celebrity.

Reich opened The Greening of America (1970) with a startling prediction: "There is a revolution coming. It will not be like revolutions of the past.... It will not require violence to succeed, and it cannot be successfully resisted by violence.... It promises a higher reason, a more human community, and a new and liberated individual. Its ultimate creation will be a new and enduring whole-ness and beauty.... This is the revolution of the new generation" (p. 2). What an

109

appealing depiction of a revolution! How could anybody say no to an insurgency of love, trust, and splendor?

Reich came across as a sincere and energetic writer, carrying a message he hoped would create the very revolution and social order he was predicting. In the minds of some critics, the coming revolution was a figment of Reich's imagination, and this was a criticism he must have anticipated. Foreshadowing this reaction he wrote, "To call this order 'fiction' is just a way of saying that the only reality man has is the one he creates" (1970, p. 425).

As a forty-two-year-old Ivy League professor and former Supreme Court clerk, Reich was no hippie. He had never participated in a war protest or a sit-in. He may have wanted the job of spokesperson for the counterculture, but he would never be able to speak as an insider. What Reich lacked in direct experience, however, he made up for in unshakable faith and optimism. Indeed, could hardly have been a more passionate and enchanting advocate.

Reich's zeal was contagious, his sincerity admirable, and his timing perfect. The success of the book also stemmed from his flair for writing accessible prose and his grasp of audience. Preaching to the choir meant he didn't have to muster evidence to justify his faith in the counterculture or his certainty about revolutionary reforms that would arise from personal growth. Reich understood that the popular imagination coveted the ideal of a good society, meaningful work, and commitment to community and personal growth. Whether you were conservative or liberal, younger or older, you could see that the major institutions of society were breaking down or already broken. Who could resist the appeal of personal growth and spiritual awakening? Who wanted to argue against living with greater consciousness, less regimentation, more pleasure? Who doesn't want to feel more connected, more in control, more aware?

Reich's embrace of the new generation's "Consciousness III" felt thrilling, even blissful—until, that is, I started poking around at the solution he was offering, which was high on hype, low on detail. His advice: "Do your own thing!" "Accept yourself!" "Be glad you're you!" No doubt these familiar platitudes appeal to the more hedonistic and self-indulgent participants in the counterculture. But wait just a minute. I thought Reich's revolution was targeted at the stress points in American culture—runaway technology, the breakdown of the social fabric, self-serving bureaucracies, the corporate state, the war machine, and meaningless work. At the brink of collapse, American culture was suffering from enormous problems. Does he expect me to believe that these problems could be solved simply by "starting with the self" (Reich, 1970, p. 241), "not judging anyone else" (p. 242), and "being completely honest" (p. 244)? Reich's idea of revolution did not sound promising to me. In fact, it sounded hollow and disingenuous, if not downright silly.

The shallowness of Reich's proposed "revolution by consciousness" was exposed by a less popular but more penetrating scrutiny of the collapsing value structure of American society: Philip Slater's *The Pursuit of Loneliness* (1970).

Writing with no apparent knowledge of Reich's book, Slater (1970, p. 148) warned that "the most serious internal danger to the new culture is the insidious transmission of individualism from the old culture, in part through confusion with the new culture's otherwise healthy emphasis on emotional expression." In particular, Slater complained about the narcissistic excesses associated with an obsessive concentration on the self. A satisfying society requires people to make demands on each other—you simply can't have everybody running around "doing their own thing." That's not to say that Slater saw anything wrong with the pursuit of joy. In fact, the cultural transformation he envisioned was one that would replace "killing and competing" with "cooperating and enjoying" (1970, p. 147).

Slater had no illusions about the magnitude of the task. "Americans have always entertained the strange fantasy that change can occur easily and without pain," bemoaned Slater, "but real change is difficult and painful" (1970, p. 144). It requires staunch commitment, profound insight, and tolerance for short-term suffering to achieve long-term goals. All living systems resist change, acting to restore balance and keeping long-standing motivational patterns in place, regardless of their dysfunctional consequences. Thus, Slater was not overly optimistic about the prospects for revolutionary change. To transform a society on the verge of collapse, a society has to change not only its institutions but also the motivations that produced them. As Slater (1970, p. 125) observed, "Change can take place only when institutions have been analyzed, discredited, and disassembled, and the motivational forces that gave rise to them, redirected in alternative spheres of gratification."

Nor can change be achieved by excluding all those for whom the new culture is counter. There has to be a place in the new for the old. "I do not believe a successful transition can be made without their participation," Slater concluded (1970, p. 126). And it's not simply a matter of replacing the old entirely with the new, the fantasy to which Reich attached his revolutionary vision; the old culture will neither topple from its own imbalance nor allow itself to be pushed into an early retirement. Those in the old culture—at least those plagued by ambivalence—must be persuaded that there are good reasons to tear down what they have spent their lives erecting (Slater, 1970). They must also be assured that there is a space carved out for them in the new order.

Whereas Reich (1970) lumped activists and hippies into a single consciousness, Slater highlighted the cleavage between student radicals and hippies. The activists were future oriented, operated according to a strict moral code, insisted on disciplined protest, and committed themselves wholeheartedly to transforming existing institutional structures. The hippies were preoccupied with inner experience and emotional expression, lived in the here-and-now, idealized love and sexuality, and intensely opposed the values associated with attachment to cultural institutions. Although activists make more noise about the corruptions in the existing system, hippies were actually chasing more radical changes. The difference is profound and serious: "One group seeks to redirect the old striving pattern to social goals ... while the other seeks to abolish the old striving pattern itself. One seeks to remake the world to make it tolerable for us to live in, the other tries to cure us of our need to remake the world" (Slater, 1970, p. 124).

What are these strivings that need either to be redirected or abolished? According to Slater, they are desires that stem from the ethos of individualism that characterizes the American persona: our slavish submission to technological progress, our profane pursuit of achievement, our automatic acquiescence to competitive spirit, our bizarre belief in controlling emotional expression, and our depraved dedication to independence. In Slater's view, the preconditions for replacing these strivings were already in motion. The momentum had swung toward a serious reconsideration of our uncritical commitment to technological progress at any cost and a clearer understanding of how individualism thwarts the human desire for community, interpersonal engagement, and shared responsibility. The job ahead was to dream new dreams based not on the scarcity assumptions of the old dreams that "brought us nothing but misery, discontent, hatred, and chaos" (Slater, 1970, p. 150), but rather an individualism subordinated to the pleasures of the personal and the group—community, cooperation, involvement, and emotional expression.

The Dawning of Interpersonal Communication

In most departments of speech or communication, public speaking was offered as "the basic course." Taught as a performance course, public speaking concentrated on developing students' skills at delivering speeches to audiences. Students were expected to learn "the available means of persuasion," to demonstrate their knowledge of how to gather and use evidence; analyze and adapt to audiences; and shape, reinforce, or alter beliefs (Bryant and Wallace, 1969).

The public speaking course had been the "bread and butter" course for the discipline for more than fifty years. Each year, thousands of students on campuses across the country had their first exposure to speech, or communication studies, through the public speaking course, which was required by many departments and often met general education requirements for oral communication competence. Now, for the first time, the course was under siege not only from outsiders, who occasionally questioned the "intellectual" foundation for the course or the special knowledge needed to teach it, but from insiders as well. In the aftermath of the New Orleans Conference on behavioral science approaches to speech communication (Kibler and Barker, 1969), social scientists were beginning to get a foot in the door of traditionally humanities-oriented speech departments and pushing for greater emphasis on face-to-face communication and interpersonal relationships. They wanted to broaden the focus of the discipline beyond speech making, rhetorical criticism, and public address.

In graduate school at Bowling Green, I had experienced a split between humanists and social scientists. The rhetoric professors insisted that the department should hang on to the public speaking course. Professor John Rickey was adamant: "We are first and foremost teachers of public speaking. That's the way it's always been. We began as public speaking teachers, and that's our special expertise. Our field is grounded on the belief that the ability to speak is essential to a productive and meaningful life. And nobody can teach speaking as well as we do. If we lose our identity with public speaking, how will we justify our existence as a unique field?"

But the behavioral science side of the department, most notably Tucker, disagreed, expressing concern that the basic course diminished the academic reputation of the department and questioning its relevance to the current cultural climate. "The public speaking course gives the wrong impression of the field," Tucker grumbled to me privately. "Don't get me wrong—being able to express yourself orally is vitally important to living a meaningful life. But public speaking is a minute part of expressive life. I know that some of my colleagues see public speaking as a service we offer to other programs, but way too often it's the only course students ever take from us. They leave with a distorted impression because they aren't introduced to the broader mission of communication studies. I doubt if that's the best service we can offer students. The public speaking course is not good public relations for the department. It doesn't recruit bright students into the major. It doesn't challenge students to look at their own interactive experiences, and they don't leave with an understanding, even a superficial one, of the field as a whole or of the importance of communication in their lives. How often will these students be asked to give a formal speech to a large audience? Yet every day they relate to friends, family, and cohorts. If they're holding a job, they interact with supervisors and colleagues. Their sense of well-being and enjoyment of life hinges on how well they relate to other people. Most of the students I see are struggling to understand themselves and give meaning to their lives. They're in the process of figuring out who they are and what they want out of life. We should be conversing with them about these issues, allowing the communication classroom to be a place where they explore how their interactive relationships contribute to their identity."

The question of how well the public speaking course represented and promoted the interests of the discipline was becoming a major conflict among speech communication professors. But undergraduate students had issues of their own with public speaking—quite different issues. Most of them weren't keen on persuasion, which they saw as a tool of oppression and manipulation. They equated persuasion with image management, control of other people's opinions, or modes of engineering sentiments. Some thought the course reduced human beings to objects; others objected to the focus on technique, arguing that public speaking was being taught as an overly calculating activity in which persuasion is construed as a technical, not an ethical problem; and still others regarded public speaking as a tool of the market and the state, the very institutional structures they wanted to shatter.

Discord among professors and resistance from students created an opportunity to reshape the speech communication curriculum. As soon as I completed my dissertation, I began to prepare for a new course, "Interpersonal Communication," which the chair at Cleveland State had put into the schedule for my first term. In light of the cultural context of the late sixties (see Ilardo, 1972; Bochner and Kelly, 1974), interpersonal communication appeared to offer a promising response to the challenges posed by faculty and students alike. The academic study of interpersonal communication and interpersonal relations already had been firmly established as an interdisciplinary field of inquiry rooted in social psychology (Allport, 1954, 1960; Gergen, 1971), the symbolic interaction branch of sociology (Blumer, 1969; G. H. Mead, 1934), and certain areas of management studies (Bennis, 1964). Thus, there was nothing standing in the way of introducing interpersonal communication into the speech communication curriculum.

In 1968, Dean Barnlund published an interdisciplinary collection of scholarly essays, *Interpersonal Communication: Survey and Studies,* the first of its kind edited or authored by a speech communication professor. A surge of excitement began to circulate about a fresh new area of study entering the speech communication curriculum. Within a couple of years, a wave of first edition textbooks on interpersonal communication hit the presses (Giffin and Patton, 1971a, 1971b; Keltner, 1970; McCroskey, Larson, and Knapp, 1971). These books began to define the scope and boundaries of the new subfield, though there were vast differences among them. Some authors took a decidedly empiricist and behavioral science orientation (McCroskey, et al., 1971), whereas others fixed attention on the human potential movement and the more therapeutic approaches to interpersonal communication (Ilardo, 1972; Keltner, 1970; Stewart, 1972).

Was interpersonal communication a fad, as some older professors warned? Would it disappear as quickly as it had surfaced? Or would this turn toward the interpersonal be remembered as a genuine innovation, an epiphany that reshaped the field of speech communication?

The new textbooks gave pedagogical legitimacy to interpersonal communication, but for the most part they didn't speak to me. I liked the humanistic and therapeutic orientation of Giffin and Patton's (1971a) book, which I considered the best of the lot. But their disregard for social and political consciousness bothered me. Their book worked from the premise that the main purpose of a course on interpersonal communication was to nurture self-expression and self-development. The goal would be to better understand the nature of interpersonal perception and to cultivate the skills necessary to form meaningful relationships with other people. At first, I found little in Giffin and Patton's text with which to quibble. I shared their interest in focusing students' attention on understanding codification and sharpening their interpersonal skills, and I thought the exercises in their book could help students get in touch with feelings and enhance their emotional sensitivity.

But I was skeptical of the sort of assertive individuality that Giffin and Patton (1971a) were promoting. Their text severed interpersonal life from cultural life, ignoring the sources of moral and value conflict in which the generational struggle in America was rooted. The rise of interest in interpersonal communication wasn't inspired simply by a desire for greater interpersonal competence or more understanding of how perception works. Many of us had the feeling that our society was unraveling, losing its moorings, on the verge of collapse, and ready to snap. We may have wanted to "go with the flow," but we also "didn't want to cop out." We were walking on a tightrope, one end gripped by our desire for a life we could truly call our own; the other by our longing to live up to some moral standard beyond ourselves. My generation had rejected conventionality, unmasked oppressive institutions, and snubbed pretentious role playing. What was left? Assuming we rejected the option of a self-absorbed, self-consuming narcissism, we had to either recover something good from a social order that had been rebuffed, destroyed, or lost, or else create something entirely new and different. This was the tension we were experiencing, the struggle of our age. I had no solution, but I was convinced that posing the question had to be a crucial part of instruction in interpersonal communication.

I would put the question of authenticity on the table for my whole class to probe, debate, and explore. Was the self enough? Didn't we need some source of meaning, some value to attach ourselves to that we shared with a community of others, something beyond ourselves? Wasn't there a risk that our absorption with ourselves, our exaggerated focus on the inner life, would descend into a pathological narcissism in which our sense of self-importance would be inflated and we would lose touch with our responsibility as citizens and members of a community? Wasn't it our nature to yearn for a sense of belonging, to feel a connection to something of value? What could offer us meaning and value beyond ourselves? We had to face up to the contradictions in which we were immersed. We wanted to come into intimate contact with ourselves, be true to ourselves, surrender our inhibitions, extricate ourselves from artificial roles, experience and express our deepest feelings, act spontaneously, and feel good. But we also wanted to elevate our social consciousness, heighten our sensitivity to others, enlarge our capacity to love, satisfy our longing for connection, achieve a sense of belonging, and live a just and moral life.

By the time I left for Cleveland, I was raring to go. The idea of teaching a course that touched students where they lived fired me up like nothing I'd ever experienced. I prepared lectures pitting Reich's optimism against Slater's pessimism and bringing into focus some of the concerns and possibilities about individualism, narcissism, authenticity, alienation, and cultural change raised in Theodore Rieff's *The Triumph of the Therapeutic* (1966), Eric Fromm's *Escape from Freedom* (1941), Rollo May's *Love and Will* (1969), and Charles Hampden Turner's *Radical Man* (1970). I also integrated materials from some of the most important and popular movies of the sixties, films that focused on cultural and personal values and on what it means to live a good life, including *Alfie, Who's Afraid of Virginia Wolf, The Graduate, Midnight Cowboy, Cool Hand Luke, Bob and Carol and Ted and Alice,* and *Easy Rider.* Like most beginning professors, I had over-prepared. Later I realized I was not only testing the students; I was also challenging myself.

The View from the Front of the Class

Looking out at the students in my class, I see the familiar signs of the youth culture. The signature feature is the hair, long and straight on male and female alike. On some women, so straight it looks as though it's been ironed; on some men, so long it has to be kept off the forehead by a bandana and away from the shoulders by a scarf or rubber band. Distinguishing boys from girls takes some effort. Several girls wear flowers in their hair and hand-strung love beads as necklaces; the boys favor Army jackets, and a few tie gypsy cummerbunds around their waists. Colors range from earth tones to psychedelic, tie-dyed rainbows. Most of these kids choose a decidedly peasant or cast-off look, though a few call attention to themselves by donning bright and wild-colored shirts or blouses. Peace jewelry and antiwar buttons are abundantly displayed, as are wrinkled T-shirts lettered with the printed slogans of the day: BAN THE BRA; PRAISE THE PILL; EVERYBODY MUST GET STONED!

A girl in the front row wears a T-shirt that reads, "Make Love Not War." To her left sits a girl dressed in a thin, see-through blouse pulled over a loose, fluid Indian-print dress that flows down to her bare feet. Sitting beside her is a boy with long, jet-black hair covering his shoulders and running halfway down his back and a thick, dark beard that makes him look like Jesus. His fringe vest covers a faded tie-dye T-shirt; around his neck he sports a medallion with the familiar antiwar symbol of an upside down bomber within a circle. An older guy in the second row is dressed in workman's overalls that make him look like Paul Bunyan. A fellow in the back row looks out from under a wide-brimmed Stetson hat. His fringed shirt, jeans, and boots remind me of a frontier settler in the Old West. As my eyes dart across the room I spot numerous examples of Army-Navy surplus and second-hand castoffs. These students seem to be making a statement about the excesses of consumer culture. Then again, I can't help thinking somebody must be making a profit on counterculture attire—the Granny glasses; hip-hugging, bell-bottomed jeans; washed-out blue work shirts; peasant blouses; red- and black-speckled bandanas; ankle-length madras skirts; love beads and primitive-tooth necklaces; day-glow love pendants; and leather jackets with American flags stitched on the back. Clearly, there's a market for authenticity and the natural look.

Generation Gap

I walk to the blackboard and write:

> If I am not for myself, who will be for me?
> If I am for myself only, what am I?
> If not now—when?
> *Talmudic Saying, Mishnah, Abot (Fromm, 1941)*

116

When I turn back toward the class, I see students in every row eager to be called on. They have their hands raised even before I've asked a question. I chuckle about how automatically they acquiesce to the hand-raising ritual of the classroom. Although I appreciate their civility, I'm surprised they don't see raising their hands as just another empty ritual.

Last week, the day before the break for the Thanksgiving holiday, one of the students started fuming about how abusive the family rituals surrounding holidays have become. "We're trying to break away from the wooden lives our parents are living," he shouted, clenching his teeth. "So why should we go home for the holidays and submit ourselves to the torture of our parents' tedious holiday rituals? They'll get all misty eyed about the first bite of chestnut dressing, the fluffiness of the mashed potatoes, and the aroma of the hot apple pie still baking in the oven. Father will compliment mother on the marvelous moist turkey, then butcher the carving, after which we'll all join in the grotesque, gluttonous debauchery. During dinner, the older folks will drink too much and begin reminiscing for the umpteenth time about what Thanksgiving was like when they were kids and how they miss the good old days even though they're much better off now; while the kids, myself included, will sit in silence rolling our eyes, biting our lips, and stuffing ourselves silly to keep from saying how we really feel."

"Do the rest of you feel that way?" I asked.

"I do," chimed in the kid in the Stetson hat. "I hate Thanksgiving. I hate how I feel before we eat, when I have to watch that stupid Macy's parade, and after we eat, when my stomach is distended and all the men withdraw to the basement to watch meaningless football games, while the women retreat to the kitchen to clean up the mess and gossip about neighbors and friends. Does anyone express any awareness of what's going on? Nope, everyone just plays their part as though they have no choice. The food is the only fresh thing at the dinner. The rest of the day is just one stale, repressive ritual. I tell you, the thought of it makes my blood boil."

Not everybody agreed, of course. Some students felt it did no good to tee off on parents that way. "What's the use?" one girl asked. "They're not going to change and neither am I. I only want to keep the peace, you know, not get any more alienated than I am already. So I grin and bear it."

A few students said they actually liked the warm family feelings that the holiday fostered. One said Thanksgiving was the only time of the year she felt comfortable being home and close to her parents. "I wouldn't think of staying away from home on the holidays," she said. "It's the closest I ever get to my parents."

But another student said he had the opposite experience. "The carving of the turkey is Dad's warm up. Once the turkey meat is sliced, I'm next. He relishes pushing my buttons. He really knows how to stick in the knife."

Still, most of the students said they felt obligated to be home with their families for the holidays, and, on the whole, they expected the meal to be pleasant and cheerful. "It's the conversation I dread," said the Paul Bunyan–looking man in the overalls. "My parents won't let sleeping dogs lie. Sooner or later, the conversation will turn to 'What are you doing with your life?' 'Are you preparing yourself for a good job?' 'Why don't you get a haircut?' I don't have the courage to tell them that I don't know which direction I'm headed. So I'll say what I think they want to hear just to get off the hook."

"My father acts like a banker," interrupted Jeff, one of the best students in the class. "He wants to know that the money he's shelling out for my tuition is going to be paid back—with interest. It's my responsibility to make him proud so he can brag about my accomplishments to his friends. The way my dad acts reminds me of one of the films you showed in class, *The Graduate.* I loved that movie. My parents are just like the Braddocks."

"Really?" I asked, expressing surprise and encouraging Jeff to continue. "How so?"

"You remember when Ben tells his dad he's worried about his future, and his dad asks him what he wants his future to be?"

"Uh-huh."

"Well, Ben says that what he wants is a different life from the one his parents are living," Jeff replied. "I feel like Ben. I'm afraid I'm going to end up miserable and lonely like them. They've lost the capacity to feel. They're numb and they don't even know it."

"Can't you see anything in their lives that brings them pleasure?" I asked.

"No, they're only interested in pleasing other people. They're constantly talking about the importance of being a nice person. They've established a set of rules they follow faithfully and insist that I do too."

"What do you mean? Can you give us an example?"

"'Don't make waves.' 'Don't be rude.' 'Follow proper channels.' 'Don't make a scene.' 'Respect authority.' They're satisfied to live a predictable life, and they want me to do the same. But that's where I draw the line. I'm not going to settle for a boring and monotonous existence. I told them that, and now there's this huge gulf between us. Most of the time we're together we sit in silence."

"I can relate to what you say about silence," bellowed Bob, a tall, skinny kid who wears one of those red and black bandanas around his forehead. "My family is one of those 'ten thousand people, maybe more' that Simon and Garfunkel are singing about in *The Graduate.* We're talking, but we're not speaking. We're hearing, but we're not listening. The noise we're making can't break through the sound of our silence. We can't understand or communicate with each other, so we don't. Instead, we hide stuff from each other. I lie to them, and they're not truthful with me either. So how could we understand each other? My dad has no notion of who I am. He doesn't know a thing about my dreams or aspirations or how I'm living my life."

"Now wait just a minute," interrupted Shirley from the back row. She's a woman in her late forties, the only student in the class over thirty. "I've heard enough of this. I've got something to say, and you may not like hearing it." She stood up slowly, drawing everyone's eyes toward her.

"I thought I could get through the whole semester without speaking," she started, "but I was wrong. I can't take it anymore. If I hear one more person bash parents or holiday rituals, I'm going to throw up."

Shirley hadn't spoken in class all semester, though she always looked attentive. I noticed that her face and neck were turning red, a sign that blood was rushing to her head. She seemed unable to contain the palpable wave of anger surging through her body.

"I want all of you to know that I'm a parent of two kids just a little older than most of you. I love my kids and they love me. I came back to school at the age of forty-four because I figured I had missed something. I saw how much my kids grew and matured in college, and I wanted to prove to myself that I could still learn and grow too. Now that my kids were out of the house, I wanted to do something for myself."

Shirley paused for a few seconds. I thought she might be losing her composure, but it turned out she was trying to muster the courage to release what she was feeling. Her anger appeared to be turning to sorrow as she continued.

"But then I came to this class and started hearing about how my generation ruined things for yours. It's our fault—all of it. We older folks don't understand. We aren't fun. We don't feel, and our lives are pathetic."

She hesitated again, clearing her throat. All eyes in the room stayed glued to her.

"What a bunch of bull!" she hollered. "You act as if you're the first kids ever to feel misunderstood by your parents. What a crock, if I say so myself. I'm not so old I can't remember thinking the same things about my parents; how they didn't understand me, how I wanted a different life from theirs, a better, more interesting and exciting life. As far as I can see, this whole idea of a generation gap isn't anything new. It's a charade, an illusion that's been created to drive a wedge between parents and children and to serve the interests of some of the industries you younger people condemn, like those on Madison Avenue."

"Are you saying you don't think there's a gap between the generations at all? I don't buy that," Jeff interrupted.

"Of course there's a gap. Younger people see things from a different point of view," Shirley replied, turning toward Jeff, and looking directly into his eyes. "But that's nothing new. I get so mad when I have to sit here and listen to you kids run your mouths off about what's wrong with your parents. You say that your parents don't understand *you*. Why don't you ask yourselves how well you understand *them*? Do you take an interest in their lives? What do you know about their dreams or disappointments or the pressures they feel? I mean, let's get real for a moment. You don't have mortgages to pay, mouths to feed, or kids to support. You haven't had to stretch a paycheck to keep the bill collectors away or worry about whether your kids would come home in a police car or you'll get a call from the emergency room. So don't lecture me about understanding unless you're willing to acknowledge that it cuts both ways."

Shirley started to sit down but abruptly changed her mind and rose again. "And another thing," she continued, "I hear all this talk about wanting to be free."

She had everyone's attention now. "The way you say it, I get the impression you mean free of all responsibility, answering to nobody but yourself. I sit here quietly and listen to you and I think about how you call people like me 'corrupted by the system, empty, and isolated.' You question the motives of everything we do and everything we seem to stand for, but you don't apply the same standards to yourselves. You think you understand the meaning of freedom, but what you're talking about isn't freedom—it's isolation, a kind of estrangement from life in which you drift from one feeling to another, one relationship to another, and one cause to another. I think many of you may be making the blunder that Erich Fromm underscored in the book we read earlier in the semester. He warned about mistaking an escape *from* freedom for freedom itself. He said that this sort of obsessive pleasure-seeking kind of freedom isn't freedom at all, except in the negative sense of being alone with yourself and facing what you think is an alienated, hostile world. Isn't that right, Dr. Bochner?"

"Fromm would agree that pleasure seeking is not necessarily an expression of a person's choice of how to act. It can become a way of trying to escape feelings of meaninglessness or insignificance. We have to be cautious about what we do to achieve feelings of belonging or security," I replied, nodding to urge Shirley to continue.

"Okay. Then I have some questions for all of you fun-loving, joy-seeking, holiday-hating youngsters who have your whole lives in front of you. Where is integrity in this ideal world of yours? Where is ethics? Where is making sacrifices for others who need or want you, people you care about? Where is your effort to understand the people you condemn? This doesn't sound like freedom to me—it sounds like self-absorption and narcissism.

"I'm sorry about ranting on like this, Dr. Bochner," Shirley said, lowering her voice, looking directly toward me, and taking her seat. "I thought I could make it through class without expressing my agitation. But sitting and listening to my classmates gripe about having to spend holidays with their parents, I couldn't help asking myself, 'What if my kids thought about Thanksgiving like that? What would I do?'"

"What would you do?" I asked.

"I'd do what Sidney Jourard [1971] recommended in the book we read. I'd drop my guard and tell my kids how I felt, how I really felt. I'd have a lot to lose, but maybe something to gain as well. At least my kids would know where they stood with me. They would know that their mother isn't fooled by all this talk about authenticity and self-actualization. I'd tell them that they can't go through life satisfying their own desires regardless of the consequences for other people like their parents, friends, and members of the community in which they live. If they think they can live a fulfilling life simply by satisfying their own desires, without exercising any boundaries, centering their lives only on themselves, without any regard to the demands placed upon them by living in a world of other people, they are in for a big surprise. How would this sort of freedom solve the problems so many of you have eloquently articulated over the course of this semester? It wouldn't rid the world of corruption, poverty, racism, or imperial governments. These are cultural and social problems. Injustices can't be remedied simply by doing your own thing." At this point she took a pensive pause, sat down, and looked across at me. "You know what I think, Dr. Bochner?"

"Well, I'm certainly getting an impression," I kidded her, trying to relieve some of the tension in the room. Quiet laughter trickled down the aisles.

"Seriously," she smiled. "I think all this whining about rituals, holidays, and family and the moaning about self-determining freedom, well, to use one of the younger generation's favorite expressions, it's a cop-out, a way of dodging personal responsibility and commitment."

The class sat in stunned silence. I looked down at my watch. "Our time is up," I said. "We'll have a lot to talk about next week."

Don't Blow It

A week later Ed, the guy who looks like Jesus, stops by my office to let me know he's prepared some notes in response to Shirley's "attack on the counterculture." I chuckle at the way he's framed it. "I'll call on you first," I tell him, and he skips out the door and down the hallway.

Ed's a highly motivated student. He never misses class and always comes prepared. He visits me during office hours at least once a week. Usually he starts with a question about the readings, but within a few minutes he's talking about his relationships and seeking my advice on a wide range of personal issues. He strikes me as a neurotic kid with a lot of promise. I see sadness in his glassy eyes. Projecting my own experience, I think Ed's pain must have originated in a troubled childhood. Ed's found a glimmer of hope and opportunity in my class, and he's transferred the role of the father in his life onto me. But I'm Ed's teacher, not his father, and my duties are different. However, Ed's placed me in a position not only to teach him about communication but also to help guide him through the crisis of identity he is going through. Should I do that? Can I?

The more experience I gain as a teacher, the more thought I give to the contradictions of the teacher-student relationship. What do we mean when we speak of a teacher-student relationship? What are my obligations to students like Ed? Should I keep my distance and insist on a completely professional relationship devoid of intimacy or particularized caring? Is this even possible, given that I can't control the feelings and dispositions that students project onto me? Should I guard against allowing myself to get close? Conversely, can I do my job well if I maintain a detached distance from students like Ed, who are seeking more than information and knowledge in the classroom?

I'm a communication professor. My courses deal with friendship, love, and family relations; intimate topics that revolve around caring and deep emotion. Besides, even if I weren't dealing with intimate topics, I would still be occupying a position of power in the classroom, a power not completely unlike that of parents, therapists, and clergy. Some teachers cast a spell on students. The students, in turn, project their problems onto their teachers. Some of them believe teachers can transform their lives or help rid them of anxiety. I did when I was a student, but not with all my teachers. I was attracted to seductive teachers. It wasn't their beauty or their sex appeal either, though that may have played a part. Mainly, it was their passion and energy that lured me. In the classroom, they were energized and evocative. They made me care about things that were important, things I'd never thought deeply about before. Don't we want our students to care about the issues with which we are dealing? Sure we do. Aren't we trying to arouse their desire? Sure we are. But once that desire is evoked, what then? We enter a danger zone. We can easily exploit the power we hold, something I feel bound ethically not to do.

Ed considers me his mentor. Is he seeking a guide, a guru, a therapist, a friend, an advisor—or a little bit of all of these? He can't say, and I don't know. What do I do now? I'm scared but also intrigued. There are no books to turn to for advice. The only thing I can do is feel my way through a maze of contradictions and dilemmas. I'm convinced that most learning takes place in the context of an interpersonal relationship. The sort of teaching to which I aspire is intellectual, but it's also personal. This kind of teacher can't tell students like Ed to get lost or to find someone else to meet their therapeutic needs. I know there are risks, but there are rewards as well. I didn't become a teacher to act like a machine and forget my own personal struggles that led me to this point in my life. I can't overlook what teachers like Brammer, Levine, and Tucker did for me. So I've taken Ed on as a project, the way a good coach nourishes a talented but immature player—by being patient yet demanding, critical yet caring, adventurous yet circumspect. I don't know if I'm doing it right.

"Ed asked to address the class," I say when the students are settled in their seats. "Are you ready, Ed?"

He clears his throat, looks at me, and begins. "I've filled my notebook with the quotes you put on the board each day. At night I read them over and over again. I try to connect the dots, see the links between the class sessions and the quotes. I guess I'm convinced there must be some method to your madness," he laughs to himself. I know he doesn't want me to think that he thinks I'm mad, so I smile back.

"This one from the Jewish Talmud, for example, brings us right back to last week. You're not going to let us off scot-free. We have to go back and look at it, look at ourselves, look at how we interacted, and what we can learn from it. You want us to metacommunicate, don't you? Isn't that your message?"

"Go on," I encourage.

"Shirley put our whole class in its place with her passionate attack on selfishness. She rained on our parade."

"Is that what you think she did?" I ask.

"Well, metaphorically speaking, yes. We were sounding so cocky and self-assured, acting as though there were no hard questions to ask about the validity of Reich's new consciousness or the generation gap between our parents and ourselves. Our whole conversation had the feel of a snowball rolling down a hill. It gradually gathers momentum until suddenly it's an avalanche and nothing can stop it. When that happens you better get out of the way. I think that's how we sounded to Shirley. We sounded as if we were saying, 'Get out of our way before you get hurt. Your generation had their chance, and they blew it. Now it's our turn.' But Shirley," he says, turning and looking directly at her, "you were having none of it. You were saying, 'That's no avalanche, it's a mirage—the kind of hallucination you might have on an acid trip. Here, let me step in front and prove it to you.' And you did—well, sort of. I can't say I agree with everything you said, but you gave me pause to think more critically about some of the things I've been taking for granted, like authenticity, freedom, and autonomy. You taught me something."

"What did you learn, Ed?" I interrupt, turning Ed's attention back toward the rest of the class.

"I learned that we have to approach the whole question of living authentically with more humility. Shirley's right about one thing—we shouldn't just spit out clichés like 'tell it like it is,' 'do your own thing,' 'love unconditionally,' and expect the whole world instantly will become a better place in which to live. People with different views from ours, people like you, Shirley—decent and reasonable people—are not-going to step aside and turn the world over to us without a fight. Heck, I'm not even sure who we mean by 'us.' Last week, I heard my cohorts express a lot of different views about the meaning of Thanksgiving, so I hardly think we've reached a unified philosophy or ideology. You've said that yourself, Doc, and so did Slater—the counterculture is a diverse community. We don't all want the same things."

"No, clearly we don't, Ed," I say. "That's a perceptive and evocative statement you made. If I could, I'd like to add something from my own point of view."

"Lay it on us, Doc," Ed says.

"First, I want to express my gratitude to Shirley for opening our eyes to the fact that changing this society will not be easy. There will always be people with different and incompatible goals, and we have to find a way to engage with them on the question of what ideals are worth championing. That's one of the reasons communication is so important. Shirley showed us that, which is why she deserves our gratitude. She didn't just sit there and take it. She had the courage to speak up, and she spoke from her heart as well as from her mind. When I looked around the room at the end of class, I could see that many of you were sitting in a state of astonishment. You seemed stunned by Shirley's honesty and courage but also because she cared enough to try to change us. She was trying to open our minds, and I think she succeeded, at least I hope she did. The point is that sometimes you have to put aside your fears and take a chance, speak your mind, and let the chips fall where they might." I stroll over to where Ed is sitting and place my hand gently on his shoulder.

"And Ed here," I continue, "he put himself on the line too. He captured one of the most important ideas I've been trying to express all semester: Life is complicated and full of contradictions, and we have to resist the temptation to settle for easy answers to complex questions. Shirley challenged us to dig deeper, and today Ed reinforced that inquiring attitude, that spirit of inquiry."

I see Shirley listening intently. She's moved up to the second row today. It's a significant shift in her relationship to her classmates and to me. "Shirley, can you help me out? Will you address one more question?"

Shirley nods her agreement.

"I'd like to hear how it felt to you to say those things and what you learned from the experience. I'm sure your classmates do too."

"Thank you for asking, Dr. Bochner," Shirley begins in a conspicuously soft voice, giving the impression she doesn't want to be the center of attention. "I don't have a lot to add to what I said last week. I was pleased to hear Ed's comments. Responses like his make me want to be part of the conversation. At the time, I was provoked and annoyed. I didn't know what would come out when I started. But once I began, I found I couldn't contain what was inside of me. Everything came pouring out, and that was scary."

"What do you mean by 'pouring out'?" I ask.

"Ha," she laughs. "Your question reminds me how I've inherited my mother's expressions. She used to say, 'When it rains, it pours.'"

"My mother did too," I interject.

Shirley continues, "As a woman and a mother, I know what it feels like to be left out of the conversation. For years I've stayed in the background and bottled up my rage. When I allowed the anger and pain to come to the surface, it came gushing out. It felt really good to get things off my chest. But afterward I had second thoughts."

"What do you mean?"

"I worried that some people might think I was lecturing them and dismiss me as another out-of-touch older person." Shirley pauses. Looking around the room, she scans the faces of her classmates as though she wants to address them directly. "But several of you made a point of seeking me out over the weekend and telling me how much you appreciated my honesty as well as my point of view. Today, for the first time, I feel a part of the class. I wish this were the first week instead of the last day of class."

"I do too, Shirley," I acknowledge. "It's as if we're just getting started, you know, coming together as a class, developing a communal feeling. And now the course is coming to an end. I only hope we can hold on to some of the lessons we've taught each other, which reminds me of one other issue I'd like to address before we finish, something that Ed said."

Ed sits up in his chair, looking pleased to get my attention. "What's that?" he asks.

"You said that the older generation had their chance and they blew it."

"I meant that's what our denunciation of her age group seemed to imply," Ed replies.

"That's the point you were making, I agree. But I want you to consider the language you used to express it, that they *blew* their opportunity. Does that remind you of anything we've gone over in the course?"

Ed rubs his forehead, and I sense the wheels turning in his head. After a few seconds he begins to stroke his beard, and then shakes his head from side to side as if to say he can't come up with anything.

"I know what you're looking for," a voice from the far left corner of the classroom interrupts. I recognize the voice of Dorothy Lenk, one of the sharpest students in the class. "You're referring to *Easy Rider,* aren't you?" she asks, fingering the love beads around her neck. An outspoken hippie who exudes warmth and understanding, Dorothy is a flower-child if ever there was one.

"That's exactly what I was thinking," I say, expressing my pleasure that the two of us are on the same wave length.

"I'm thinking of the scene right before the end of the movie," Dorothy continues. "Billy is all excited about hitting pay dirt. They've just sold the drugs, and he's overcome with joy. He says, 'We're rich, man. We're free,' or something to that effect. But his sidekick, Wyatt, the guy played by that dreamy Peter Fonda, thinks the fortune they've made is fool's gold. He tells Billy, 'We blew it. We all blew it.'"

"Why does Wyatt consider it fool's gold? He doesn't say that, does he?" I ask.

"No. The movie leaves the meaning open and ambiguous. But that's what I took from it. Fool's gold makes you think you're rich but sets you up for a big disappointment."

"But they are rich, aren't they? I mean they've made a big score, and they have all this cash?" I'm urging Dorothy to dig deeper.

"Yes, that's true literally. They are rich. But I'm using fool's gold as a metaphor, like you taught us."

"Go on."

"Is it okay if I read something that I wrote in the journal I'm handing in today?"

"Yes, of course."

"Let me find the passage." She pauses, leafing through her thick course binder. "Here it is: 'Billy seems to think that being rich will make him free, that this pot of gold will buy him the American Dream. But Wyatt knows it's not that easy to achieve personal fulfillment. The way I see him, Wyatt is this deeply introspective guy who really loves America. He's biking across the country with a real sense of purpose—to find the America that is in his heart. He even calls himself Captain America and wears a flag on his leather jacket. He wants to feel connected, whether it's on a farm, at a commune, in a brothel, a cemetery, or even in jail. Riding on his bike is the closest Wyatt can get to freedom, but I think he realizes at some point that he can't live his whole life biking across the highways of America. A person has to make a contribution; his life has to have a meaning or a purpose. So when he and Billy collect the cash, Wyatt feels empty inside. Dealing drugs can't buy him what he's longing for, the kind of peace of mind and genuine selfhood he seeks. He realizes he hasn't dodged other people's games; he's only learned to play them better. In the final analysis, he and Billy are no better than any other outlaws. They blew it. They took to the road to cut themselves loose from the uptight, hateful, and mean-spirited elements of the dominant society, only to find the roots ran deeper than they thought. They couldn't break free.'"

"Wow, that's a deep analysis, Dorothy. I love the way you've integrated what we've been talking and reading about throughout the semester. But your interpretation is so dark and sad."

"That's how I saw it, Dr. Bochner. I came away very dejected. When they all got killed at the end, I cried and felt overcome with hatred toward those repulsive southern rednecks. They reminded me of some of the reactions I've witnessed at antiwar and civil rights protests. We're out there marching for peace and social justice, and some people drive by and shout at the guys I'm walking with, 'Why don't you get a haircut?' How absurd and trivial! We're talking about killing and oppressing people, and all they're worried about is the length of our hair, as if our nonconformity is on a par with their violence and hatred."

"Isn't there anything hopeful you can say?" I press.

"Not in *Easy Rider*. That film is shot through with tragedy. But this class gives me hope. I will try to remember the quote you wrote on the board, especially the words, 'If not now, when?' There's no time to waste. We have to act now. Wyatt was waiting to find the right people, at the right time, in the right place. Sadly, he never made it. I don't want to blow it. I want to be true to myself, but not only to myself. As long as there's such abundant suffering in the world, I feel I have to answer a call beyond myself, a call to care for and help others who need me."

After class, I grab my mail at the department office and head home. Arriving at the apartment, I flip on the stereo and open a letter from the editor of *Speech Monographs,* Dr. Tom Scheidel. He informs me that the article I submitted from my dissertation has been accepted for publication. "Yes!" I cry out. "I did it."

This is my first solo publication. Dr. Scheidel attached one review with his letter. The associate editor, whose name remained anonymous, wrote, "I think this is a good study, but frankly I don't understand the methodology. The multivariate statistical analysis is light years ahead of anything I know. The paper is well written and it looks to be a competently executed study."

I'm elated by this news. I feel as though I've arrived. I walk to the kitchen and pour myself a glass of wine to celebrate.

Thoughts about today's class intrude on my delight. I can't get my exchange with Dorothy out of my mind. I wonder, *Is my elation any different from Billy's? Is publishing another form of fool's gold?* Dorothy's metaphor sticks. It won't let go of me. I can't help thinking my victory is a fraud. After all, the journal editors accepted a paper they didn't understand. How should I feel about that?

I hear Don McLean's voice blaring from the stereo:

> Oh, and there we were all in one place,
> A generation lost in space
> With no time left to start again …

CHAPTER FIVE

Double Bind

Selling Out or Risking Ruin

> Life has an inner calculus, which is the passage of existence through
> time, through one state into another, by leaps and by infinitesimals, from
> one mood to another, from one person to another, from one embrace or
> struggle to another, to its final summation and dissolution.
>
> *Jules Henry (1971, p. xvi)*

Dreary Days

This morning, the *Cleveland Plain Dealer* featured an article on the cloudiest cities in America, which turned out to be Pittsburgh, Syracuse, Cleveland, and Seattle. I grew up in the first, attended graduate school in the second, and began my life as a professor in the third. The shape of my destiny points in the direction of Seattle, a city renowned for serial killers, suicides, and coffee houses. I make a mental note to resist the temptation to complete the cycle.

I close my eyes and imagine gentle sun rays enveloping my body. I hear birds singing merrily, and see myself staring in awe at the miracle of sun-kissed roses and vibrant tulips. Basking in the light and warmth of a dazzling sunny day, I feel alive, alert, energized.

I open my eyes, raising the curtain shielding the truth. Reality sinks in. I'm not living in Maui. This is Cleveland. You have to wait a long time for a day like that in Cleveland. In winter, the sky here is saturated with a leaden overcast that drains the human spirit. By early November, the howling winds begin to blow across Lake Erie in a Toledo-to-Buffalo direction, and lake-effect snow piles high in the eastern suburbs. Occasionally, the sun wiggles through the clouds, momentarily filling my heart with hopeful anticipation, only to be snuffed out by gloomy clouds sweeping across the sky, dimming the light and whisking away my last glimmer of optimism.

The succession of dark, cloudy days takes its toll on me. It doesn't help that most of my work day is spent on the seventeenth floor of a concrete-tower build-ing, which houses the library as well as most of the classrooms in which courses are taught. I don't know whether to blame my blue funk on the weather, my restless desire for new adventures, a dearth of inspiring colleagues, the absence of a campus atmosphere, or the transition from graduate student to faculty status.

As a graduate student, I could count on finding cohorts hanging around the department, even late at night. I cherished our talks about the future of the field, the latest communication research, and whatever new books we were reading. Together we formed a circle of gossip and rumor that cemented our friendships, helping us temporarily to forget our worries about how little money we had and whether we would land a decent faculty position when we finished. I miss the bantering and rumor mongering. I took it for granted that this sort of collegiality and friendship would always be a part of university life. I'll admit that an undercurrent of competition existed among us, but these rivalries never hindered our collegiality. We rooted for each other to publish, finish our dissertations, and secure good jobs. Nevertheless, we were eager to get out of Dodge as quickly as possible and could hardly wait to graduate. Now, a little more than a year after graduation, I sit and grieve the loss of innocence and friendship.

The grim state of the country wasn't helping either. In mid-September, a Washington, DC, grand jury brought indictments against E. Howard Hunt, G. Gordon Liddy, and five professional burglars they had hired to break into the Watergate Hotel in June 1972 for the purposes of bugging the headquarters of the Democratic National Committee. One of the burglars was James W. Mc-Cord, an employee of the Committee to Re-Elect the President—aptly referred to as CREEP—and a former CIA agent. For four months, the press had been vigorously investigating the possible ties between the Nixon White House and the break-in at the Watergate. Responding to the pressure, Nixon sent his press secretary, Ron Ziegler, out to clear the air. Ziegler scoffed at the "unfounded accusations," referring to Watergate as "a third-rate burglary" and accusing the media of blowing the event out of proportion to gain political advantage in the upcoming election (Anderson, 2006).

Right from the start, the whole affair smelled bad to me. Nixon had a long history of "dirty tricks," dating from his days as a vice presidential candidate when he accepted illegal campaign contributions. I eagerly anticipated a day when even President Nixon might have to "stand naked," as Bob Dylan (1965) might say. The aftermath of the indictments turned up the pressure on the Nixon White House but had little effect on public opinion. A poll conducted in October 1972 showed that half the nation still didn't know the location of Watergate or to what the term referred (Waldron, 2012). On the evening of October 27, 1972, Walter Cronkite presented a fourteen-minute *CBS News* report on "The Watergate Scandal," concluding that "Watergate has escalated into charges of a high-level campaign of political sabotage and espionage apparently unparalleled in American history" (Martin, July 17, 2009). Cronkite's report reinforced my darkest suspicions, but came too late to affect the presidential election. On November 7, Nixon was re-elected by a landslide, receiving more than 60 percent of the popular and 96 percent of the electoral college votes—and leaving me in a foul mood.

A Book to Change Your Life

"I'll get it," Brenda calls to me when the doorbell rings. A few seconds later, she enters my study. "Here, this is for you," she says, handing me a large, thick, square package. "The mailman couldn't fit it through the slot."

"Oh, it's from Barb," I say.

"Good. Maybe she can cheer you up," Brenda replies, zipping up her heavy down jacket and pulling the hood over her head. She takes her mail with her and heads for the door. "I'm off to the library. See you after work."

I pull off the packing tape and open the brown envelope. A letter sits on top of something wrapped in newspaper that feels like a book. I open the letter first:

Dear Art,

Here's a little present for you. Let me warn you—this book may change your life. I know it's changed mine. Hurry up and read it so we can talk about it.

Norman and I are deeply discouraged by the election results, but Norman says to tell you to hold on. They're going to get that lying crook Nixon yet.

I'm nearly finished with my dissertation. I'll call next week. Happy reading!

Love, Barb

A book that will change my life! Coming from Barb, a person not prone to hyperbole, that's quite an endorsement. I tear away the newspaper and remove a thick paperback. On the shiny white cover, the blue and black lettering reads, *Pathways to Madness* by Jules Henry. I glance briefly at the back cover and read, "A masterpiece ... Totally absorbing ... A remarkable book," then turn past the dedication page, where I spot a single sentence on an otherwise blank page:

"Life lures us with small favors to commit great crimes."

Quite an opening! Small favors—are these the pathways? I wonder. Great crimes—is this the madness? Is madness a crime—something produced, something avoidable? Or is the madness to which he refers our madness—life's madness—the fact that our wrongdoings are enticed by such small pleasures? Are we still living in the Garden of Eden?

I move eagerly to the "Preface," where Henry (1971, xi) says, "This book is not only a study of pathways to madness but also, indirectly, an account of some changes in myself." The changes to which he refers reflect not only how he was transformed by his research but also by his mental and emotional state, "the sense of doom, of helplessness" in the world at large that affected him deeply and sharpened his understanding.

This is the first time I have read an account by a social scientist in which the link between the researcher's subjectivity and his observations of other people is acknowledged. Henry not only admits to these feelings, but he also attributes positive consequences to them. Rather than corrupting or biasing his capacity to understand these families, he claims that these deep emotions improved his understanding.

Is Henry conceding the fallibility of objectivity? Wouldn't these dark feelings of helplessness and doom jeopardize the validity of his perceptions? By divulging his mental and emotional state, isn't he making himself vulnerable to charges of bias? Won't critics question his impartiality?

Erving Goffman comes to mind. Goffman was a fieldworker, but unlike Henry, he never put himself on the page. He never disclosed how he was feeling or how his fieldwork or the state of the world personally affected him. Come to think of it, I know precious little about Erving Goffman the person. Would it alter my admiration for Goffman if I knew him more personally or if he had divulged his state of mind? Of course, I did form impressions of Goffman. He strikes me as clever and nimble, but also as aloof and unfriendly. I doubt he likes people. He comes across as a snob. Still, I identify with his anger about the precariousness of social life. Sometimes, I feel that way too. *Am I projecting my anger onto him?*

I don't perceive Goffman as disinterested, though. His books definitely take a point of view. He presents a resolute indictment of how society undermines personal integrity, how people learn to conserve appearances even while recognizing the necessity of tearing them down. But as a fieldworker, he insists on keeping his distance. Standing above and apart from the individuals and institutions he studies, he never abandons his sociological persona. His maneuvers as a fieldworker are strategic and theatrical, orchestrated to reveal the profound weakness of the social fabric and to document the ever-present opportunity for personal degradation and humiliation. He gives the impression he is there, immersed in the scenes he is describing, but you never see him and you rarely feel as though anything he witnesses touches or changes him. Without unveiling his own face, Goffman cleverly unmasks the deceits of everyday life.

Is distancing a trait to be admired in a researcher? Am I reading too much into Henry's candid disclosure about his state of mind? The way I see it, Henry is positioning himself both within and outside the families he is studying. He will be both *apart from* and *a part of* the study he is conducting. But is this kind of self-conscious engagement appropriate?

I've never had to think deeply about these questions. I took for granted what Tucker taught me—that the researcher must remain impartial and free of any personal or political bias. Tucker's words still ring in my ears. I hear him railing against experimenter bias. He scorns the widespread ignorance of demand characteristics and measurement error. His embrace of objectivity and neutrality is firm and uncompromising, and he socialized me to covet these values as well.

Reading Henry, I'm having second thoughts. Bateson's (1951) description of perception and codification enters my mind. If we only perceive the product of our perceptions, then the idea of an untarnished objectivity is an illusion. Any "truth" out there in the world has to make its way through human perception, codification, and translation. The known is inextricably connected to the knower, the observed to the observer, and the self to others. What is known has to be processed through a knower; what is observed is mediated by an observer. Isn't it crucial, then, to observe the observer, to gain entry into the subjectivity and consciousness of the observer? Isn't that what Henry is doing by disclosing the changes he went through over the course of his research and the state of mind in which he labored to tell what he had observed and learned?

Henry's book gives me pause to question the categorical commitment to objectivity and the value-free social science into which I'd been socialized. The questions he raises about conventions of social science methodology and writing practices unnerve me. I don't know how I'm going to resolve the dissonance I feel.

As I read on, I find that Henry was not inclined to stop there. If he had opened a Pandora's Box by inserting himself into his research text, well, he may as well shatter some of the other illusions under which social scientists labor. In only a few introductory pages and a brief methodological appendix, Henry produces a pointed critique of virtually every methodological principle of positivist social science, undermining much of what I had been taught in graduate school.

What Everybody Knows

I had been taught that social scientific knowledge is advanced by conducting controlled experimental studies in which independent variables are manipulated and effects on dependent variables are measured. But Henry doubts the meaningfulness of experiments (1971, p. xv), stating:

> **I am repelled by the artificiality of experimental studies of human behavior because they strip the context from life. They take away from it the environment, without which it has no meaning, without which it has no envelope.**

I had been schooled in the hypothetical-deductive method, a system of inquiry that emphasizes evidence-based hypotheses deduced from previous research. In social science, the cornerstone of the hypothetical-deductive model is the literature review, a synthesis and analysis of previous research from which one's hypotheses are inferred. Under this model, scientific progress is conceived as a linear, building-block process in which all possible outcomes are preconceived and stipulated prior to data collection. I was required to pose hypotheses in advance of inquiry, to formulate predictions deduced from the logical consequences of my hypotheses, and to collect data against which the accuracy of these predictions could be tested. But Henry disputes the necessity of deciding what is important in advance of research (1971, pp. 459–460):

> **It was obvious to me that if I were to start naturalistic observation with a pre-conception of what was important, I could not learn very much beyond my preconceptions.... I felt it was scientifically unsound to "pre-think" the data, and I felt sure that when the record was finished I would be able to make sense of it.**

I had been taught to use advanced statistical tools such as factor analysis to produce typologies or taxonomies of behavior that could be used to synthesize varieties of behavior. But Henry (1971, pp. xv–xvi) takes a stand against typologies:

In this book, I offer no "typologies," because human phenomena do not arrange themselves obligingly in types but, rather, afford us the spectacle of endless overlapping. Hence I have no family "types" and no statistics, only intensive analyses of the variety of family experience. The less we know about family life the easier it is to set up categories, just as the less data we have the easier it is to write history.

I had been encouraged to follow social science orthodoxy, in particular the ideal of reductionism—that science and scientific theory advance by reducing complex phenomena to simpler explanatory variables. The data reduction methods I had learned were designed to develop parsimonious explanations of the variance, reducing complex wholes to simpler parts. But Henry (1971, p. xix) offers an opposing point of view on scientific orthodoxy and reductionism:

A purpose of this book is to get away from reductionism. Orthodoxy impoverishes life—life itself, and the description of it. I want to show how rich existence is, even though it often appears that it is rich merely in misery.

I had been taught that the researcher should never participate directly with subjects. In the presence of the researcher, the subjects would act unnaturally. They would become cautious and guarded. But Henry (1971, p. 458) believes this concern is vastly overrated:

When the observer is in the home ... the family becomes accustomed to him.... Though a family may wish to protect itself from the eyes of the observer, its members cannot remain on guard constantly and everywhere, for the strain is too great ... much of the time the subjects do not even know what one should inhibit or conceal.

I had been taught to master the technical language of communication theory in order to establish my credibility and authority as a knowledgeable researcher. I learned that jargon was a badge of membership in the club and a form of shorthand that speeds communication among the community of scholars, improving efficiency and effectiveness. But Henry (1971, p. xxi) denounces the use of jargon in social science writing:

I have tried to keep technical language out of this book, not only because it is ugly and incomprehensible to most people, but because it is ugly and incomprehensible to me.... Everyday language is usually clearer than the technical vocabulary. Renouncing it and searching for clarity in ordinary language was good discipline, for it compelled me to rack my brains for what I really wanted to say.

But Is it Science? Is it Research?

Jules Henry's oppositional stance on orthodox social science methodology caught me off guard, shaking my faith in science. The hypothetical-deductive model of scientific inquiry had never been presented to me as optional. I had been taught that empiricism was synonymous with scientific method; it was the *one* and *only* *way* to produce scientific knowledge and advance communication theory. In graduate school, I'd been led to believe you either embraced scientific method or you looked for a different kind of work. The choice wasn't between one set of goals and another, or one methodology and another; it was between science, on the one hand, and the arts and humanities on the other. Science was science. The application of scientific method didn't depend on whether you were aligned with the harder physical sciences or the softer social sciences. If you chose science, you were obliged to seek law-like regularities and causal relationships through the application of the scientific method.

The orthodox view left no room for metaphysics. Measurements were what counted. "If it can't be measured, it doesn't exist," Tucker insisted when he introduced us to operationalism (Bridgman, 1927). But how do you measure meanings? Because meanings are not accessible to our senses, we can't rely on sense data. Thus, in behavioral science, meanings are reduced to or replaced by measures of behaviors that can be observed, counted, and measured. "We can't accept fuzzy musings about what something means," Tucker professed. "Just tell me the operations by which you're measuring your concepts. That's what gives them meaning—the operations."

Now, for the first time, I was presented with an alternative to empiricism. Henry's version of social science was driven by a completely different set of goals and procedures. He wasn't interested in producing laws of social behavior akin to the Law of Gravity. Instead, he wanted a social science that could yield interpretive understanding, one that "made sense" of the complexity of everyday life by relentlessly examining the commonplace, relying on an investigator's "intoxicating curiosity," and combining "disciplined observation with a comprehensive interpretation of life in its complex interrelations" (Henry, 1971, p. xv). Henry's interpretive approach did not prescribe a universal methodology; rather, it called for diligent scrutiny of detailed observations carried out by a thoughtful investigator "racking his brains" to try to understand what was going on and figure out how to represent his interpretations in language. Henry's unorthodox interpretive social science focused on phenomena that were left out of mainstream social science. Bits of behavior were considered secondary to configurations of actions and events placed in a context—in a place and at a time. Rescued from obscurity, emotional and subjective experiences now took center stage.

But was this really social *science*? According to Henry (1971, p. 460), if science were considered the process by which the seemingly infinite variety of the universe is made orderly, then he was doing science. But why quibble over the meaning of the word *science*? Henry underscored the importance of close and systematic observations in the natural world—naturalistic observation—and the process of making sense of these observations, interpreting what they mean. In Henry's world of inquiry there is no need for hypotheses and nothing to be gained by experiments, statistics, typologies, predictions, control, or excessive jargon. What is required is "a writer" who can put together configurations of values, emotions, and actions, marshaling the evidence and presenting the facts to demonstrate their significance (Henry, 1971, p. xxi).

The idea of conceiving of communication research as the product of a researcher who is both a fieldworker and a writer excited and intimidated me. I knew that I wanted to study people, not objects, and deep down I doubted the wisdom of treating communication as an object. If communication is the human process by which people create meaning and value, then our methods of inquiry need to be meaning-rich. But empiricism had transformed interactive communication into an object in order to subject it to the kind of inquiry that could produce facts, test hypotheses, and assess theories, disregarding the fact that communication is an intersubjective, meaning-making process. Where meaning is concerned, one is studying people, not objects. Human meaning making cannot be reduced to bits of behavior. Thus, the study of sense making has to proceed along lines quite different from behavioral science. It is a human science, not a behavioral one.

But the lines Henry was suggesting felt daunting to me. I was confident I could learn the empirical part—observing interaction, interviewing participants, writing everything down, and synthesizing all of it after the fact. But Henry was able not only to invent lively metaphors and elegant concepts but also to make life come alive on the page. In *Pathways to Madness*, family members became characters, experiences became scenes, conflicts became dramas, and meanings were revealed through evocative stories and incisive essays. As a writer, Henry rose to a majestic level akin to great artists, composers, and novelists.

Every page I turned increased my admiration for Henry. His razor-sharp critiques of the cultural contradictions under which families labor cut to the chase, revealing a sensitive and deeply insightful mind caught in a web of its own, trying to work through an infuriating anger that parents can do these terrible things to children, while also expressing a tender understanding and empathy for these inadequate parents whose lives had been shaped by the deficiencies of their own parents and the stress our culture imposes on them. Henry was not only a keen critic, perceptive analyst, and imaginative theorist; he also was a talented and evocative writer—a highly gifted storyteller. As I moved through the book, I sat in awe of the combination: a moving and gifted writer sufficiently poignant and eloquent enough to be a novelist while sufficiently disciplined and theoretical enough to be a social scientist.

I was attracted to Henry's project, but I doubted whether I had the ability to do this kind of work. Would I be able to write well enough? If I couldn't do it well, would I want to do it at all?

And what about my career aspirations? I had invested so much in the orthodox version of social science. Three publications were in press, and I had two others ready for submission to journals. I was developing a network of contacts with the best quantitative methodologists in my field and felt confident that once my publications were in print, I would be considered a rising star. Why would I turn my back on this? Was I afraid of success? I knew I had a tendency to grow restless and want to move on to something new. Was I being too suggestible? I had a lot to lose by relinquishing my credentials as an expert statistician and rigorous methodologist. I can't just walk away and never look back, I thought. People expect certain things from me.

I felt like the man who realizes the evening before his wedding that he really doesn't love the woman he's about to marry. He phones her to say they need to call off the wedding. She agrees, saying she feels the same way. They can be friends, but they're really not in love with each other. He feels relieved. As they continue to talk, however, they begin to worry about all the other people who their decision will affect. "But what about all the people who have come from the four corners of the country for our wedding—the relatives, our friends, your colleagues?" she asks. "We can't disappoint them. And what about my parents? They've spent so much money for the service and reception. They'll be so embarrassed. Aren't we being selfish?" So they decide to go on with the wedding.

The Boss

"The boss wants to see you when you get a chance," Laura says, looking up from her desk. Laura is the administrative assistant to the new chair of the department. Dean Soules kept his word. The department hired a new chair and a tenure-track assistant professor last year and has approval to hire on two new tenure-track lines this year.

The new department chair is Dr. Peter Levitt. Peter strikes me as exactly the right person to stir things up and jumpstart the department. He's young for a department chair, my guess about thirty-seven or thirty-eight, but his energy and enthusiasm are contagious, and he's a cheerful and upbeat person. Peter smiles a lot, and his wide grin exposes two large dimples that pleat his cheeks. His dark brown eyes fluctuate between gentle flirtation and arresting authority, giving the impression of a man with a cunning charm. Peter is well connected in the field, having received his PhD at the University of Wisconsin, widely recognized as one of the top graduate programs in communication.

At his interview, Peter impressed me with how easily he moved between respect for the old and attraction to the new. Of the three candidates, he was least threatening to the old guard in the department. He may have won them over with his charisma, but more likely it was his diverse background. A die-hard empiricist was not going to sell, and Peter was the only candidate who could move deftly between social science and humanities without intimidating either. In his PhD work, Peter had focused on mass communications with an emphasis on "effects research," but prior to attending Wisconsin, he was headed for a career in theater. His BFA and MFA in theater were both completed at the renowned Art Institute of Chicago—the Goodman Theatre. I never did get the story of how or why he had converted from the arts to the social sciences, but the fact that he had planted one foot in the humanities and the other in social sciences was appealing. On the whole, the decision was a no-brainer: Peter was by far the best fit for this department. Still, I don't think any of us knew what we were getting.

The faculty search was my first exposure to the way hiring decisions are made in the academy. You get two days with a candidate, sometimes fewer. You can read their publications and, in smaller departments, talk with them one-on-one, face-to-face, for about an hour. You get to hear them give a research lecture and teach a class. The finalists all come with hyperbolic letters of recommendations, suggesting that they walk on water. Each candidate is primed to present a brilliant "job talk" and be on their best behavior. During the interview, the department faculty adheres to an unwritten rule not to question the candidate aggressively or to give a bad impression of the department.

On the basis of this highly sanitized ritual the department chooses a person they can expect to live with as a colleague for anywhere from seven years to a lifetime. It's a flawed and imperfect process fraught with error. Maybe it only seems that way to me because I'm new at this.

Take Peter, for example. He's been my department chair for five months. I can't say I really know him. There were things I really liked about him when he interviewed—his sense of humor, openness, and drive. I still see these attributes, but now I see many more things as well, behaviors that I couldn't possibly have anticipated from the brief time we spent together on the day of his interview. For example, I never expected he would assume such a fatherly manner toward me, which makes me uncomfortable. I'm not looking for a father, especially not at my workplace. He's my supervisor, someone with experience in the field and political savvy. That's all good, but he acts as though he wants to be my life counselor too—not only mine but also Brenda's. Don't get me wrong; I believe Peter has my best interests at heart. He impresses me as a benevolent and honest person. In fact, he's gone out of his way to toss new research opportunities in my direction. But his domineering style bothers me. I don't want to become emotionally attached to him like a son to a father. That's what bothers me—his desire to bond emotionally. I feel safer keeping my distance, maintaining a professional, collegial relationship. I've thought of telling him how uncomfortable this behavior makes me, but the thought of bringing it up feels threatening. I don't feel I can say anything without making myself vulnerable. I can't afford to take the chance of insulting him or making him angry at me. After all, he does have fate control over me.

Maybe it's me. Like I said, I'm new at this. Sometimes I'm not sure exactly how I'm supposed to act. And it's not as though I don't have issues with my own father. Isn't one overbearing father enough? Now that I think of it, I can remember how my father's impatience and frustration with me was highest when we were working on something together. He would insist that I do things his way, and I would insist on doing them my way. Inevitably, I'd screw up, and he'd get enraged. Submitting to authority has never come easy to me. When I became a professor,

I figured that I would rarely have to deal with authority—that's one of the things that attracted me to university life. But here I am, right back where I started.

Saying Yes When You Want to Say No

I enter the chair's office and see Peter sitting behind the oversized desk, puffing on a vile-smelling cigar. His legs are propped up on the desk, and he's shuffling through a stack of computer printouts sitting on his lap. The thick smoke circling around him conjures up the image of bootlegging criminals, illegal bookmaking operations, and backroom politicians cutting deals. Why is cigar-smoking so appealing to short and stout men? Is it the eroticism of the long, thick, wet stogie? Or is it the macho-image it conveys? The cigar bestows virility and power often lacking in the appearance of short men. A cigar in the mouth, even when unlit, seems to confer a more confident masculinity. A couple of weeks ago, I told Peter that cigar smoke made me nauseous. He sat there in disbelief; then went on and on about the mild and sweet aroma of a good cigar. I told him that I must not be sufficiently cultured because I didn't smell an aroma; I smelled a stench.

"What's up, Peter?" I ask as I enter. "Laura said you wanted to see me." I approach his desk and stand across from him.

"Yeah, yeah, I do. Pull up a seat," he says pointing to a spot next to him. I drag a chair from in front of the desk to the place where he has pointed. "I've been looking over some printouts from the postelection polling data John and I collected."

"John?" I ask.

"John Benson in political science. Don't you know him?"

"I've seen him around the halls, but I've never met him."

"Well, you're going to next week. I've asked Laura to set up a meeting for the three of us. John and I are starting a new research project, and we want you to be involved in it."

"What's the project about?" I ask.

"The Watergate burglary," Peter replies emphatically. "Have you been following the news?"

"Yes, of course. I'm obsessed with the whole case. I can't wait to see Nixon get nailed. He's such a liar."

"Tricky Dick a liar? Are you serious?" Peter kids.

I laugh too and say, "Eventually this one may bite him. He won't have Checkers to blame this time."

"I don't know where it's going to lead, but the pressure is mounting. Something is going to break soon."

"What have you heard?" I ask.

"Nothing you don't know already if you've been reading the papers and watching TV. That's just the point: Everything we're learning about Watergate is coming through press and media coverage. The press is shaping public opinion, and they're acting like sharks circling for the kill. My gut tells me they're prowling for something big, and they're not going to stop until they find it."

"Did you hear Cronkite's report?" I ask.

"No, but I read about it," Peter replies. "He was stoking the fire by asking where the money came from to pay these burglars and who gave the orders."

"It was quite a dramatic report. He called Watergate a sinister case of political espionage, or something to that effect."

"That's what I mean. The press is not going to let go. This could be the biggest story of our time. There is talk that the Senate is just waiting to see whether the burglars and their accomplices get convicted, and nobody doubts they will, since they were caught red-handed. I'm betting that as soon as the verdict comes down, the Senate is going to start hearings on Nixon's campaign activities, and all hell is going to break loose."

"And you want to be ready to study the hearings?"

"I don't want to wait that long. I want to start as soon as possible. The *New York Times, Washington Post,* and *Los Angeles Times* have assigned investigative reporters to dig up facts, and they've been breaking new stories every week. And you've seen what Cronkite and Eric Sevareid are doing, giving Watergate major air time on the evening news. I want to follow the story as it unfolds in the public realm. It's a great opportunity to measure how public opinion is shaped by the media coverage. That's why I need you."

"You need me?"

"Yes, you," Peter replies emphatically. "I want you to develop the survey instruments and the sampling strategies and to supervise the data analysis. John and I will help with the development of the questions, but we'll rely on you to do your thing with the statistical analysis. I've read your papers. I don't know much about statistics, but I can tell when someone does. You're very good at it, very knowledgeable, and we're going to need you not only to supervise the data analysis but to write the methods sections of the articles we produce. I can promise you, we're going to churn out a lot of studies." Peter stops abruptly and stares at me. He's chewing compulsively on the end of his cigar, waiting for me to say something. But I don't know what to say.

The next few seconds feel like an eternity as I sit frozen in uncomfortable silence. I'm flattered that Peter wants me to be part of his research team, but this sounds like a huge commitment. Besides, survey research holds little interest for me. Can I say that to Peter? He's counting on me, and I can't take a chance of landing in the boss's dog house. However, I'm not sure how much help I can be. I wasn't trained as a survey researcher. I know just enough to want to stay away from survey research. Surveys are difficult to do well. They pose challenges not encountered in well-controlled experimental studies. It's difficult to get a representative sample, you need skillful interviewers, it's hard not to arouse suspicion and to suppress demand characteristics, ethical quagmires are abundant, and, most of all, you need to have a clear idea of what you're trying to find out from your respondents.

"Will you join us on this study?" Peter asks impatiently, breaking the silence and waking me from my wandering thoughts.

"Yes, I'll be glad to help in any way I can," I say, trying to sound enthusiastic but probably exposing my hesitancy.

When it comes to research, Peter and I are not on the same page. Peter likes to study events that are still in the process of unfolding—Watergate is a prime example. But who knows where this investigation is going to lead? How do you plan a study with such diffuse boundaries? No wonder Peter calls this work "firehouse research." The researchers act like firemen responding to an alarm—they rush to the scene not knowing what to expect. There is no time to meet and plan a strategy. But that's not all bad. After all, the firehouse researcher is focusing on real-world problems—crises in the making. In the best examples I've seen, researchers go out in public and mingle with people who are witnessing the events being studied as they unfold (Lang and Lang, 1953). But firehouse research tends to assume the respondents' immediate reactions are their most meaningful ones. That's a questionable assumption.

Here's another thing that bothers me about firehouse research. If an event is still unfolding, how do you know what questions to ask? You can get people to talk about what they're experiencing, and that's a good thing, but when you start asking everyone the same questions—chosen in advance—without any assurance that these are the right questions to ask, what you get may not be of any value. I have serious doubts about whether researchers can know in advance which questions to ask in the middle of an event. The best tack might be to assume the research goal is to find out what questions need to be asked. But that's not how it usually goes. Often the researchers end up asking the same questions they've asked in previous media effects research, ignoring or bypassing the unique character of the event, which may be the most important quality to investigate.

"Good, I'm delighted," Peter says, that irresistible smile covering his face. "We'll make a great team. Oh, one more thing I want to give you before you leave," he adds, shuffling through some open envelopes on his desk until he finds the one he wants and removes a letter from it. "Here, take this with you," he continues, handing me the letter and a manuscript from his end basket.

I start to read the letter, but Peter interrupts. "Take it to your office," he says. "It's a letter from the editor of *Journalism Quarterly* and a couple of reviews. They want me to revise and resubmit the manuscript. Read the comments from the reviewers and check in with me tomorrow. We can talk about it then. I want your advice about how to respond."

"What sort of advice are you looking for?"

"The reviewers raised questions about the survey methods and the data analysis. I was thinking maybe you could rewrite the methods section for me. You're really good at that. Really and truly, I don't know how to respond. If you think it would help, I'll give you the data decks and you can run a new analysis. I have the computer printouts if you want to see them, too. Let's not bother with it now. Give me a buzz tomorrow and tell me what you think. Oh, I'm so excited to have you on my research team."

I leave and go to my office, where I sit and read the reviews of Peter's article and the editor's letter. I glance at the discussion of method and the tables displayed in Peter's article. There are some elementary errors in the analysis that aren't all that fixable. I don't know if the paper is salvageable, but how can I tell that to Peter?

I never realized how much data snooping survey researchers do. I remember Tucker warning us about data mining. "Sinful what they do," he would say. "If you keep fishing, sooner or later something will bite. But that's not how science works. These data miners ought to be prosecuted." Then he would laugh from his belly, and we could tell he was exaggerating. *Maybe I should call Tucker and ask him what to do. No, I know what he'd say. He has no tolerance for scholars who bend the rules.*

I feel anxiety coursing through my body. *How did I get myself into such a mess? I don't want to be on a media research team. Watergate holds intrigue for me as a citizen, not as a researcher. Interpersonal relationships—that's what moves me, that's what captures my heart. I want to get back to Henry's book. He's opening my mind to so many new possibilities. If I take on all these new projects with Peter and his political science buddies, what time will be left over to finish reading and reflecting on Henry or to complete my own research projects? Left over? I don't want my own work—the things I really care about—reduced to leftovers. They should be my highest priority, not something I get to only after I've finished working on Peter's projects.*

Am I blowing this whole episode out of proportion? Maybe I could just tag along on the Watergate project. Peter's article has some merit, and he's studying important political events. Besides, I may be young, but I've had a lot of experience writing the methods and procedures sections of social science articles. I can probably finesse it enough to get Peter's articles by the reviewers. But would that be ethical? *Take it easy, Art. Think this through. Peter's a powerful person. He knows a lot of important people in the field. He can open doors for you. You don't want to get on his bad side, do you? But what do I have to do to stay on his good side? Is it worth it? Am I selling out?*

My head throbs. I've got Excedrin headache number ninety-nine. I reach into my top drawer and grab the bottle of aspirin. I down three tablets quickly. Then I grab my jacket and my copy of *Pathways to Madness* and head for the door, leaving Peter's materials on my desk.

My Double Bind

Over semester break, I finished reading *Pathways to Madness*. I wrote notes in the margins of almost every page. I can see I'm going to need a new copy, because many of the pages already are frayed, and the front and back covers are unraveling from their binding. Barb thought I was going to tell her how grateful

I was for her gift, but when she called, I told her I was in a state of high anxiety. "You've upset the applecart, that's what you've done," I said. She laughed and told me to relax.

"You're the one person I know in our field who could appreciate Henry's depiction of how pattens of relational pathology reveal themselves in interpersonal transactions. Henry has that same kind of keen mind as Goffman and Laing, but he's more humane than Goffman and more sympathetic than Laing."

"He's a better writer than either of them and a more meticulous researcher too," I reply.

"So what's the problem?" Barb asks. "You sound really agitated."

"You know."

"No, I don't."

"Didn't you tell me this book would change my life?"

"Yes, but I meant in a good way. He reminded me of things you've said about not being so parochial about the discipline—the way he combines anthropology, psychiatry, and literature."

"I'm speaking on a more personal level. I was getting along fine before I read this book. Now I'm questioning everything."

"Isn't that a good thing?" she asks.

"Ordinarily, I'd agree. But, there's something I haven't told you yet. Temple University has invited me to campus for a job interview."

"That's great. I'm happy for you."

"And they're searching for a methodologist—an empiricist. They have a relatively new PhD program and need someone to teach methods courses and supervise quantitative dissertations."

"You can do that. You're a better methodologist than anyone I know, other than Tucker."

"I could do it, but is that what I want? Statistics don't capture my heart and soul. I want to do fieldwork and to write theoretical essays like Henry's. I don't know if I have the talent, but I want to give it a try. Feeling the way I do, I'd be interviewing at Temple under false pretenses."

"Couldn't you do that *and* statistics?"

"Oh Barb, that's just like you—insisting on being inclusive."

"If you were in touch with your feminine side, you wouldn't be feeling this conflict."

"Is it okay if I do that later? I've got bigger worries than my underdeveloped feminine side right now."

"There you go again, putting it off. I've been telling you for years that if only you'd nurture your feminine side, everything else would fall into place. But relax, Art! You have the rest of your life to bring these two regions into harmony." She laughs.

"Thank you. Now where were we before we got distracted by your concern for my feminine side?"

"You were talking about the dilemma you were facing. From the sound of it, you're going through something of an academic crisis of meaning."

"Ouch! When you say it like that, I sound like some guy over forty who just bought a hot red sports car. But I admit that it does feel like a crisis of meaning. I don't think I can live an academic life without a sense of devotion to something that matters. I need to feel like I'm on some kind of a mission. I can't merely go through the motions."

"We both know a lot of people who do, but that's not in your character structure or mine," Barb says.

"That reminds me of the part of the book where Henry talks about the professor who acts as if he's an effective teacher, though he's really not, because it's the only way he can keep going year after year."

"Henry's big on the necessity of illusions. He says we need illusions to keep us sane."

"The story about that professor got me thinking about how difficult it would be for me to act that way. Henry says we have to be careful about which illusions we choose to live by. Some are downright dangerous. If you're constantly trying to pull the wool over other people's eyes, sooner or later you pay the price. It's your own eyes that are shielded. You can't see what you're doing to yourself."

"Are you saying that you're going to refuse the interview at Temple? That's really admirable, Art."

"Not so fast. I didn't say that. You want to make it simple, but it's not. I'm confused about what sort of academic identity I should embrace. I feel as though I'm turning myself inside out. At Cleveland State, everybody looks upon me as a methodologist. I'm the statistics guru of the department. My chair wants to involve me in some of his survey research because he doesn't have sufficient quantitative skills. He thinks I'm some kind of genius because I can explain the meaning of his findings, produce elaborate charts and graphs, and write up the methods section of his articles using sophisticated jargon that he doesn't know the first thing about."

"What a shame."

"Wait! It gets worse. I'm receiving invitations from major universities all over the country to give lectures on methodology, and I'll probably have four or five more articles in press over the next six months."

"And they're all quantitative, right?

"You guessed it."

"A star is born," Barb teases. "Can I tell people I knew you when you were a struggling youngster wearing tie-dye t-shirts and running around with holes in the soles of your shoes?"

"It's not funny, Barb. I feel like a fraud."

"You've really dug yourself a hole this time. You can't go to Temple because you'd be enacting a sham. But if you stay at Cleveland State, you'll feel as if you're selling out. You'll lose your soul. It's a Laingian knot, isn't it?"

"And a double bind. I'm damned if I do and damned if I don't. And I can't climb in a hole and stay there. I have to do something, take some kind of action."

"This is where the rubber hits the road—communication theory applied to one's own life."

"Now you know why I hate you."

Jules Henry as a Theorist of Interpersonal Relationships

In spring 1973, I lectured on Henry's book for the first time. "This is not popcorn reading," I warned the students in Advanced Interpersonal Communication when I handed out copies of a few readings I had selected from the book. "Henry will stretch your mind, and he may help you expand your vocabulary. He's a brilliant theorist and an evocative writer. Think about your own families when you read the accounts of the families he studied."

In my first lecture, I told students that Henry's work towered over other attempts to draw conclusions about mental illness from direct observations of families in their home environment. "While many researchers look upon the mundane details of everyday life as trivial, Henry shows that concentrating on common, everyday family activities can produce profound insights that escape researchers who restrict observations of families to a clinic or to controlled empirical studies. Some researchers think that only careful control of variables can yield authentic data, but Henry shows how much can be learned when a researcher shuns the artificiality of the laboratory and enters the places where the phenomena of interest occur naturally—inside the family.

"Before I look at some of the conclusions Henry reached, let's briefly review his methodology. Who can summarize how Henry approached the families he studied?"

I call on my old friend Shirley, who has come full circle since the introductory class. She sits in the front row and participates frequently in class.

"He spent between five and eight days with each family," she says. "One of the families provided a room for him. At the other three, he showed up in time for breakfast and stayed all day, until they had retired for the evening."

"How many families were there?" I ask Shirley.

"Five," a male student shouts from the back of the room, and I grimace disapprovingly at his rude interruption. "I'm sorry," he says.

"But Henry only went to four of them." Shirley interjects. "He had an assistant who did the fifth."

"That's right," I say. "Who can tell me what he did while he was with the families?"

Nate, the boy in the back of the room, raises his hand, and I call on him, trying to signal that I'm not holding a grudge. "He acted like someone who was a friend of the family or a relative, and he kept a record of everything. There wasn't much detail in the field notes we read, but I imagine he wrote copious comments."

"Yes, he says that he wrote everything down that he could remember, no matter how tangential it seemed at the time," I reply. "What about his writing strategy? Was there anything unique about it?" I spot Ed sitting right behind Shirley. "Ed, what do you think?"

"I loved what he did with theory. He introduced us to each family with an essay that highlighted some quality of family life that is important in all families but particularly crucial in the family he was about to describe. In the Jones family, it was quarreling, anger, and the importance of circumspection. In the Rosenberg family, it was sham and the various orders of truth; and in the Metz family, it was how love gets communicated or whether it gets communicated in the way it was intended."

"That's excellent, Ed. You've pinpointed how Henry uses these essays as framing devices that help us better understand the families we're about to observe. Though the essays can stand on their own, they become even more valuable when we see how they can help us grasp the meanings of the patterns of interaction in the particular family to which he links them. These are profound exemplars of how communication theory can be applied to families. Now I want to go over some of his conclusions about the interactional dynamics of normal and disturbed families."

I grab the stack of handouts on the desk in front of me and distribute a copy to each of the students:

Conclusions from Jules Henry's *Pathways to Madness*

1. *Family interaction is highly complex. So many things happen at the same time that it is difficult to make sense of it all. Where do things start? The birth of a baby initiates a circle of action and reaction in which the baby's responses to the parents cause each of them to respond to the baby's responses. No single bit of behavior can be understood in isolation from the configuration of jointly enmeshed behaviors in which it is embedded. Thus, the task of separating cause from effect becomes extremely difficult, perhaps impossible.*

2. *The differences between disturbed and normal families are not as substantial as one might imagine. Disturbed families enact much the same routines of everyday life as the rest of us, and, with only a few exceptions, their behavior falls within the limits of what is considered normal. It is these exceptions—the occasions when they exceed normal limits and go to extremes—that we find upsetting and deem pathological. Even in the sickest families some signs of health exist—alleviating conditions that mute the pain. It is important to see the strengths in even the most disturbed families and the weaknesses in even the healthiest ones.*

3. *There is more cruelty and less compassion in "miserable families." Cruelty is a function of vulnerability, for without vulnerability, cruelty would be impossible. Disturbed families fail to understand the importance of compassion. In Henry's opinion, the "judicious application of compassion" (1971, p. 449) is essential to maintaining the health of the family.*

4. *In disturbed families at least one person is viewed as an enemy and treated like an opponent. Usually, the scapegoat is one of the children and the other children—the ones not treated this way—are better off.*

145

5. *Too often, family members do not know how to restrain their reactions when it is necessary to do so. They fight when they ought to submit, and they practice the subtle art of entrapment by appearing innocent when they are guilty of triggering other family members' emotional impulses, what Henry calls "turning the other person on" (Henry, 1971, p. 449).*

6. *In disturbed families, the means of satisfaction are distorted. For instance, spouses may substitute the affection received from a child for what is lacking in their own relationship.*

7. *Disturbed families take life too seriously. There is too little joy and not enough humor in disturbed families. They seem to suffer from a "compulsion to murder pleasure" (Henry, 1971, p. 452).*

8. *Crucial differences are discounted. Henry calls this "pathogenic leveling," a form of "concordant misperception" in which sick children are treated as if they are well, young kids act as if they are adults, and strangers are treated as if they are relatives or friends.*

I give the students several minutes to read over the handout, after which I continue, "Our time is almost exhausted for today, but we're not finished thinking about Jules Henry's work. Over the weekend, I want you to apply to your own family some of the conclusions he reached. Many of you have referred to your family as 'dysfunctional,' but you haven't had a language or concepts through which to speak concretely about the patterns of dysfunction you perceive. I don't like the term 'dysfunctional family.' In fact, I find the ease with which people use that term revolting. If all families can be considered dysfunctional—as many of you seem to suggest—then the term loses any unique meaning or application. And if you really believe that families inevitably become dysfunctional, then why do so many of you say you look forward to creating your own family? That isn't rational. Henry wants us to emphasize strengths and weaknesses, and he gives us a language to begin talking about both of these. I want you to go down his list and identify which ones apply to your family. You may want to think of the absence of a weakness as a strength. Try to be concrete, and come to class with specific examples that you feel comfortable sharing in class. That's it for today."

After class I retreat to my office and write some notes into the teaching journal I'm keeping:

Am I asking too much of these students? I haven't told any of my colleagues what I'm doing in this class. I'm afraid they'd think I was intervening into the personal lives of my students. I can hear the voice of one of my senior colleagues reprimanding me for crossing boundaries. "This is the life of the mind," he would admonish. "Their personal or family lives should be of no concern to you." But this course isn't math or chemistry. Undergraduate students aren't drawn to courses in interpersonal or family communication because they want to theorize or develop concepts to be applied in research. Students come to these courses because they're trying to figure out how to live better lives. And they can't do this if we only educate them from the neck up, ignoring their emotional and sensual lives. Anyhow, does it really matter whether I ask them questions that probe their personal lives and family experiences? Aren't they going to ask themselves these questions anyway? If I cite the latest research findings about the relationship difficulties experienced by children of divorced parents, aren't they going to think, "I'm one of the people he's describing"? Isn't it better to bring these concerns into the classroom and let students engage their fears and feelings openly? Their stories about their family life help me understand what they need from me and from their cohorts; it makes me a better and more compassionate teacher, more cognizant of the resources from which I must draw to reach them.

I place my journal in the bottom drawer of my desk and begin gathering materials to take home with me. As I do, episodes in my own family history flash through my mind:

My sister and I are twins. After we were born, my older brother was sent to live with my grandparents for a short time. He was five years old when he was arbitrarily removed from the family. When he rejoined us, he took charge of sibling relationships. By the time I was five or six years old—the time of my earliest memories—he was dominating my sister and me. Shorter, lighter, and weaker, I had no chance in the fights he would pick with me. He would pin me to the ground, overpower me, and make me surrender.

But wrestling was not our only form of relating. We both loved competitive sports. He would challenge me to one-on-one basketball and wiffleball, which was a game designed as a substitute for baseball playable in tiny backyards like ours. He was more than a foot taller and fifty pounds heavier. I had no chance to win these games, but I was not a quitter. Refusing to yield quietly to his strength, I competed feverishly. Although the outcome of these games never varied, I did my best to prolong them. I felt alive and energized when we were competing, and I wanted to hold on to these feelings as long as possible. Inevitably, the game ended, and the excitement vanished. What I didn't realize then was how meaningful this time and contact with my brother was for me. By the time I was twelve years old, he had moved out of our little house for good, and I had lost a playmate and rival who motivated me.

What did these games mean to my brother? I never took the risk to ask him, and he never brought up his experience of our play with me. I can only hazard a guess. On the surface, he was the master and I was the slave. He could rejoice in victory, whereas I was left with the sorrow of defeat. But the master needs the slave: The slave is the relational source of his power—as long as the slave continues to deliver what the master demands or needs from him. The pattern of the relationship must be kept within certain bounds. Is this why my brother never let me win, not once? He won each and every contest. Was his strength compared to mine also a source of vulnerability for him, one in which a single loss could crush him? That's the way it looks to me now, that winning (or my surrender) was as important to him as playing was to me. For my brother, ours had become a hostile-dependent relationship. He depended on me as a source for the expression of his anger and hostility.

147

I can't help thinking how awful it must have felt to be shipped across town when my sister and I arrived, after being the center of attention for five years. How could my brother resolve his doubt about whether parents who love him would do this? What could he do with the anger and resentment he may have felt? One thing he could do was take it out on me, degrade me—a source of his humiliation—to mitigate his pain. Oddly enough, I don't recall feeling degraded. This was the only time it felt as though we had a family connection, a link to each other as brothers.

I make a note to myself to write down these thoughts in my journal as soon as I get home. I want to present them to the class on Monday as an example of what Henry called "distortion in the means of satisfaction"—how we learn to achieve satisfaction from patterns that twist or disfigure our connections to people whom we love. I clip the note to the top of my course file, gather the remaining papers and books, and head out of my office.

Tonight I'll be giving more thought to my relationship to my siblings and parents. I've asked students in my class to examine their family's patterns of communication, so I feel obliged to share stories and analysis of mine as well. Examining one's life—isn't that what a liberal education should encourage? Who could object to that? Not that I'm naïve—I understand that the mining of memory can open old wounds. The challenge will be creating a pedagogy that won't infect but could heal. "Do no damage," Tucker used to say when we talked about the ethical obligations of a professor. If he were here, I would ask him how far to carry that principle. I would say, "I want my classroom to be a place in which we converse about things that really matter; where we ask how we can live better lives, where we examine our lives together and draw meaning from our experiences. I don't think you can do that without taking risks."

Tucker would look me in the eye and say, "Go for it. What are you waiting for?"

Chapter Six

Paradigms Shift

Dark Side of the Moon

There is no dark side of the moon really. Matter of fact, it's all dark.
Roger Waters (1973)

"We're looking principally for a methodologist, a person to direct empirical dissertations," Murray Halfond said when he called to invite me for an interview at Temple University. Murray did not come across as an in-your-face, dominating type of leader as Peter had been at Cleveland State. He spoke slowly in a soothing, gentle voice that gave the impression of a caring and understanding person who would rather listen than talk. Prior to becoming chair, Murray had served as director of the Speech and Hearing Clinic, and his well-practiced clinical persona seemed perfectly suited for a person occupying a position in which one's capacity to remain unruffled would be tested.

"We need someone on the cutting edge of statistical analysis, and your credentials impressed our search committee," Murray continued. "Will you come to campus for an interview?"

"I'd love to. I'm eager to meet other members of the faculty and see the campus," I replied.

"Is there anything else on your mind?" Murray asked, signaling we were nearing the end of the conversation. "Any questions I can answer now?"

"What about the interpersonal area? Will I be free to develop courses on close relationships?"

"If that's what you're passionate about, by all means. Take me, for example. I'm keenly interested in self-talk, how and why people talk to themselves."

"You mean intrapersonal communication?" I asked, delighted to hear Murray join teaching to passion.

"Yes. I've developed an intrapersonal course and now I'm planning one on dreaming and dream analysis. At Temple, if you are immersed in a topic and make a good case for it, you can get new courses approved without much difficulty."

"I'm glad to hear that."

"But I should emphasize that the main thing we need is a sequence of empirical research methods courses for our graduate students. If you join us, methods will be your principal responsibility." I was pleased to hear about Murray's off-the-beaten-track intrapersonal courses, but after we hung up I thought about how unequivocally he had stated the department's need for a methodologist and wondered whether I had revealed too much about my other interests.

As the date for my interview—early February 1973—drew closer, I grew increasingly anxious about how I was going to present myself. I wanted out of Cleveland. The thought of another winter or two of cloud-covered skies, howling winds, and snow piled three feet high on the sides of the highways was demoralizing. Temple had a PhD program, a more accomplished faculty, and a reputation as a progressive university with a strong college of arts and sciences. A faculty appointment at Temple would move me up the academic ladder. Murray had indicated that my credentials might be sufficient to get my foot in the door, but was this a door I wanted to walk through? I would be losing the freedom and flexibility I'd enjoyed at Cleveland State, where I was a big fish in a little pond. Tucker used to say, "Be careful what you wish for!" Would the identity of departmental methodologist satisfy me?

In preparation for the interview, I did my homework. At Temple, the department was called *speech* and was divided into two areas that functioned independently, rhetoric and communication, and speech pathology and audiology. The lower-level curriculum in rhetoric and communication was dominated by speaking courses: persuasion, argumentation and debate, voice and articulation, and advanced public speaking. Upper-division courses focused on the history and criticism of rhetoric and public address. Given my background and interests, this was not good news. Undoubtedly, my comfort level would be challenged at Temple, where the social science aspects of communication studies took a backseat to the traditional humanities orientations of the field. The communication area appeared to be sorely neglected and understaffed; only a couple of offerings on communication theory and systems approaches to communication had made their way into the catalogue, and only one other faculty member identified as a social scientist. Without colleagues who shared my interests, I worried that I would feel lonely and isolated at Temple. However, Murray indicated that new courses could be developed, and I had confidence in my ability to persuade colleagues to expand the social science offerings.

Neither the catalogue nor the documents on the graduate program suggested that the rhetoric and communication area offered an innovative program prepared to break new ground or forge a unique view of the field. On the whole, the curriculum at Temple seemed conventional and uninspiring. One exception, however, did catch my eye—a course on "The Rhetoric of Science" taught by Professor Herb Simons. The idea of subjecting science and scientific method to rhetorical analysis and criticism intrigued me. Do scientists persuade, or do data speak for themselves through the application of scientific methodology? Jules Henry (1971) positioned himself on the side of interpretation. The value-free objectivism of empiricism, however, insinuates that the "meanings" of data arise from the application of criteria-based methodological rules and practices beyond interpretation. In other words, methodological rules produce "brute data" whose meanings cannot be called into question by offering other interpretations or readings. The scientist is only a mouthpiece for brute data, only an instrument who carries meanings without judgment as if data speak for themselves.

The idea of science as rhetorical fascinated me. At first blush, rhetoric of science had the potential to bring the two worlds of inquiry (Snow, 1959) together, joining the humanities orientation of rhetorical studies with the social science perspective of communication studies.

I had met Herb Simons previously. In December 1972, he called my room at the Speech Association of America convention in San Francisco, announcing that he was recruiting me to apply for a faculty position. We scheduled a brief meeting that ended up lasting several hours, during which we covered a wide range of academic issues. "Herb and I hit it off immediately. We talked like old friends," I told Brenda later that night. "I'm not sure why—probably something ethnic, since we're both Jewish. He talked a lot about his research interests and didn't show a lot of interest in mine, but he's charming, witty, and has a keen mind. I found myself absorbed by the conversation, but a little scared too. He likes to tear ideas apart, and he's good at it."

Frowning in disapproval, Brenda replied, "You're not making him sound all that attractive."

Laughing, I decided to tread carefully. "I know my description makes him sound like another ego-driven, dominating intellectual, and I'm aware how much you dislike academics who insist on being center of attention and seem to be perpetually performing. But there is something enchanting and original about Herb too. He's passionate, amusing, and has a flair for irony that I don't see very often. He can stretch me. I need a colleague who can inspire and challenge me, someone I can learn from. I don't have that at Cleveland State."

"I understand. You want a colleague who could mentor you. That sounds good in theory. I just don't want you to become one of those self-absorbed academics in love with the sound of your own voice."

Scientific Revolutions

A few weeks before my interview, Herb phoned. "I thought you might want to come to my graduate seminar while you're here for your interview," he begins. "We're reading Thomas Kuhn's *Structure of Scientific Revolutions*. Do you know the book?"

"Yes," I lie—sort of. I do know of the book. I've seen it cited, but I've not read it.

"Good, then you'll come and join the conversation. Okay?"

"Sure, I'd love to," I lie again, worried that I am digging a grave for myself. I feel as if I'm back in graduate school preparing for an exam. Except this time I haven't taken the course or read the book.

The next day I buy a copy of *The Structure of Scientific Revolutions* and lock myself away in my office to study it. The book turns out to be a much tougher read than expected. Kuhn's examples are drawn mainly from chemistry and physics—Einstein, Galileo, Lavoisier, Newton—sciences largely unfamiliar to me. At first, I struggle to understand each case. Then I realize I'm missing the forest for the trees. Mastering the physics and chemistry cases is not all that important. The big picture—that's what I need to grasp.

Soon the big picture comes into focus. I scribble notes throughout the text and highlight evocative quotations. Sitting at my desk, I begin to type furiously in a stream-of-consciousness fashion:

> Kuhn is challenging the fundamental premise of progress in science—the building-block model of science. He is saying that science doesn't evolve cumulatively, brick by brick. Progress isn't gradual and continuous—it's abrupt and irregular, akin to a fissure that breaks sharply from its foundation. The building-block model gives the impression of an orderly and precise progression in which science moves closer and closer to something called "truth." Each research study aims to add on to the ones that preceded it. But history tells a different story, says Kuhn, one that reveals a chaotic process of change during which the stability of science is punctuated by "revolutions" that suddenly revise and replace the entire "disciplinary matrix" or "paradigm" of scientific beliefs that preceded them. "[T]he new paradigm, or a sufficient hint to allow later articulation, emerges all at once, sometimes in the middle of the night, in the mind of a man [sic] deeply immersed in crisis" (Kuhn, 1970, p. 90).
>
> Contrary to the prevailing story line, scientific revolutions aren't merely add-ons that append existing knowledge. According to Kuhn, they radically revise the entire constellation of beliefs and practices in the research community. Revolutions shift the foundation and shake the earth; the same data now are seen through a different lens, one that reframes the meanings of key scientific terms, the puzzles and methods deemed central and appropriate to inquiry, and the perspective through which the discipline is viewed. As Kuhn observes, "The normal-scientific tradition that emerges from a scientific revolution is not only incompatible but often actually incommensurable with that which has gone before" (1970, p. 103).
>
> Kuhn starts with a discussion of what he calls normal science, "research firmly based upon one or more past scientific achievements that some particular scientific community acknowledges for a time as supplying the foundation for its further practice" (p. 10). Normal science defines the phenomena, the body of theory, and the methods applicable to address the puzzles of the field. For most of us, graduate school constitutes our indoctrination—some call it socialization—into the community of scholars practicing normal science in our field. We are given concrete, relatively standard research exemplars that promote the shared theoretical beliefs, research practices, and taken-for-granted premises of our "disciplinary matrix" (1970, p. 182). By the time our socialization is complete we will have internalized and developed the mind-set of a normal

152

scientist. We will understand the work of our discipline in the vernacular of the paradigm that governs it.

For the most part, our work as normal scientists takes the form of what Kuhn calls "mop up work" (p. 24). We are taught to stay within the framework of the paradigm. Straying too far from home, trying out novel approaches or new ideas, we are told, will threaten our opportunities to publish our work in prestigious (if obscure) journals. We become worker bees whose main function is to maintain the stability and growth of the disciplinary matrix, to feed and nourish the paradigm. Our audience is a small, sometimes minute, community of highly specialized experts who speak in the same tongue—a shared vocabulary inaccessible to the world at large. Together we form "a specialist society" replete with our own technical journals and unique jargon. When our socialization is complete, we will have internalized a commitment to this society and adopted the mind-set of our discipline.

This image of a scientific community and its cumulative progress within a disciplinary matrix is complete as far as it goes. But it doesn't go far enough. "Normal science does not aim at novelties of fact or theory, and when successful, finds none," writes Kuhn. "New and unsuspected phenomena are, however, repeatedly uncovered by scientific research, and radical new theories have again and again been invented by scientists" (1970, p. 53). Researchers inevitably recognize that more than one theoretical explanation can be applied to a given set of data even within a well-established paradigm. Moreover, occasions arise when no existing theories appear capable of explaining the data. In these moments, when anomalies cannot be explained by existing theories within the prevailing paradigm, an atmosphere of crisis develops that opens the discipline to a clash between the old paradigm and new contenders for paradigmatic status. Kuhn calls these periods "extraordinary" because they signify a turning point during which the field experiences the kind of vulnerability that undermines the practice of normal science by weakening confidence in the ruling paradigm and thus opening the flood gates to a wave of new possibilities for abrupt and radical transformations in the constellations of beliefs and values that have defined it: "The proliferation of competing articulations, the willingness to try anything, the expression of explicit discontent, the recourse to philosophy and to debate over fundamentals, all these are symptoms of a transition from normal to extraordinary research" (Kuhn, 1970, p. 91).

A scientific revolution is a revision of a field's disciplinary matrix—a paradigm shift that transforms the field's view of the world in the aftermath of a crisis of confidence in the paradigm's ability to deal with annoying anomalies. Kuhn's explanation of how this revision process works departs radically from the building-block picture of scientific progress and undercuts the premise that science necessarily progresses in a fashion that moves closer and closer to "truth." He rejects the methodological dogma of logical positivism that promises progress through the rigorous application of scientific method—*truth through method*. "That is not the way a science develops," writes Kuhn (1970, p. 40). His account of episodes of major theory change in the history of science dashes the logical positivists' hopes for something akin to a "neutral observation language"

153

into which the predictive consequences of conflicting theories could be translated in order to choose rationally between them.

The cases Kuhn discusses show that there is no methodological algorithm that can settle theoretical clashes. The "facts" used to decide between competing theories during these *revolutionary* episodes in science are not independent of a theory that defines them as "facts." There is no *neutral observation language* capable of translating the "facts" (or terms) of one theory into that of another. Because one theory is, in Kuhn's terms, "incommensurable" with the other(s), there is no set of rules under which a rational judgment could be applied to decide which is best. Thus, when we choose one theoretical explanation over another, our choice is not based on rules but on values or something akin to "sociopolitical factors" such as self-interests, pressures to conform to prevailing disciplinary dogma, or any beliefs beyond pure knowledge seeking. Whereas logical empiricists had looked upon "neutral observation language" as a solution to the problem of theory choice, Kuhn argues convincingly that such an amorphous language is incapable of providing "objective" decision rules for settling theoretical controversies. There is no such thing as theory-free observation.

When one theory competes with another it is not simply a matter of comparing each theory to the world. Each has to be compared to the other *and* to the world. Thus, the debate between paradigms inevitably becomes circular. As Kuhn (1970, p. 93) notes, "Each group uses its own paradigm to argue in that paradigm's defense." Thus, the choice of a paradigm is not a simple matter of deciding on the basis of objective proof or something akin to a neutral observation language. When paradigms clash, a communication failure is unavoidable because "communication across the revolutionary divide is inevitably partial . . . the proponents of different paradigms practice their trade in different worlds" (Kuhn, 1970, pp. 149–150).

Advocates of one paradigm cannot think in the terms of the other paradigm's language. Nor can the language of one paradigm be translated into the language of the other, even if the same words are used. Aristotle and Galileo, for example, use the term "motion" to refer to fundamentally different things. For Kuhn, this "incommensurability" means they not only practice in different worlds; "they see different things when they look from the same point in the same direction" (1970, p. 149). Kuhn is not saying they can see anything they choose or that what they look at has changed, only that "in the areas circumscribed by the terms of their theory, they see different things and see them in different relations one to the other" (p. 149).

I stop typing and lift myself out of my chair. Scratching my head and picking at threads of my beard, I begin pacing back and forth in my office, talking to myself:

Kuhn's argument is both disturbing and exhilarating. I feel rage rising from the pit of my stomach as I think about my indoctrination as a graduate student. I'm grateful to Tucker for his inspirational teaching and his belief in me. He introduced me to Goffman, Laing, Mead, and Bateson, but his commitment to the methodological paradigm of empiricism blinded him to the possibilities that the achievements of these nonconforming, inventive theorists opened. Tucker used these imaginative theorists to turn me on, seducing me with appealing ideas about close relationships, the self, authenticity, and intimacy, but when it came time for the "serious" work of research, he insisted on a commitment to the positivist paradigm. He prepared me to become one of the worker bees who keep the paradigm alive. I don't know if he did this consciously, but that is what I've become—another janitor mopping up at the end of the day, a custodian holding a PhD.

Kuhn doesn't say much about the social sciences, but his analysis of "normal science" seems to fit communication research. My little social network is a small and rarified community of technicians. We understand data analysis and stay on top of the latest advances in multivariate techniques. We don't have trouble publishing in our field's rarified journals, though we doubt that colleagues without our erudition—its skills and vocabulary—can understand what we write. When you look closely at our work, you wonder, what does this work really have to do with human communication? We treat communication as if it were an object in order to carry out rigorous studies and develop sophisticated and precise measures. That's what the objectivist paradigm forces you to do. You hide your eyes from ideas about communication that don't allow precise measurement. You disregard what you know in your heart and soul—that communication has something to do with how we come to think, feel, and act in certain ways by using language: having conversations with others and ourselves, developing relationships and attaching meanings to interactive experiences. What we need is a paradigm of interactive communication.

The trouble is that once you're invested in the ruling paradigm, it feels risky to change. This is what you were "trained" to do, all your best friends do it, you've established a reputation, and you're moving up the career ladder. Why would you give that up for something so uncertain? There's no interpretive community, no communication journals inviting research articles anchored in and written from an interpretive point of view, nobody specializing in interpretive methodologies. Besides, you may turn out to be no good at it. Heck, I'm not even sure what "it" is, except something nebulously referred to as an interpretive paradigm. In my present disheartened state, I may not be thinking straight. If I abandon the empiricist paradigm—turn in my membership, so to speak—will I be committing academic suicide?

Kuhn talks about paradigm change as a crisis of faith, a conversion from old to new, as if it were some kind of religious reformation. If that's the case, well, I'm on the verge of becoming a nonbeliever. Realizing how convinced I was that my methodological acumen could get me closer and closer to truth propels me into a state of ironic despair. Kuhn identifies the source of the illusion by which I was living my academic life. Science is about solving puzzles, not about achieving truth. Normal science, especially in the social sciences, is an indoctrination, a shakedown, a pressure to conform or else. Our careers depend on it. You can't get published if you don't abide by the conventions of writing and analysis the paradigm authorizes.

I waver between feeling downcast and feeling elated. Kuhn places human subjectivity at the center of scientific progress. It feels thrilling and liberating to demystify science. Most of us think that what separates science from other forms of inquiry is its method, *a set of objective procedures and criteria that assures rationality and guarantees an accumulation of knowledge. This is why we treat science with such reverence. But Kuhn blurs the distinction between objectivity and subjectivity and between facts and values. When Kuhn equated a paradigm shift to a "gestalt switch," I was reminded of Bateson's ideas about codification. What is out there in the world—in reality—has to be processed through an elaborate codification system that inevitably transforms it. Cognitive barriers stand in the way of seeing things that are there. Each of us develops "habits of mind" that become entrenched and dispose us to interpret what we see in a particular way. Once our habits of mind take root, they are difficult to dislodge. Yet if we are to see and make sense of a new idea or paradigm, this is exactly what must happen—our entrenched habits must be displaced. The moral of the story Kuhn tells is that there simply is no way to distinguish unequivocally between what is in our minds and what's out there in the world—no rules we can follow, no methods to guarantee validation or truth. Scientific method does not make it possible for the mind to transcend the skin. It turns out that science can't stand above the contingencies of language and perception or outside the circle of historical, cultural, and autobiographical interests.*

Our reverence for science is largely a function of the rhetoric of objectivity and value neutrality, which has produced an idealized and exaggerated view of science. The problem is not with science but with an idealized and deferential view of science that obscures its human, subjective, institutional, and relational qualities. Kuhn argued that science's highest standard was not objectivity or "truth" but rather the concurrence of the community—solidarity in the social network of scientists. Of course, to say that science has not lived up to its ideal of objectivity does not mean that science isn't useful. Far from it.

Maybe what needs to be changed is the rhetorical flourish of science. I'm thinking I should tell Herb's class that, rhetorically speaking, what science needs is less talk about rigor and more about imagination, less conversation about objectivity and more about community, less discussion about methods and more about paradigms. Then again, maybe that's not the best strategy to adopt if you're a candidate for a faculty position as a methodologist!

Sunset

July 8, 1974. I lie on the floor in the living room, my head and neck propped up by two big cushions leaning against the wall. I'm alone in our second-floor duplex. Well, not quite alone. Across the room the amplifier blinks in the darkness as the stereo blares out the space-rock music of Pink Floyd's *Dark Side of the Moon* (Gilmour et al., 1973), an album that elevates music to new plateaus of breathtaking artistry. It's a technological masterpiece of art-rock, an emotional and aesthetic triumph. I'm immersed in the music. I feel as if I'm inside it, as if it's playing me.

I lean over in the darkness and feel for the tiny box on the floor. I strike a match in the dark and relight the joint I've been working on for the past hour or so. This

156

is a routine I've been practicing a lot lately. Inhale deeply—as deeply as your lungs can take it—hold the smoke as long as you can, then exhale slowly. I repeat the sequence several times until I feel my eye lids wanting to close. I reach for the ear phones strategically placed on the floor beside me. I want the full effect—to merge the inner space marijuana creates with the outer cosmos of Pink Floyd's trippy imagery and sound. Soon the long, spacey instrumentals carry me away. I float through a peculiar mental space in which I see myself trying to connect revolving stars that keep spinning away from me. I think I know where I am; then I don't. How can the familiar feel so strange?

Earthy Matters

I can't believe it's been fifteen months since my interview at Temple. So much has changed since then. The interview went well—at least I thought it did. I presented a "job talk" nobody understood, but I did it with such flair and energy that it didn't matter. I talked the talk—canonical correlations, multiple regression, structural equations, multivariate analysis of variance—and danced around the front of the lecture hall with a spring to my step while the audience gave blank stares on affirming faces, content to fake interest and appreciation. I recall thinking that they were thinking, How can anyone be so turned on by this dull stuff? Well, I guess it won't kill us to have one of these guys. In the individual meetings with faculty members I turned on what one faculty member later called "Bochner's boyish charm," listening intently to each person's stories, professing enthusiasm for everyone's specialty, and establishing rapport by kibitzing and assuming a relaxed appearance. By the time I left, I felt certain I had aced the interview.

Then a strange thing happened. Five weeks went by without a call or a letter. I waited and waited. This is strange, I thought. Why haven't they contacted me? Finally, one day, the first week in April, Murray called and told me the department had decided to go in a different direction. "We hired a rhetorical critic," he told me. "But we're still considering you. I have an appointment to see the dean next week. I'm going to ask him to give us another line. If he agrees, we want to offer you the position—that is, if you're still interested."

"Yes, I'm interested," I replied, puzzled by the whole scenario. Is this how academia works? They advertise for one thing and hire for something entirely different? Or is this just a reflection of the department's resistance to empirical research?

"Okay, then, I'll get back in touch with you after my meeting with the dean," Murray said.

I didn't hear from him again until the first week in May. The news was good, but the timing was bad.

"I want to accept, Murray, but I can't in good faith resign this late in the year. It would be too late for my department to search for a replacement."

"I'm really sorry to hear that, Art. Everybody here really likes you. You're a good fit for us."

I didn't know what else to say. I wanted the position at Temple. Even with all my doubts about the curriculum and the maddening hiring process, I had prepared myself mentally to leave Cleveland. After a long silence, I took a stab at an optional plan, the only alternative that came to mind. It's a long shot, I thought, but what do I have to lose?

"If you're willing to offer me a contract to start a year later, I'll accept. It would mean I'd be a lame-duck professor here for a year, and you'd have to wait until then for a methodologist."

"That's a brilliant idea, Art," Murray replied, sounding positively gleeful. "I don't know why I didn't think of it. Let me run it by my colleagues and the dean. I think they'll go for it." This time Murray called back the next day, and we sealed the deal.

A new academic life awaited me at Temple. Fifteen months. You only have to survive the next fifteen months, I said to myself. When I told Peter I was leaving and would not consider a counter-offer, he acted miffed and wounded. He took it personally—as if my decision to leave reflected a failure on his part. Within a month, he told me I was no longer a "full" faculty member. "I don't want you to attend faculty meetings or serve on any committees," he said.

Fine, I have nothing more to prove at Cleveland State, I thought. So what if I was the person who created the communication program and developed the curriculum? I'm already forgotten. I guess universities have short memories and no loyalties.

I got over the hurt quickly and reframed my remaining time at Cleveland State as a long, relaxed experiment in pedagogical freedom. They couldn't fire me, and I would not be bucking for a raise. Sid had released me from everything but teaching. Chains unlocked, I was free to try out new modes of experiential pedagogy. Beginning in Auburn, New York, where I taught high school, I had fantasized about taking a crack at teaching in a radically different way, setting up a less hierarchical structure and creating a different world of experience in the classroom, but I lacked the courage to give it a go. Now nothing stood in the way.

In fall 1973, I took the handcuffs off. I taught a nonverbal communication class in a dance studio, a small room where students were surrounded by mirrors on all four walls. The opportunities afforded for students "to see themselves" were abundant. I also offered an advanced interpersonal course limited to twelve students. I modeled the course after the T-Group methodology originated at the National Training Laboratory in Bethel Maine (see Grogan, 2012), where I had taken a two-week workshop on "learning blocks" the previous summer. The purpose of the course was to "become a group" and "analyze ourselves." I participated as one of the group members. I had never gained so much access to what students thought or felt nor shared mine as openly. Teaching had never been this much fun or this rewarding.

Eclipse

The heartbeat pulses through my ears. I recognize the end of "Eclipse," the song that concludes *Dark Side of the Moon*. I stand up and shuffle over to the stereo to restart the album. Plopping back down on the floor, I hear the pounding heartbeat again, the throbbing essence of the human condition. The opening heartbeat sounds stronger, stouter, swifter. At the end of the album, the heart weakens, beating slower, sounding frailer, fading away until it is gone and the last words spoken on the album interrupt, "Now there is no dark side of the moon really. It's all dark."

I lay in pitch-blackness, listening to this gloomy album. Misery depicted beautifully, angst never sounding so lovely. No dreamy vision of paradise here; no hippie hopefulness. Only despairing observations of the cold, confused, chaotic world of reality—madness, war, politics, aging, death. As the album begins again, I hear the opening heartbeat quickening, the tempo rising, then the lyrics, "I've always been mad," followed by a snippet of maniacal laughter, the kind reminiscent of the sound of hilarious glee echoing through the halls of an insane asylum.

I think of Brenda. The thoughts hurt; they cut deep: What did I miss? How could I not have seen this coming? Do we ever really know what is going on in another person's head, even a person we love? The lyrics of "Eclipse" haunt me: "The lunatic is in my head.... There's someone in my head but it's not me." So close to the bone, so near to Brenda's words the night it started: "My mind is racing ahead of me; I'm just trying to catch up."

Anomaly

We had eaten dinner at the home of our best friends, Jane and Frank. After dinner, we smoked a little pot—a few tokes; nothing extreme. We'd done the same thing dozens of times. A little pot to take the edge off—a good conversational starter. But this time was different.

Brenda never did much talking. She was shy in public and introverted even in the presence of familiar friends. Occasionally, I would nudge her to talk more. "I'll talk when I have something to say," she'd reply. It wasn't as if she withdrew or acted bored. Brenda was always alert—watching, taking the world in, sensitive to everyone's feelings and needs. After a night out, she would debrief by analyzing the conversation on the way home. Sometimes I felt if she had a special sensitivity, a gift to see what was really going on. In the academic world, you don't see many Brendas. Either she didn't have much ego or her ego flourished in a space unknown to me. Often I would urge her to hire an agent and submit her poems for publication.

"You have an uncommon gift for poetic language—the way you create and use metaphors, sensuality, sound, and imagery. I don't understand why you refuse to send your work off for review."

"You don't get it, Art. My pleasure is in writing the poems. Seeing them in print means nothing to me."

She was right—I didn't get it. But the nights she read her poems to me were special. She was letting me into a secret world that she shared with nobody else. It was one of the ways she made love to me.

I'll never forget that first episode. Before we finished passing the joint, Brenda took the floor. With a surge of emotional intensity, she seized control of the conversation, her speech sprinting past the three of us at electrifying speed. Shifting swiftly from topic to topic, her sentences skated across the room, fragments of thoughts running round and round like a carousel circling at high velocity. She wasn't making much sense, but I couldn't help feeling mesmerized by the euphoric wave of pleasure pulsing through her expressions. When I picture the scene in my mind, I recall the rush of words, the feverish pace at which she spoke, her wide-eyed, open-mouthed smile when she tried to catch her breath, and the intense concentration it took to try to keep up with her. The three of us sat frozen in awe of the speed and passion of her speech. She was a raft being carried downstream by the current. Without a guide and with no paddlers, she was at the mercy of the waves thrusting her over a treacherous precipice. "I can't keep up with my sentences," she said at one point. "I'm chasing as fast as I can, but I can't catch up."

"You're talking so fast. We can't keep pace. You're tiring us out," I said.

"I can't help it, and I don't really want to stop it. It's thrilling. I've never been happier." I didn't want to stop her either. Her vitality was exhausting but also intoxicating.

"I've never seen Brenda like that," Jane whispered to me when we got up to leave.

"Neither have I. What was in that pot?" I teased.

On the way home, Brenda told me that she had never seen so clearly, and her ears were flooded with sounds and sensations she'd never heard before. She continued to talk nonstop, and at one point made an astounding observation. "I think Jane's attracted to me. I can tell by the look in her eyes, the way she stares at me."

"Don't be ridiculous, Brenda. We were all staring at you. It was hard not to, the way you were carrying on. But it was fun. I enjoyed you."

"Jane isn't the only woman interested in me. I've seen others give me the same look. I think I may be a lesbian."

Her statement was so out of character that I didn't know how to respond. I said nothing, and Brenda quickly moved on to another topic.

We went to sleep at 1:00 a.m. In the middle of the night the sound of a typewriter woke me up. Half asleep, I automatically reached toward Brenda's body and immediately realized she wasn't there. Of course not; she's in the next room typing, I realize. Why? What the hell is going on? I reluctantly climbed out of bed and staggered down the hallway.

"Are you all right?" I asked, interrupting her typing.

"Never felt better, honey."

"What are you doing up at this hour?"

"I'm not sleepy. I slept enough."

"How can an hour be enough sleep?

"I don't know. I just don't feel tired. You know I haven't been sleeping as much lately. But look here. The poems are pouring out of me."

She handed me a stack of pages, poems neatly typed on them. "I'm too tired to read these now. I'll look at them in the morning," I said.

"That'll be great. I'll have a lot more by then. The poems are writing themselves. I'm just trying to keep up with the transcription," she laughed. Scratching my head, I retreated to the bedroom. *I don't get it. She usually works for weeks on a single poem before she shares it with me. But I can't deal with this now. I'm too tired.*

In the morning, the stack of poems was twice as big, and Brenda had retreated to the kitchen. Noticing all of our pots, pans, and dishes stacked on the kitchen counter, I asked, "What are you doing?"

"I'm rearranging the housewares and utensils. We need to be better organized. I can never find things when I want them."

For the next two weeks Brenda worked at a feverish pace, organizing and re-organizing not only the houseware but also the furniture in every room, files of receipts and bills, books and journals in the bookcases, staples in the cupboards, and racks of magazines. Declaring open season on every object in the house, she became obsessed with orderliness and neatness—folding and refolding towels and linens, underwear, socks, shorts, and blouses. She took two or three hot showers a day and washed her hands repeatedly. During this period, Brenda was in perpetual motion, occasionally expressing her exhaustion at night but unable to sleep more than a couple of hours at a time. Waking earlier and earlier, she acted unfazed by lack of sleep. Adrenaline rushed through her like a deer chased by a mountain lion. She flew around the house with boundless energy. After the first couple of days, I felt alarmed, worried that Brenda's behavior was spinning out of control. From the beginning of our relationship, I had been aware of a few of Brenda's obsessive behaviors—twirling and pulling out strands of her long blonde hair repeatedly, washing her hands compulsively—but she was taking these behaviors, and new ones, to a whole other level. Soon I became worried sick.

Hindsight

Had Brenda been sending a distress signal the night of our dinner at Jane and Frank's? How had I missed her call for help? Would more awareness have made any difference? She was a different person that night—true enough—but how different? She was acting more self-assured, zealous, and assertive. Why should that worry me? In the context of a pot-induced conversation, she seemed perfectly normal. Actually, I felt roused and refreshed by Brenda's sudden gusto and burst of effervescent energy.

161

I search my memory for the point at which Brenda crossed the line between genius and madness. The initial obsessions had seemed mild to me, never interfering with her capacity to hold a job, excel in school, compose eloquent poems, or meet family responsibilities. What pushed her over the edge?

I can look back in hindsight and locate telltale signs—her family history, mild obsessive behaviors, inhibition and discomfort in public, passivity, and lack of ego. But Brenda's extraordinary competence, intellectual gifts, command of language, and sense of responsibility overshadowed these personal dispositions. After her mother's death, she became legal guardian of two younger sisters, approaching the duties of this obligation as if she had been called to them by a higher authority. Disappointing her sisters was not an option. She carried out the details of her responsibilities meticulously, performing her surrogate parent role in a loving and protective manner. She never missed an allowance check or tuition payment, a birthday card or holiday gift. The girls were constantly on her mind. They lived with us during most summers and holidays and built a trusting and affectionate bond with Brenda, openly confiding their hopes, dreams, and fears. Privately, Brenda worried whether her sisters eventually would be able to live independently after they turned twenty-one, but she was determined to let go and allow them to stand on their own.

Several weeks before Brenda's first manic episode, her youngest sister turned twenty-one, ending her legal obligation to them. Now she could turn her mind to other matters.

Downward Spiral

Three weeks after its abrupt beginning, Brenda's first manic episode skidded to a halt. Near the end she became increasingly agitated and hostile toward me. One night she picked a fight, saying she would not be coming with me to Philadelphia because she was taking a lesbian lover—her supervisor at the library at which she worked. She stormed out of the house and didn't come back until the middle of the night. The next evening she acted as if I were a complete stranger. Her hands twitched, and she paced nervously through the house like a cat in unfamiliar surroundings. Confusion etched on her glassy-eyed face, she seemed to be totally losing touch with reality. I tried to stay calm, but panic coursed through my veins. When I approached and tried to reassure her, she backed away, hurled a vase across the room, and warned me not to come near her. Naively trying to shake her out of her delusional state, I screamed my name and hers, reminding her we were married.

"We are not. I don't know you. You're scaring me," she yelled back. Before I could react, she ran into the bedroom and hid under the bed.

I spent the night on the living room couch. At dawn, I walked cautiously into our bedroom. Brenda was sound asleep on the floor near the bed, the first time she had slept through the night since the beginning of the episode. I walked over, picked her up, and placed her gently on the bed. Ten hours later she was still asleep. I questioned whether I should interrupt her deep, unbroken sleep. Realizing that she'd had nothing to eat or drink for twenty hours, I made a sandwich and a cup of tea and brought them into the bedroom.

"I'mmm not hunggry," she said faintly, after I nudged her awake. "I feel weeeak and draained." She spoke deliberately, laboring over each word.

"Okay, darling. I'll leave the food here on the table, and you can eat when you get up."

For the next several days Brenda confined herself to the bedroom. She would get up to go to the bathroom and brush her teeth; then head right back to bed. It was as if the mental exertion of the past five weeks had run down her battery, and her body was trying to recharge. "All I want to do is sleep," she said. I had to force her to eat a few crackers and take occasional sips of chicken soup. "I'm not hungry," she insisted every time I approached her with food.

Each day I grew more impatient and panicky. Brenda was in no shape to go to work, and she seemed to be losing interest in everything but sleeping. "You have to regain your strength so you can go back to work," I said one morning, pleading with her to eat.

"I'm not going back to work," she replied, as if leaving her job was of no consequence.

"You mean until you feel better, right? That's what I told Sheryl when I called."

"No, I'm never going back. I don't want to work there anymore. Tell Sheryl I quit."

Brenda stopped answering the phone, reading books and newspapers, and writing poems. Listless, she showed no interest in work or recreation of any kind. "I don't want to talk or see anyone," she announced one morning when the phone rang. "You should be careful too," she warned. "I'm certain our conversations are being recorded."

The swing from rapturous high to despondent low had been swift and dramatic. Slowed to a baby's crawl, Brenda struggled to form coherent words or sentences. Drenched in despair, she cried for hours on end, but couldn't say why. On the few occasions she left her cocoon, her gait was awkward and unsteady. She wobbled across the room like a child taking her first steps. Eventually, she started referring to me as "Daddy." "Can you read me a story, Daddy, while I sit on your lap?" she asked. Shaken by the sight of my beloved transforming into a little girl in front of my eyes, I felt as if the quicksand of melancholy were pulling both of us under.

What's Next?

"The lunatic is in my head." Roger Waters's voice sends a chill down my spine. Is there a lunatic in everybody's skull? Am I at risk of losing it too—releasing the lunatic in my head? Are you? What happens when the lunatic surfaces, and doctors are called on to take a look? Waters answers, "You raise the blade, you make the change, you rearrange me til I'm sane." They made Brenda's father sane, didn't they? The surgeon lowered the blade, lobotomizing him, bringing his madness under control, condemning him to a life sentence in a mental institution.

Lost

Your life rolls along smoothly. It makes sense. You are moving ahead. The forward momentum feels good. You don't question it. The paradigm is working. It gives you the illusion of predictability and permanence. One chapter foretells the next. The story is sufficiently familiar to feel secure, sufficiently puzzling to hold interest. You think you know the plot and have a notion where it's leading. Some days you feel as if you've been here before; other days you feel as if you're making it up as you go along. Neither feeling threatens you. There has to be a little mystery in every story, you tell yourself. Go with the flow. There, far off in the distance, you catch a glimpse of an ending toward which your story is pointing. But you're in no hurry to finish. The ride is more important than the destination. You don't want to miss anything on the way. You expect a few bumps along the road, but you've done your homework. You have a map—you're prepared.

Then one day an anomaly appears out of the blue. You come to a place that isn't on your map. You can turn left or right or continue straight ahead. You don't know which way to turn. You look behind you, and all you see is thick, dense fog. The road back home disappears from view. Vanished, gone—it's nowhere to be found. You turn back and gaze ahead. Which path do I take? You hesitate, unsure.

Each path is a different story, leading you in a different direction. But there are no signposts. There is nobody to guide you, no book or map to show the way. Fear and doubt engulf you. You feel lost and scared. Darkness moves in. You hear the sounds of nocturnal creatures approaching. You can't stay put. You must decide.

Am I Dreaming?

If I had become a stranger to Brenda, who had she become to me? How can I express what it feels like to wake up beside someone you've slept with every night for five years, a person with whom you've planned a life course, revealed your past and plotted your future, shared your history and your destiny, released your pain and pleasure, disclosed your dreams and fears, opened your heart and mind, trusted with your secrets and your fantasies, confided in, explored with, banked on, and not know that person, feel as if she is a stranger, as if the two of you have no shared past? How can I tell you what it feels like to one day be a husband and a partner, and the next day be a father and a caregiver to the same person?

You're twenty-eight years old. You have most of your adult life ahead of you when, suddenly, with little warning, a tidal wave of fate sweeps into the harbor of your consciousness, taking your breath away, jolting your frames of reference, ripping away your moorings, carrying your anchor out to sea. Suddenly life's impermanence reveals itself. What can you really count on? Everything feels uncertain, undependable, unreliable. At a moment like this, when you're overcome with confusion, despair, and dread, you can lose your bearings. You begin to doubt your grasp on reality. Is this real? Is it a dream, a bad dream—a nightmare? As soon as you wake up everything will be back to normal. You'll see.

Can I please wake up now?

Fading Away

Things were getting worse each day. Brenda was disintegrating in front of my eyes. Her agony was palpable. I couldn't stand by and watch her disappear in a haze of depression. I had to do something—but what? I had no frame of reference, no model or paradigm to guide me. At first I assumed her sadness would pass. Soon I realized the trajectory was downward; it wouldn't simply lapse. Her life was losing its life. When she kept insisting she was all right and didn't need to see a doctor, I felt obligated to respect her viewpoint, but I also realized I couldn't trust her self-perceptions. Wasn't Brenda really saying, "Please allow me to be crazy"? If I consented, wouldn't I become a coconspirator in her attempt at existential suicide? How long would it take for her to turn into a silent figurine? I couldn't allow that to happen.

Brenda's condition, whatever its cause, was beyond me. She needed professional help. To whom should I turn? That question tormented me. On the surface, the answer seemed simple: Take her to a qualified doctor. After all, I had no experience with serious illness of any kind, and everything I knew about "mental illness" I had learned by reading books by antipsychiatrists and social theorists (Foucault, 1965; Laing, 1965, 1967; Szasz, 1961). But these books posed a serious challenge to the medical model, revealing the ways in which medical practices and technologies reduce a person to a diagnosis, nullify autonomy and personal responsibility, and promote labels that stigmatize and victimize. These dehumanizing practices mattered to me, especially in my work as a communication theorist. I had learned to recognize the ways in which unconventional or nonconforming behavior become pathologized—for example, "different" turns into "sick," bringing shame, humiliation, and self-hatred to a person who needs acknowledgment, validation, and support.

I didn't want to think of Brenda as "ill." I was trying to hold onto my image of her as a normal, even gifted person. Looking back on the whole episode—her sizzling highs and lifeless lows—I arrived at a new insight. This was not a breakdown; it was a breakthrough! Brenda never wanted to be in the rat race. She was trying to release herself from the burden of normality.

But if what I was observing was not an illness, what was it? What sort of life did this "breakthrough" point toward? In her current state, Brenda couldn't care for herself or for others, she couldn't be an equal partner in a relationship, and she was incapable of structuring her own life. Those weren't tears of joy I was hearing, and she wasn't celebrating a form of emancipation. Quite the contrary, she had been delivered into disability. Tortured by my fear of yielding to the pressure—that conventional medical treatment would humiliate and stigmatize Brenda—I wrestled with my resistance to thinking of Brenda as mentally ill. Was this struggle for Brenda's benefit or for my own? Why couldn't I let go? Was I afraid to admit that defining Brenda as mentally ill diminished my own self-worth?

I feared that surrendering Brenda to the medical model of psychopathology would place her at the mercy of scientific objectification. The source of Brenda's problem would be viewed as organic and located in her brain. Objectifying her illness as a "nervous breakdown," her doctors would treat her disordered and disorganized behavior as if it stemmed from a mechanical failure that had little if anything to do with her personal and subjective life. They wouldn't concern themselves with something as subjective as loss of meaning.

I didn't want Brenda's subjectivity to be ignored. But I could no longer hide my eyes from the fact that she was fading away. Philosophizing about her phenomenological experience failed to take into account the obvious bodily consequences she was suffering. Her pain could not be alleviated by an act of will. I wanted Brenda to be seen both as a subject—a person "subjectively" experiencing something deeply despairing inside her—*and* an object—a body observed "objectively" from outside her, a body running down or failing in some important way. Wasn't there some way to understand her subjectivity and her embodiment as inextricably connected?

Context

In 1968, a few months after Brenda and I met, we had visited her father in the VA hospital in Rochester, New York. He wore a double-breasted suit from the 1950s and repeatedly asked us whether we thought Eisenhower would be re-elected. Frozen in time, he drifted in and out of our conversation, speaking slowly, in a low monotone, as if he had been tranquilized. He sat motionless, a blank stare covering a face from which all emotion had been erased. He didn't laugh or cry, smile or frown. He showed no anger and no sorrow. The lobotomy had ended his emotional suffering.

I fantasized what it would be like to live a life on such an even keel—no ups or downs, no arousal or deflation, no self-pity, no inflated self-importance. Simply a flat, steady existence. I pictured a zombie, then a robot. Does either have a self?

I felt the weight of Brenda's family history on my shoulders. Although lobotomies were no longer being performed, I had read horror stories about electroshock treatments and new drug therapies. I was afraid of what might happen to Brenda if she were hospitalized. Free to drug, manipulate, or experiment on her, institutional psychiatrists could do permanent damage to her mind. I still held out hope that her incredible intelligence, command of language, and creativity could be restored. I didn't want to see her end up like her father, confined to a hospital the rest of her life. I was worried that she would be recruited into the role of mental patient and be subjected to treatments that would exacerbate her condition and prolong her misery. On a personal level, I was afraid to face the possibility that the life we had built together was crumbling and we would never be able to restore it. I felt lost and alone. Still, my love for Brenda meant I had to get over my own fear and confusion. This was not the time to theorize Brenda's phenomenological experience. I couldn't simply say she needed to be understood, that her bizarre behavior, mood shifts, and delusions were an intelligible response to an existential crisis. Whatever the source of her ontological crisis, something had to be done about it. I had to make the call.

Nightmare

The sound of bell chimes leading into "Time" rings through my ears. The chord frictions of David Gilmour's disquieting guitar resound through the curves of my consciousness. Layers of clock noise—chilling ticks, haunting tocks, a shrill alarm clock—flood my senses, rousing me from my dreamy, sonic journey. The echoing eternal chime of time breaks my trance. It's a frightening wake-up call.

I peer into the darkness and think about how time eludes our consciousness. When we're kids, we feel as if we have all the time in the world. We play, we have fun, we amuse ourselves. The days seem long; they linger and pass slowly. We're in no hurry to get on with our lives. Then, one day, all of a sudden, we find we've grown up and begin feeling "older." Time begins to move more swiftly—or so it seems. Life feels more serious, precious and finite. We have important things to do, and we act as if we're in a rush to do them. Still, we carry over some of the playfulness of childhood. Too often, we "fritter and waste the hours in an offhand way" (Waters, 1973) as if we have time to kill.

When the band sings "waiting for someone or something to show the way," I think about how lost I've felt recently, how much waiting around I've been do-ing—not finding my way, assuming "someone" or "something" would come along to point me in the right direction. I've been walking around in a dream-like state. You know how in a dream you find yourself in the middle of something? You don't know how you got there, and you don't know where it's going. Then you wake up before it's over. Sometimes you wish you could go back to sleep and finish the dream; other times you're relieved to be out of it. You wouldn't dare go back.

Maybe a dream is more lifelike than we think. At this time last year, I thought I knew where I was heading. I thought I'd been preparing for a life as a professor, the life for which I'd been groomed. The offer from Temple University was a natural progression of the order of things. It fit squarely within the professorial paradigm.

But the orderliness of the professorial paradigm couldn't contend with the kind of chaos into which I had plunged. Confronted by the anomaly of Brenda's sudden illness, I had become Kuhn's vulnerable scientist, "a man deeply immersed in crisis" (Kuhn, 1970, p. 90). The paradigm through which I anticipated and looked forward to the future couldn't accommodate the novelty of Brenda's collapse. Brenda had stood at my side through the stress and pressure of graduate school. Struggling to make ends meet, we kept to a tight budget, resisted material pleasures, and graduated free of debt. She sheltered me from the storms of anxiety and self-doubt that occasionally raged within me. When I was upset, she comforted and calmed me. When I felt jubilant, she shared my thrill. She was my editor, my confidant, and my lover. We were content to live apart from most of the rest of the world, in a dyadic reality defined by mutual tenderness, vulnerability, and passion. Together we laughed and cried, sang and danced, worked and played. We marched side-by-side at antiwar and women's and civil rights' protests, attended concerts, carried on at parties, and performed at poetry slams. Sometimes we laughed at ourselves; other times we took ourselves way too seriously. We mourned our losses and celebrated our victories together.

Then the lunatic came into her head. Oh, how I miss the Brenda I had known. I want her back. I don't know if I can make it without her. I'm losing confidence in my entire constellation of beliefs.

Up and Down, Round and Round

Eventually Brenda agreed to check herself into a psychiatric hospital on a voluntary basis. After the first two days, I consulted with the staff psychiatrist, Dr. Friedman.

"We're not sure. It's going to take some time to see how she responds to medication," the tall, slim, female psychiatrist told me when I asked for a prognosis. She spoke deliberately, choosing her words carefully. "Brenda had a breakdown, a psychotic episode," she continued. "Psychologically, we regard the hallucinations and delusions you witnessed as a defensive screen, a way of protecting herself by disappearing from reality."

"Do you know what caused her breakdown?" I asked.

"No, we don't know what triggered the episode. It could have been building up to this for years. Something deep down frightened her. Her family history suggests a genetic factor may have predisposed her to psychosis. We'll learn more once her symptoms are mitigated. We've started her on a high dose of Thorazine to suppress the psychosis. She may have to take this high dosage for several weeks or a month before the psychosis is completely relieved. You will notice that she is sleepy and a little sluggish. Over time, these side effects and others should diminish."

"Are you saying this drug can cure the psychosis? Will she get back to normal?" I asked expectantly.

"'Cured' is not a word we use here in reference to psychosis. We are optimistic that Brenda's psychosis can be controlled by drugs."

"Controlled, but not cured?" I asked, agitated by her measured response. "Are we splitting hairs, Dr. Friedman?"

"I wish I could give you a definitive answer, but I can't. There's so much we don't understand about psychosis. I'm confident Thorazine will arrest her symptoms. But once a person has an episode like Brenda's, the odds increase that she will have additional episodes. I understand you want to know whether she can return to a normal life. If you mean the life she had before the breakdown, I doubt it. But if you are asking, 'Can she hold a job? Can she function in society? Will she stay in touch with reality?' I think the outlook is good. It depends largely on how she reacts to the medication. You'll need to be heedful of the fluctuation of her moods, and we'll need to monitor the effectiveness of the drugs carefully. Every month she'll need to come in for tests so we can evaluate her blood chemistry and alter prescribed dosages accordingly."

"Are you saying she'll need to take drugs for the rest of her life?"

"Yes, her recovery will depend on getting the dosage right. Once the symptoms are in remission, she can begin psychotherapy. Quite often, the drug dosage is reduced. But Brenda can't abruptly stop taking medication. That would be highly dangerous. She'd be right back where she started."

By the end of the first week, Brenda's depression had waned, and her chart recorded her condition as "stable and improving." Her appetite returned, she stopped crying, and she was interacting more normally. "I'm making a lot of friends here," she told me. "It feels good to be taken care of. I want to stay as long as possible."

"I'm glad you're feeling better," I replied.

"I do feel much better. Happier, I mean," Brenda confirmed, yawning repeatedly as she talked. "I'm thinking now that I'll go back to work at the library when I leave here. I miss the women at work. Sheryl came to visit this morning, and she said I could have my job back when I get well."

After ten days, Brenda was released from the hospital. At home, she seemed calm and composed, and I felt hopeful about recovery. I took her quietness as a sign that the old Brenda was returning. I noticed that her face was puffy and her belly, normally flat as a pancake, looked bloated, like an inflated balloon. I assumed she'd been well fed at the hospital and, given the lack of exercise and abundant sleep, she'd put on a few pounds. I was impressed that she seemed to have established an equilibrium, an even keel that gave the appearance of normality. Soon I would realize that this was wishful thinking.

If the Thorazine and Stelazine—a second weapon in the psychiatrist's arsenal of antipsychotic weapons—that Brenda was taking had chased away her demons, it was not without a cost. She complained bitterly about how the drugs made her feel. "I can't wake up. I'm always drowsy. I can't concentrate. The cataloguing I do is detailed work. I'm making mistakes I've never made. It's so frustrating. I feel incompetent."

"We'll talk to Dr. Friedman, honey. Maybe she can lower the dosage." I tried to reassure her. But Friedman insisted Brenda needed the amount she was taking.

I felt as if I were walking on egg shells. Sure, Brenda was quiet and cooperative, but that was because she was being tranquilized into a hushed state of immobility.

It hurt me to see her like this. When she walked, she shuffled across the living room rug, dragging one foot after the other. When awake, she might as well have been asleep, because she was constantly yawning and rubbing her eyes. I recalled my visit with Brenda's father. How different was this? Is Thorazine a liquid lobotomy? "I feel out of it most of the time," she announced one morning matter-of-factly. "There's this fog creeping over my mind." I worried that Brenda would start altering the dosage on her own. Then I worried she wouldn't. One day she did. I couldn't blame Brenda. I'd rather be a crazy person than a zombie.

Another two-week hospitalization followed. Then another.

Between Paradigms

All that is now
All that is gone
All that's to come
and everything under the sun is in tune
but the sun is eclipsed by the moon.

The album ends. I toss aside the earphones and sit up in the silent darkness. I think about how I will be leaving for Philadelphia in three weeks and must brace myself for the move.

I am living between paradigms. The old paradigm still has a hold on me. I can't shake free from the grip of the past. The new paradigm revives me, rousing my hunger for adventure and change. It urges me to show faith in its promise.

I've met a woman, Linda, with whom I can play and be an equal, and I'm staying with Brenda as well, taking care of her as if she were my child. Both women are coming with me to Philadelphia. My personal life exists in a liminal space between two women—two lives—as different as night and day. My professional life parallels this split between old and new. I vacillate between the comforting pretense of objectivism and the daring obscurity of subjectivity.

Time marches relentlessly forward. A person can live in the chaos of paradigm clash for only so long. Inevitably, an old paradigm gets replaced by a new one, "the sun is eclipsed by the moon" (Waters, 1973).

Chapter Seven

Taking Chances

> Doubtless, much of our thought was fumbling and
> undeveloped. Certainly, hardly any of it was unmarked by
> quarrel. But "the move toward meaning" has proved a proper
> revolution: sweeping, durable, turbulent, and consequential.
> *Clifford Geertz (1995, p. 115)*

Good books nourish me. As a boy, I read books to escape into worlds of experience and fantasy removed from the painful reality of my home life. I identified with the plight and bravery of heroes, thinking of myself first as one character and then another. Imagining what it would feel like to overcome the physical hardships and indignities of their demanding quests, I envisioned myself as the valiant Ivanhoe (Scott, 1819) fighting to rehabilitate my reputation on behalf of people I love, and then the tragic Jean Valjean (Hugo, 1987), rising above the temptations of evil, willing to suffer noble defeat for the sake of laudable ideals. Later, as an adolescent seeking direction for my life, I turned to books again, immersing myself in fictional realities that depicted life's existential dilemmas (see Chapter 2). Camus's novels (1946, 1947) drew my attention to the impermanence of life and the wrenching awareness of the passage of time that plagues human beings. Aware of the absurdity and incomprehensibility of life, we nonetheless must act and make decisions. Sooner or later trouble comes to everyone. Then what?

In college and, later, in graduate school, I steadily moved away from fiction. Introduced for the first time to the social and behavioral sciences, I feasted on the writings of Maslow (1962), Rogers (1961), May (1953, 1969), Frankl (1959), Fromm (1969), Laing (1961, 1965, 1967, 1969), Goffman (1959, 1961, 1963, 1966, 1967), and Bateson (1958, 1972). These writers plunged beneath the surface of human experience and subjectivity, discovering there how intricate, ironic, and fateful life could be. I appreciated that they weren't making things up; they were dealing with concrete experiences, observing people in their everyday lives, exposing vital complexities and contradictions of actual lived experience. They made me stop and ponder my own life, helping me think through and cope with many of the conflicts I had endured as a youngster. I learned that reading books could be soothing and healing. Later on, I recognized what I had been doing as bibliotherapy, an attempt to heal my emotional and psychic wounds by reading (Haley, 1973). When I think about my life as a professor, I realize that's what I want my teaching and research to do: help other people heal and cope, question themselves and ask what it means to live a good life.

Now, in the middle of my own personal and professional crisis, I know no place to turn other than to books. I believe books can save me. They have in the past. Why not now? That's what I need—books that can feed my hunger to set things right, fill what is missing, and rehabilitate me.

The Bookstore

As I walk toward the Temple bookstore, I reflect on my academic life. I'm thankful to have earned my degree in communication. On the one hand, I have a creative freedom and flexibility I probably wouldn't enjoy as a sociologist or a psychologist. The boundaries of communication studies are fluid and diffuse; they touch virtually every aspect of human life. On the other hand, the lack of rigorous boundaries breeds insecurity. I've noticed a huge inferiority complex among rhetoric and communication scholars obsessed with the goal of establishing communication as a "real" discipline. I understand the protective function of their discourse on disciplinary legitimization, but these conversations bore me. I have an urge to say, "Let's get on with the work. If we do meaningful work, it will get recognized." The big question for me is, What makes one's work significant and meaningful?

What if someone stopped me on the street right now and asked, "Hey, Art, you're a communication professor, right? So tell me, what are you interested in? What questions fascinate and inspire you? What's the most meaningful work you can think of doing as a communication researcher?" What would I say? I know the conventional answers to this question. I can recite the mantra of the social science paradigm of communication inquiry, give the party-line answers about prediction and control, the connections between properties of messages and attitudes and opinions, models of social and communicative influence, compliance-gaining strategies, and so on. But these aren't the issues or questions that speak to me these days. They don't touch me where I live.

My life feels chaotic and out of control. Is anybody really in control of his or her life? I've been living under the threat of a collapse of meaning, and I feel the weight of an existential imperative to chart a new course and destination for my life. I'm not talking only about my personal life, because it's no longer a part of me that I leave at home when I head to the university. Indeed, my personal life keeps trickling into my life as a professor. It's tough to play the role of a professor when the rest of your life is falling apart. Sometimes I feel as if my life is unreal; other times it feels too real. Brenda's breakdown put me in touch with the fragility of the human condition. I want to understand and deal with these feelings, not deny or run away from them.

The limitations and possibilities of the human condition are what call me to the life of a communication professor these days. When Brenda withdrew from the everyday, mundane world of ordinary life that sustains most of us but no longer

172

felt important to her, I experienced her breakdown as a loss of meaning. The patterns of our communication were radically transformed by her actions and my reactions to them, and we found ourselves in an entirely different relationship. Our joint past seemed to have vanished completely. Without a shared memory of the past, how can we possibly plan a future together? In light of this experience, I want to understand the vulnerability of a person's structure of meanings, what sustains and threatens meanings, and how intimate partners can use communication to keep despair and dread at bay.

I didn't foresee Brenda's illness, nor could I have anticipated how I would react to it. I feel a moral responsibility to stay with her until she has recovered sufficiently to manage her own life, which will take some time. I willingly accept the responsibility of acting as Brenda's caregiver. I don't ever want to feel as if I've abandoned her, but I've learned that a caregiver is not in an equal relationship with a person requiring care. I don't want to arrest my desire and need for a life partner.

When I reflect on these circumstances, I hear myself saying I don't ever want to have to go through anything like this again. At the same time I recognize that what I experienced is an enduring part of me that I'm still going through. Some of my friends tell me to get over it. "Move on with your life," they say. What does "move on" mean? A person inevitably faces unforeseen circumstances over the course of a life. Ideally, these circumstances bring out the best in a person. But the ideal is not necessarily the real. Confronted with the unexpected and unknown, a person may act badly or cowardly in the moment of truth. What then? The person may be riddled with dread, despair, and regret. Whatever he or she did will live in the person's memory, and he or she will have to find a way to accept the bad as well as the good. It's part of who the person is and what the person has become. Fortunately, a person is never finished becoming, not as long as he or she lives.

I'm just babbling to myself, I think as I enter the bookstore. Stepping through the door, the first things I notice are the cardboard signs identifying the different sections of the store. I enjoy browsing the different discipline sections, checking out which books are being used in various social science courses. I'm constantly on the lookout for books that cross the boundaries of different disciplines. They appeal to me the most.

The journal project I completed for Dr. Hilyard (see Chapter Three) opened my eyes to the extensive diversity and scope of communication research. I became convinced that communication is an activity and an idea that stretches across the social sciences and humanities. Communication would never be a subject restricted to a single discipline; knowledge about communication would always be spread across the arts and sciences. Thus, I'm constantly searching for books in allied disciplines that bear upon my own interests, texts I may one day use in my own courses.

Scanning the sections in front of me, my eyes are drawn to a purple paperback in the anthropology section, *The Interpretation of Cultures* (1973) by Clifford

Geertz. After I finished Jules Henry's book, I wanted to immerse myself in the literature of interpretive social science, but I never got the chance. This book may be a good place to start.

I skim through the first few pages until I come upon an astonishing statement in the last paragraph of Part I: "Believing, with Max Weber, that man is an animal suspended in webs of significance he himself has spun, I take culture to be those webs, and the analysis of it to be therefore not an experimental science in search of laws but an interpretive one in search of meanings" (Geertz, 1973, p. 5).

I can't recall where I've run across that phrase before—webs of significance. Maybe it was one of Tucker's lectures. I think he used the phrase "webs of meaning" when he lectured on the symbolic interactionists' theory of the self. Webs of significance, webs of meaning—they're the same thing to me. What a powerful and incisive metaphor, the web of meaning. I picture a spider's web of meaning and think about how we humans use symbols to create intricate structures of meaning in which we ultimately become suspended. We're caught in a trap of our own making, hoisted by our own petard.

I think about how I'm wedged in one of those webs of significance, the covering law paradigm of science (Hempel, 1948). Isn't science a symbolic structure of meaning? Isn't what I'm still going through in my personal life another one? Geertz's distinction between a search for laws and a search for meanings captures the oppositions I have been feeling but couldn't articulate. Thoroughly prepared by my academic training to conduct rigorous scientific experiments, I had been indoctrinated into a reductionist and objectivist paradigm that embraced a search for laws. Initially, the success I was experiencing as an empiricist thrilled me. I had confidence in my ability and had earned the respect of other researchers I admired. But something was missing. The work I was doing was technically competent, rigorous, and well executed. But as time passed, I had grown increasingly disenchanted and disappointed with the building-block nature of what I was doing. I was losing faith in the work; it wasn't meaningful any longer. These weren't the puzzles that stirred my heart. I couldn't see myself mopping up for the rest of my professional life.

I felt like the title character in the film *Alfie* (1966): "What's it all about, Alfie?" he asks himself. Is this all there is? Experiencing the despair of Brenda's descent into depression, I felt as if I had lost a soul mate and an intimate relationship that gave my life meaning. I wanted to understand that loss of meaning and how one rises from the ashes. But I didn't see any possibility of achieving that goal through questionnaires or experiments. After reading Kuhn, I wanted something more from my research life than just the buzz of a worker bee. Deep down, I knew that social science experiments created artificial contexts and simulated experiences. They forced you to objectify communication and decontextualize meanings. I kept hearing Bateson's voice whispering in my ear: "without context there is no communication" (1972, p. 402). I wasn't sure I had the courage to break from a career path that had been good to me, but I knew I had to find work to do that inspired me.

Returning to the text, I swallowed hard when I read Geertz's (1973) unequivocal rejection of the search for laws as a goal for scientific anthropology.
He audaciously shuns operationalism (see Bridgman, 1927), the essential and
indispensible first principle of objectivism's methodological paradigm, calling
it "a methodological dogma that never made much sense so far as the social
sciences are concerned" (1973, p. 5), and he pronounces it "largely dead now."
Where was I while operationalism lay dying? I must have slept through the news
of its impending demise.

Though I felt a tad defensive, I couldn't wait to read more. I wanted a fuller
picture of how to go about a search for meanings. What questions would I ask?
What procedures would I follow? How would I know when I got it right? What
would an interpretive research monograph look like? I purchased the book and
headed home to read it.

Interpreting Cultures

The Interpretation of Cultures (Geertz, 1973) intrigued and baffled me. I couldn't
decide whether Clifford Geertz was a journalist, storyteller, social scientist, or
philosopher. He expressed an aesthetic imagination that promoted a "literary
turn" for anthropology, but he refused any impulse to turn away from concrete
public events, drift into an embrace of intuition, or let sentiments run amuck. He
equated the writings of anthropologists with fiction—"something made," "something fashioned" (1973, p. 15)—yet cast the anthropologist into the privileged
position of interpreter of other people's interpretations and held to the image
of anthropology as a science. He rejected the practices governing the scientific
orthodoxy of anthropology while dodging the question of the rules by which
the interpretive anthropologist is bound: "you either grasp an interpretation or
you do not, see the point of it or you do not, accept it or you do not" (1973, p.
24). He displayed a unique talent for making distinctions, and at the same time
he specialized in blurring categories. Little wonder that I found it difficult to pin
down how one would carry on as an interpretive social scientist.

Still, I believed that there was something fateful about discovering *The Interpretation of Cultures.* I needed a new source of inspiration that could awaken me
from the numbness I had been experiencing. I didn't want to keep going through
the motions; I wanted to believe the thoughts and feelings I had encountered
when I read *Pathways to Madness* (Henry, 1971) were not mine alone. I fantasized a secret, closeted community of interpretivists, scholars in possession of
the "wild intoxicated curiosity" of which Henry (1973, p. xv) spoke. There had
to be a core of academics somewhere who wanted to immerse themselves in
the study of the existential dilemmas ordinary people experience in the course
of their everyday lives, people trying to make sense of the difficult choices and
unanticipated blows of fate that came their way, much as I was doing in the
aftermath of Brenda's illness.

I perceived Clifford Geertz as a kindred spirit. He was taking on the establishment in his field, trying to formulate something new, different, and meaningful; opening up rather than closing down what can count as significant social science research. Of course, the idea that human meanings are created discursively—through interactive experience—was not new. In the early twentieth century, the symbolic interactionists (G. H. Mead, 1934; A. M. Rose, 1962) had pointed to the importance of symbols in the creation of meaning and value (see Chapter Three). But after World War II, mainstream social science became a methodological (and largely quantitative) paradigm that couldn't accommodate the interpretive space in which meanings take on significance. As long as methodological positivism held a privileged and largely unquestioned status, meanings would be neglected, bracketed, or put aside in the name of science. That is, until Clifford Geertz and his vision of interpretive anthropology resuscitated the search for meanings.

It was not a stretch to extend Geertz's appeal to study meanings ethnographically to my field, communication research. I could see no important difference between culture and communication. Culture is semiotic; it's a system of symbolic meanings, a communication system. The term *culture* "denotes an historically transmitted pattern of meanings embodied in symbols, a system of inherited conceptions expressed in symbolic forms by means of which men communicate, perpetuate, and develop their knowledge and attitudes about life" (Geertz, 1973, p. 89). If you want to know culture, you have to put yourself in the middle of it, embed yourself in the significant contexts in which cultural meanings are being negotiated, validated, and/or produced. In other words, you need to be an ethnographer.

Geertz's exemplary interpretive anthropologist is an ethnographer who attempts "first to grasp, then to render" (1973, p. 10) cultural meanings as if reading and interpreting a text. For Geertz (1973, p. 9), "Analysis is sorting out the structures of signification ... and describing their social ground and import." The goal is interpretation, a thick description (Geertz, 1973) of the meanings comprehended by a close reading of cultural texts such as rituals, practices, leisure activities, customs, value systems, kinship relations, staying as close as possible to the experience of those studied, applying what Geertz terms "experience-near concepts."

Isn't this what Jules Henry (1971) was doing—putting readers in touch with strangers (and a world unfamiliar to most of us) by applying experience-near concepts such as sham, vulnerability, gratification, and circumspection, structures of signification that make each family's peculiarities sensible? He was not studying an exotic culture, only a family culture, but he was putting himself in the middle of uniquely significant family contexts in which cultural meanings of "family" were being produced and reinforced. He was "grasping and rendering" each family's system of meanings.

In communication theory, I had been teaching students that the codes by which people perceive, interpret, and react to each other and to objects in the world are their structures of signification, their frames of interpretation and meaning, an idea I extrapolated from Bateson's work (1972). Now I was beginning to see connections among the writings of Bateson (1972), Henry (1971), and Geertz (1973). Each was an ethnographer, each emphasized patterns and structures of meaning, and each thought quantification was overemphasized and of limited applicability in the social sciences.

I recalled how Bateson liked to admonish social scientists "to stamp out nouns" (1972, p. 334). In that spirit, I interpreted Geertz's critique of the concept of culture to imply that culture was not a noun but rather a verb. The main question about culture's significance was an epistemological and communicational one: If you want to know culture, you study what culture does. You ask how culture inscribes, activates, and/or changes meanings. You look at people reflecting on the significance of their lives, and in the process you engage in an ongoing construction and negotiation of personal and cultural meanings.

Geertz makes the modest claim that the intent of his argument is to "cut the concept of culture down to size" (1973, p. 4). Grinding an ax against the influence of British functionalism (Radcliffe-Brown, 1952, 1957) and French structuralism (Levi-Strauss, 1958) on how anthropologists construe culture, he winces at typologies, belittles predictions, snubs grand narratives, frowns upon cultural universals, and shows little interest in abstraction. They represent the wrong intellectual agenda for anthropology, an escape from the reality of the incompleteness and essential contestability of cultural analysis and knowledge claims. What is needed is a new paradigm, a shift from prediction and control to interpretation and understanding, from the thin descriptions of hypothesis-testing empiricism to the thick descriptions of meaning-centered interpretivism, from positivism to hermeneutics, from operationalism to *verstehen,* from structures and functions to meanings and interpretations, and from twitches to winks (Geertz, pp. 6–7).

According to Geertz, the heart of social science is not laws but meanings, and the trail to grasping meanings is not blazed by experiments but by ethnographies. Nor is operationalism an instrument in the ethnographer's toolbox. Geertz considers operationalism as dead and in no need of resurrection. Interpretive ethnographers seek to "bring us into touch with the lives of natives" (Geertz, 1973, p. 16). They have no stake in appropriating strangers' experiences in order to build social theories. Nor do they put much weight on predictions. Instead, the ideal to which anthropology (or any other social science) should aspire "is the enlargement of the universe of human discourse" (Geertz, 1973, p. 14). Thus, the objective of engaging in better, more humanizing conversations with "natives" replaces the goal of predicting and controlling them. "We are seeking, in the widened sense of the term in which it encompasses very much more than talk, to converse with them," writes Geertz (1973, p. 13), "a matter a great deal more difficult, and not only with strangers, than is commonly recognized."

Interpretive anthropology places symbolic communication at the center of cultural inquiry and positions the researcher in the middle of the action. You have to form relationships with the people you study, walk in their shoes, and learn to see the world through their eyes.

I was familiar with some of the classic ethnographies, but I'd never thought of fieldwork in the terms Geertz was using to describe it. Still, a vocabulary that emphasized rigorous methodological rules and systematic procedures had shaped my life as a researcher. Geertz was persuasive but also elusive. He expressed lofty ideals in eloquent idioms, but when I tried to grab hold of the idea of thick description, it kept slipping away: You try to clarify what is going on, you diminish the puzzlement, you tap into the lives of strangers, you access the conceptual worlds of the people you are studying, you answer deep questions, you refine debate (Geertz, 1973). These are noble goals, but how would I know when I had achieved them? I was left with the question, What does meaning mean? I didn't intend this as a hostile (or de-meaning) question. On the brink of a Kuhnian paradigm conversion, I wanted my commitment to interpretive social science to be grounded on tangible and concrete methods of inquiry.

In his essay on "thick description," Geertz (1973, p. 5) advises, "if you want to understand what a science is, you should look in the first instance not at its theories or its findings, and certainly not at what its apologists say about it; you should look at what the practitioners of it do." I decided to take his advice.

Considering Geertz to be a leading practitioner of interpretive anthropology, I turned to Chapter 15, "Deep Play: Notes on the Balinese Cockfight" (Geertz, 1973), and asked, How does he work? What does Geertz do? Based exclusively on his written text, I arrived at the following tentative conclusions:

1. Geertz chose an overlooked cultural event saturated with meanings, the cockfight, that had the potential to reveal what being a Balinese man "is really like" (1973, p. 417). He makes the case for the symbolic significance of the cockfight with humor and panache: "To anyone who has been in Bali any length of time, the deep psychological identification of men with their cocks is unmistakable. The double entendre here is deliberate" (p. 417).

2. Geertz went to great lengths to establish his authority as an accepted and trusted outsider. He tells the story of a raid by policemen with machine guns on the semisecret location of cockfighting matches that he and his wife were witnessing. Following the anthropological imperative, "When in Rome ... ," he and his wife did what everyone else did: they panicked and ran. Recruited into a performance of innocence familiar to natives, Geertz and his wife stood out from the crowd as "white men." Quickly noticed by a policeman, they were rescued by their host of five minutes who vigorously defended them as American professors there to write a book about Bali. "The next morning the village was a completely different world for us," writes Geertz. "Not only were we no longer invisible, we were suddenly the center of attention, the object of a great outpouring of warmth, inter-

est, and most especially, amusement" (1973, p. 416). Having sided with the villagers against the police, Geertz and his wife were now regarded as one of them.

3. Geertz provided "thick descriptions" of "The Fight" and the rules under which it operates, including the melodrama surrounding each interval and the climax, the activity of the handlers and the umpire, and the cockfight's function as a mode of connecting "the excitements of collective life and those of blood sport" (1973, p. 425) as well as the complicated rules of wagering and keeping score that prop up the magnitude of betting and the uncertainty of the outcome.

4. Cockfighting in Bali is interpreted as a moral contest in which men risk their masculinity, laying their public selves on the line—their pride and honor, their composure and indifference—in what Geertz (1973, p. 437) calls "a dramatization of status concerns." He enumerates seventeen facts in support of this thesis, indicating that "concrete evidence ... is both extensive and unmistakable" (p. 437). The moral meaning of the cockfight, however, is not only a sociological formation but also a sentimental education: "Balinese go to cockfights to find out what a man, usually composed, aloof, almost obsessively self-absorbed, a kind of moral autocosm, feels like when, attacked, tormented, challenged, insulted, and driven in result to the extremes of fury, he has totally triumphed or been brought totally low" (p. 450).

5. The cockfight is portrayed as a dramatic text, an artful performance, a local production, and a peculiarly Balinese frame of self-understanding that brings Balinese subjectivity into focus, showing how they make sense of their status hierarchy and, thus, providing "a metasocial commentary upon the whole matter of assorting human beings into fixed hierarchical ranks and then organizing the major part of collective existence around that assortment" (1973, p. 448).

6. Geertz claims that the local people, not the ethnographer, are the ones who do the interpreting: "It is a Balinese reading of Balinese experience, a story they tell themselves about themselves" (1973, p. 448).

7. Carefully qualifying his conclusions about the meaning of Balinese cockfights, Geertz considers interpretations as partial and restricted truths open to challenge and debate. He shows no interest in generalizing his analysis beyond the local culture of Bali and cautions against inflating the importance of the cockfight: "The cockfight is not the master key to Balinese life, any more than bullfighting is to Spanish" (1973, p. 453).

8. Geertz does not discuss the historical evolution of the cockfight nor try to reduce the spectacle of cockfighting to rudimentary causes; rather, he looks at the cockfight as a drama or story, analyzing it as he might any work of art by asking what it means.

Science or Literature?

I came away from this exercise with a better grasp of interpretive anthropology but couldn't decide whether interpretive anthropology was science or literature. It seemed to fall somewhere in between. Insofar as it concentrates on the meanings of a text, interpretive anthropology turns toward literature and literary criticism. But insofar as it concentrates on observing events in the empirical world—collecting data, accumulating facts, and drawing conclusions—interpretive anthropology preserves ideals and attributes of scientific inquiry.

Clearly the kind of "empiricism" the interpretive anthropologist practices is vastly different from the positivist empiricism into which I had been recruited as a graduate student. I had been taught to search for invariant factors, underlying structures, and determined outcomes; and to maintain my distance and objectivity, staying emotionally and physically detached from the field of observables to which my work was addressed, looking down on it from a more or less universal standpoint, applying standardized and methodical criteria in order to get in touch with the true nature of things—that is, to produce "value-free" knowledge. The kind of social science Geertz practiced, however, did not subscribe to these principles. The interpretivist's charge is expressive and edifying rather than reductive and generalizing. Bound by no hard and fast rules of procedure and unburdened by any attachment to the rhetoric of scientific objectivity, the interpretivist feels free to muddle along with no criteria laid out in advance, relying on the persuasive power of thick description rather than the coercive force of methodical procedures. Whereas the empiricist plants himself squarely outside and above what he observes, the interpretivist dives into the middle of things, where the action is.

Believing that you can't know what it feels like to be native or what things mean to natives simply by observing them, the interpretive anthropologist participates in cultural activities as if she is a native—thinking like a native, walking in a native's shoes, and doing what a native does. In other words, she takes every opportunity to get as close to the experience of what it means to be a native as she can. She realizes that truth is ambiguous and elusive; that there are different kinds of truth; and that there is no picture of truth that can stand on its own, free of values, contexts, and cultural frames. Thus, the truth to which the interpretive social scientist aspires is a necessarily contestable, situated, and partial truth.

How different is communication studies from anthropology? Both disciplines are grounded in the question of how symbols function to organize perception, construct meanings, and sustain social order. Both can be viewed as interpretive fields in search of meanings.

Sometimes I feel frustrated by the divisions among the social sciences and humanities, and the ways in which, once divided, the departments and fields protect and defend their turf. At times, I feel as if I'm a social psychologist or a sociologist; at other times, I am drawn to psychotherapy and philosophy. Now,

I'm attracted to interpretive anthropology and ethnography. These turf divisions don't make sense to me. Looking around the conference table at a recent department meeting, I asked myself, "Do I belong here? I'm not a rhetorician; I don't have an interest in studying speeches or theorizing about argumentation, and I find history for history's sake utterly dry and dull."

I'm not saying that I've jumped on the interpretive anthropology bandwagon. I still have doubts. Is this a viable approach to social science research? Is it respected? Can I do it? But what I've read so far does inspire me. I'm attracted to the idea of contestable truth and thick description. I'd like to take a crack at this new kind of social science writing that tries to take readers into the heart of the experience that is being described. Going through Brenda's breakdown with her, I can't help but see the whole event as an existential and moral crisis. If I were to write about it as a crisis of meaning, I'd want to include myself in the experience I would be describing.

Geertz bears an affinity to Goffman, but I see a difference. Goffman is more anecdotal, and many of his examples provide only brief snippets of interaction. Geertz is deeper, more seductive, passionate, and aesthetic. But Geertz also is a clever fox, and sometimes I get the impression he's a little too slick and crafty. He keeps talking about looking at Balinese life as if he were Balinese, and he says that "deep play" is a Balinese interpretation of Balinese experience, "a story they tell themselves about themselves" (1973, p. 448). But I'm not buying that. I'm not saying his interpretation of the meaning of the cockfight is wrong; I'm just not willing to say it's their interpretation of themselves. Their voices aren't in it. They aren't coauthors, and I know they wouldn't speak in the vernacular of anthropologists—Geertz speaks for them. He does present a convincing case about the internal logic of the cockfight and its moral story of concealed aggression and brutality. But he doesn't offer alternative interpretations, and he doesn't discuss or qualify his own capacity to see them as they see themselves. I appreciate his effort to speak like an insider, but he's not Balinese. He observes their participation but not his own. Isn't the interpreter a crucial part of what he or she interprets? As far as I am concerned, Geertz is on shaky grounds when he becomes a part of what is being analyzed and understood and then acts as if he is not. If we're going to shift our understanding of a researcher's connection to what is being observed and studied, then we need also to focus on understanding how the researcher influences the observables and how, in turn, they affected the researcher.

Social Science as History

It is the rare social psychologist whose values do not influence the subject of his research, his methods of observation, or the terms of description.
Kenneth J. Gergen (1973, p. 311)

I have talked with countless graduate students drawn into psychology out of deep humanistic concern. Within many lies a frustrated poet, philosopher, or humanitarian who finds the scientific method at once a means to expressive needs and an encumbrance to free expression.

Kenneth J. Gergen (1971, p. 312)

A few weeks later, I received a package from the office manager in the communication department at Cleveland State. "These journals came for you," she wrote. "I assume they arrived before you changed your address. Good luck with your new position. We miss you. Patti."

In addition to a couple of communication journals, the package contained the latest issue of the *Journal of Personality and Social Psychology (JSPS)*. Among empiricists in communication, *JSPS* was celebrated as the top journal publishing empirical research on social interaction. In our eyes, no journal maintained higher standards of rigor and excellence than *JSPS*. An article in *JSPS* could lift a fledgling scholar like me to the summit of the field—or so I thought. I had never mustered the courage to submit any of my work there.

Skimming through the contents of the journal, I arrived at a peculiarly titled article, "Social Psychology as History." The author was Kenneth J. Gergen, a social psychologist whose work was familiar to me. He had published a chapter with David Marlowe on personality and social behavior in the second edition of *The Handbook of Social Psychology* (Lindzey and Aronson, 1968), which I had read while studying for my doctoral exams. At the time, I couldn't believe my good fortune. I already had decided that my dissertation was going to focus on predicting the outcomes of group decision making on the basis of the Mach IV personality measure (see Chapter Three). Marlowe and Gergen's (1968) chapter provided a thorough review of the literature, calling attention to important methodological and conceptual issues, and assessing the promise and limitations of attempting to predict social behavior based on personality measures.

After graduate school I kept up with Gergen's work on self-consistency and self-presentation (Gergen, 1969, 1971; Morse and Gergen, 1970). In my communication theory classes at Cleveland State, I referred to his book, *The Concept of Self* (1971), in lectures on the self as constituted through communication. As far as I could tell, Gergen was one of the most creative and prolific experimental social psychologists doing work connected to communication. He had a keen understanding of the connection between social interaction and the development of the self. His research was well designed, rigorous, and original, and it was placed in the most prestigious experimental social psychology journals. He had held a faculty appointment in the Department of Social Relations at Harvard and was now on the faculty at Swarthmore, an elite private university not far from Temple. Given the rigor and prestige of the journals and books in which he published, Gergen had achieved an enviable status as a respected experimental social psychologist within the first ten years of his career. I assumed he had a steadfast commitment to experimental social psychology's scientific mission of developing laws of human interaction. Nothing in Gergen's background or

182

previous publications suggested he had serious doubts about the capacity of social psychology to fulfill its mission as a science. Nor did he strike me as a rebel, someone who would rise up and speak out against the most taken-for-granted assumptions about the nature and function of his discipline.

Was I ever mistaken! "Social Psychology as History" was a bolt of lightning crashing against the foundations of social psychology's edifice of scientific orthodoxy. Gergen presented a pessimistic and sweeping impeachment of social psychology's misguided longing to be a "true" science. Social psychology cannot be a science, according to Gergen (1973, p. 31), because "unlike the natural sciences, it deals with facts that are largely unrepeatable and which fluctuate markedly over time." After seventy-five years of experiments on social psychology, no laws of social interaction and few repeatable facts had been established. Referring to social psychology's obsession with establishing general laws of social behavior as "misdirected" and "unjustified," Gergen portrayed social psychology as an historical not a scientific field because behavior patterns are influenced by changing social events and by the feedback social psychologists disseminate when they publish their research.

The feedback loop endemic to social psychology and other social sciences ironically encourages the very instability of scientific findings that stands in the way of establishing social psychology as a scientific field that can produce brute evidence of stable causal relationships between events or variables. Over and over again, social psychologists find that public reaction to research findings annul the very principles on which their research is based. When people are "enlightened" by learning the results of psychological experiments, they may react against how social scientists have understood or explained their behavior and, over time, alter the results. Women told they are "more persuadable than men," for example, may retaliate by becoming more resistant to persuasion, reversing previous findings (Gergen, 1973, p. 311). Indeed, "blacks, women, activists, suburbanites, educators, and the elderly have all reacted bitterly to explanations of their behavior" (Gergen, 1973, p. 314).

Gergen ran through a litany of examples of the vulnerability and mortality of social psychological theory in the face of "enlightenment effects," changing historical and cultural circumstances, ideological commitments, doctrinaire biases, and the shifting sands of standards of moral and/or ethical behavior over time. He concluded with the bold declaration that "the study of social psychology is primarily an historical undertaking. We are essentially engaged in a systematic account of contemporary affairs. We utilize scientific methodology, but the results are not scientific principles in the traditional sense" (Gergen, 1973, pp. 316–317).

What's going on here,? I wondered. Ken Gergen isn't a novice researcher trying to make a name for himself, nor is he a renegade social psychologist turning his back on the field. "Social Psychology as History" isn't an act of desertion; he isn't signaling his departure from the field, though I imagine Gergen will lose some friends, and a few orthodox social psychologists will condemn him as a defector.

He isn't giving up on social psychology, only trying to face up to the limitations of social psychological inquiry. The article strikes me as an act of conscience and commitment. Gergen doesn't come across as angry or antagonistic , and he doesn't express his criticism in a harsh or abrasive voice. His argument is carefully reasoned and delivered in a cool and objective tone. He wants a social psychology he can believe in, one that can contribute something good to the world and in which he can work authentically. He wants a less myopic and more sensitizing social psychology, one that concedes the importance of situational and historical contexts and acknowledges social psychology's need to connect more broadly and purposefully with political, cultural, historical, and philosophical inquiry.

What a courageous and daring act of conviction and honesty. Ken Gergen has nothing to gain and everything to lose by writing this article. His is a socially perilous kind of truth because he is bound to suffer repercussions. He is not going to come away from this truth telling unscathed. Henry (1971) calls this kind of fidelity the "truth of courage," acknowledging that this kind of ethical truth is the province of people who recognize their strength. Referring to the truth of courage—truth in the face of fear of retribution—as "self-maximizing," Henry (1971, p. 108) says, "Every time a person takes his timidity in hand and tells the truth while his heart flutters just a trifle, he is so much the better for it—he feels."

Ken Gergen wants to shift the ruling paradigm of social psychology away from a search for laws and toward a historical, political, and cultural consciousness of contemporary social life. He offers a compelling case against empiricist social psychology's search for laws of human interaction. In that respect, he goes beyond Clifford Geertz's rejection of anthropology's law-centered paradigm of investigation. But Geertz's attempt to build a new and quite different anthropology aimed at the search for meanings and grounded in "thick descriptions" is one that breaks more completely with the past than does Gergen's. The term "meaning" does not occur in Gergen's sketch of a historically grounded social psychology, and he stills holds to much of the old paradigm's methodological vocabulary of stability and causal relationships. Perhaps his is just the beginning—the first crack in the armor of social psychology—and much more is to come. Now I ponder, What is to come for me? Why don't I have the courage to break with contested research traditions and methodologies that no longer inspire me? What's holding me back?

Born to Run

The Temple University campus is located on Broad Street within the sprawling inner-city decay of North Philadelphia that local residents refer to as "the black ghetto." The guarded parking lots are too expensive for someone at my salary level, so one of my daily chores is hunting for a parking place. Beyond the two- or three-block radius of Weiss Hall, the building that houses my office, the neighborhoods are unsafe. I can make the drive to my home in East Falls in about half an hour. Some days it takes almost as long to get to my car. I had two tape players stolen during my first year. When I arrive at my car, I'm never sure what I'm going to find.

You would think I'd want to take the scenic route home along the lush East River Drive. But most days, I choose to drive right through the eye of the storm. I turn north on Broad Street and pass through the slums that stretch all the way to Chelton and Germantown Avenues. I see the sorry sites of poverty and social decay, block after block of them—abandoned, vacant, and dilapidated homes engulfed by unkempt vegetation; stripped and deserted automobiles; sidewalks littered with rotted wood, broken glass, and foul-smelling trash; and teenage boys and older men loafing on street corners, looking as if the restless desire within them is about to burst. Race riots took place here in the mid-1960s, and I get the impression that when the conflict ended, nobody bothered to clean up the mess. Now the streets and neighborhoods have the look of a place abandoned in a hurry. The people who left never came back, never even looked back. Mostly they were white people who fled to the suburbs and took the corridor of retail enterprise with them. Some black people left too, but as soon as they landed in new neighborhoods, the white people moved away. This tale of residential segregation is a familiar story in urban America. As soon as black people start moving into a neighborhood, insecure and anxious white people leave, extending the reach of what some people call the "Black Belt." Often, what white flight leaves behind is a climate of despair and hopelessness. Here, on the streets of inner-city Philadelphia, stretching farther and wider than anywhere I've witnessed firsthand, the drama of residential segregation is performed in scenes of wretched poverty, hopelessness, and urban decay. I wasn't shocked to hear last week that Philadelphia has the highest rate of juvenile crime in the country.

Why do I take this route home? I don't know for certain. I guess something from my past pulls me in this direction. I'm reminded of some of the sections of the Hill District and Homewood in Pittsburgh where I grew up. The Philadelphia ghetto seems a lot worse, though, and making this drive each workday keeps me aware of how privileged I am.

On the ride home, I tune the car radio to WXMN, 88.5, operated by the University of Pennsylvania. Between five and eight o'clock each night, it broadcasts "energy music," a program that features avant-garde and New Age music. It routinely plays the music of some of my favorite spacey musicians—Tangerine Dream, Can, Klaus Schulze, and Sun Ra. Admittedly, it feels weird to drive through the rubble and ruins of North Philadelphia neighborhoods listening to the cosmic sound of Sun Ra chanting "space is the place." On second thought, I imagine that quite a few of the men I pass on these streets would delight in a trip to Sun Ra's "Omniverse."

Turning my car into the driveway of my home, I am greeted by the sound of keyboards and thundering drums rumbling out the open side door of the house and drowning out the mellow sounds of the New Age music coming from my car radio. It's not unusual for my girlfriend, Linda, to pump up the volume on the stereo when she loves a song. She covets the sensual thrill of feeling encircled by music. Free to dance wildly across the room, she throws her arms into the air, belts out lyrics at the top of her lungs, and gyrates her hips as if she is trying to keep a hula hoop aloft. When she gets like this, her energy and gusto—her lust for life—is contagious.

Linda and I have very little in common, yet I am hopelessly attracted to the intensely sensual and erotic space in which she dwells. She and I purchased this house together and have shaped it into an earthy home—a cozy, comfortable environment designed for relaxation and meditation. As an undergraduate, Linda majored in Eastern religion and became devoted to the ideals of cosmic harmony and spiritual fulfillment aligned with her understanding of Taoism and Buddhism. Convinced that hers is the Age of Aquarius, Linda became an experience junkie. She couldn't resist anything that offered a setting for expanding consciousness, reducing inhibitions, exploring sexuality, dropping ego attachments, or living in the moment. You name it, and she's tried it—psychedelic drugs, encounter groups, yoga and meditation, massage, palmistry, channeling, primal screaming.

"God lives in each of us," Linda declared shortly after we met, staring at me with a mystical look on her face. "Each individual is a divine self. If you accept the presence of God in your heart, you will awaken dormant powers within you. That's the path to spiritual perfection." At first I argued with her, citing Alan Watts's notion of "the myth of myself" (Watts, 1996/1973), but Linda and I weren't on the same wavelength, and it was no use and no fun to dispute her deeply ingrained beliefs by means of an academic argument about how everything is tied together and functions interdependently.

"You and your friends, you know what's wrong with you?" she would ask. "You're hypercerebral. You're not in touch with your bodies or your feelings. You're just talking heads. You don't believe in the wisdom of your own experience or trust your own feelings. If it isn't written in a book, you don't care about or believe it. And you're so negative—you're always criticizing stuff. What's the fun in living that way? You can't ever be satisfied or happy."

Linda had a point. I hung out with a crowd of highly critical leftist intellectuals, and, of course, there was no disputing the fact that my friends and hers lived categorically different lives. Whereas Linda lived in a world of pleasure-seeking self-fulfillment, a touchy-feely, here-and-now in which everyone was responsible for her own life circumstances and everything bad or good in the world was viewed through the prism of individual consciousness, I lived in a world of perpetual struggle and unapologetic concern for social justice, fairness, and equal opportunity, a critical, skeptical, and future-focused consciousness directed at shared empowerment and cognizant of the corruptions of the lust for domination, greed, and fame.

Linda was prepared to play at a moment's notice; I felt guilty if I wasn't working nearly all the time. "You take life too seriously," she would say.

"You don't take it seriously enough," I would reply.

"Why don't you laugh more?" she asked.

"Why don't you cry more?" I answered.

"You're not in touch with yourself," she insisted.

"You're not in touch with anyone else," I argued back.

In Linda's world, there were no victims, only people forced to relive the mistakes of a past lifetime in order to rid themselves of bad, and create good, karma. "No victims?" I shouted at her one day. "What do you call the Jews who died in the gas chambers at Auschwitz? Do you think they were brought there for karmic development?" But I was wasting my breath.

"You pay too much attention to the material world," she snapped back. "This life is only a blink in time. It's the mystic realm beyond that really matters. That's where they'll find peace and harmony." Like her other New Age friends, Linda thought any sort of activism or participation in political causes was a distraction from the quest for spiritual perfection, which could only be achieved inwardly. It wasn't the world that needed changing; it was one's consciousness of the world. I thought I would throw up if I heard one more of her friends say "reality is what you make it."

One day, I reached my threshold and barked, "Yeah, well, tell that to the guys I pass by every day on my way home, the black men hanging out on North Broad Street who have no money, nothing to eat, and no place to sleep. Tell them it's only an illusion and everything will be okay when they perceive reality differently." But Linda and her friends merely shrugged their shoulders and chuckled, looking at me like I were some kind of unenlightened carnival freak. Later, after her friends left, Linda expressed her disappointment in me. "You just don't get IT." And she was right. I didn't.

But when I asked, "What is the IT that I'm supposed to get?" all she could say is, "You'd know it if you had IT."

I didn't feel a need to defend my belief that the world in which we live was saturated with sorrow and injustice. I loved work—my teaching and research—and I cared deeply about trying to do something about the social injustices circulating through the world. These activities gave meaning to my life, something for me to do. I didn't see the quest for spiritual fulfillment as an end in itself, and I had far too much conviction about relationality and interdependence to buy into the notion that everything should or could be reduced to individual experience. So I guess I didn't get IT. As far as I was concerned, Linda and her New Age friends hadn't been liberated from the material world; they had simply withdrawn into hiding.

Yet there was something mysterious, fresh, and seductive about Linda that pulled me toward her, something I'd never experienced before. Linda wanted no part of the heady, intellectual world of university life that I inhabited. Instead, she invited me to take up residence in her world of sensual and bodily pleasure and to concentrate my energy on the world of actual, here-and-now experience. In that space, the pressures of the everyday world that had troubled, alienated, and frustrated me disappeared—at least for a little while. I wasn't persuaded that sexual ecstasy and drug-induced euphoria were the channels toward spiritual fulfillment, but they did introduce me to a side of myself I had never explored so intensely, a space a world apart from the intellectualized, controlled, and hyper-rational academic self.

"Let go of your ego," Linda whispered in my ear. "You can do this. Think of Jim Morrison [1971] and break on through to the other side." And I did. And I liked it there. It was an optimistic and hopeful place to dwell, a place devoid of the tragedy and suffering of everyday life. We sang, danced, and immersed ourselves in the glow of love, peace, and harmony; and talked about cosmic unity, ultimate purpose, and the meaning of life. But in the morning, after I had dried off from our euphoric swim and the waves of positive emotion had run their course, I realized this was not a mode of lived experience that could sustain me for long. It was not in the structure of my character to be uncritical as a matter of principle or to detach myself from the political, social, and emotional causes that were important to me. I had learned from Linda that more grounding in my own personal experience was something I needed and wanted, but I would never be satisfied with making my own self-fulfillment the singular goal of my life.

"Come on in and dance," Linda shouted to me through the window. "Hurry up. I want you to hear this."

"Who is that you are listening to?" I asked, grabbing my bag, jumping out of my car, and jogging into the house. The music had a strong beat. The thunderous drums and copious keyboards vibrated from the speakers, and Linda, as usual, had the music amplified about as loud as she could play it without blowing out the receiver. She grabbed me as soon as I entered the door, and we rocked our way uninhibitedly across the living room. "Just dance," she yelled into my ear, trying to be heard above the music. "We can talk later." I couldn't make out most of the words, but I immediately felt the raw power and passion of the music, which was energetic and heart thumping.

"Tramps like us, baby we were born to run," Linda bellowed over the music as the first cut ended, embracing me tightly.

"Wow, that's a sexy sound," I whispered in her ear. Breaking our clench, I marched over to the stereo, turned the volume down, and picked up the album cover, which read, Bruce Springsteen, *Born to Run* (1975). The front cover featured a picture of a smiling, relaxed, and casually dressed Bruce Springsteen leaning against one of the members of his band while holding an electric guitar loosely in his left hand just below his hips. Turning the wrap-around cover revealed the identity of the other guy, Clarence Clemons, intensely pouring his soul and guts into blowing the saxophone.

"Springsteen, is he the guy we heard up at the Main Point last year?"

"That's him. That's Bruce. Isn't he fantastic?"

"I'll say," I agreed, pulling out the page of lyrics from inside the album. "He is really intense. I've got to stop and listen closely to the whole album." But before

I could even begin, Linda had the sound wailing from the speakers and booming across the room.

"You can study the lyrics later. Right now, let's just dance and have some fun," Linda said, snatching the page of lyrics out of my hand and pulling me toward her.

After Linda passed out on the couch I did study the lyrics. I stayed up most of the night listening to *Born to Run,* playing it over and over again. When Bruce sang, "I want to know if love is wild and I want to know if love is real," a shiver ran up my spine. I felt the music coursing through my blood, rattling my bones, and settling in my gut. I recalled what it felt like to believe love was real, then to question it, and then to lose it. *How deeply rooted must love be in order to be trusted?*

There is nothing particularly cerebral about *Born to Run.* The songs are raw, and Bruce delivers his message nakedly. "I'll love you with all the madness in my soul" is an expression of the passionate, uninhibited desire unleashed when a person gives everything he has. He conveys an unrestrained experience of being alive, freed from the everyday demands and pressures that keep one's zest for life contained, under control, and locked in. Bruce's rough, raspy voice makes the quest feel urgent and desperate. "We gotta get out while we're young. Tramps like us, baby, we were born to run." It doesn't matter how old you are—Bruce is only twenty-four—this could be your last chance to make a better life. If you don't "get out while you can," you'll be stuck forever, condemned to dead-end jobs and failed relationships.

"This town rips the bones from your back," he warns, a callous and cruel environment destined to lead to despair and meaninglessness. Hope and liberation are somewhere down the road, so if you don't want to end up a loser living a boring life, you better get going. But Bruce also makes it clear that the journey will be demanding. "I'm a scared and lonely rider," he wails, and love is "so hard and filled with defeat."

I felt the hardness and pain every day as I tried to figure out how to go on in the face of Brenda's absence from my life without feeling overcome by sadness, remorse, and regret. Initially, she had withdrawn from me psychologically. Then, a few weeks ago, after we dissolved our marriage, she left physically, moving back to Cleveland to be closer to her friends.

But Bruce reminded me that pain was not all I felt about the loss of Brenda's love and companionship. On "Backstreets," he recalls the broken vows of an everlasting love and commitment. "When the breakdown hit at midnight, there was nothing to say ... and I hated you when you went away." I had never acknowledged the anger I felt when the Brenda I'd known and loved "went away," deserting me emotionally. It wasn't Brenda's fault. She couldn't help it. Regardless, I felt betrayed and had no outlet for my anger, however irrational the source of my hostility might have been. Now, sitting here in the darkness that Bruce finds so appealing, I realize that I have to find a way to escape the entrapment I'm feeling.

The characters in Bruce's songs are wanderers and runners; they take to the street, gunning their engines, going full throttle, searching for something, demanding something more out of life, some meaning or purpose, some connection to something and/or somebody—a dream or a lover. They feel trapped in dead-end jobs, botched relationships, boredom, and rootlessness. For most of them, life was bound to end badly. Maybe they had waited too long, expected some "savior to rise from the streets," assumed they had no choice but to accept what fate had already chosen for them, and lacked the courage or determination to create a dream-fulfilling answer to Bruce's desperate question, "What else can we do now?"—something other than rolling down the window and letting the wind blow back their hair (Masur, 2009).

I'm not particularly fascinated by cars, and I've never been on a motorcycle, but something about Bruce's music felt close to the bone of my existence. Maybe it was my working-class roots or the appeal of the darkness of the night—I had never been a morning person. More likely, it was the tension and urgency of his message. I was wounded, but I wasn't dead. I had no choice but to find a way to live with my sorrow. I was "a sad and lonely rider," but I didn't need to act as if that's all I was or ever would be. An honest life is destined to be riddled occasionally with confusion, contradiction, loss, and suffering. Bruce offered me hope that I could rise above the devastation by trying to make it real, quit hiding, and strive to "get to that place I really want to go" personally and academically. Perhaps our dreams always are at least a step ahead of us, but we shouldn't give up the chase.

Bruce's music touched me where I lived. I felt as if he were speaking directly to me, one working-class kid to another, heart to heart. His songs echoed what I had learned from Viktor Frankl (1959) more than a decade earlier: A person can find meaning in suffering. Indeed, life is a search for meaning: it's about taking chances, about striving for connection, virtue, and love. It's about giving everything you've got.

I felt intoxicated, energetic, and alive. *Born to Run* was my wake-up call. Time to take to the road and "breathe the fire [I] was born in."

Chapter Eight

Between Obligation and Inspiration[1]

> My knowledge of everyday life has the quality of an instrument that
> cuts a path through the forest and, as it does so, projects a narrow
> cone of light on what lies just ahead and immediately around; on
> all sides of the path there continues to be darkness … the reality of
> everyday life is overcast by the penumbras of our dreams.
>
> *Peter L. Berger and Thomas Luckmann (1967, p. 45)*

I walk swiftly through the open door and take my usual position on the soft, black leather couch sitting against the windowless wall. For the "client," a therapist's couch is a significant symbol drenched in meaning, carrying the weight of history. True to form, this one is no ordinary couch. You don't sit *on* it; you sit *in* it. The couch prompts a memory of the bean bag chairs of the sixties—a prominent hippie symbol of freedom. They looked cushy and comfortable but turned out to make your butt sore and your back stiff, a reminder that freedom comes at a price. I can't help wondering why my therapist had chosen this style of couch. Shouldn't a therapist's couch provide something more than an illusion of freedom?

I think of the couch as the third person in the room. We've developed a relationship replete with the ordinary ups and downs of any extended interpersonal bond. After six months of therapy, I can talk freely about our relationship because we're doing much better with each other than we had earlier in our relationship.

We got off to a rocky start. Right from the get-go I felt as if the couch were manipulating me. Don't get me wrong, I'm not trying to inflate my importance to the couch. I realize that the couch's "behavior" was part of a larger conspiracy, a scheme to weaken my defenses. In a state of relaxation, I would be more likely to come out of hiding—open up, reveal hang-ups, and express feelings.

I was on to Dr. Milton's plot and would have none of it. Determined not to give in to the couch's demands, I made the couch my opponent. When the couch insisted that I slouch or recline, I vowed to find a way to sit up. Damn it, I was going to find a way to sit tall at the corner of the couch. I twisted, I turned, I even propped myself up on cushions. Still, I could not sit up straight, which made it impossible for me to look directly at Dr. Milton, eyeball to eyeball. As my frustration mounted, I looked in desperation for another place to sit, but Milton had outfoxed me. There were no other seats in the room. Unless I sat on his lap, I was stuck on the couch.

"This couch is horribly uncomfortable," I griped to Milton in one of our early sessions.

"I'm sorry you feel that way," he replied calmly. "Many of my patients tell me they like it. They say it helps them relax. But you know, Art, you can't please everyone."

Milton had seen right through me. When he said, "You can't please everyone," he wasn't talking only about taste and preference in couches. He was making a therapeutic intervention. Did I try to please everyone? Did I have the courage of my convictions? Did I understand that I couldn't completely control other people's reactions to me and that the more I tried, the more frustrated I might become? Unobtrusively, Milton had slipped in a teaching moment. He wasn't really sorry about my reaction to his couch, but he wasn't disingenuous, either. He must have been waiting for just the right opportunity to make a therapeutic move. My complaint provided an opening, and he seized the moment to fish for deeper meanings of my relationship to the couch, to him, and to other aspects of my life. But he wasn't going to explicitly point out what it all meant. This was not a classroom lecture. We were in this together, and that meant I had work to do as well. He was hoping our little exchange about the couch would kick-start a self-reflective loop.

Unlike the couch, therapy sessions never stay in the room, at least not for the client. Milton knew I would take the bait. Driving home around the darkened curves of East River Drive, I couldn't get the session out of my mind. I had to make a decision about whether I was serious about therapy. I couldn't just go through the motions. Milton was letting me know he wasn't there to please me. If I wanted to benefit, I had better learn that pleasing each other was not the goal of therapy. The more I thought about our exchange, the more I marveled at how gently he had introduced his hypothesis about my "other-centeredness." He had trusted my capacity to pick up on his subtlety.

Our exchange over the status of the couch marked the real start of therapy. Together for three or four sessions, we had not yet broken the ice. Milton must have seen that my grumbling about the couch was emblematic of my resistance to therapy. He was waiting for me to acknowledge what he already knew: I was not committed to giving myself over to the therapeutic process. I was faking it. I was here alright, but I wasn't really *here.* That's why I couldn't see what he saw—that the couch was giving me away. My wiggling and fidgeting showed I was uptight and on edge. I wanted to keep my distance. I felt vulnerable in the presence of an old, seasoned therapist whose job was to ask questions and make interpretations. Deep down, I was afraid he would humiliate or shame me. So I tried to exert control over our sessions. But Milton was way ahead of me. Maybe it was time to lower my shield.

Why Therapy?

You may be wondering what made me seek the counsel of a therapist. I suppose my reasons are no more urgent or unusual than anyone else's. I thought I had reached a breaking point. On a personal level, I was still despairing about the loss of my first love. A lover is supposed to protect and guard his beloved from harm, but I had failed to shelter Brenda from the storm of psychic trauma that blew her away from me. Worse, I had not acted competently. Experts on psychic trauma say that a moment arises when you realize something is terribly wrong with your partner. The scene flashes clearly through my mind—now. Brenda had never taken center stage the way she had that night at Jane and Frank's. The spectacle of that evening is burned into my brain. Someday, the wound may be barely noticeable, but the scar tissue will never go away. In the moment of truth, when I might have been able to save her, I didn't see what was right in front of me. I didn't want to believe or admit that something this bad was happening to Brenda—and to us. Like many partners recruited into a care-giving role, I didn't want to imagine a life together significantly different from the past.

One of my cohorts in graduate school conducted his dissertation research on the phenomenon of perceptual defense (Baudhuin, 1970, 1973). His study focused on how people defend themselves against seeing or hearing things they can't comprehend or tolerate within their worldview. In order to minimize or reduce anxiety, perceptual defense prevents threatening stimuli from entering conscious awareness (Erdelyi, 1974; McGinnies, 1949). When faced with anxiety-arousing circumstances, we are likely to act in a self-interested manner, protecting and defending ourselves against full recognition of what is going on. In my situation with Brenda, I may have reasoned that nothing really had changed. In a day or two, she would return to normal. Perceptual defense is an active process that remains out of awareness and paradoxically allows or encourages inaction. I didn't have to do anything, as long as I refused to admit to myself that something needed to be done. Unfortunately, perceptual defense can produce dire consequences—as I found out. Relational life demands accountability. Eventually, you have to deal with the consequences of inaction. You can't stay in denial forever.

I still fantasize about Brenda's return to a full and healthy life, though I know she's never coming back to me. She has returned to Cleveland, while I'm here, trying to move on. Will she always live within me? Milton says a time will come when my grief will be filed away, like the manila files of research articles stored in the drawers of my filing cabinets. When I want or need to summon a memory, I reach into the past and retrieve the file, but most of the time the file just sits in the drawer benignly indifferent to my earthly concerns. Can therapy help me file away the guilt and grief still consuming me?

On a professional level, I am living a double life, torn between my obligations and inspirations. I have gone over and over the web of contradictions within which I am living, but to no avail. For the first time since I left home and started college, I am stymied, unable to solve the riddle of what to make of things on my own. I am stuck, muddled, and confused. What if these feelings don't change? What if they become worse? Talking to myself isn't working, and the books I'm reading aren't helping either.

I can't keep living exclusively in my head. Life wasn't meant to be lived so stoically. I need a new storyline, but I haven't been able to compose one on my own. I fear I am drifting toward a life that may exclude everything but reading, writing, and teaching, with an occasional romantic fling thrown into the mix. I am determined not to let that happen. My hope is that someone with a fresh perspective can offer me new ways to think about myself and understand what's going on in my life.

Opening

I ask a psychologist neighbor unconnected to the university to recommend a therapist. I also make a list of names from the Yellow Pages. Unable to resist my academic impulses, I go to the library and look up these names to see which therapists have published scholarly articles. I am excited to come across several publications by a Dr. Jay Milton. He writes about how paradoxical injunctions can be used to counteract a patient's knotted contradictions. I'm impressed by his practical applications of communication theory and by a Batesonian kind of edginess to his writing. My decision is made.

"I'm here to make a new life for myself," I tell Milton at our first session.

"Well, I'm glad you haven't set the bar too high," he chuckles. "A new life, that's awfully abstract. What's wrong with the life you're living now?"

"That's a long story," I say, not knowing where or how to begin.

"We have another forty-five minutes today. Is that enough time to get started?"

Burying my face in my hands, I think about how to tell my story. I don't know how much to tell. I'm not ready to spill my guts to a stranger regardless of his credentials. But we can't just sit here for the rest of the hour. I have to break the irritating silence permeating the room.

When I finally look up, I am distracted by the sight of Milton's intensely focused eyes staring at me. He's a handsome old chap. I wonder whether I'll look that good when I reach his age—about sixty-five, give or take a year or two, I'd guess. He has a few soft wrinkles beneath his eyes and some minor flabbiness sagging from his neck, but his soft face is long and lean, and a dimpled chin makes it look as if he's perpetually smiling. A few white whiskers peek through an otherwise closely shaven face.

"I'm a social scientist teaching in a department of speech," I say, hesitating. "I've had some success publishing quantitative research, and my work is being noticed."

"Good for you," Milton interrupts, giving me a breather.

"In terms of my productivity as a scholar, yeah, I guess that's good. Publishing came relatively easy. At first it was challenging, but now I'm bored. I don't consider what I'm doing worthwhile. My heart isn't in it."

194

"Are you saying you don't want to conduct research any longer?"

"No, that's not it at all. I think research can be thrilling. I want to continue doing research, but not the kind of hypothesis-testing, experimental, quantitative research that I was trained to do. There's nothing wrong with these methods *per se*. I just don't believe they can be used to get to the vital questions of communication that revolve around sense making and how people go on with their lives after they've suffered through traumatic events. I want to understand relationships—love, friendship, marriage, families—and I don't believe I can accomplish that with surveys and questionnaires."

"People change all the time. Isn't this just a sign you're evolving as a scholar?"

"That's a generous interpretation. I do think I'm evolving. But here's the rub: I was hired to teach graduate students to be empiricists and mentor them through quantitative dissertations. I'm supposed to be an exemplary empiricist, a model for my students to emulate. Don't get me wrong, I love teaching and I don't mind being a model for the students, but if I were free to choose, this isn't the kind of work I would model. As far as I'm concerned, my published work is trivial. Oh, it's competent enough, but it doesn't represent my values or core beliefs about how communication works and the ways in which ideally we should study it. Every time I stand in front of a class and extol the virtues of empiricism, I'm betraying myself."

"Oh my," Milton winces, acknowledging his understanding of the dilemma I'm expressing. He seems to be listening to me as attentively as I listen to music.

"I'm glad you appreciate the quandary I'm facing."

"Tell me more. How have you been dealing with this situation?" Milton asks.

"Not very well, I'm afraid. That's why I'm here seeking your counsel."

"Therapy is a big step to take. Can't your friends and your partner help you?"

"No, they can't," I say definitively, resisting his attempt to talk me out of therapy. "My partner, Linda, tells me in no uncertain terms that she doesn't want to hear about my academic angst, and I can't talk about my identity struggles with colleagues or my circle of academic friends. I worry most about my colleagues, except for my good friend, Herb. He appreciates my work ethic and commitment to the field, but I can't trust that other members of my department wouldn't hold this against me. You probably think I'm paranoid."

"It turns out that paranoid people quite often are right," Milton smiles. "Other people are out to get them."

Milton and I have a good laugh together over the "validity" of paranoia and then get back to work. I try to impress upon Milton that I feel as if I'm standing at the crossroads. I'm afraid the whole foundation of my life could crumble. I need help figuring out how to unknot the tangle of contradictions I am experiencing. I tell him that I feel imprisoned in the identity of an empiricist and yet reluctant to give up the status. How can I turn my back and walk away now? Wasn't this what I had always wanted?

"For the first time in my life, my father is proud of me," I declare. "It doesn't matter that he has no idea what I really do. Well, maybe it does—a little," I add, "but I know deep down I've earned his respect. I work long hours, and I'm not satisfied with anything less than my best effort. This is a character trait I inherited from my father. It's his legacy. But his respect is not enough to sustain me."

Milton made a point of telling me that he wanted to hear more about what my father had passed on to me. I was not ready to go there, however, so I shifted the topic back to a more comfortable zone, returning the conversation to my paradigm shift. I told him about my admiration for ethnographers like Goffman, Henry, and Geertz. "They're bending the categories," I say. "They write like novelists, but they observe everyday cultural and family life, making truth claims about the empirical world. They're blurring the categories of social science and humanities."

Milton responds by observing how my body language changed when I started talking about my enthusiasm for the new paradigm: "What did you call it, interpretive social science? Why, your whole face lit up, and I thought you were going to burst at the seams," he kidded.

"That's just the point," I confirm. "My trademark as a teacher is my passion and enthusiasm for what I teach. But you can't fake caring about something—at least I can't. I just don't see how I can continue promoting empiricism to graduate students. I'm already acting in bad faith, and it's making me sick. I'm becoming a snake oil salesman."

"So you want to teach and work authentically, but you feel it's too risky."

"That's right. I don't want to feel like a fraud, but I have students who are counting on me," I continue. "Two students came with me from Cleveland State to do PhD work at Temple, and a third joined a year later. What would I tell them? 'I'm sorry, I've changed my mind. Forget everything I taught you?' And what about my social network of friends? Many of my good friends are empiricists. They're the leading methodologists in the field. They see me as one of them. I would be betraying them if I openly rejected empiricism. Besides, I don't know who my audience would be if I started writing interpretive social science. I don't know a single communication scholar who identifies with that term. So who could I count on to acknowledge and support my work? Where would I publish? The whole idea of bending my professional identity sounds preposterous. Am I crazy to be thinking these thoughts?"

I paused to take in the meaning of the words that have been spilling out of my mouth. Was this really me talking? I feel as if the words were speaking me. Hearing the echo of my own voice, I realize how fragile my attachments are on both sides of the divide. Milton and I sit in silence for what seems like a couple of minutes. Time is running out on the session, but all I can think to say is, "Can you help me?"

"The choice seems pretty clear," Milton replies. "Carl Rogers [1961] used to tell his clients that eventually they would have to decide whether they want to be accepted for what other people want them to be or rejected for who they really are." He peers into my eyes for a moment; then turns away and points his index finger at the small clock sitting on the end table next to him.

Tick Tock

I grew to hate the way therapy sessions ended. No matter how much we accomplished, it wasn't enough. I wanted more—more time, more talk, more analysis, greater understanding.

Isn't there something more that can be said, something that will make the session feel finished? I suppose the end of a therapy session is like the end of life. It is bound to seem incomplete. At the end of each fifty-minute hour, Milton's methodical nod at the clock reminded me that he was in charge. Occasionally, I would try to sneak in another utterance and a question or two, but it was no use. The session was over when Milton signaled it was over. These frustrating endings were designed, I guessed, to teach me that every moment was precious, some were wasted, and none could be done over. As the weeks passed, I became more aware of and haunted by the ticking clock. The sessions seemed to get shorter and go faster. There was never enough time.

Yin and Yang

The couch episode showed me that Milton had something to teach me. Gradually, I was becoming enchanted by the way therapy worked. Milton had perceptions about my perceptions, and I had perceptions about his perceptions. Therapy took place at the intersections of these jointly constructed metaperceptions and, of course, the feelings that we attached to them and shared with each other. For a relationship junkie like me, therapy produced the ultimate high. I was a participant observer in an interpersonal laboratory. Not everything was rosy, though. I had to bracket my alarm about how much money this was costing and my skepticism about the wisdom of the peculiar rules under which we operated. Milton insisted upon these rules: We would never be friends or have contact with each other outside this room (unless we met accidentally or a dire emergency occurred), and we would never exceed the fifty-minute hour. At one point, I asked him if we could record our sessions and write and share our reflections on the recordings. "Each of us should keep our own therapy diary," I proposed one day, but Milton flatly rejected the idea.

"This is not an academic exercise," he said. "I'm sorry, but there are certain rules we cannot violate." Although therapy was supposed to make you healthier outside, in the "real" world, the therapy sessions were restricted to the self-contained bubble of the room in which we met and the relationship between Milton and me that took place exclusively in this setting.

Over the next few months, Milton helped me unfreeze some of my views. I began to understand that my professional life was deeply entangled with my personal life. In both realms, I had split and divided parts of myself. Brenda had been quiet, serious, and detached. Linda was outgoing, playful, and a relationship junkie. Yin and yang! Empiricism appealed to my urge for prediction and control, stability, facticity, and objectivity. Conversely, the new interpretive paradigm appealed to my longing for understanding; creating meaning and value; and acknowledging the importance of improvisation, contingency, multiplicity, and subjectivity. Yin and yang—again!

"You must find a way to bring the two sides of yourself into harmony," Milton advised as our session drew to a close that day, and he gave his familiar nod at the clock. "Our time is up." In therapy as in life, the clock never stops ticking.

The Dream

"I had a disturbing dream last night," I begin the next visit, allowing my body to sink into the flowing fold of the couch.

"Tell me about it," Milton replies, bobbing his head and leaning forward.

"I was walking alone along an undulating hiking trail covered with fractured chunks of moss-coated slate and nestled in a dense forest of mountain maple, yellow birch, and fir trees. My face was flushed from exertion. I looked like a long-distance runner trying to muster the strength to make it to the finish line. A low-hanging fog was moving in, making the trail hard to see. I kept looking around, disoriented. 'Why can't I find a tree with a painted blue blaze?' I whispered to myself. I stopped to study the small map I was carrying, but it was of no use; I was hopelessly lost. 'How am I going to find my way back to the trailhead where my car is parked before it gets dark?' I mumbled. I had some water and a tiny flashlight, but no other supplies. The howling wind made me shiver, and I realized the light jacket I was wearing would not be warm enough if I had to stay in the forest overnight. I kept telling myself not to panic, but negative thoughts and fears shuffled through my mind: *Nobody knows I'm here. I could freeze to death.*

"Turning a corner on the trail, I came to a place where the road forked. I didn't know which way to go, though I vaguely recalled coming upon a similar fork in the road on my trip up the trail earlier in the day. Was this the same place? It looked familiar, but I couldn't be certain. No matter, I couldn't remember whether I had turned left or right on my trek up the mountain. I was facing a critical choice: one way was the right way and would lead me out, but which one? Right or left, which trail should I take? I felt as if my life depended on making the right choice. Frozen by indecision, I couldn't move.

"Looking up toward the heavens, I prayed for divine guidance to free me from my vacillation. Suddenly a face appeared in the misty sky above me. Through an opening in the trees I recognized the image in the darkening clouds as Ray Tucker's face.

"'Go to the right,' Tucker instructed.

"'How do you know that's the way back to the trailhead?'

"'Trust me. I have your best interests at heart.'

"'I do trust you, Dr. Tucker, but my life may be at stake. You always insisted we should base important decisions on data and evidence.'

198

"'That's right, Art. Follow the empiricist's credo: gather sense-data, trust your observations, preserve objectivity.'

"'I don't have time to quibble over methodological details. If I don't make a decision soon, it will be too late.'

"'Calm down, Art. You only need a moment or two. Take a few steps down the trail to the right. You'll see that the trail is worn and bare from many people walking on it. Then retrace your steps and walk a short way in the other direction. There you'll find high grass and weeds growing over an unmaintained trail. That's your clue. In one direction, thousands of boots have marched down the trail. In the other direction, there are no footprints to follow. Only a few hikers have ever gone in that direction, and it's likely they lost their way. You don't want to follow the less-traveled road, do you? There's no telling where that path will lead.'

"I followed Tucker's instructions, and within a few minutes had my answer. The two trails fit his description exactly.

"'Thanks, Dr. Tucker. You're a savior,' I bellowed into the air and started running swiftly down the trail to the right. Before I could go more than a few dozen feet, however, I heard a second voice, which I only faintly recognized. I looked up and was shocked to see Dr. Levine's face."

"Levine?" Milton puzzles, taking me out of my relived dream state.

"Don't you remember? He was my undergraduate philosophy prof. I took that great course on existentialism from him."

"Right, right, now I recall. He's the one who showed the Bergman film to your class."

"That's right. He had a great influence on me," I say, opening my eyes. I am surprised to discover myself in a reclining position on the couch.

"Don't stop, Art. I want to hear the rest of your dream."

"Well, here's where things get really hairy."

"Go on, go on, Art," Milton encourages from the edge of his seat. "What did Levine say?"

I lean back and close my eyes again, attempting to put myself back into the space of the dream. Tonight, for the first time, I'm one with the couch. I continue: "'I'm disappointed in you, Art.' That's what Levine said, and the echo of his voice reverberated through the gap in the surrounding mountains.

"'Why are you disappointed in me? What did I do wrong?' I cried out like a little boy submitting to a scolding by his daddy. 'Have I made the wrong choice? Am I headed down the wrong path?' I asked.

"'I can't tell you that, Art.'

"'You mean you won't help me?'

"'Only you can decide which trail to take,' Levine said, his voice trailing off. The image of his face started fading away.

"'Wait, please don't leave,' I begged. 'I'm lost, and I may die if I choose the wrong road.'

"'Why are you so afraid of dying? Everybody dies. Remember what I said in class: It's not whether you exist; it's how you exist that matters.'

"'I know, I know everybody dies,' I stammer. 'But I don't want to die feeling lost. My death would be meaningless.'

"'You aren't lost, Art. You only think you're lost. Besides, a meaningless death usually is the product of a meaningless life.'

"'But if I die tonight, I will have been deprived of an opportunity to live a meaningful life.'

"'Every moment is precious. You are confusing a meaningful life with a long life. Short lives can be meaningful and long lives meaningless. We talked a lot in the existentialism course about what gives life meaning. Don't you remember?'

"'You mean about choice and freedom?'

"'Yes. Can you recall what you learned about choice?'

"'You taught us that a person is defined by the choices he makes. We express our freedom through our choices. Our actions give our lives meaning.'

"'That's right. So it's your responsibility to make this decision. Nobody can make this choice for you.'

"'You mean I shouldn't have taken Tucker's counsel?'

"'That's not for me to say.'

"'I'm so worried about making the wrong decision.'

"'What makes you so sure there is one right decision?'

"'The trails go off in different directions. They won't end at the same place. One will lead me away from my goal.'

"'Listen to yourself, Art. You keep worrying about what will happen in the end. Perhaps that is the source of your suffering. You're ignoring what's happening right now. You're mistaking the forest for the trees.' Levine burst out laughing at his own joke, which I didn't find funny in my present state. Then he started coughing uncontrollably. I flashed back to the sound of the dry, hacking cough that used to interrupt his lectures. I guess he never quit smoking that pipe of his—strange that an existentialist philosopher would take such poor care of himself.

"'If you mean I'm not dealing with this problem, you're right,' I replied as soon as Levine regained his composure. Talking to Levine was slowing me down and giving me pause to reconsider my decision. 'To be frank, Dr. Levine, you're confusing me. You say there may not be one right decision to make and I may only think I'm lost. How can that be true? Don't you see how scared I am? My anxiety is at a fever pitch.'

"'I shouldn't need to remind you that anxiety has a purpose. It tells you that something is at stake. This may be the most meaningful moment of your life. You don't realize how lucky you are to have to face this predicament. It's a gift. I doubt if you've ever been as fully aware of your existence as you are right now.'

"'So you admit that my predicament is real. I am going to die if I make the wrong decision.'

"'I can't say. How would I know?'

"'I assumed you came to help me, like you did once before. In class you used to make my head spin. You never gave us answers, but your questions helped us recognize the source of our confusion.'

"'Okay, then, here's a question to ponder: What makes you think the two roads are so terribly different?'

"'One is well traveled; the other is not. I've seen that with my own eyes.'

"'How perfect is that knowledge?'

"'I don't understand. What do you mean by perfect knowledge?'

"'That's the point, isn't it, Art?'

"'You mean that our knowledge can never be perfect?'

"'The knowledge you speak of is *human* knowledge—in your case, a product of what you saw with your eyes in your specific circumstance.'

"'But it is clearly evident that the two trails differ in precisely the way Dr. Tucker predicted.'

"'You are confusing evidence with truth. What is evident may not be true.'

"'But I saw it with my own eyes. That's a fact.'

"'Yes, a fact, indeed. But what does that fact mean? You are in a forest, Art. A forest is steeped in mystery, and the secrets of the forest are not made available to us through facts. What appears as factual to you may only be a product of your own imaginative reconstruction given your predicament.'

"'But I know what I saw.'

"'Why are you fighting me, Art? Don't you understand that your experience of each road has been limited by what your eyes could see and interpret? You've traveled only a short distance in each direction. How can you tell what's around the next corner? Are the two roads really so different? Along each road, you can find living things and decaying things, signs of life and signs of death, new life cropping up and past life decomposing. The two roads are alike and they are different. Each road has its own special charm and promise, complete with risks and rewards.'

"'You make my predicament sound astonishing. You want me to stand here in awe of the secrets of life and death revealed in the forest. As a philosopher, you can afford to indulge in such wonderment, but my dilemma is practical. I can't take both roads. I must choose, and the strain of that choice feels unbearable.'

"'Do you really think you can know the consequences of the choice you make in advance? Life doesn't admit absolute certainty. Life involves contingency, chance, and fate.'

"'I just don't want to regret later on that I didn't choose the other path.'

"'You can't be released from the mystery of the unknown, the path you could have taken but didn't. There are no do-overs. The choice you make will set the rest of your life in motion. You won't have a chance to come back and do it over again.'"

"'So if both paths are riddled with uncertainty, how can I make a rational choice?'

"'I've given you all the guidance you need. It's time for me to leave. The choice in front of you is about who you take yourself to be.' Suddenly Levine's face faded

201

from view. Left behind was the surrounding sound of Levine's voice, his final words echoing repeatedly across the forest: "The choice in front of you is about who you take yourself to be.'"

Who Do I Take Myself to Be?

"I woke up trembling and bewildered. A few seconds later, though, I realized I had been dreaming. 'Whew, I'm awake. I'm alive.' The dream had seemed so real. I sighed, exhaling a deep groan of relief. But my reprieve was temporary. As the day wore on, I kept asking myself what Levine meant when he implied the incident could have been an illusion—you know, not real—and that my choice was about who I took myself to be. I mean, only a fool would go down the unkempt path that showed no sign of life. Wouldn't that mean sure death? I would be taking myself to be a dead man. What do you think, Dr. Milton? What does my dream mean?"

"I think this is an important dream!" Milton exclaims. "You shouldn't belittle Levine's departing words. Undoubtedly, they originate deep in your unconscious, which is ahead of your conscious level of experience. You need to figure out what your unconscious is trying to tell you."

Eyes now wide open, I wiggle my way into a halfway seated position. Milton has a deadly serious look on his face. Is this my therapeutic moment of truth? I wonder. I feel my stomach starting to roll the way it used to when my father would approach me in an agitated state. I remind myself that Milton is not my father. He is on my side. He is just trying to make sure I don't evade the lesson in the dream. But what is the lesson?

"You began by saying that the dream was disturbing," Milton continues. "What disturbed you about it? What made you tremble?"

"I felt under extraordinary pressure to make a choice, yet frozen by a fear that I might make the wrong choice and die in the forest. I looked to my mentors for direction, but each pointed me in a different direction. Then they disappeared. At the end of the dream, I was alone and still lost. When I realized it was a dream, I was relieved that I had awakened before I could find out whether I had survived. I've read that if you die in your dream, you'll soon die in real life."

"Do you think the dream was literally about survival?" Milton questions.

"If not literally, then I guess metaphorically. Hmmm, I suppose it reflects my desire not to feel dead."

"Uh-huh," Milton encourages.

"I'm referring to the deadening feeling I've disclosed in here before, how I feel when I betray my deepest values and commitments by going through the motions, acting as if I'm really devoted to empiricism and quantitative research."

"Why do you call your feeling deadening?" Milton puzzles.

"I think of it as a kind of death in life. I'm alive, but I may as well be dead. I'm so disgusted with myself." I stop to take in my own words for a moment.

"Disgusted?" Milton interrupts.

"Disgusted that I'm hiding my real convictions—I'm ashamed. I feel inauthentic, a fake. It's disgusting that I don't have the courage to stand behind what I believe."

"So the dream is a wake-up call?" Milton smiles at the connection he is drawing.

"I suppose you mean the dream rouses me from the living dead. I'm grateful for that observation. Now I'm a *grateful* dead person! Ha!" We laugh in unison; then Milton resumes his therapeutic stare.

"Tell me more about the vision of Tucker and Levine that came to you in the dream." Milton prompts.

"That seems pretty straightforward to me. Tucker and Levine represent an expression of the paradigm clash I've been trying to resolve—you know, empiricism and interpretive social science."

"Two roads you could travel down in your professional life?"

"Yes, of course. The crux of the dream is the whole question of which path to take to get me out of the forest safely."

"Safely? Oh, so you want to make a safe choice. Is that what you're saying?"

Milton's question startles me. I've wanted to see myself as a risk taker—within some limits of course—but he's making me ponder whether I'm protecting something, wanting to play it safe.

"It's like I've said before, Milton, academics talk like liberals and act like conservatives. And empiricism is radically conservative. You are supposed to plod along, following in the footsteps of the researchers whose work your research follows. In the dream, I am relieved when Tucker takes me by the hand and leads me down what looks like the right path, the well-worn, well-trodden trail, out of danger. Revolting how easily I acquiesce, isn't it?"

"But then along comes Levine."

"Yeah, he messes everything up! Just when I'm on my way out, he comes into the picture and tries to change the frame."

"Oh, are you sure he's not saving you?"

"Saving me? At the end of the dream I haven't made a choice, which means I may die or suffer mightily overnight in the forest. Levine confuses me. He questions whether the whole mess even is real."

"Well, it is a dream, you know!" Milton grins.

"And then he suggests the audacious notion that the two roads are alike—sort of—and I should more fully appreciate the enveloping mystery of each road and the forest as a whole."

"Cheeky of him, wasn't it? I'd like to meet this guy," Milton kids, then pauses. "But, Art, you know what?"

"What?" I urge.

"I have met him."

"You have?"

"Yes! Right here in this room." Milton hesitates. "He's you!"

"Me?"

"Yes, Tucker is you too, and he always will be a part of you. He rescued you at a time when you needed a father and a mentor. But you've played Tucker, and that part may have played itself out. I believe Levine represents the person you want to be. He appeals to your desire to confront the mysteries and contradictions of life and to use your imagination. It's all right there in your dream."

"But I haven't been able to put Tucker behind me."

"No, you haven't. You feel obliged and loyal to Tucker, the way any good son would out of respect for his father. But sooner or later, every son has to find himself and make his own way as free of guilt as he can. We can't relive our father's lives. We have to live our own."

"Is that why Levine insisted that I'm not lost, that I only think I'm lost?"

"In a manner of speaking, we're all lost—and not lost. We're trying to find our bearings, the meaning of our existence, in a universe that refuses to talk to us or tell us what it wants from us. A few weeks ago, you described yourself as torn between your obligations and your inspirations—beautifully said, I should add. And in your dream, Levine reminds you that death is not the problem. Life is the problem. How did he put it?"

"It's not whether you exist; it's how you exist!"

"Yes, that's it. Within the contingencies and blows of fate over which you have no control—like Brenda's illness—you choose how you exist. You commit to something, something you can believe in and care about. That's what releases you from the kind of boredom you were resisting by coming into therapy. You want a meaningful existence or you wouldn't be here, taking this abuse from me," he kids. "So the way I see it, you're not lost. You're scared, as anyone would be who is moving from one mode of being to another or, as you like to say, from one paradigm to another."

"Though I haven't made that move yet. At the end of my dream, I'm still on Tucker's road."

"But you've hesitated. You're wavering. You're not too far down the road to reverse your course. Levine says your predicament is a gift. That's your unconscious talking, the source of your genuine desire. The gift is right there in front of you. You just have to accept it."

"Trouble is, Levine can't guarantee I'll survive if I go down the other road."

"No! I think he's trying to show you that it's not a question of whether you survive but whether you thrive. What's exciting is that you don't know where that road, the untraveled road, will lead."

"You say exciting. I say terrifying."

"Sometimes we desire things that both excite and terrify us. Nobody leads a meaningful life without ever encountering terrifying moments and experiences." Milton pauses and brushes a lock of his shiny white hair off his forehead. "If you think about everything we've talked about today, that it came to you in a dream, you have to be amazed. When I look at you through the dream, I can't help but see Art, the dreamer. Metaphorically, it all may boil down to the future you're dreaming for yourself."

"You mean to try to make my dream into reality? How very Disney of you, Milton—make your dreams come true! Wish upon a star! Sorry, but I'm too tied to earth for that."

"Ha. I'm glad you haven't lost your sense of humor," Milton grins. "You know that's not what I mean. Not literally, not at all. Not this dream. I'm talking about committing to your dreams." Milton stops abruptly and nods at the clock. I look at him eagerly, awaiting a conclusive ending to our session. Please don't end without saying something more, I think.

Milton gestures at the clock and says, "The choice in front of you is who you take yourself to be."

Note

1. An earlier version of this chapter was published as "Between Obligation and Inspiration: Choosing Qualitative Inquiry," *Qualitative Inquiry* 18, (2012), pp. 535–543. DOI: 10.1177/1077800412450152.

Chapter Nine

Disconnecting and Connecting

Seeking a Home in Academia

> I wish that the college I bound my identity over to had introduced
> me to my heart. I wish it had set mercy and compassion
> before me as idols, instead of Athena's cold brow.
> *Jane Tompkins (1996, p. 220)*

Breaking Up

June 24, 1984. Weiss Hall, Psychology/Speech Building, Temple University.

I pause to take a break. I've been cleaning out and packing up my office, rummaging through files of syllabi, student seminar papers, lecture notes, drafts of old convention papers, professional correspondence, and three cabinets of photocopied articles and chapters that I started accumulating in graduate school—a stash of academic stuff. I'll be moving to Tampa, Florida, in a couple of weeks, where I'll start my new faculty position at the University of South Florida.

Hard to believe I've been at Temple for ten years. Where did the time go? I came as a scared but ambitious assistant professor. I'm leaving as a tenured full professor. I arrived never having taught a graduate course or served on a dissertation committee. Before departing I'll have completed supervision of my fifth PhD student, and I've served on more than a dozen dissertation committees.

I've been treated well at Temple. Murray nurtured and guided me through my first seven years. He kept his word about shepherding my proposals for new courses through university committees. Our department became one of the first communication programs to offer courses in marriage and family communication as part of its standard undergraduate curriculum and to teach communication theory from a Batesonian perspective. When Murray stepped down as chair to return to full-time teaching, I lost a major source of support. But that's not the reason I decided to leave.

My divorce from Linda was finalized last year. Once we moved in together, marriage became more like a foregone conclusion than a measured decision. Our relationship centered on having fun, not on planning a future together. In retrospect, marrying Linda appears to have been the most impulsive decision of my life, but as Kierkegaard (1959) observed, life can be understood backward but must be lived forward. On the whole, we had six delightful, fun-filled years together, but our differences eventually proved too large to overcome. What brought us together could not keep us together. Linda pleaded over and over for more "quality time" with me. She couldn't understand what compelled me to work such long hours. She liked to sleep late, awaken slowly, amble through the afternoon, and stay out at local bars until closing time. "Why can't you ever take a day or evening off?" she'd complain. "Other people don't work such insanely long hours."

I tried to make Linda understand that I couldn't help myself. "A work ethic courses through my veins. For me, work is play," I'd tell her. "You find drinking and hanging out in bars fun. I don't. The bar scene mesmerizes you, but it doesn't appeal to me in the least." These differences made a difference.

Our joint friends tell us they don't understand what went wrong. "We don't want to take sides," they say. I insist that "nothing went wrong, and there are no sides to take. Linda and I had our time. We aren't the kind of couple destined to stay together forever. Each of us wants to move forward and make a different life for ourselves."

We were one of those couples whose marriage simply reaches an end. At a certain point, we had drained what we could offer each other. I realize, in hindsight, that I came into our relationship in a traumatized state, as did Linda. Each of us had endured a long stretch of sorrow over the demise of a previous marriage. When we met, we fed off each other's need to awaken the torrid passion suppressed by grief. We came together seeking adventure and release from the emotional control we had been forced to bear. A fire ignited under these circumstances eventually gets smothered by the mundane realities of sharing a life under the same roof. Our wires crossed and we burned out. Try as we might, we couldn't rekindle the flame.

But divorce didn't only end our marriage; it also tore me away from the network of social support that I had shared with Linda. I was surprised to find I had not only lost a partner but also a support system. In the absence of their validation, Philadelphia no longer feels like home to me. I need to make a clean break and begin a new life elsewhere.

I will not find it easy to leave. I'm a city boy with working-class roots, and Temple is the archetype of an urban, commuter university. On the Temple campus, you won't find a tree-lined quadrangle bordering beautiful buildings with stone or marble facades, modern dining facilities, food courts, lush and exotic gardens, or state-of-the art exercise facilities. Nor is Temple a pedestrian-friendly campus. Students and faculty don't linger or hang around after class. Most students come to class directly from work or shuttle off to a job right after class.

Only a couple of residence halls exist on campus, and most of Temple's physical plant is nestled between dangerous urban neighborhoods. I never feel unsafe during the day, but the evenings can be scary. The daunting presence of security guards at the entrance of every campus building creates an intimidating atmosphere of surveillance and scrutiny. The intention of the heightened security is to make students and staff feel safe, an admirable goal. But after viewing Francis Ford Coppola's stunning film *The Conversation* (1974), I began to doubt the administration's explanation of how far these "security measures" were being extended. Coppola's film questions whether we really know precisely where, when, and by whom we are being watched. When cameras started appearing outside and on top of buildings, I thought the administration had gone too far. Did we really need Big Brother's bird's-eye view to protect us? This is a college campus, not a military base.

I arrived during a period my colleague, Herb Simons, later referred to as "Temple's Golden Years." By the mid-1970s, the PhD program had begun to achieve national visibility, and we were able to recruit and support talented and ambitious students. The department was situated in a large College of Arts and Sciences with a strong liberal education mission and little emphasis on majors. Our undergraduate courses drew a broad mix of students from across liberal arts departments—history, psychology, philosophy, sociology, and so forth. And Temple gave more than lip service to its mission to serve disadvantaged and inner-city populations. The administration started actively recruiting "nontraditional" students—blacks, Hispanics, Asians, older and disabled students—long before diversity became a trumpet call in universities across America. In the mid-1970s, few universities could match Temple's minority student population.

I love teaching Temple's rough-around-the edges undergraduates. They haven't attended the best high schools or grown up in families who demanded commitment to education, but what they lack in background they make up for in desire and moxie. Quite a few are first-generation college students fulfilling a dream. They want to be the first in their families to earn a college diploma, which they see as a ticket to upward mobility.

My undergraduate courses pulsate with energy and excitement. The best word I can come up with to describe the feel of these classes is *spirited*. My challenge is to create an environment in which the students feel safe to release their energy. I try to facilitate a psychological and interactive classroom climate that allows the truth and meaningfulness of students' lived experiences to emerge. These students are hungry for the nourishment of acknowledgment and good conversation. They don't sit on their hands passively, waiting to be told the "truth." They're engaged and lively kids itching for opportunity and determined to have something good happen to them. "We haven't had other teachers who asked about our experiences," some of them tell me, wide eyed with appreciation. The stories they write in my courses—stories about drug abuse, eating disorders, fatherless families, living in poverty, being surrounded by crime and prejudice—evoke strong reactions and heated discussions and debates with classmates. Our conversations move in unpredictable directions. I have to trust the process, counting on the students to make their way constructively through the discord that arises. After all, most of them have seen and dealt with much worse. Although the students treat me with respect, they don't cower in my presence. They offer a different kind of intelligence from what we typically reward in university teaching: They are more street smart than book smart. They may lack the polish of students at schools like Penn or Penn State, but they are more lively, animated, and thrilling to teach.

Maybe I'm romanticizing the Temple students. I'll admit that I have to work hard to access and adapt to their frame of reference. I want to meet them where they live, but many of them live in a place that is culturally foreign to me. Yet despite our cultural differences, I see myself in many of them. I want to be their Levine, a professor who encourages them to take themselves seriously, giving them a chance to make it in a city that is largely indifferent to their struggles. I can't completely explain their appeal to me, though I know this: they make me a better teacher.

Temple's golden days didn't last long. Like many of its peer institutions, Temple misjudged the potential for future growth, intense competition for students, and capacity of the economy to support lofty goals. New programs and new faculty were added too quickly and without adequate resources to sustain them through tough times, and enrollment projections missed their targets. By the late 1970s, Temple was plagued by shrinking enrollments, insufficient endowments, inadequate facilities, reduced state appropriations, a weak national economy, and low faculty morale. On two occasions, 1977 and 1982, legislative gridlock delayed passage of a budget, and Temple was forced to pay hundreds of thousands of dollars in interest on temporary bank loans (Hilty, 2010).

The budget crisis came to a head in 1979. Faced with a projected revenue shortfall of $8 million, Temple's central administration issued letters of "provisional retrenchment" to twenty-three tenured faculty members. Although the budget shortfall was reconciled and the administration rescinded the letters the following year, faculty morale had been shattered. A dark cloud hung over smaller departments like mine, creating despair and pessimism about the future. Plans to hire new tenure-line faculty were shelved; and budgets for equipment, travel, and graduate student support were slashed or frozen.

At the national level speech communication departments faced severe cuts, threatening program shutdowns. Several had been folded into other units, losing their independent disciplinary identity. I began to worry this could happen at Temple. We were mainly a traditional speech and rhetoric program, and our departmental publication record was not particularly impressive—more than half of the faculty were not research active. I admired Temple's commitment to urban education and working-class students, but I was growing tired of coming to a workplace immersed in doom and gloom. When I returned from a sabbatical term at Michigan State in the spring of 1980, my marriage was on the skids, and the department was teetering on the edge.

In January 1982, the dean of Arts and Sciences announced that enrollments had dropped by more than 15 percent. Another budget crisis loomed on the horizon. I was thirty-seven years old and a full professor. If I was ever going to leave Temple, now was the time. But it would have to be the right situation. I wanted good colleagues, a university on the rise, and a school immune from the virus of perpetual budget crises. I fantasized a position in a department on the make but not steeped in tradition, one that was open to shaping a unique graduate program along the lines of interpretive social science. Given the restricted market for senior professors, this would likely be my last move, so quality of life was an issue. I didn't need a big city, but I didn't want a small college town either. The cultural vitality of Philadelphia had spoiled me. Ideally, I wanted a locale that would include fine dining, live theater and music, a dynamic cultural center, and a diverse population. Did a place meeting these requirements exist? Would it have an opening for a senior professor?

Greener Pastures

By 1982, the United States had experienced a thoroughgoing "southernization" (Schulman, 2001). In the aftermath of defeat in Vietnam, scandal at the Watergate, terrorism at the Summer Olympics, a hostage crisis in Iran, double-digit inflation, escalating oil prices, and long lines at the gas pumps, distrust in government had reached epic proportions. The country was ripe for radical change. An anti-big-government, pro-private-enterprise, nationalistic attitude took hold, shifting political power from the "elite" establishment of the Northeast to the Sunbelt, where an expedient, doctrinaire, conservative politics, promoting tax cutting and free-market capitalism, had co-opted a resurgence of religious fundamentalism (Schulman, 2001). While the Northeast continued to be mired in economic stagflation, the Sunbelt basked in economic prosperity. Several factors contributed to the significant population migration from the Frostbelt to the Sunbelt during the 1970s. First, the attractiveness of low-wage, nonunion areas of the Southeast hastened a major relocation of manufacturing jobs during the downturn in the economy. Second, city dwellers fed up with rampant crime, urban decay, energy shortages, and bad weather looked upon the South with its lower taxes, affordable mortgages, and cheaper energy as offering a better quality of life. Third, the amenity-rich, safe-haven, Sunbelt retirement villages enticed elderly people—the fastest growing demographic in the country—to move south (Frum, 2000; Schulman, 2001).

In preparation for entering the job market, I consulted books in the field of futures studies, including several on the New York Times list of best-selling, non-fiction books (Toffler, 1970, 1984; Naisbitt, 1984). Most of the futurists were predicting an expansion of American industry in the South and Southwest and a declining influence among the big, urban megacities. California and Florida were identified as two of the bellwether states of the future, along with Colorado and Arizona.

I was fortunate to receive verbal offers from two schools that met my criteria, one in Florida, the other in Arizona, two states with booming economies and expanding state university systems. Dotted with a collection of arid and semiarid plants from various regions of the world, the campus at the University of Arizona looked like an arboretum. Dining in an open-air campus restaurant in the middle of February, I looked up at the tantalizing mountains surrounding me and wondered how anyone could resist the temptation to put down the books and go for a hike or a downhill ski. During my interview, my campus tour guide walked me down a long, grassy mall bordered with rustling palm trees, proudly pointing to the tidy, integrated landscape and architecture, with its eye-catching red-brick buildings. The stunning contrast with Temple's disheveled appearance made me feel as if I had entered an alternate universe. *Was this a university or a resort?*

My second interview took place at the University of South Florida (USF), a campus that felt a lot more familiar. The department of communication was housed in one of the oldest buildings on campus, the facilities were unimpressive, and the buildings looked as if they had been impulsively thrown together on the spur of the moment. USF was a commuter university bereft of a campus personality, but during my visit I learned that the university had acquired extensive land surrounding the present campus—nearly two thousand acres. What was visible appeared small, dull, and uninviting, but campus planners had a vision for the future. My hosts informed me the state legislature had approved and funded a new USF medical school, and the university's master plan was to develop nationally recognized graduate programs. "We're bringing in top scholars to build these programs," Provost Greg O'Brien declared during my interview. "Communication is one of the programs we are targeting to add a PhD program. With your reputation and publication record, you would be an ideal person to lead that effort."

Walking across campus at the end of the interview, my eyes were drawn to the brilliant sunshine, fluffy white clouds, and deep blue sky—Florida blue they called it. It was mid-February, yet in every direction I looked, I saw lush green grass and leaves on the trees. I wanted to plop on the ground and allow the sun's balmy rays to warm my chilled northern bones, but I didn't want to make a spectacle of myself. "This is a low-tax state," the department chair declared during my interview, "but salaries tend to be lower here than in other parts of the country. The state charges a toll for the sunshine," he kidded.

One of my friends joked that Florida wasn't meant to be inhabited. Trying to dissuade me from going on the interview, he insisted that Florida had no character. "I have just one word for Florida, Art: 'Plastic,'" he mocked, seizing on what he knew was one of my favorite lines in the film *The Graduate* (1967). "That's my image of Florida—fake, flat, and inauthentic," he continued. "You'll dry up like a prune in a place like that."

I brushed off my friend as a biased source, but driving around the city during my visit, I glimpsed what he was talking about. Tampa looked like one sprawling strip mall. Aside from an old Cuban cigar-making area of town, the city lacked personality or a cultural persona. It wasn't a beach town or retirement community, but it wasn't a thriving cultural metropolis, either. The museums and theaters were unimpressive, and virtually no night life existed outside the "old town," Ybor City, which, aside from a small, struggling bohemian subculture, had become largely a nightlife haven for adolescents and young adults. Could I get used to this? Had I been spoiled by Philadelphia?

Returning from the interviews, I knew in my heart that my days at Temple were numbered. Temple and I had "come to distances," and it was time to say goodbye (Cohen, 1967). Despite my reservations about leaving the vibrant urban culture of Philadelphia for the laid-back coastal charm of Tampa, the grass looked greener in Florida—much greener! Every time I walked into Weiss Hall, I'd feel a knot in my stomach. What was causing this anxiety? Was it sorrow? Was I grieving? Was I guilty of betrayal? Had I failed to keep a promise to people who had put their faith in me? Though I could rationalize that Temple had failed me more than I had disappointed her, I couldn't overcome the perception I was a traitor. I felt as if I were breaking up with a lover. How do I say I'm leaving? How do I tell her my feelings have changed? I have to leave, but a piece of me will always stay here and a piece of you will always be with me. That statement felt true but self-interested. Does every meaningful departure carry with it a sorrow akin to loss or death? Is this why I dread good-byes?

Weiss Hall had been my academic home for nearly ten years. Now it felt remote and alien. Living in limbo, I stayed home to work as much as possible and didn't take on any new graduate students. I missed the golden days, when I could hardly wait to get to school and feel the positive energy of the graduate students. How fondly I recall those long, sometimes heated conversations with students about the future of the field and the kibitzing, teasing, and playful ribbing in which we engaged. What fun! Those days were gone, and they weren't coming back. The quality and commitment of the students had declined markedly as the program took on a more regional cast.

Though my mind was all but made up, I wanted to do the right thing, the professionally ethical thing. I scheduled an appointment with the dean of Arts and Sciences to go over my options and give Temple a chance to make a counteroffer. Before meeting with the dean, I turned down the offer from Arizona. The interview there had gone well, perhaps too well. Shortly after I returned to campus, the chair of the search committee phoned to tell me the position had been upgraded to "department head" with no term limit. I could tell this was an energetic, rising department that would make a lot of noise in the discipline, but my interview with the president scared me. I got the strong impression that Arizona was a university with a philosophy of top-down decision making and little commitment to faculty governance. Within the previous two years, several eminent empiricists had been appointed to the faculty in communication. Within a short time, they had wrestled control of the department away from their humanist colleagues in a contentious takeover that upper administration supported. I would be walking into a hornet's nest. Major decisions about the future of the department had been made already. The focus of the department was going to be communication science in the positivist, quantitative research tradition. If I accepted this position, I would be right back where I started. Levine's words stuck in my mind. The identity I would need to assume at Arizona was no longer "who I took myself to be." Though I still had one foot in the closet—continuing to teach statistics and research design courses at Temple while deepening my immersion in interpretive perspectives on the human sciences—I knew I could not go to Arizona under the false pretense that I was wed to a positivist's worldview. Moreover, I didn't see myself as an administrator. I had enough trouble managing my own life; I didn't fancy supervising other people's lives.

"What can we offer to keep you here, Art?" the dean asked. "If it's a question of salary, we can match and possibly exceed what South Florida has offered."

"Salary is important. It's nice to know you're valued, and salary is one of the ways to keep score. But money isn't the main issue for me."

"Tell me what is."

"I'm concerned about the future of the graduate program. Support for graduate students has been steadily declining, and we're no longer able to recruit top students. I need to know this condition is temporary. What can you tell me about the future of the graduate program in rhetoric and communication?"

"I'm afraid I can't be optimistic. As you know, we've had a lot of budget issues the past few years. Enrollments have stabilized, but the competition for students is fierce. We're not anticipating any rapid expansion, and we expect the legislature to continue to decrease funding to state universities. Besides, I'm not even sure your department will remain in Arts and Sciences. Some members of the School of Communications and Theater believe your department belongs in their school."

"I appreciate your candor, though I'm disappointed to hear this," I say. We continue to chat cordially for a few minutes. Both of us realize the outcome. When I return to my office I check the mail and find a letter with my USF contract along with a package. I open the package and slip on the enclosed USF T-shirt. The lettering on the shirt says, "Communication: We do it with meaning!" The shirt fits perfectly.

Disconnections

I'm beginning to realize why I feel so sad. My sorrow is not so much about leaving as it is about the lack of connection I feel here. I have one dear friend, Herb Simons, and another friend who is a much younger colleague. He's packing to leave too, heading for Southern California.

When I started cleaning out the drawers in my desk this morning, I took a last look at the eleven names on the list of telephone numbers of the departmental faculty. I tried to conjure an image of each of them as if they were characters in a story I was writing. In most cases, I couldn't. Four of the people on the list have not been sighted all year—at least I haven't seen them. The other seven have been around from time to time, but two of them haven't spoken to me in several years. I've exchanged pleasantries with some of the others, but I can't remember a single significant conversation with any of them—ever. I earned tenure here and was promoted twice, but I would venture a guess that most of my colleagues have never read anything I've published. Over the years, we've had some big fights in the department, and these conflicts created a huge split between factions of the department. I could tolerate the divisions, but what really bothered me was that we never talked about them, never tried to face them head on. We let the conflicts simmer below the surface. Apparently, we don't have the stomach for metacommunication. One of my colleagues told me that he had started taking Valium before faculty meetings to prevent his rage from boiling over.

Last week, the chair held a party at his Center City condominium for me and the other departing colleague, Eric Eisenberg. It was a very uncomfortable evening. Were they celebrating our departure? More than half the members of the department didn't show up. The ones who did come didn't seem to know what to say. Neither did I. They gave me a leather briefcase. The chair said it was "a token of our appreciation." Did that mean they were glad I was leaving? Opening the briefcase, I found nothing inside. No farewell speeches were given, either. I used to say to Murray, "I'm grateful that you leave me alone." So why should I expect things to be any different? It's hard to get to know somebody you always leave alone. And that's just it: They don't know me, and I don't know them.

I never realized this was what I was signing on for when I committed to "the life of the mind." Are all departments like this? In a few weeks, I'll be off for Florida, leaving behind ten years of sweat and hard work. Right now, I feel as empty as that briefcase. What difference would it have made if I had never been here at all?

After "Social Psychology as History"

That's enough reminiscence. I need to get moving, get these cabinets and book-shelves cleaned out and the files and books packed. So far, I've filled three boxes that I labeled "Interpretive Social Science," and I'm starting another one. Some-day I may get to tell the story of how I educated myself as an interpretive social scientist, and these materials will come in handy. I reach down and pull a thick file from the bottom drawer of my cabinet tagged "Gergen-Schlenker debate." I think about how this now-obscure conflict between two social psychologists came to mark a turning point in my academic life.

It's remarkable how fateful and contingent my life seems as I look back in hindsight. I think of Levine exhorting me to take myself seriously; Dr. Smith holding one assistantship in reserve just in case someone like me came along; Tucker taking me under his wings as if I were his own son; Hilyard getting me out of his hair by shipping me off to the library, where I discovered a treasure trove of work on communication outside my own discipline; Brenda's illness bringing the impermanence and unpredictability of life into stark relief; Goffman (1959, 1963, 1971), Henry (1971), and Geertz (1973) opening my eyes to a horizon of new possibilities for interpretive social science; Milton healing my wounded soul, clarifying my options, and urging me to honor my genuine interests wherever they may lead; and coming across Ken Gergen's "Social Psychology as History" (1973), after which my teaching and research were never the same.

The yellowed and wrinkled notes in the file tell that story: The publication of Ken Gergen's "Social Psychology as History" (1973) was a watershed moment that steered me into uncharted waters. Gergen (1973) had touched a nerve by questioning the fundamental premises of the positivist research agenda in social psychology. If social facts are historically and culturally contingent, as Gergen (1973) had argued, then the notion of an orderly accumulation of scientific knowledge of social behavior is highly doubtful for at least two reasons. First, the events social scientists seek to explain are not stable over time; second, as social scientists, we cannot enact the kind of objectivity akin to the natural sciences because we are inside what we are studying and, thus, bring our values and biases to our observations and interpretations of data. The only thing scientific about the field is its methods, which do not yield scientific explanations akin to those in the natural sciences (Gergen, 1973). Gergen's critique convinced me that social psychology had become a doctrinaire field based on the shaky foundation of methodological dogma, the same dogma that Kuhn (1970) had rejected as the grounding for the kind of linear progress that positivist science seeks.

Kuhn (1970) had predicted that a field whose major premises are challenged can expect to be thrown into chaos, a condition under which three things are likely to occur. First, confidence in the ruling paradigm will be weakened. Second, fundamentalist devotees attached to the old paradigm, sensing their life's work is being called into question, will launch a vigorous defense of the old paradigm. Third, the floodgates will be opened to a wave of new possibilities. This is precisely what happened in the aftermath of Gergen's critique of social psychology's methodological paradigm.

In the decade following the publication of Gergen's article a chorus of critics voiced concerns about the premises and practices of the "received view" of knowledge. Unimpressed by the achievements of experimental and social psychology, proponents of new paradigms began to speak of "a crisis of confidence" and call for radical transformations in the goals and aspirations of social science (Coser, 1975; Cronbach, 1975; Elms, 1975; Gergen, 1976, 1978, 1980; Israel and Taijfel, 1972). They expressed misgivings about experimental manipulation and deception (Harré and Secord, 1972; Kelman, 1972; McGuire, 1967, 1973; Ring, 1967; Tajfel, 1972), questioned the social relevance of laboratory fact finding (Helmreich, 1975), doubted the possibility of establishing a cumulative social science (Cartwright, 1979; Gergen, 1978; Smith, 1972), rejected the premise of transhistorical prediction (Gergen, 1976), found fault with the image of humanity and individualism underlying psychology's application of empiricism (Harré and Secord, 1972; Hollis, 1977; Sampson, 1975; Shotter, 1975), and deconstructed the correspondence theory of knowledge on which logical empiricism is based (Rorty, 1979).

215

Social psychology's mainstream could not afford to allow this repudiation of the field's foundational premises and institutional practices to escalate. Immersed in a mounting crisis, loyalists had a lot on the line. They had devoted their careers to a logical positivist agenda now under siege from numerous directions. By openly revealing the field's insularity, narrowness, and historical contingency, Gergen had opened a Pandora's Box that threatened to splinter the solidarity of the discipline's practitioners. This threat had to be nipped in the bud.

Within a few weeks—and continuing over the course of several years—conservative voices of the mainstream rose to defend and fortify social psychology's scientific premises (e.g., Greenwald, 1976; Harris, 1976; Manis, 1976; Schlenker, 1974, 1976). In its first issue of 1974, the *Journal of Personality and Social Psychology* published Barry Schlenker's shrill and condescending defense of social psychology's search for covering laws, invariant constants, and transhistorical facts—as the lead article, no less! Schlenker (1974) characterized Gergen's critique as exaggerated, confused, flawed, and inappropriate. According to Schlenker, the case for social psychology as history was "philosophically unsound" (p. 12) and riddled with "misconceptions about the nature of science" (p. 2). Expressing unbridled optimism about the future of social psychology, Schlenker conveyed an unimpeachable reverence for science and accused Gergen of holding social psychology to an unreasonable standard for such a young science. Where others saw a crisis, Schlenker saw a rough patch endemic to all developing sciences trying to establish themselves. Social psychology may be a young and immature science, he concluded, but the field eventually will put these difficulties behind it and grow into a respectable and valid scientific field. Reinscribing the building block metaphor discredited by Kuhn (1970), Schlenker ended by affirming his commitment to the paradigm and calling out those unwilling to make the necessary sacrifice: "The construction process is well underway," he decreed, "and will not be abandoned simply because the stones are heavy and the construction difficult" (1974, pp. 14–15).

Gergen (1973) had indirectly interrogated the question, What kind of life is social life? He arrived at the conclusion that social life is grounded in historical consciousness and cultural contingency. Knowledge about social life—the kind of knowledge that social psychologists attempt to accumulate and disseminate—has a social life of its own insofar as it makes its way into the public consciousness. Once "enlightened" by the findings of social research, people can react by resisting or negating them, and thus, threatening the stability of findings and generalizations over time. Moreover, every age has certain issues or problems endemic to its time and different from previous and subsequent generations. A conscientious social science ought to be concerned about how the work of the field relates to the problems of its time. A social psychology divorced from human affairs—politics, morality, ethics, happiness—would likely be trivial, irrelevant, or useless. Even if one thought some social knowledge could be timeless, wouldn't it be worth considering knowledge that is time-bound? Couldn't such knowledge be useful?

216

According to Kuhn, in the event of a paradigm clash, "each group uses its own paradigm to argue in that paradigm's defense" (1970, p. 93). It is not surprising, then, that Schlenker simply rehashed the principles of positivist philosophy of science. He showed no interest in the problems of his time; indeed, he was stoically unconcerned about how social life (or social science) works in tandem with social research. Instead, he clung to an implacable faith in a disinterested, cumulative scientific method directed at laws of social behavior. Curiously, Schlenker supported his belief in transhistorical regularities in social behavior not by reference to a litany of experimental research findings in social psychology but by the lasting influence of writings about social life by Greek, Roman, German, French, and English philosophers, whose observations he called "hypotheses."

Schlenker impressed me as one of a throng of busy specialists and technical experts—I know many in my field—who believe that the nature of a scientific discipline is clarified by concentrating on its method. Thus, his argument was confined to "the nature" of scientific explanation, regularity, and abstraction. Applying the restricted worldview of positivism, Schlenker implied that the progress of a scientific field is simply a matter of doing more science, keeping busier and busier, collecting more and more data. It didn't seem to matter to Schlenker what data are collected or whether these are relevant to understanding the social difficulties, contradictions, or problems men and women experience in contemporary life. Indeed, Schlenker offered no grounds under which one could reasonably question either the validity or usefulness of the methodological paradigm of social psychology. In light of his fetish for data, any challenge to empiricism would always invite a response that called for more data to be collected under the same premises. Within the closed system of positivism and the closed-mindedness of advocates such as Schlenker, one is hard-pressed to figure out what would count as a legitimate challenge to the domination of the positivist paradigm of research in social psychology. How would one ever know whether the positivist agenda was failing? What would count as falsifying evidence?

Reading between the lines, I detected a scary subtext in Schlenker's article. He made no attempt to mask his disdain for those who would dare question the positivist agenda. The metamessage went something like this: "Leave us alone. Brush up on your science and (positivist) epistemology. Show a greater willingness to work harder. Stop being so negative!" The way I read it, the goal of his article was to discredit Gergen (as naïve, unsophisticated, pessimistic, and uninformed) and dodge the whole question of social psychology's historical and cultural contingency. In the left-hand margin of Schlenker's article, I had written the following question: "Isn't there room for more than one scientific research agenda for social psychology?"

I interpreted "Social Psychology and Science" as a warning to other malcontents. If you're frustrated by social psychology's lack of scientific achievements, it's because you don't understand the nature of science. By reminding readers that attacks on the scientific status of social disciplines have been made before—Gergen's is nothing new—Schlenker (1974) appealed to the solidarity of the discipline and its consensus on the privileged status of positivist epistemology. It was time for the discipline to close ranks and get on with the hard work of doing scientific research, building the "pyramid" of scientific knowledge. The question of whether social psychology can be improved by adopting the historical consciousness that Gergen was seeking is not a question worth taking seriously.

When I started graduate school, I was told that a discipline was a "community of scholars" searching for the truth in a circumscribed domain of collective concern. My professors promoted the idea that a discipline was an evolving community of conversation, deliberation, and inquiry. As a human group, a community of scholars was supposed to do something more than protect the status quo. After all, one's discipline would not remain the same over time. Today's graduate students shape tomorrow's future. What a discipline can become is as important as what it has been in the past. A community of scholars was (supposed to be) a dynamic society respectful of its past and traditions but pointed toward the future, not just "being" but also "becoming"—renewing and reinventing itself, staking out opportunities to expand its mission and scope of influence.

In graduate school, I also was taught to be critical. "Doubt, test, challenge," I was told. But for traditionalists like Schlenker, the impulse to question must be weighed against the demand for loyalty to one's discipline. "Don't make waves," Tucker said to me one day when I complained about one of my other professors. "You have everything to lose and nothing to gain. It's not rational." I guess, then, you could say that Gergen's critique of social psychology's scientific status was not rational either. He was "making waves," engaging in an act of disloyalty. Couldn't he have seen this coming? Wouldn't he have known the mainstream would mark him as an infidel, a danger to the solidarity of the field? Schlenker (1974) was the chosen assassin. His job was to discredit Gergen, show him to be fickle, nitpicky, unsophisticated, and unscientific.

I wonder, am I reading too much into this? Do I see myself in Ken Gergen? Am I afraid that I will be responded to in the same demeaning fashion if I express my own convictions about the poverty of communication science—discredited and cast out of the discipline?

In the months following the publication of Schlenker's article, I eagerly anticipated a follow-up from Gergen or someone sympathetic to his point of view. After all, Gergen had acknowledged the helpful advice of a dozen other social psychologists in preparing his article. I assumed some of these scholars would come to his defense. The gossip mills were churning in Temple's division of social psychology. "There's a lot of turbulence in the field right now," a colleague in social psychology told me. "Gergen rocked the boat. He's got guts. Others not so sympathetic say 'he's got a lot of nerve,' as in 'who does he think he is?'"

I waited patiently for each issue of *JPSP* to arrive, only to be disappointed. As it turned out, nothing more came of "the great debate," at least not on the pages of one of social psychology's elite journals. Apparently, the editors of the journal had washed their hands of the whole matter, giving Schlenker (1974) the last word. Solidarity trumped innovation. More than two years later, a newer and less-esteemed social psychology journal published a symposium inviting both Gergen (1976) and Schlenker to participate (1976). By that time, however, I was already deeply immersed in an intense reading program inspired by the "crisis of confidence."

Convinced that the logic and standards of positivist philosophy of science could not judge fairly the legitimacy of an interpretive social science, I set out to study the philosophical roots of interpretive social science. According to Gergen (1973), the phenomena of social psychology are historically and culturally embedded, and this renders the social sciences "unlike the natural sciences." In response, Schlenker (1974, p. 12) had argued that Gergen's critique was "philosophically unsound," and thus the case for fundamentally distinguishing between the social and natural sciences was without foundation. But Schlenker had stacked the deck by supporting his "philosophical" arguments exclusively with testimony from positivist philosophers of science such as Hempel (1965), Kaplan (1964), and Nagel (1961). Gergen was no help here, because he had not rested his case primarily on philosophical discourse. Was there a philosophical grounding for dividing the social sciences from the natural sciences? What would philosophers working outside positivist philosophy of science say about this issue? I assumed that Gergen was not the only maverick social scientist intent on breaking new ground and introducing alternatives to positivist social science. Others must be waiting in the wings. Where were these other dissenting voices?

Rigor and Imagination

I toss the Gergen-Schlenker file in one of the boxes, lean back in my chair, and close my eyes, allowing memories to flood through me. The Asilomar Conference Center near Monterey Bay, California, comes into view. I see myself walking near the beach with Carol Wilder, a professor from San Francisco whom I met there at a conference on multivariate statistics in 1977. I'm there to give a paper on "Multivariate Analysis of Variance," coauthored with Mary Anne Fitzpatrick (Bochner and Fitzpatrick, 1980), my first doctoral advisee. Carol is there to find out what all the fuss over multivariate statistics is about. By the end of the first day, both of us are bored to tears and decide to take a walk on the beach.

"What are you doing at this conference?" I ask as we stroll along the beautiful, rocky coastline. The sun is setting, casting long shadows across the crystal-clear water. Two dogs are splashing in the water, reminding me of my German shepherd, China. How she would love this!

"I'm not sure. I'm not on the program, and I've never conducted a quantitative study. You could say I'm a curious onlooker. I heard that multivariate statistics was the cutting edge of analyzing communication data, so I came to check it out." Carol bends down and cups some of the soft sand in her hand. "Nice here, isn't it?" She notices how entranced I am by the scene. "The California coast really is special."

"Sure is, and really different from Cape Cod, where I vacation in the summertime. No big rocks there, but a heck of a lot of sand." I think of the rising sand dunes China and I play on during the summer. Why does anyone work when they could be doing this? "Then I take it you're not a methodologist?" I ask, returning to the previous topic.

"No," she chuckles, amused by my observation. "I did my dissertation on the rhetoric of social movements. I'm a sixties survivor, an over-thirty hippie trying to find my place in the university."

"You think you can find a place here with these folks? They don't exactly strike me as aging hippies."

"Ha!" she laughs. "You got that right. But I figure I better get with the program, because there's not much future in rhetoric. That part of the field is dying. I want to be where the action is. Besides, I'm just up the road at San Francisco State, so it didn't cost me much to get here."

"What do you think so far?"

"I confess, I'm in way over my head. To me these guys—they're practically all guys, you know—they're speaking a foreign language." I grin at her sardonic observation, knowing she has a point. She smiles back at me. "But that's not the biggest problem."

"Oh, what is?" I wonder if I'm sounding like Milton.

"I don't see what any of the stuff they're talking about has to do with communication. The papers I've heard belong in a statistics book. In fact, most of them could work comfortably in a statistics department. But I shouldn't be so negative. I'm just going to have to bite the bullet and learn it."

"I hate to be the one to tell you this, but multivariate analysis is not something you can learn in your spare time."

"I realize that. But what choice do I have? I don't want the field to pass me by."

"I think you're asking the wrong question: What do I really want to do?—that's the question you should be asking. What kind of academic identity are you seeking?" I gulp quietly as I ask these questions, realizing how close to home they hit.

"I don't know whether it's academic, but I think there's a frustrated journalist in me."

"Can you think of a way to put that passion to work?"

"Actually, I have already. I did an interview with Colin Cherry that was accepted for publication in *Human Communication Research* [Wilder, 1977]. I had a blast doing that." The excitement shows in her voice. "Hey, it's getting dark," Carol cautions. "We better get back to the conference center."

"Okay, but first let me suggest an idea. You're at San Francisco State, right?" I ask as we reverse direction and head back.

"That's right." Carol's eyes shine in the dimming light. I can tell by her dilating pupils that she really wants to hear this.

"That means you're a short distance from Palo Alto, the location of MRI, which used to be called the Mental Research Institute. Call the MRI and get an appointment with Paul Watzlawick or John Weakland. I could see you doing a series of interviews with the family therapists there, maybe even a book of interviews. That would be so cool."

"You think I could do that?"

"What do you have to lose? Who knows, someone there might be willing to put you in touch with Gregory Bateson. I heard he's living in Santa Cruz and his health is failing. He's one of my heroes. Weakland was a colleague of his when they were working on the double-bind theory of schizophrenia. You see what I'm getting at?"

"Yes, of course. These folks are applying communication theory. If I could get my foot in the door, this could lead to something amazing," she says, beaming from ear to ear. I can see that nothing is going to hold Carol back.

And nothing did. Within a few weeks, Carol had met and interviewed Paul Watzlawick (Wilder, 1978) and struck up friendships with John Weakland and Heinz von Foerster (Wilder, 1988). Within a few months, she had gained access to Gregory Bateson and was planning a national conference at Asilomar to honor his legacy (Wilder-Mott and Weakland, 1981).

Forming Warm Ideas

I open my eyes and walk to the bookcase where I store the volumes of special importance to me. I plan to pack these books last, with exceptional care. I take *Rigor and Imagination: Essays from the Legacy of Gregory Bateson* (Wilder-Mott and Weakland, 1981) from the shelf and turn to my essay, "Forming Warm Ideas" (1981). I am surprised to find a copy of the paper I read at the conference, a condensed version of the published piece, folded inside the first page of my chapter. I recall the weekend I locked myself in my office and drafted that paper, Levine's words circulating through me, wanting finally to express who I took myself to be:

> Like man [sic] himself, [social] science, a creation of man [sic], is unfinished, inconstant, and mutable. The public audience of science commonly assumes that the work of science is to "discover" laws by strictly applying a formal set of rules called the scientific method to observable phenomena called facts. Thus, in ordinary usage, the term scientific is equivalent to factual; the scientific method stands for the objective procedures through which truth is established; and scientific evidence is thought to be infinitely authoritative.
>
> Of course, many people know better. They recognize that the public image of science is a fiction. After all, scientists are human beings. The phenomena that (social) scientists seek to describe are not completely separate from the scientists themselves. The boundary separating internal from external, or subject from object, is drawn arbitrarily. Scientific observations cannot result in objective descriptions because the phenomena observed must be *subjected* to the process of observation in order to be seen and described. Einstein convinced many of his contemporaries that a physicist's frame of reference conditioned observation, making it a relatively rather than absolutely

objective process. Heisenberg further established the idea that scientific activity is recursive by noting that what had been seen also changes the one who is seeing. To these points can be added the vexing question of how observed and observer are transformed as time passes between observation of phenomena (so-called externals), recording of observation as "raw data," descriptions of these data as findings in formal scientific documents, and disseminations of the documents throughout a scientific community. How do these processes—observing, recording, reporting, disseminating—alter the original conception of the "findings"? The end products apparently can never be anything more or less than maps of maps of maps, to borrow Bateson's expression. No pure or simple facts, only apprehended appearances.

Phenomena cannot speak for themselves. They must be spoken for persuasively if science is to advance. Nowhere is this evidenced more clearly than in Feyerabend's (1975) controversial description of the Copernican revolution in physics. Galileo establishes that the earth moves, an outlandish assertion at the time. He accomplishes this feat not by producing unequivocal facts but by using ingenious argumentative ploys, trickery, and even propaganda. So preposterous and counterintuitive was his thesis that no amount of rational deliberation or "hard" facts would have captured the eyes and ears of his contemporaries. Even if they had been available, facts would have had no compelling force, as the epistemology of the day would have prevented observers from seeing them. Galileo had to change the way reality was understood and talked about. Orthodoxy would not turn the tide. So, he *ad hoced* his way through the case, defusing the cosmology of his day and subverting historically derived cognitions by conducting a propaganda campaign, magically maneuvering the facts and shielding an interesting hypothesis by taking liberty with the rules of scientific method. He was sloppy, devious, and superficial, and his muddle-headedness turned out to be bliss (Feyerabend, 1975). What would have happened if he had proceeded according to the rules, if he had let the facts speak for themselves? Feyerabend (1975) answers,

> Galileo succeeds because he did not follow these rules; his contemporaries, with very few exceptions, overlooked fundamental difficulties that existed at the time, and modern science developed quickly and in the "right direction" . . . because of this negligence. *Ignorance was bliss.* Conversely, a more determined application of the canons of scientific method, a more determined search for relevant facts, a more critical attitude, far from accelerating this attitude development, would have brought it to a standstill. (p. 112)

II

I am attempting to establish these three ideas:

1. *Scientific activity—observation, analysis, reporting, etc—is inherently codificational, symbolic, communicational.* All phenomena, no mat-

ter what we call them, are literally appearances. As Bateson implies (1972), we never see the territory because we cannot step onto the terrain without transforming it into a map. Science, then, is inescapably representational.

2. *Scientific progress, especially theoretical advancement, requires ingenuity, passion, intuition, and/or courage. It is doubtful whether these fall under the category of skills to be honed. Certainly, strict insistence on rules will not encourage imagination. Theorizing must be deformalized. The only common denominator among imaginative theorists seems to be artful dodging.*

3. *Science is an open system. Like other developing systems, it continually changes. At each juncture in its evolution a particular science will be confronted by conflict accompanying its changing context. If strict rules are set and followed unyieldingly, adaptability will be threatened, creativity impaired, and progress halted. Direct clashes of ideas will not be easy to tolerate, but without them a science dies, its story ends.*

III

My point is that a science of living things must be aesthetically reasonable, rhythmical, and qualitative, which brings me to a set of distinctly interpretive principles of social science inquiry that I call "Bateson's Rules of Thumb":

1. Study life in its natural setting, being careful not to destroy the historical and interactional integrity of the whole setting.
2. Think aesthetically. Visualize, analogize, compare. Look for patterns, configurations, figures in the rug.
3. Live with your data. Be a detective. Mull, contemplate, inspect. Think about, through, and beyond.
4. Don't be controlled by dogmatic formalisms about how to theorize and research. Avoid the dualisms announced and pronounced by particularizing methodologists and theorists. (They'll fire their shots at you one way or another anyhow.)
5. Be as precise as possible, but don't close off possibilities. Look to the ever-larger systems and configurations for your explanations. Keep your explanations as close to your data and experience as possible.
6. Aim for catalytic conceptualizations; warm ideas are contagious.... We need imagination, not rules; intuition, not technique; warm ideas, not cold facts....

Particularly in the social sciences, where the question of the measurability of phenomena and lawfulness of behavior is so troublesome, what we need is inventive people, not conformists; fertile thinking, not rigid rules to follow. Why must we insist that empirical concepts be assessed and interpreted in terms of quantities? Bateson argued that "quantities are precisely *not* the stuff of complex communication systems," yet we continue to judge concepts mainly according to the criterion of quantifiability.

The question is how to warm to the task of thinking catalytically. At the present time quantification rules. In my opinion, when quantitative methods control thinking, a social field of inquiry runs the risk of being not a marketplace for exhibiting, exchanging, and evolving ideas but rather a depository for dumping instruments, tools, and techniques.

Reflections on a Mentoring Friendship

The sound of a ringing phone awakens me from my reflective reverie. I reach up to my desk from my crouched position on the floor and grab the receiver from its cradle.

"Hello," I answer, clearing my throat.

"Hi Art. Glad I caught you at your office. Do you have time to talk?" I recognize the voice of Bill Rawlins, a former student, now on the faculty at Penn State.

"Sure, Bill," I say. "It's great to hear your voice. Hold on a second." I rise and move toward the chair behind my desk, hopping over several boxes and swinging the cord from the phone around with me. Bill and I always have great conversations, and I want to be as comfortable as possible while we talk. "There, that's better. What's up?"

"I'm just calling to wish you the best on your move to South Florida."

"Thanks, Bill. Sweet of you to think of me, and kind of uncanny that you would call right at this moment."

"What do you mean?"

"Today's my last day in this office. I've been packing books, and when you called I was thumbing through the volume from the Bateson Conference. There's a great picture of you in that book. Damn, you're handsome!"

"Yeah, man, there's one of you too in that hip, brown leather vest you used to wear." We both laugh.

"That conference was so pivotal," Bill continues. "I remember the day you told me about it. I had been taking this course on Kenneth Burke with Dennis Smith. It was late in the afternoon, and I was heading out of the building after class. You came bounding down the stairs, grinning from ear to ear. You stopped me in my tracks on the stairwell, hollering from the floor above. I can still recall the conversation:

"You shouted, 'Carol Wilder just got the funding to hold a conference at Asilomar in honor of Gregory Bateson!'

"'No!' I shrieked as you caught up to me. And you had this look on your face like a parent holding a gift behind his back.

"'Guess who else is going to be there?'

"'Who?'

"'Kenneth Burke!'

"'Holy shit.' I couldn't believe it.

"'Hell yeah!'

"We stood there high fiving, hugging, and celebrating on the staircase as if we had just won the lottery. People passing on the steps thought we were crazy. They couldn't have known what it meant to us to bring together Bateson and Burke, what a watershed moment this would be. Here were these two aesthetically informed, deep-thinking, profoundly original risk takers, the kind of intellectuals you and I embraced, and they were going to be there on the same platform. I wanted to freeze that moment, you know, make the feeling last, but I had to run to catch my train.'"

"It seemed as if you were always running to catch a train," I interrupt.

"You got that right. Graduate school was no walk in the park. Sandi would get me up at a quarter to five in the morning, and I would stagger to the corner to wait for the bus to get me to the train station to catch the Metro that would take me to the 30th Street Station in Philadelphia, where I would grab the subway to the Temple campus. It cost me ten dollars a day in 1975, and my assistantship only paid three thousand."

"That's the same stipend I was getting in 1968. 'Slave labor' we used to call it."

"It wasn't enough to pay the bills—that's for sure," Bill replies.

"As I recall, you didn't come to Temple to study with me."

"That's right. My intention was to study social movements and activism with Herb Simons, but destiny intervened. He went off to Iowa on a study leave and I met you."

"I've always wondered how I came across to you, given my quantitative orientation at the time."

"To be candid, I had been forewarned. Jack Orr, a professor of mine at Delaware and a graduate of Temple, had described you as a fierce empiricist. 'Bochner, he's intense, really intense about social science.' I had this image of a short-haired, crew-cut, button-down guy, a number cruncher, sort of a 1950s nerd, you know, a guy wearing high pants and thick glasses. The first time we met, you blew that all away. You couldn't have been more different from what I expected. You came into the mailroom, looked at me, and said, 'Hey, you're Bill Rawlins. You're going to be in my class.' You stood and talked with me for a while, and we totally clicked. We flat-out clicked. And I'm thinking all that time, this long-haired, bearded, hipped-out guy—shit, man, you mean this is Art Bochner? No way!"

"That's hilarious, Bill," I say, laughing so hard I'm shaking and tears are forming in my eyes.

"We just totally clicked right from the start," he continues. "But that's not to say there weren't moments you scared me. I remember being outside of class one day. I think we were on break, and you had just mentioned six books right before the break—this book, that book, another book. So my head is spinning, and I'm thinking I'll never be able to read that number of books and articles quickly enough. You walked out and noticed me standing alone with this dejected look on my face. 'What are you looking so glum about?' you asked. After I told you, well, you paused, put your arm around me, and said 'Relax, Bill,' I've been at this for ten years. You'll get to it in plenty of time.' That comment lifted me right out of my funk."

"I would have been in a permanent funk if I'd had your kind of commute every day."

"It was physically taxing, no doubt about it. But I was on an existential journey."

"What do you mean?"

"I mean a quest to live a more reflective, authentic life and to appreciate the mysteries of being alive. I don't know exactly how to define it. I was growing up and broadening my horizon, searching for something that would give my life meaning in the long run. Graduate school opened my eyes to new possibilities and opportunities. It put me in touch with the choices I had about what kind of person I could become."

"That sounds something like what the phenomenologists mean when they talk about the ground of one's being," I say. "How would you describe this quest? What moved it along?"

"Good questions. I've always loved to read. As an undergraduate, I read a lot of comparative literature. Then I came into your theory class and started reading all this social science that focused on how social life actually is lived, which also is the essence of literature, only social science wasn't fiction. In your theory class, we talked about the good life and how the mission of the human sciences ought to be to improve the human condition. You placed meanings and values at the center of communication studies, and that touched me where I live and breathe. Right on, let's do work that makes life better, helps people become more aware and better understand their everyday existence."

"Did it bother you that we were looking at these issues within the frame of empiricism?"

"That never entered my mind. I thought you were giving us what Burke [1941/1967] called 'equipment for living.' Certainly, the frame in those days was the hypothetico-deductive model, but you were such a reflective person and the readings were so wide and sweeping. I never experienced what you were saying as an attempt to impose some kind of imperial authority. The scientific methods part was not all that central. You wanted us to wrestle with some of the constrictions on human happiness and how communication could be used to cope with the contradictions of everyday living. I took these issues to heart."

"At what point did you know the academic life was what you wanted?"

"You used to say, 'A PhD is not a career, it's a way of life.'"

"Yeah, I learned that from my advisor, Ray Tucker," I interrupt.

"In those days, you'd quote him a lot. Anyway, after a short time I could see that graduate school wasn't going to work for me unless I gave myself to it completely. I had some tough choices to make."

"That's when you came to me with your confession, right?"

"You mean about playing in the band?"

"Uh-huh. I remember thinking how courageous you were to speak that candidly with so much on the line."

"It was a decisive moment, that's for sure. I realized I couldn't give myself fully to these two separate worlds—a life as a musician and an academic life. I had to make a choice, at least in the short run."

"The way you dealt with your love for both worlds spoke volumes about you as a person, about your character. I saw the extent of your commitment to an academic life and realized you were going to be an exceptional student. Of course, I couldn't help but notice the angst you felt about giving up your place in the band, because music was in your soul."

"Yeah man, playing music energizes me. I wanted you to know I was serious about my work, like you, but my life as a whole extends beyond my work as a teacher and scholar. A year later, I got a call from my friends asking me to come back and play after the tragic loss of their drummer. I thought I could handle it at that point, so I agreed, and it turned out the whole experience of playing in the band on weekends animated and invigorated me. When you and I got to know each other better and you invited me to your house, I witnessed how much you love music—love to listen and be moved by it—and I thought, right on, he gets how important music can be, how it can rouse and electrify."

Bill's voice intensifies as he talks about his love for music and playing in the band. His enthusiasm is contagious, and as we converse I feel myself emerging from the sadness in which I had been immersed. "I love hearing your enthusiasm and passion when you talk about these things," I say.

"You know, Art, when I look back at that first year I think how lucky I was to get through it."

"Tell me more about that period," I encourage.

"Right from the beginning I felt humbled. I was thrown into this cohort of indelible and unforgettable characters," he chuckles. "They could have been characters from a novel, right off the page."

"You mean Dorothy, George, and Linda?"

"Ken and Betty too. They scared me—the way they seemed to know everything. They were well spoken and carried themselves with this aura that said, 'I belong here.' They seemed to have all the jargon down. Maybe they were performing for you, but I wasn't sophisticated enough to see that. I was very tuned into ideas but wasn't practiced in expressing myself—you know, acting the part."

"Yeah, but you had this rural authenticity that was charming and real, to say nothing of your keen intellect and drive."

"It didn't feel charming to me. I felt like a babe in the woods, and I was feeling intense pressure from old friends who didn't get why I was doing this. They had real jobs, decent raincoats, and money in their pockets."

"At what point did it come together for you? When did you start feeling that you belonged?"

"I don't know that there was a precise moment, though I do recall one night in your theory class. We were discussing Kuhn's *The Structure of Scientific Revolutions*. I asked whether anyone had ever studied the implicit subtext of the book, how the book itself represents the idea of the book? I blurted out something like, 'Isn't Kuhn using his theory about how paradigms shift to shift a paradigm, the paradigm of scientific progress?' And you dignified my question. You acknowledged me, took me seriously."

"That was just like you, Bill, to see the ironic and metalevel of things," I interrupt.

"I guess that's how my mind works. But what I was getting at," Bill picks up where he left off, "is what an important part of teaching that is—dignifying students, I mean! That's what I try to do when I teach. It was a small moment in the total scheme of things, but I remember thinking, yeah, I can do this. Art thinks I can. I'm growing as a thinker and I love the challenge."

"'Do what you love.' I say that to students all the time. 'Go with your passion. If this isn't what you love, find another line of work that is.'"

"But getting back to your question, Art, I tell my students that the comps are a major turning point. It all came together for me when I took my comps. That was the smartest I had ever felt. When I completed comps I felt prepared for whatever came next. I knew I wanted to do something empirical on friendship that would involve thick description and interpretive methods of inquiry, something that centered on communicative practices of friendship, how friendship is accomplished."

"Remind me how you settled on friendship as the topic for your dissertation."

"It started in the middle of your seminar on close relationships. You had us read this article, 'In Search of Friendship' by a Canadian anthropologist, Robert Paine, which was published in the anthropology journal *Man* [1969]. I think of it as a representative moment of how you help students educate themselves."

"What do you mean?"

"It's your method of teaching graduate students. I doubt if there was anyone else in our field who at that time could have handed me that essay. That article changed my life. It absolutely galvanized my intellect, capturing the love I have for my friends and at the same time the questions and quandaries I had been facing as I became more and more an academic and found myself dislocating myself from my friends and from my past."

"I opened the barn door, or Paine did, and you took off."

"Yeah man, but it was not a smooth ride from there. I wasn't sure how to translate all these great ideas into a dissertation project. Like a lot of students, I expected you to shape it for me, but you didn't seem to want to do that. I guess you thought I'd be better off figuring it out for myself."

"Ha! You give me more credit than I deserve. The truth is I didn't know what to tell you. I'd never done a project like yours. We were making it up as you went along. I knew that nobody in our discipline had done what you were doing—an interpretive study aimed at thick description—and if you could pull it off, you'd break new ground for interpersonal and relationship research."

"In the meantime I experienced some dark days. You'd meet with me whenever I asked, but I couldn't get you to tell me what to do. Then one night Sandi said, 'I don't think Art's going to tell you how to do this, and I don't think you want him to.' That was another turning point."

"That's a great story, Bill, one that every graduate student should hear. Of course, some students need more guidance and hand holding than others. I had no doubt you would figure it out, but I also knew I couldn't leave you stranded on an island."

"You were available when I needed you, which showed during your sabbatical."

"Fate was on our side. You had a job interview at Hope College, and I was on leave not far away at Michigan State, so we planned a summit on your dissertation."

"Another decisive moment," Bill interrupts.

"I didn't do much."

"I needed to talk through what I was doing. You were my sounding board. You listened, heard it, and told it back to me, and I left totally rejuvenated."

"I was lifted too. Suddenly it dawned on me that what you had done was to create a new methodology for how to study and analyze relationships—interviewing couples separately, then together, and again if possible, and building a dialectical theory, the first of its kind, from the texts of the interviews [Rawlins, 1983a, 1983b]. At the time, I was completing a draft of my essay on interpersonal bonding [Bochner, 1984], discussing some of the contradictions that couples have to cope with in close relationships, and here were these data, these texts that you had produced, which showed friends in the process of dealing with some of these dilemmas, socially constructing a frame for understanding what was happening in their lives."

"In retrospect, I can see how we were in sync, like a couple of jamming musicians."

"Social science already had breadth; you were giving it depth, which was sorely needed. I was thrilled by the prospects of what this could mean for the future of social science inquiry on long-term relationships. You were blazing a path for others to follow. You might never get the credit you deserve for it, but I knew in my heart this was an epiphany for those of us who wanted to do a more personally meaningful kind of social science."

"Damn, that's a mouthful. I'm glad you feel that way."

"And I have data to prove it, namely the two monographs you published in our discipline's mainstream, empiricist journals [Rawlins, 1983a, 1983b]. Publishing interpretive studies in positivist journals that favor quantitative research—that was quite an achievement. You set an example for others to follow."

"Art, I wish we could keep talking, but I've got to start for home. Brian and Sandi are waiting on dinner for me. Before I go, can you bring me up to date on 'Perspectives on Inquiry,' the essay you said you were starting to write last time we talked?"

229

"I'm sorry. I had no idea it had gotten so late. You should go. We can discuss my chapter next time we talk."

"Can you give me a quick preview of your thesis?"

"I'm claiming that we need to change the terms of our argument with empiricists. Our dissent should not be about methods but about purposes. Now you better go, Bill. When I get time for a real break in a couple of weeks, I'll call and fill you in on the details. We'll take an academic interlude and try to keep the conversation going, as Richard Rorty [1979] would say."

CHAPTER TEN

Life's Forward Momentum

> But in a story, which is a kind of dreaming, the dead
> sometimes smile and sit up and return to the world.
> *Tim O'Brien (1990, p. 225)*

The phone conversation with Bill Rawlins awakens memories of other Temple graduate students. Seeking communion with these memories, I close my eyes, turning my thoughts inward and floating along the river of my past. At first, unfocused images rush past me. Then abruptly they slow and I see myself standing in front of a room full of familiar faces. I dwell on each face for a moment, imagining myself reliving a special moment that we shared together. I linger for a while in each scene before returning to the original room of faces. Surveying each face, I continue down the river of memory, attempting to organize and draw meaning from the swirling images. Some of the memories make me chuckle; others bring tears to my eyes. I see longing and hunger in these faces, a desire to cram as much experience and knowledge as they can into the brief time we have together. As I glance across the room, the faces suddenly begin to blur and fade. Gradually, each face dissolves into mine. Frightened by that image, I open my eyes for a few seconds to break from it. When I shut them again the room is still there, but now it's empty except for one face that is partially hidden from view. The image narrows, zooming closer. Slowly, a clear image of the face emerges. "Carol, Carol Gifford? Is that you?"

Opening my eyes again, I think about how fortunate I've been to cross paths with so many talented and fascinating students. It felt exhilarating to retrieve memories of them—the enchantment, challenges, even the disappointments and uncertainties of a life of teaching and mentoring. Without students there is no teaching or learning, and clearly it was my connection to these particular students that gave stability and conviction to the fragile meanings that sustained my academic life at Temple. Their faces had been significantly folded into my own. In important respects, our lives were comingled. Perhaps the disappearance of their faces—each slowly dissolving into an image of my face—signaled that our work together was finished but that I would carry what I had learned from them forward. It may also have suggested that my memories would never be perfectly clear. They were as much inventions as they were representations. Each recollection was a re-creation of what I had observed or experienced. How much of what we remember is a product of our imagination? How much of recollection is re-creation? The images seemed real enough—vivid in their immediacy—but they were, after all, images, symbolic re-creations mobilized by the workings of mental and perceptual phenomena.

Still, one face, a distinct one, remained in the room, and I knew that was no accident. Of all the students I'd encountered, Carol Gifford had left the most indelible impression. Why did her image linger after all the others had left? Was our work together incomplete, unlike my other students?

Carol Gifford wasn't the most intellectually gifted student, nor was she the most ambitious one, though she was by no means lacking in smarts or bereft of drive. But these weren't the most important things about her. She possessed something more significant, something I equate with character.

What does it mean to say a person has character? Doesn't everyone have character? Certainly, everyone has some unique characteristics that, taken together, form the person's individuality. Novelists and playwrights seek to develop fully formed characters, individuals with depth, purpose, and physical and emotional idiosyncrasies. Ideally, the reader or viewer can recognize each character's intentions, motivations, and vulnerabilities. And not all characters are good. Some are evil. The good ones often reflect another sense of character, what I call moral fiber. In a good play, one or more of the actors usually face a situation in which their character is tested. This is when character (in the sense I mean it) shows itself. When a person must act under duress, make a critical choice in a situation in which no option appears clearly desirable— between a rock and a hard place—that's when character comes to the surface. If a person lives long enough, sooner or later some unforeseen circumstance—some blow of fate—will arise. When life's contingencies weaken and make her vulnerable, that's when her character is tested. What will she do to preserve her dignity and integrity?

In 1979, I promised Carol I would pass on her story to future generations of students and scholars so that they could learn from it. I suspect that's why she is still hanging around my consciousness. I haven't yet satisfied that vow. 'The time is now,' I hear her saying. Oh, how I wish Carol were here in the flesh to tell the story herself, but she's not. I have to tell it. Unable to bring Carol back to life, I believe the best I can do is make an effort to be true to the plot of her life and allow you to experience what it was about her that made such a lasting impression on me. I want to breathe life back into Carol symbolically, show you her humanity—her human *being*—as I experienced it: what she evoked and awakened in her relations with others; how she enacted freedom, refusing to put aside her own convictions and desires in order to satisfy other people's expectations; and the openness and trust with which she faced the burdens life dealt her.

Urgent News

When Carol returned to Temple to complete her undergraduate degree she was approaching her fortieth birthday. "I hate when they call me an adult learner," she told me the first time we met. "Yes, I'm older than most of the other students, but I feel that I'm as eager, energetic, and capable as any of them. We're all students.

It's not as if some of us are adults and others are children or adolescents. Besides, I refuse to think of the years I spent raising my daughter as a sacrifice I made on the altar of motherhood. Those years weren't wasted. I knew what I was doing then, and I know what I'm trying to do now. I'm here to get an education so I can make my mark on the world. If my years as a mom put me behind schedule, so be it. I'll just have to move faster and recover the time I lost."

Eventually, I learned that once Carol made up her mind, there was no hurdle she couldn't leap over. She hit the ground running and moved swiftly through her undergraduate coursework, establishing herself as one of our best students. In the middle of my course on family communication, she asked me to be her advisor and informed me that she wanted to apply to the graduate program. "My goal is to complete a doctorate," she said. "I don't know whether I'll teach, but I want to do research that will help families understand the importance of communication and maybe do community work."

I became Carol's mentor, and she moved steadily through her undergraduate and MA programs, and the coursework for her PhD. In September, a few weeks before she was scheduled to sit for her comprehensive examination, Carol came to see me during my office hours. She entered with a worried look on her face.

"What's wrong?" I asked.

"I have breast cancer," she blurted out, still standing near the door of my office. "Now there, I've said it. I've been agonizing over how to tell you," she continued, walking toward my desk.

Shocked by her disclosure, I fumbled for words. "Are you okay?" I asked. I felt overcome with sadness, but was determined not to upset her by being too emotional. *Is this the right way to respond?*

I instinctively stood. She reached toward me, and I held her tight while fighting back tears. "Sit down," I said, motioning toward the chair next to my desk and pulling up a seat next to it for myself. "Tell me more. How long have you known? What's the prognosis?" I feel as if I'm firing questions at her without thinking. *Why am I being so direct when I know I should avoid upsetting her?*

"I only found out last week, but I should have known much earlier. I made a terrible mistake."

"What do you mean?"

"About a year ago I felt a lump in my breast when I was showering. I went to my doctor and he felt it too. 'It a hard lump, but quite small,' he told me. 'It's likely a fibroid cyst that will disappear over time. Let's just keep an eye on it, and if you notice it getting bigger, come back.' I was relieved that he wasn't alarmed, so I went home and put it out of my mind. Then, last month I touched it again and got worried, because it felt bigger. I went back to the doctor, and this time he ordered tests. A few days later I received a call to come to his office. Next thing I knew he was telling me the lump was malignant cancer and had spread into the lymph nodes. That means the cancer is at an advanced stage. They want me to start chemotherapy immediately."

"That idiot doctor."

"I don't blame the doctor," Carol said. "I blame myself." She paused to catch her breath. "Actually, I'm trying not to blame anyone. What good would that do?"

"I see your point, but I can't help thinking he should have erred on the side of caution. Are you going to have surgery?"

"I'll have a lumpectomy, but nothing radical. The big worry is how much the cancer has spread. I have to admit that the prognosis doesn't look good. But there is something positive to come of this, I think."

"What do you mean?" I asked, doubting whether cancer can ever be a good thing.

"I have a dissertation topic!" she said smiling. "I want to study marriages in which the wife has been diagnosed with breast cancer. Frankly, my husband and I have not been dealing well with this. We're having lots of conflicts, and some of the conversations have been extremely difficult. He's as unsettled as I am, and our fights are affecting our sex life, our communication, and our happiness. We're committed to making our way through the maze of cancer, but right now, I can't say we're coping effectively. I want to understand how families deal with breast cancer. I've met a couple of women at the oncology center who are going through this, and they've shared amazing stories with me. I can see that I'm not alone—other women have many of the same difficulties communicating with their husbands that I'm experiencing."

"That's a great idea, Carol. It will make a fantastic dissertation project."

"I knew you'd say that, so I've already started reviewing the literature and thinking about how to conduct interviews. I want the husbands in the project too. I'm so glad you trust me to do this, Art. For the first time I feel that I have a calling, something I can contribute to help others as well as myself."

"Then let's do it. We can have a meeting to outline your prospectus together whenever you feel ready."

"I'm ready when you're ready."

Carol completed her comps and prospectus within a few months and started conducting interviews the following winter. As far as I knew, the study was moving along well. Occasionally, she left notes in my mailbox bringing me up to date on the interviews and on other literature she was finding on her topic. She didn't talk about the chemotherapy treatments, and I didn't inquire about them. I suppose I was intentionally avoiding the topic. She was the first person I'd known who had been diagnosed with cancer. Later I would wonder how I could have allowed myself to stay in the dark so long. Couldn't I have offered her greater comfort, acknowledgment, and companionship? Had I abandoned her, left her to suffer the indignity of chemotherapy treatments alone?

If Not Now, When?

In early May, Carol called to schedule a face-to-face meeting. I assumed we would use the meeting to talk through an outline of the chapters of her dissertation. As it turned out, she had other things on her mind.

"I have something I need to say to you," she began, and I noted the worried look on her face. "I could have told you over the phone, but I wanted to tell you in person." She was staring directly into my eyes and her forewarning sent an ominous chill down my spine.

"I've stopped the chemotherapy treatments," she stated abruptly, pausing to gauge my response as she slowly brought her eyes level with mine.

"Does this mean the cancer is in remission?" I asked, hoping for the best but fearing the worst.

"No, Art. The cancer is still there," she said without a hint of the dejection I was feeling upon hearing this news.

"Then why are you stopping? What are your doctors advising?" I asked in rapid-fire.

"The doctors want me to continue the drugs, but I've decided against further treatment. The drugs were giving me mouth sores, infections, and nausea. I lost my hair and was throwing up constantly. I couldn't walk from one room in my house to the next without having to sit down and rest. When I looked in the mirror, I didn't recognize myself: 'Who is this person I'm looking at? I want the old Carol back. Where did she go?'"

"Oh, Carol, that's horrible. I'm so sorry." I said. "But isn't chemotherapy your best hope of survival?"

"Yes, it is. From the beginning, though, I realized chemotherapy was a long shot and the cancer was eventually going to kill me. But I wanted to finish my dissertation and squeeze out as much time with my family as I could. Then I found I couldn't do either very well while I was in treatment. I couldn't concentrate on my research, and I was becoming a burden to my family. That's not how I want to live. So I decided, while I'm alive I'm not going to let my whole life revolve around being a cancer patient. 'No more drugs for me,' I told my doctor last week, and hopefully no more nausea, chills, and fever! I want to be able to enjoy my daughter and my family. I've rented a cottage on Long Beach Island, and my daughter and I are heading down there next week. We'll stay the entire summer, and my husband will be there on weekends."

"You're very brave." I said, wondering whether that was an appropriate thing to say at this time.

"No, I'm not. If I were brave, I'd stay on the medications and try to tough it out. Maybe I'd be the miracle case or at least get a few more years of life if the cancer did go into remission."

"How has your family reacted to your decision?"

"They'd like to keep me around as long as possible. However, they don't want me to suffer. It's a terrible contradiction—one of life's burdens that nobody relishes having to face. We've talked through the options, and we've cried a lot. It's been good for me to get things out into the open and to experience the people I love really listening to me. I told them what I'm telling you, that cancer taught me a lesson. I've learned what's important in life and what I want. Cancer has deepened my capacity to differentiate between what is essential and what is trivial. I've thought a lot about the quote you gave us from Primo Levi [1985]: 'If not now, when?'"

"Actually, it originated with Hillel the Elder. It's one of my favorites," I interrupt.

"And mine too," Carol continues. "My family is probably tired of hearing it from me. I've used it as my main argument for going off these crippling medications. I've had to remind them that when you are stricken with a fatal illness, you can't hide any longer from the finiteness of life. *When* becomes *now*—or never! Knowing that cancer will kill me makes each day take on greater urgency. Ironically, though, as you realize that the number of days remaining in your life is shrinking, your awareness of what you want to do with the days you have left expands. You become aware of the limits of life but also of the freedom you may not have exercised. I'm mindful now that I've bit off more than I can chew. As a result, I've had to make some tough choices. The first was to shift my identity away from that of a patient and to reclaim my desire to complete my life on my own terms. I know not everyone would look at it this way, but the way I see it chemotherapy would extend my life, but it would not complete it. I could still end up feeling as if my life were incomplete."

"I have to write this down," I say, jotting notes on a yellow pad. "The importance of feeling one's life is complete," I repeat, talking as I write. "What a keen distinction, Carol. I want to remember that. It's something few of us ever imagine but most of us truly desire—the feeling of completion at the end of life. It reminds me of the question I've asked students in my seminars—you know, about what it means to live a good life."

She smiled, apparently recalling the discussion. "Yeah, our class had a vigorous debate about it but couldn't come to any agreement."

"Well, I think you've given one possible definition of a life well lived. Death ends a person's life, but it doesn't necessarily complete it. You're suggesting that a person may have an opportunity to do something that makes her believe her life is complete before she dies."

"Yes, I know that's what I want—a sense of completion. In one of your seminars we were talking about Erikson's [1968] theory of identity crisis, and you said something about the desire to be the author of your own life or at least to feel that way. As I've gone through this experience I've returned to that idea time and again." I take notice of how animated Carol is as she says these words and how she's speaking with more ease and composure.

"Can you elaborate? What does it mean to author your own life?"

"I'm planning to author the last chapter of my life. I won't allow my doctors to write it, not any longer. Their intentions are good; they're polite and they sure know a lot about this illness. But there's a big gap between us. They treat my body, but they ignore my soul. I don't think they really want to know anything beyond what the blood tests and scans are telling them. I would love it if they acknowledged the wider context of my illness, but they don't. They can't seem to understand anything beyond a patient's body. They see cancer as a disease that spreads from one organ to the next. What they don't see is how it spreads beyond the body, interrupting the course of a patient's life and threatening to contaminate her whole life world. Maybe it would be different if my doctors let me into their hearts or if they talked with me rather than at me. I doubt if that would save me, but it might alleviate the loneliness I feel when I'm in their presence.

"The loneliness, that's the most terrifying part of this whole experience, even worse than the chemotherapy. I've had enough of all this, the loneliness and isolation of the medical treatments, the physical pain, the emotional conflicts at home. I have to put a stop to it, change the momentum, and turn in a different direction. Don't get me wrong—I have no illusions; I know I can't cure myself of illness. But I can at least try to author this last chapter of my life, providing the people closest to me consent to the plot I have in mind. It hasn't been easy, but I've forced myself to look back over my whole life and see where it was leading, so maybe I can bring it to a fitting close. That's how I made the decision to spend the last months of my life in intimate contact with my family, especially with my daughter.

"The other day, I was sitting in my office at home meditating on the predicament I was facing. I recalled your lecture on the importance of creating firm and lasting meanings. It really hit home, what you said about how human beings are the only animals that have to create their own meanings and how these meanings had to be convincing enough to feel a sense of purpose and security in the world."

I respond, "That was Ernest Becker's idea of *Homo Poeta* [1968], the poetic challenge we all face in creating meanings that can sustain us." As soon as I say this I want to take it back. This is not the time to intellectualize Carol's epiphany. Professor Bochner is not who I want to be in this conversation.

"That's the question I asked myself: What meanings truly sustain me?" Carol continues, ignoring my intrusion. "Which meanings can provide a sense of completion to my life? Suddenly what I wanted became clear to me. My family is an expression of the meanings that have sustained me. What we have become as a family is something I helped cultivate. To some degree, every family creates itself, and my family is no exception. I like to think of myself as the conductor and our family as my greatest composition. Some of my friends tell me, 'Carol, your family is a real piece of work'—and I have to agree." Carol chuckles to herself, and I crack up too.

For a moment I feel a sense of comic relief from the heaviness of the conversation. In the momentary silence, as we pause to catch our breath, we stare into each other's eyes with a sense of recognition that this is one of those conversations that will live on in the memory of each of us. The conversation feels like a door opening between Carol's mind and mine. I feel as if each of us is thinking and feeling our way into the other's house of being, touching each other's humanity. I wonder whether I'm up to such a momentous task, something for which my professional duties had not trained me. She's definitely making it possible for me

237

to experience her experience, which is touching me deeply, but this is the closest I've been to another person's death, and I feel utterly helpless and ill prepared.

"That's it in a nutshell, Art. I want the last chapter of my life to be a meaningful conversation with my family. They represent the meanings that have sustained me and what I will be leaving behind. At the very least, we are a cocreation, one of which I am really proud. They've listened to me say these things, and they're supporting me one hundred percent."

"Meaningful conversation, that's a wonderful ideal, Carol. For what it's worth, I'm convinced you've made the right decision. The affirmation of your family seems crucial."

"But I am worried about one thing," Carol declared, her furrowed brow catching my attention. She proceeded cautiously, saying, "I'm concerned that I may not finish my dissertation before I die. I'm going to work on it at the beach and hope to have it nearly finished by the end of the summer. But if I don't finish, I hope you won't be disappointed in me."

I wipe the tears forming in the corner of my eyes with the tips of my fingers. "Disappointed? Are you kidding? I could never be disappointed in you, Carol. I'm as proud of you as any student I've ever known. You're the first student to work with me who has chosen to study something so emotionally close to her own lived experience. Regardless of what happens to you this summer or next year, I will be sharing your story with other students and colleagues the rest of my life. I will tell them how you chose to study the marital relationships of women with breast cancer because you were a woman with breast cancer who experienced conflicts in your marriage that you had not anticipated. Your work and your story will be an inspiration to other women and students." I paused and looked away, clearing my throat. *Am I acting appropriately?* I'm talking about a future that she will not share with me—am I making her sad? When I looked up, I saw a big grin covering her face. I continued, "You've emboldened me. From now on, I'm going to insist that students who work with me follow your lead by doing research that is personally meaningful to them, projects that originate in their own personal experience."

"I'm so relieved to hear that, Art. Now I can go away for the summer with a clear mind. Even if I don't finish, I'll know that the story of the struggles women like me face will not end with my death."

In the middle of the summer, I received a card from Carol inscribed with the following brief message. "Life is good. I'm blessed to have this precious time with my family. Walking on the beach each day with my daughter, I am in touch with the mystery and majesty of the universe—the crashing waves, the endless sky, the sounds and sights of nature's splendor. I realize my life is but a blink in time, a twitch on the face of eternity. Love, Carol."

One day, early in the fall semester, I received a call from Carol. She told me she was in the hospital and wanted to see me the next day if possible. "There isn't much time left," she said. "The doctors say that I may not live more than another few days. I want to see you before I die, Art. It's important to me. Can you visit tomorrow?"

"Yes, of course. I want to see you too."

Peace of Mind

Readying myself to visit Carol in the morning, I sit in the stillness of the night, reflecting on the enduring meanings of our conversations and my first close encounter with a dear friend standing at the edge of death. The imminence of Carol's death made our connection feel intimate in a way I'd never experienced. I didn't know what to say or how to act, but I trusted Carol to lead the way. She had become like an older sister to me, and I took my cues from her, counting on her to guide me. In her presence I was the student and she was the teacher. I wondered whether other people occupying my side of an end-of-life relationship felt as helpless and uninformed as I did. Death is inevitable, yet we do little to prepare people to interact compassionately in close-to-death relationships, when the caregiver needs to feel useful and affirming. Do we assume that one "naturally" knows what to say or do? Or are we so terrified of our own death that we can't tolerate the practicing of dying? Most of the time, we distance ourselves from death, refusing to face the tragic contradictions of life as a symbolic creature. Split in two, torn between a finite body and a symbolic self, we invest enormous energy hiding from the most basic truth of human existence (Becker, 1973).

Carol taught me that living close to death did not necessitate turning away from life. She was determined to squeeze the most meaning out of the remaining days of her life. Funeral services remind us that "in the midst of life, we are in death . . . ashes to ashes, dust to dust." Carol seemed to be saying "in the midst of death, I choose life." Resisting the alienation of chemotherapy treatments, Carol exercised her desire for renewal by refusing further treatment. The temptation to feel alive in the midst of dying was too alluring. When death announced itself, calling out, "Here I am," Carol answered back, "I will not settle for an empty life." Cancer was going to kill her, but she wouldn't allow it to deaden her spirit. Instead of keeping the idea of her own death at a distance, she allowed it to be a part of her ongoing consciousness. Death had inched closer and closer until it was standing right in front of her. Now she could, without delay, evaluate her life and make plans from the standpoint of her own finitude. Procrastinating away her life was no longer an option. Knowing her death was imminent, she was freed from any question about what to do about death. The only question that mattered was what to do about life, the same question all of us face, whether we are at the beginning, middle, or end of life.

I recalled the dream in which Dr. Levine reminded me that a long life was not necessarily a meaningful one (see Chapter 8). But what is a meaningful life, and how can we know it's meaningful while we're living it? Carol wanted to conduct research that could be useful to other people faced with a crisis similar to the one she had been forced to endure as a married woman with breast cancer. She wanted to leave something of value for other women and other families—a legacy. Her body would not live on, but her influence and helpfulness could, as could the virtues she had instilled in her family.

Ernest Becker (1973) refers to this urge to produce something meaningful over the course of one's life as "an immortality project." In *The Denial of Death* (1973) he analyzes the ways in which humans seek "heroism," a term he uses synonymously with the ideal of a personally meaningful life. What each person needs, argues Becker, is to feel secure in her self-esteem, to achieve and maintain "warm feelings" about herself. Because a person's self-worth is constituted symbolically (Becker, 1973, p. 3), and most of us are not consciously aware of what we want or need to achieve it, we have to rely on the societies in which we live to establish a reward structure that can fulfill our earthly need for heroism. But culture rarely gives its members their due. The cultural hero system is not designed to meet each person's desire to achieve a sense of cosmic specialness. What a huge strain it can become to justify yourself as an object of primary value in the universe (Becker, 1973). "We disguise our struggle," writes Becker, "by piling up figures in a bank book to reflect privately our sense of heroic worth. Or by having only a little better home in the neighborhood, a bigger car, brighter children. But underneath throbs the ache of cosmic specialness no matter how we mask it in concerns of smaller scope" (1973, p. 4).

Carol had risen to the occasion by searching her own lived history for clues about how she had rained her particular talents on the world (especially in the context of her closest relationships) and how these talents had been expressed over the course of her life. The meanings that sustained her were personal, though they appeared to rest somewhere between the secular and the sacred dimensions of her life. Her family was a living embodiment of the expression of the meaning of her life and the legacy she would be leaving behind when she died.

I didn't have Carol's precious family experience on which to ground meanings that could sustain me. I wasn't even convinced that a person ultimately could recognize something akin to what Becker (1971, p. 187) called "authentic talent" and discover once and for all "how to work it on the world." Life seemed to me too saturated by chance and contingency to anticipate that degree of self-awareness. I had grown up in the presence of a father whose sense of self-worth rested mainly on his work. Living in his presence and watching him paint signs, I saw a man who appeared happiest when he was working and who insisted on completing each job, no matter how small, as well as he could. He needed to make a living to feed his family, but his greatest pleasure was not derived from the modest income he earned but rather from the praise he received from his clients. He didn't have to tell me that my work should reveal my integrity and self-discipline. He showed it to me every time he painted a sign. There were many ways in which I wanted my life to be different from my father's, but this was not one of them.

I wanted to do work that had integrity and, thus, could give me warm feelings about myself. I wanted my work to contribute to making a better society and a more meaningful life for myself and for other people, especially those who enter life without some of the advantages with which I was blessed. As a graduate student, I had been drawn to social science because it seemed to be the best way to bring philosophy down to earth. Philosophy was too divorced from life as it actually is lived in this world. The empirical study of human beings and human life, however, offered the possibility of producing knowledge that was relevant to maximizing human meanings and promoting life itself as a value by focusing on the creation of human meanings. But eventually I realized that disciplines like psychology, sociology, and communication promoted a restricted view of empirical research. Groping for scientific respectability, these disciplines assigned priority to method and precision on the atomistic model of the physical sciences (Becker, 1968), producing narrowly focused technicians who accumulated mountains of data largely for its own sake. This was no longer the kind of social science that I could believe in and find meaningful.

Carol Gifford's candor, vulnerability, and trust in me made me feel in my heart what I knew in my mind: Life is not endless, and one can never be fulfilled without acting assertively on the sources of meaning within one's self. Some of these sources of meaning will be inherited, and many will have been socially conditioned. But I firmly and resolutely rejected the notion that the meanings to which a person is attached reflect the kind of repetition of the past that Freud (1915) had theorized. As Otto Rank (1958) had observed, the belief in a strict determinism repudiates personal autonomy, closes down possibilities for change, and negates life itself. Carol's decision to reject chemotherapy in favor of what she believed to be a fitting completion to her life distinctly expressed what Rank (1945) had called a "will to change." She had taken a stand on who she took herself to be. Approaching the crossroads of life and death, she chose continuity and a meaningful completion over the invasive treatments that had interrupted and endangered her striving to put something meaningful into her world and take something meaningful out of it. Listening to Carol bravely affirm the importance of what she could still do to make her life feel complete, I had witnessed a person taking control of her life and making it her own by filling it with meanings of her own making. She couldn't alter the facticity of human mortality, but she could transform the discontinuity and pain she had been experiencing into the kind of continuity, connection, and completion that would bring peace of mind to her as she neared the end of her life.

An Academic Pause

It's hard for me to know how much Carol's will to change affected my own. Carol's illness occurred during a period when I was continuing to struggle with the integrity of my own work. Compared to the adversity that Carol had faced, my academic struggle seemed trivial and unimportant. Nevertheless, this was the life I was living, and the question of how well I could live it mattered to me.

In fact, watching how Carol coped with her circumstances made it even more significant to me. As a witness to Carol's allegiance to the life she had lived—to the truth of that life—I viewed her actions as an affirmation of what living a good life could mean. Accepting Carol's invitation to participate as a significant other in the final chapter of her life, I felt as if I was touching a dimension of the human condition that had so far eluded me. Nothing in my life as a social scientist had prepared me for the heartbreak and sorrow that I was feeling. I felt at once both scared and edified. I was afraid I would fail to live up to Carol's expectations, but I was also buoyed by the urgency and poignancy of her responses to her illness and impending death. I was learning about the human condition as it can be lived at the end of life, and the "knowledge" I was gaining was not the result of distance, objectivity, or abstraction. I was witnessing something akin to what Becker (1971) called "the birth and death of meaning," and I was more convinced than ever that he was correct to say, after Karl Mannheim (1958), that social science should seek to "show the way toward a better society and a more meaningful life" (Becker, 1968, p. 308) and that "all of science, as the Enlightenment understood, is thus a moral problem" (p. 365).

Preparing to go off to a new academic home at the University of South Florida, I stood at a crossroads. I longed to do work that focused on what a good life could mean and how it could be lived. But could such a "moral" project fall within the boundaries of social science? I couldn't help posing the obvious question: If the quality of our lives rests on our capacity to achieve a sense of significance—warm feelings about ourselves—shouldn't "the problem of meaning" be the central concern of the social sciences? Ernest Becker thought so. In *The Structure of Evil* (1968) he called meaning "the proper superordinate datum" of the social sciences. The philosopher Charles Taylor (1977) agreed: the human sciences, according to Taylor (p. 101), are sciences of interpretation that must deal with "forms of meaning." We cannot come to understand human life as meaningful within an empiricist orientation grounded on the ideal of verification and resting on "brute data," the validity of which is not open to further interpretations. "We need to go beyond the bounds of a science based on verification," writes Taylor (1977, p. 125) "to one which would study the intersubjective and common meanings embedded in social reality." Instead of findings grounded in brute data, social science should involve readings of meaning (Taylor, 1977).

In the late 1970s, I had immersed myself in the literature on the history and philosophy of the social sciences and was both surprised and delighted to find a harmonious synthesis of viewpoints emphasizing the systematic study of meaning and placing the agents and channels of meaning as well as the understanding of meaning at the center of a new paradigm for the human sciences (Berger and Luckmann, 1967; Cicourel, 1974; Dallmayr and McCarthy, 1977; Gadamer, 1975; Garfinkel, 1967; Geertz, 1973, 1980; Gergen, 1982; Grossberg, 1979; Harré and Secord, 1972; Mischel, 1969; Pompa, 1975; Rabinow and Sullivan, 1979; Ricoeur, 1971; Rommetveit, 1980; Rosnow, 1978; Sampson, 1978; Schutz,

1967, 1970; Taylor, 1977; Toulmin, 1969; Weber, 1947, 1958). I was craving an opportunity to make the case for a meaning-centered focus in communication research.

As luck would have it, Gerald Miller and Mark Knapp, two senior scholars in communication, invited me to contribute a chapter to the first edition of *The Handbook of Interpersonal Communication* (Knapp and Miller, 1985). When the editors sent me an outline of the book, however, I discovered that all of the other chapters would be authored by hard-boiled empiricists. I was faced with a dilemma. On the one hand, I had an appealing opportunity to introduce judicious alternatives to traditional empiricism and, thus, widen the scope of "scientific" research on interpersonal communication. On the other hand, I had to be careful not to alienate the readers and colleagues I was trying to persuade. Beginning in the mid-1970s, several researchers working outside the positivist establishment had made valiant attempts to broaden the boundaries of empirical research on communication (see e.g., Cushman, 1977; Cushman, Valentinsen and Dietrich, 1982; Pearce, 1976; Pearce and Cronen, 1980) only to find themselves ridiculed and dismissed by more powerful insiders. Within the mainstream there still was strong resistance to expanding research on interpersonal communication beyond laboratory studies aimed at prediction and control and focused on individual differences, strategic behavior, and social cognition. But writers such as Cushman and Whiting (1972), Cushman (1977), Pearce (1976), and Pearce and Cronen (1980) were persistent and resolute. By refusing to give in to disciplinary pressures to conform to a singular perspective and instead offering reasonable alternatives to the dominance of the covering law paradigm, they contributed to a growing "ferment in the field" (see Gerbner, 1983; G. Miller, 1983). From my perspective the field was in flux. Certainly, the logical positivists (O'Keefe, 1975) were still in command, but the crisis of confidence in social psychology (see Chapter 9) had leaked into communication. Interpretive scholars were introducing alternatives and expressing discontent, and the flood gates appeared ready to open.

There was a side of me that wanted to offer something new and daring. After reading Kuhn (1970), I understood that sciences are never finished products. The time seemed ripe for change. But there was another side of me resisting the temptation to throw caution to the wind. Kuhn (1970) had emphasized that the conventions holding together a scientific community command loyalty and change slowly. The struggle to innovate can lead to bitter battles and acrimonious debates. Up to this point, my professional life had been aimed principally at achieving credibility as a quantitative researcher and experimentalist. Though I had written discreetly critical essays about the empiricist paradigm (Bochner, 1978; Bochner and Krueger, 1979, 1981), I was still considered a trustworthy insider. This gave me some latitude for improvisation, but I couldn't afford to get carried away. The editors were not going to look favorably on an essay that would undermine the handbook's partiality to empiricism and the covering law model of social science. Given my desire to advance an interpretive and critical perspective on interpersonal communication, I was walking a tightrope between tradition and innovation. I wanted to develop the case for an interpretive perspective on interpersonal communication that focused on how interactants perform and negotiate meaning, but I intended to make the case without taking an oppositional stance.

My strategy would be to make the differences between empiricists, interpretivists, and critical theorists less of a big deal than they seemed at the time. Out of the thicket of differences, I would seek common ground. I would attempt to reassure empiricists that allowing different perspectives on interpersonal inquiry to flourish was not akin to giving comfort to the enemy. Interpretivists were not against science and not out to destroy the field. I would try to change the terms and vocabulary of what had been disputed: This was not a quarrel about method but about purpose. I would argue that interpersonal communication is a subject that can be legitimately approached in several different ways, described in several different vocabularies, and studied with several different purposes in mind. It was my view, as it was Bateson's (1972, 1979), that a uniquely correct scientific perspective does not exist because "natural events and processes always lend themselves to a variety and multiplicity of descriptions, depending on one's point of view" (Toulmin, 1981, p. 368).

During a study leave in 1980, I had immersed myself in the writings of Richard Rorty (1979, 1980), which greatly influenced the direction of my handbook essay. Rorty sought to replace the phrase "reality as it is in itself"—the metaphysical distinction between appearances and reality—with something akin to the pragmatists' distinction between "more useful" and "less useful." Truth is not a goal of inquiry, according to Rorty, because truth is considered absolute, and the justification for truth is always relative to a community of inquirers, to the purposes of the community to which it is answerable and the context to which it is applied. It is the standards of acceptance the community develops and endorses (for the time being) that justify their beliefs. We can never be certain that we have achieved truth because the standards of acceptance the community apply are fallible. Thus, according to Rorty, truth becomes a trivial concern about which there is little to say. A concept of truth can be "useful," but it cannot be invoked as a way of explaining research practices or standards of justification.

Applied to the human sciences, Rorty's version of pragmatism starts with the question, What do we want to do with human beings? It then examines the modes of description—the vocabularies—that are useful for our particular purposes (Rorty, 1982b). In my handbook essay (Bochner, 1985), "Perspectives on Inquiry," I argued, after Rorty, that predicting and controlling their behavior is only one of the things we want to do with human beings. For example, we may want to interpret and understand them, making sense of their actions and meanings, and we may want to transform the social conditions within which they live, making a more just and virtuous society (Bochner, 1985). In other words, the phenomena of interpersonal inquiry should be viewed not only as *facts* but also as *meanings* and as *values*. As the aims of inquiry shift, so does the language within which we situate our research and by which we evaluate its outcomes. Thus, the goals of prediction and control, interpretation and understanding, and criticism and social change should not be construed as competing modes of conducting research that match qualitative against quantitative methods, objectivity against subjectivity, or rigor against imagination. They are merely preferences for approaching our subject matter from different points of view and with different purposes in mind. In Rorty's words, these different views are "not issue(s) to be resolved, only ... differences to be lived with" (1982b, p. 197).

It is never easy to clear a path within a grove of differences, but I was convinced that one way to do it was to reframe the terms of the discussion. Although conflicts between interpretivists and empiricists usually center on which *methods* should be used to study human beings, the dissention can be boiled down to *preferences for different vocabularies*—that is, different ways of describing and doing things with human beings. To quarrel over method is to have a goal in common, but to disagree about how best to achieve the goal. But interpretivists and empiricists do not agree on a goal. Empiricists usually want to predict and control human behavior, whereas interpretivists want to understand human beings and help them decide what to do. These different goals belong to different universes of discourse. Empiricists use a vocabulary that expresses the values of objectivity, moral neutrality, the search for facts, and the kind of understanding that explanatory theories and covering laws provide. Interpretivists speak in a vastly different tongue. Their work is couched in a vocabulary that emphasizes horizons of meaning, moral reflection, subjectivity, embodiment, and empathy.

By acknowledging more than one legitimate goal to which social science inquiry can be addressed, researchers free themselves from the chains of a monolithic model of research practices that can sabotage the unique opportunities provided by recognizing and validating the multiple goals and perspectives that exist in the study of social life. Research in the human sciences should be oriented toward not only facts but also meanings; under not only the rule of rigor but also the inspiration of the imagination; to achieve not only better predictions and more control but also peace of mind and social justice; from not only the position of neutrality and distance but also the standpoint of caring and vulnerability; toward not only the production of conventional research texts but also the performance of creative, artistic, and dialogic modes of representing lived experience.

As I was working on this essay I realized I was writing it as much for myself as for the readers of the handbook in which it would be published. It was highly unlikely that my argument would reach the young scholars and potential interpretive social scientists for whom it might truly make a difference—the deck was institutionally stacked against us. The insiders' views held a privileged status, and the slanted view of the book's chapters would likely be an expression of the power they held to police the field. I kept my goals modest in the hope that things might change slowly but surely. Perhaps I was making a mistake by not staking out a bolder and more revolutionary position. In the world of scholarship in which I was immersed, there was now widespread agreement that the doctrine of scientific method and objectivity was a contestable narrative designed to preserve power. Kuhn (1970) had instigated a renewed interest in the sociology (and social construction) of knowledge by showing that the official story of scientific progress is not at all the way in which scientific knowledge is made, leading to a vigorous skepticism toward official ideologies of objective methodology. By the mid-1980s, some of the most venerable ideas about scientific knowledge and truth were being challenged and deconstructed. As early as 1969, Toulmin had observed that the "facts" scientists see are inexplicably connected to the vocabulary they use to express and represent them. In 1984, Lyotard had debunked the belief in a unified totality of knowledge, questioning whether "master narratives" were either possible or desirable. Then poststructuralist and deconstructionist writers, such as Barthes (1977), Derrida (1976, 1978), and Foucault (1970a, 1970b), effectively obliterated the modernist conception of the author, altering how we understand the connections among author, text, and readers. Under the influence of Bakhtin (1981), the interpretive space available to the reader was broadened, encouraging multiple perspectives, unsettled meanings, plural voices, and local and marginalized knowledges that transgress against the claims of a unified body of theory; and Harstock (1983) and Harding (1986) promoted the unique and too often silenced standpoints, particularities, and literatures of women.

In the aftermath of these developments, how could one possibly hold onto a monolithic ideal of social science inquiry? I was convinced that the goal of social science ought to be the moral one of enlarging and deepening a sense of community, human solidarity, and social justice. The making of a better world ought to replace objective knowledge as the principal purpose of research. This goal would echo Rorty's (1982b, p. 202) sentiments that "what we hope for from social scientists is that they will act as interpreters for those with whom we are not sure how to talk. This is the same thing we hope for from our poets and dramatists and novelists."

On Life's Forward Momentum

Driving to the hospital, I felt unsure about how to talk with Carol. What would I say? What did she want from me? What could I provide for her? There were no theories to guide me and no personal experience from which I could draw. I was a stranger to end-of-life conversation, completely lacking the typifications that a person normally can depend on in his or her encounters with other people (Schutz, 1967). Given the urgency Carol had communicated in our brief phone conversation, I anticipated that this would be the last time I would see her. How does one prepare for a final conversation with a person he cares about?

I had started out as Carol's professor and advisor, but eventually I realized that what I could teach her paled by comparison with what she had taught me. She

246

had helped me understand that death is not the enemy of life and had shown me that to be human is to be oriented beyond the body toward the kind of "healthy repressions and immortality-ideologies" that Ernest Becker (1973) had talked about. Now I wanted to assist her, to do something substantive for her, but what? All I had to offer at this point, with so little time left, was my presence. Could that be sufficient?

As I turned into the hospital parking lot I tried to conjure an image of the scene that would soon take place between us. My mind flashed on movies that depicted dying patients hooked up to whirling machines, delaying the inevitable end of life. Carol wouldn't allow that, I assured myself. She will have thought through what she wants from the people closest to her, leaving as little to chance as possible. And she will tell us what she wants. Knowing Carol's competence comforted me, but I still felt uneasy about what I was going to find when I got to her hospital room. What's going on up there? I worried. The only images I could summon came from B-minus movies. I imagined a scene shot in a grim and lifeless hospital room. Family and friends huddle around a hospital bed, wailing frantically. The camera slowly pans between two of the witnesses, revealing a dying patient lying motionless on the bed, moaning and groaning. Oh stop it, Art! I tell myself. You know these scenes are disgracefully unrealistic. Cleansed of the grisly sights and foul smells that can accompany the decay of the body, Hollywood's version of death is dramatic, spectacular, and hasty. Rarely do they show the slow, methodical slide into coma or the long, agonizing, sleepless days and nights survivors endure as they await a loved one's final decline into death.

Besides, Carol's voice on the phone sounded strong and sturdy. She didn't sound like someone fighting for her life or gasping for a last breath. I have to take my mind off worst-case scenarios. Her words, however, left no doubt that she was close to the end of her life. Carol was not inclined to exaggerate. If she said, "There isn't much time left," I better get there fast.

Entering the hospital, I feel the urgency of the moment and quicken my pace. Responding to my query at her desk, the receptionist says, "Carol Gifford, let's see. Gifford, Gifford, here she is, Carol Gifford, room 488. Take the first elevator on the right."

I feel nervous as I walk—more slowly than usual—down the long corridor of the fourth floor. There is no mistaking this place for anything other than a hospital—the white walls and ceilings, the vinyl-tiled floors, the sterile smells, the whirring and clanking of the ventilation system, the occasional hacking coughs bouncing out of the rooms, the nondescript paintings hanging on the walls, one no different from another. Is anyone ever comfortable in a place like this? I can hear my heart beating and feel my pulse quickening. Following the arrows pointing to 450–499, I turn the corner and spot a group of people—five or six—clustered together about halfway down the hallway. Seeing me approach, one of the men breaks away to greet me. "Hi, Dr. Bochner. Bob Gifford, Carol's husband. I don't know if you remember me."

247

"Of course, I do," I reply. "We've met at several departmental functions. I'm glad to see you again, though I wish the circumstances were different." My words trickle out awkwardly. I feel stiff and self-conscious, as if I have to weigh every word I speak. *Watch what you say, Art.*

"I'm grateful you could make it today. Carol has been so looking forward to talking with you. Go right in. She'll be so happy to see you."

Immediately upon entering the room my eyes meet Carol's, and for a few seconds we stare at each other like two good friends taking in the moment of renewal after a long absence. "I'm so happy to see you."

"Me too," Carol exclaims. I am amazed by the sight of her animated and vibrant presence. Instead of the prostrate and ailing woman I half-expected to see, Carol is sitting up in the middle of the bed with her legs crossed in front of her and her hands clasping a yellow pad of paper parked on her lap. A light blue hospital gown is draped around her, covering everything except her bare arms and feet. The only overt sign of illness is two prongs of soft plastic tubing inserted into her nostrils. I presume that the tubes deliver sustaining concentrations of oxygen.

"It is so great to see you, Art. I have so much to tell you." Her energy and enthusiasm startle me.

"I want to hear everything," I say. I realize that I'm standing above her, and she has to look up at me, so I walk toward the chair at the foot of her bed.

"No, no, no," she says. "Come sit next to me on the bed." When I scoot next to her, she reaches out her right hand. I squeeze her hand and she squeezes mine, looking directly into my eyes again. Suddenly the heartbreaking seriousness of the moment overcomes me. Not wanting her to see the flood of tears streaming down my face, I turn my head away.

Carol reaches behind her and retrieves a large box of Kleenex tissues. "Here, take as many as you want," she says. I can't believe that she's taking care of me. I take a handful of tissues and wipe away the tears.

"I've gone through three boxes of these today. Everyone who comes in here breaks out in tears," she says, smiling. "I just keep dishing out the Kleenex, one after another." A wide grin covers her face, which glows with amusement. The irony of the visitors' vulnerability is not lost on her.

"Why does that thought make you smile?" I ask, relishing an opportunity to lighten the conversation.

"This may sound perverse," she says, "but it's wonderful to know that people you love are sad that you're leaving and will miss you. Actually, I have mixed emotions. I don't want my friends and family to feel sorrowful and heartbroken. I wish we could have a party and merrily celebrate all that we've meant to each other. But in my present condition I can't dance, and, besides, it brings me a lot of joy to know I've done some good in this world and somebody will remember me. One thing people don't realize about illness is that it's not all a calamity. Some of it is funny. I don't know. I really shouldn't laugh about this, but it's kind of funny to see everyone break down like this in my presence, though there is one thing that bothers me about it."

"What's that?" I ask.

"It's something we discussed in your interpersonal class—the way people distance themselves from death. They can't do that when they come in here. I don't hide the fact that within a few days I'll be gone. I'm not telling them that to be mean. I've asked my closest friends to come here to say goodbye to me so we could all have closure. But I think what's happening is that I'm making them anxious."

"Well, most people do love life and find the thought of leaving it unpleasant."

"I love life too!" Carol says definitively. "But I don't find death unacceptable."

"You've had to face it, and most of us haven't."

"So you mean I have an advantage because I'm dying?" Carole grins again. She is obviously enjoying playing with these ironies.

"Hmmm, this is certainly turning into an edgy conversation," I kid. "I'll tell you why I'm sad. Because I'm losing a playmate. I won't have you to converse with any longer. I'll miss your playfulness and the way you turn ideas inside out."

"That's quite a compliment, Art. Trouble is, given my future, I don't know whether I'll miss it or not." Her face glows again. I think to myself how much I want to remember the twinkle in her eyes. "But I'll tell you this," she continues, "I'm not afraid. Knowing that I'm this close to the end of my life, I feel much more in touch with the mysterious and the sacred. As you know, I've always been a bit of a control freak, but when it comes to death it's obviously not something that can be neatly ordered and treated rationally. When I was younger, I was hungry to know the answers to why we're here—you know, what's the purpose of creation anyway? Now it occurs to me that it's simply something we're not supposed to know. It's like you taught me: life is filled with contradictions, and the best we may be able to do is face them with a degree of openness and trust."

"Is that what your faith does for you?" I inquire.

She takes her time responding to my query. "I'm not sure. Certainly, it seems like the best choice open to me for accepting some of the burdens of life and facing death with hope. But I didn't ask you here to talk about death or about my religious beliefs. I just wanted to say good-bye, face-to-face, and make a request. There's something I want you to do for me."

"Tell me," I say, suspecting that she's given considerable thought to any request she might make of me.

"I want you to continue the work that I've started. I don't mean that you have to write another dissertation. From what I hear, you've already done one." She chuckles at her own joke.

"Whew, that's a relief. I wouldn't want to go through that again," I kid back.

"Seriously, this work I've started on women with breast cancer and their family communication is very important to me. I've got all my files and notes sitting in that box over there by the corner." She points to the far end of the room. "I want you to take the whole box with you when you leave. I have drafts of the first few chapters, and the questionnaires and interview notes are in there too. You can think of this as a gift but also as a reminder. I don't want you to forget what I was doing when the academic life I was planning came to a halt."

"I'm flattered you would trust me with carrying your life's work forward."

"So you'll do this for me?"

"Yes. I'll do what I can. It won't be as notable as if it came from you, a woman with breast cancer herself, but conceivably I can put your project and your life in its proper context and perspective. Other people need to know how you coped with your illness and how you decided to complete your life."

"Thank you. I'm really grateful to have this closure," Carol says, her face bathed in a radiant grin.

Carol and I continued to talk for another fifteen minutes or so. She told me about the funeral service she had composed, including the music, and a tribute she'd written to her friends and her family. We laughed about how even at the end of life she was still planning things. I promised I would attend the funeral service, and she also informed me that her daughter was now a freshman at Temple and would be stopping in to see me from time to time. I could see that she was tiring and needed some rest. I felt exhausted too. We hugged one last time, and she handed me a few more tissues. I would need them on the ride home.

Arriving at my car, I put the heavy box of papers, files, and notes in my trunk and blew my nose. Driving home, I kept thinking about how important it was to Carol to give me the box containing her research and writing and to be reassured that someday others might benefit from the work she had started. When I arrived home I took the box up to my study and placed it in front of my desk. I sat down in my chair and picked up the copy of Ernest Becker's *Denial of Death* (1973, p. 285), which was resting next to the typewriter. I flipped to the last page and the mysterious two sentences with which he ended the book: "Who knows what form the forward momentum of life will take in the time ahead or what use it will make of our anguished searching. The most that any one of us can seem to do is to fashion something—an object or ourselves—and drop it into the confusion, make an offering of it, so to speak, to the life force."

CHAPTER ELEVEN

A Twist of Fate

> We are all too ready to forget that in fact everything
> we do with our life is chance, from our origin out of
> the meeting of spermatozoon and ovum onwards.
> *Sigmund Freud (1910, p. 137)*

> How long must he wait?
> One more time for a simple twist of fate.
> *Bob Dylan (1975a)*

"How did you feel about USF when you first arrived?" Carolyn Ellis asks as the two of us sip white wine in her living room. One of her dogs, a Jack Russell named Ande, sits on my lap, and a Rat terrier named Likker lies prone on hers.

You may wonder what I'm doing here. Well, we didn't arrange a date, if that's what you're thinking. Instead, we called a "meeting." Presumably, we are getting together to discuss ways of connecting the graduate programs in sociology—Carolyn's department—and communication, my department. But academic meetings between two people rarely take place in such a beguiling setting—soft music in the background, wine and cheese on the table in front of us, dogs on our laps. There's more here than meets the eye. I think both of us know that, but we aren't saying so, not yet anyway.

My Lucky Day

> The first time ever I saw your face,
> I thought the sun rose in your eyes.
> *Ewan MacColl (1957)*

I met Carolyn at a lecture she presented in the College of Business several weeks before. Little did I know what was in store for me that fateful morning when I read an announcement in USF's student newspaper about a lecture on "systematic sociological introspection," to be presented by an associate professor of sociology.

"Grab a yellow pad and follow me," I said to a couple of graduate students hanging out in the hall in front of my office.

"Where are we going?" one of them asked.

"To hear a USF sociologist talk about introspection as a social science methodology."

"I thought you told me the sociology department was weak," the student replied, a look of puzzlement crossing his face.

"They have that reputation, but the title of this talk fascinates me. Let's go see and hear for ourselves."

It is remarkable how much of a human life can turn on chance. Many of us live under the illusion that we can plan the course of our lives, and a good deal of life does seem to be under the control of the plans we make and carry out. But when we look back, usually we can find a single incident, a coincidental encounter, or an unforeseen event that colored and steered everything that followed. Our lives may rest on little more than a "tissue of contingencies" to use Richard Rorty's (1989) nimble expression. By a stroke of luck, or caress of fate, this was one of those precious days after which nothing in my life would seem the same.

I had never heard the term, "systematic sociological introspection," and the name Carolyn Ellis didn't ring a bell, either. Frankly, I didn't know what to expect. I entered the small, tiered classroom and took the last seat in the last row, about twenty-five feet from where the podium stood.

"She's really cute," I overheard one of my graduate students say to the other. I silently agreed. As I looked around the room I felt a strange sense of anticipation in the air, as if something special was about to happen. When Carolyn Ellis began to speak, I felt my heart flutter. For a second, I thought it had skipped a beat. I trained my eyes on her, taking in every expression and gesture. I didn't want to miss a word, but I was fighting to avoid the distraction of her magnetic energy that made me feel as if I were being pulled across the room toward her. She appeared to be having the time of her life. Her talk felt more like a dance than a lecture, one in which she was totally absorbed in the moment and basking in the glow of the attentive eyes cast on her.

This was a serious talk. She was challenging ingrained and deep-seated prejudices against the intrusion of introspection and subjectivity into scientific sociology. *Right on,* I thought when Carolyn urged a sociology that centered on emotionality and embraced detailed lived experience. But "Oh no," I muttered under my breath when she let herself get carried into a defensive posture, trying to shield herself against the slings and arrows of mainstream sociologists who might not consider her work "real sociology" because it wasn't sufficiently rigorous or generalizable. *Come on, Carolyn, you should know that if you play by their rules, then you're going to have to play their game. You're giving away too much. Besides, their rules don't apply to the kind of sociology that you're endorsing when you speak about representing patterns of lived experience in ways that make them assessable and readable. "In the form of stories," you say, and you're so right. That's exactly what's needed, but it's precisely not what the project of traditional empiricism is about. Empiricists use lived experience as the ground from which to abstract fixed generalizations in order to exert some control over life's uncertainties. But stories usually make us care about the person whose story is being told and about the story itself, which matters dearly to the storyteller. As an interpretive sociologist, you're not trying to stand above the story; you're standing under it, trying to under-stand it, or beside it—to be with it—to sympathize with the pain and suffering that has been endured and to envision what can be done to make life better.*

Settle down, Art, I tell myself. Why am I getting so annoyed? She's not the one to blame for the depreciation of lived experience and the overemphasis on concepts, order, and control. This is a system of thought into which nearly all social scientists are socialized. Give her a chance. She's trying to make a case for a different kind of sociology without alienating the people she's trying to persuade.

I turn my attention back to Carolyn and hear her say, "I write these stories through a mode of systematic introspection to try to understand the intersection of personal and social aspects of emotions and to invite you, my readers or audience members, to enter these experiences with me and the people in my story, feeling what we may have felt or imagining what you would have felt or done in similar circumstances. In that way you have your emotions to examine, which is the best way I know to convey to you what emotions feel like."

"Oh my," I mumble to myself, "now she's giving my lecture about how social science needn't be restricted to representing the world of others but could become a way of using our experience in other people's worlds to reflect on our own experiences and to make our readers reflect on their own lives, putting themselves in the shoes of the other(s). Damn she's audacious. I have to meet this woman."

When she launched into stories, I became fully immersed in the moments of lived life and loss she shared. Writing from inside her own experiences, Carolyn read selections of narrative from a book on which she was working (Ellis, 1995) that expressed what it felt like to live as a caregiver and lover, over a nine-year period, with a partner who died after a long struggle with emphysema and then to suffer the sudden loss of her brother, who was on his way to visit her when his airplane crashed into the Potomac River in Washington, DC (Ellis, 1993). As I listened, I felt as if I were riding a roller coaster of emotions—first exhaustion and burnout, then hope and trust, then shock and numbness, and finally sorrow and uncertainty. She didn't try to sugarcoat the terrible and crucial struggles in which she had been immersed, wrestling against emptiness and isolation, fighting to create meaning and purpose out of the chaos of a life shattered by loss and saturated with grief. The stories kept me close to the events and the feelings surrounding them, and were crafted to make it difficult, if not impossible, to distance myself from the experiences and the emotions attached to them.

When Carolyn ended by confiding that "I needed to write these stories to work my way through the pain and be transformed by the truth of the stories," I felt a rush of optimism rushing through my body. *Yes! This is what social science needs to become in order to make a difference in the world—daring, intimate, embodied, and evocative.* The stories Carolyn was telling were not so much about people as on behalf of them. I was envious. She was doing what I had only theorized, bearing witness to the wreckage of human suffering, showing what it might mean to live well while afflicted by loss, inviting her readers to become witnesses themselves, refusing to hide behind academic jargon, and making us feel the truth of her stories in our guts.

As Carolyn finished, people in the room sat in stunned silence. I couldn't imagine that her talk was anything like what faculty in the College of Business had anticipated. Speaking into the silence, Carolyn invited the audience to respond. "Now I'd like to open this session for questions and responses from you." Watching from the back of the room, I could see that nobody was ready to speak. Worried that the session might end without my making contact with her, I stood and raised my hand. She called on me immediately.

"Dr. Ellis, thank you for that wonderful talk. I agree with you—social science does need more heart and emotion. I have only one small point to make. You seem to accept the terms that orthodox social scientists use to describe and evaluate their work: objectivity, validity, reliability. You spent a great deal of your time trying to convince us that your work is sufficiently scientific and can be appreciated by applying these same criteria, albeit by expanding the potential meanings of these terms. This ends up making you sound very defensive. Why not drop all the science talk? Take it for granted that your stories matter. The stories are raw and intimate; they make me care about you and about other people who experience this kind of loss, and they put me in touch with a wide range of my own emotions. All the talk about science and validity only distracts you and your readers from the human sense of suffering and loss you communicate so beautifully."

A look of surprise covered Carolyn's face. "That's not normally the reaction I get to my work," she began. "Most of my critics question whether what I'm doing is science, so I'm accustomed to defending the rigor and systematic manner in which I work. I try to anticipate the objections that will be raised and respond to them. But I have to admit that it would lift a great burden from my shoulders if more orthodox sociologists approached my work the way you do. On the other hand, you sound like one of those postmodernist "language is everything" people. I'm not convinced that any one thing is everything. I, uh …"

I interrupted her to say that I didn't see myself as all that extreme in my view of language and to urge her to view her work as a form of empirical research that bridges the humanities and social sciences. "The stories you told today are drawn artistically," I observed, "much like a novelist would tell them, and they produce a kind of therapeutic experience and sympathetic response for the reader or listener that is alien to conventional social science but common in the humanities, where questions about what is good and of value are highlighted." I paused to catch my breath, thinking maybe I should quit while I was ahead. But Carolyn seemed attentive to my every word, which encouraged me to go on.

"The stories you told are not made up; they depict events that really happened, and like a good social scientist you're trying to stay as close to the facts as you can. But unlike fact-centered empiricism, your kind of sociology urges social scientists to get real, which means not to shy away from experiences that resist rational control and conceptual explanation. Your stories take us where many people fear to go—into the messy, ambiguous, and difficult regions of lived experience, where life is dark, hot, and uncertain. Most of us feel vulnerable and scared when we enter this zone, and we usually try to avoid or run away from it. But you enter calmly and compassionately with your eyes and your heart wide open, helping us understand that the joy of life is not restricted to pleasure and fun but includes accepting and dealing with everything life can throw at us, including pain and suffering. That's why I say the whole question of whether your work is sufficiently scientific is trivial."

We exchanged a couple of more comments before other people entered the conversation, and I backed away. I had come on strong, hopefully not overbearing or obnoxious, but strong enough to justify apologizing for hogging the floor or sounding overly critical. I didn't feel I could leave without making more personal contact. Carolyn's talk had focused on her relationship with a partner, Gene Weinstein, who had died and, ironically was a scholar I had cited in my dissertation. Was she involved in another romantic relationship now? I had to know. How weird that we had worked on the same campus for six years and our paths had never crossed.

I waited until the crowd around Carolyn had scattered and she was packing her papers to leave. Approaching her slowly, I introduced myself; then added, "I hope I didn't offend you."

"On the contrary, you gave me a lot to think about, which I appreciate," she replied, grabbing her purse off the back of a chair. "Are you walking out this way?" she asked, motioning toward the parking lot.

"Yes, I'm going toward my office in Cooper Hall."

"Good, let's walk together." I breathed a sigh of relief, taking her request as a sign that she wanted more contact with me.

We walked slowly through the parking lot, continuing our conversation. "I really did admire your talk. You have a real talent for storytelling."

"Coming from a language person, that's quite a compliment," she said, sounding amused.

"Actually, I'm not so much a language person as a communication person. I'm chair of the communication department."

"You are? What a lucky coincidence." I love the way her eyes light up and the uninhibited way in which she expresses her exuberance. "I'm the graduate director in sociology, and I'm really trying to develop the qualitative research program. I heard communication is initiating a qualitative PhD program, and I've been meaning to get in touch with someone there. Would you be willing to explore some possible ways in which we could connect our two programs?"

"That's a great idea. Maybe we could get better acquainted by exchanging some articles we've published between the two of us. I'd love to read some of your work."

"That sounds like a good way to begin. Let's do it."

The next day, we began a form of flirtation and courting distinctive to academics—exchanging publications and work in progress. Carolyn started by having a student drop off a few of her publications in my departmental mailbox. I responded in a typically competitive fashion by instructing one of my graduate students to deliver reprints of various articles throughout the day. Every time Carolyn showed up at her mailbox, she would find another article or book chapter of mine. Quickly catching on to the rules of this little game, Carolyn sent over additional articles throughout the week, including a draft of an essay on emotional sociology. "If you have time, I'd really appreciate some feedback on this manuscript," she jotted on the cover page.

Carolyn's invitation was both appealing and intimidating. Responding in writing to her manuscript would provide an opportunity to show off my skills as a reviewer, but at the same I might risk offending her and spoil my opportunity for romance. Was she looking mainly for praise and affirmation? How would she respond to a thorough critique, including line-by-line editing, which I do routinely when I'm reviewing article submissions that show promise?

I decided to throw caution to the wind and provide a thorough review, critique, and edit. When I finished, virtually every page included marginal comments, line editing, and suggestions for reorganization. "This is an article that has the potential to reshape how sociologists think about and practice the sociology of emotions," I typed on a page I attached to the draft. I continued:

> Your essay has the potential to shift the field from a rational actor to a narrative paradigm and to sensitize sociologists to their own emotion work as researchers. To achieve this goal, however, the story you tell—by the way, I think all good theorizing involves a storyline—has to keep the reader moving along, turning the page, anticipating what may come next, showing respect for the past but also revealing the deficiencies in the rational-actor model. Be bold—call for a new paradigm that addresses how emotions work and what meanings people draw from them in actual lived experience. The stories and anecdotes you tell are powerful—obviously this is your strength. But the stories need to be more deftly integrated with the conceptual and theoretical material. I call this narrative smoothing. I've tried to make suggestions throughout the manuscript about how you might accomplish this goal. To reiterate what I said at your lecture, you can drop the defensiveness. That's not your authentic voice, and it only plays into the resistance to this kind of work among traditional social scientists. Make them play on your home field. Do this by setting the terms—your terms—for understanding and appreciating this kind of work. Don't retreat into their criteria for what counts as sociology or science. I know that you believe in this work, so don't back down. Emotional sociology is a powerful idea and fits extremely well with how I see the future of interpretive social science. In short, it's not what you're saying but how you're saying it that will make or break this article.

I read over what I'd written, then added hesitantly, "I hope you still like me when you finish going through my edits and comments." I'm probably destroying any chance for a romantic relationship, I thought. But this is who I am, and I want Carolyn to know from the outset how seriously I take this work. If she's the person I think she is, she'll appreciate the feedback I'm giving her. If she's testing me, well I'm testing her too.

The day after I sent my review, I had my answer. Carolyn phoned to thank me for the review and tell me how excited she was to get back to work on the article. "You've bolstered my confidence. Dropping the defensiveness feels liberating. You hit the nail on the head. All that scientific mumbo jumbo doesn't speak to me and probably won't speak to readers who might be drawn and open to emotional sociology. Defending myself has become a meaningless ritual in my writing, and I need to rid myself of it once and for all. I hope you'll take another look when I finish the next draft."

"Of course," I replied. "I probably sounded a lot more negative than I intended. I envy your ability to put embodied emotional experience on the page. There's an immediacy and rawness to the way you tell stories that puts the reader in the place of the people and experiences you're describing. I can see that you're not really inclined to be defensive. It's refreshing to see someone respond to feedback the way you do. I admire your spirit and determination."

"That's music to my ears. Now that I've seen the affinity between your work and mine, I'm more determined than ever to link our two graduate programs," Carolyn replied. "Can we schedule some time to explore possible connections?"

"Sure. Do you want to set up a meeting while we're on the phone? I have my calendar here."

"How about coming over to my house on Wednesday night, about eight o'clock? We can have a glass of wine and talk through a bunch of possibilities."

"I'd love to."

"Great, I'll send over directions to my house. I can't wait to have you meet my dogs. They're my family. You're okay with dogs, aren't you?"

"I adore dogs. I have a German shepherd named Martina. I want you to meet her sometime too."

The day before our meeting, I received a package in my mailbox that described the graduate program in sociology. On the top of the package was a yellow Post-it note with a handwritten message: "I'm so glad we found each other." I pinned it to my bulletin board, where it remains today.

The Meeting

Talk is the kiss of life.
Anatole Broyard (1992, p. 54)

"During that first year at USF I had a lot of conflicting feelings," I say, taking a sip of wine and pausing to organize my thoughts.

"I take it you missed Philadelphia," Carolyn infers. "I sure missed New York during my first year in Florida. Here try some of these," she adds, pushing the small plate of melted brie and crackers toward my side of the table.

I gently nudge Ande off my lap and reach for the snacks Carolyn's prepared. "Oh, that's good!" I utter, savoring the rich taste of the warm, softened cheese dissolving in my mouth.

"Umm, one of my favorites," she agrees, joining in on the treats. "I'm afraid when you get to know me, you'll find I'm a habitual nibbler."

"That doesn't scare me," I kid. "I'm a person who lives to eat. In Jewish families, sharing good food is an expression of love. I'll bet I can out-nibble you." The fact we are talking about things and activities we care about isn't lost on me, nor is the metamessage about getting to know each other better. *Isn't that really why we're here?*

Moving back to our unfinished topic, I say, "I missed the energy of the city, my friends, and the intensity of the Temple students. They were so uninhibited. But other things bothered me more."

"Sounds like you were really unhappy."

"Not so much unhappy as conflicted. On the one hand, a huge boulder had been lifted from my shoulders. I was no longer branded as the departmental methodologist. I had been liberated from teaching statistics and research design once and for all."

"That must have felt good."

"It did. I felt energized, free to follow my inspiration, and I was happy to have escaped the resistance to change that had frustrated me at Temple, but ..."

"Oh, oh, I hear an 'on the other hand' coming," Carolyn interjects.

"You know I wouldn't have been conflicted if things were perfect."

"Let me guess what it was."

"Okay."

"Your colleagues didn't immediately warm to you."

"That certainly was one of the factors. I felt paranoid my colleagues were watching me, weighing everything I said. They doubted whether I was truly one of them. But getting a cold shoulder doesn't quite capture the complications. I had been naïve to think I could come charging into USF and push immediately for wholesale changes in the curriculum. It was going to take a long time to gain trust. On top of that, the department lacked the resources necessary to put an interpretive social science program together."

"What sort of resources do you mean?" Carolyn asks.

"The department lacked a passion for research. My colleagues primarily saw themselves as teachers, not scholars. They were dedicated and effective instructors, but only one or two had the kind of desire for research and writing that burned inside of me. I've never been convinced that you can create a desire for research. With a few exceptions, most people either have it or they don't."

"I had the same feelings about my department. Coming out of a top graduate school, I couldn't understand why so many of my colleagues were not doing any research at all. Eventually, I realized that quite a few had been hired before USF became a comprehensive research university."

"Then you know what I was facing. I thought I had come to the wrong place. I was worried that my dream could turn into a nightmare. I didn't know what to do. What would you have done if you were in my shoes?"

"I would look upon the situation as an ethnographer, setting out to learn the local culture, which is what I did when I came to USF. I was a brand new PhD, so my situation was considerably different from yours. But I can remember saying to myself, 'Oh my gosh, this may never be a place I can ever feel at home and pursue my academic dreams.' You're still here, though, so something must have changed."

"Something did change. The chair of the department resigned to take a position in Arizona."

"Was this part of your dream?" Carolyn teases.

"Ha," I laugh. "Far from it! His resignation actually heightened my anxiety. I was the only research-active full professor in the department. I looked around the table and realized that if I didn't make myself a candidate for chair, one of the associate professors would likely be appointed, which would dash my hopes for an interpretive program. But department chair was not part of my dream. I didn't want to become a 'suit,' if you know what I mean."

"Yuck," Carolyn replies, sticking out her tongue. "I would never want to do that job."

"I felt the same way at the time, but be forewarned: circumstances can change how you feel about things."

"Not when it comes to being a chair. That's not for me. Anyway, you must have reframed your view of chairing a department."

"That makes it sound too easy. You see, I held in my mind this other rigid dichotomy—either you're an academic or you're not, and administrators aren't truly academics. When I went to sleep at night, I'd hear the voices of Berger and Luckmann [1967] whispering, 'Don't forget that you take on the characteristics and attitudes of the people with whom you talk.' I was terrified that I'd become one of them—a suit."

"I can picture that," Carolyn chuckles. "But I guess you learned to live with your terror," she teases.

"This is my fifth year."

"That's a long time to spend doing something you're not crazy about."

"When the chair resigned, my perspective changed. I couldn't convince myself that I would be able to create an interpretive social science program unless I became chair, and without that program I would never be content at USF. Suddenly chairing the department looked like a great opportunity, perhaps my only chance to put this kind of program together."

"But if you were perceived as an outsider, how could you possibly win an election for chair?"

"Oh that's a long story. I don't want to bore you with a tale steeped in departmental history and politics."

"How about the Cliff's Notes version?" she grins. I love how attentively Carolyn follows my stories. *She sure has beautiful blue eyes. And oh, those dimples when she smiles.*

"I composed a speech in which I revealed a lot of my biography and conveyed my dream for the department—that our reach would exceed our grasp."

"And that won over the doubters, eh?" she says in an ironic tone of voice.

"Actually it didn't. Well, maybe one or two minds were changed. That's where things became political. The department couldn't reach a consensus."

"I guess the other candidate gave a good speech too," Carolyn grins.

"Ha!" I don't know if you'd consider him inspiring, but he was predictable, steady, and a considerate person. He had been in the department for a long time and had built a lot of trust. I ended up with a couple of votes more than he did, but under the department's governance rules I needed more than a simple majority. Eventually the vote count was reported to the dean and he made the decision."

"You must have really had your work cut out for you. Being chosen over the home town favorite can be mighty contentious."

"I had to work hard to heal the wounds and hurt feelings of some faculty. It took a couple of years, but eventually I earned their trust and we came together. Now my dream is close to becoming a reality. In August, our first five PhD students will enroll. I'm planning to offer my first seminar on narrative inquiry. I'd like to use some of your stories in that course. Are any of the stories you told at the lecture published yet? I didn't see them among the articles you sent me."

"No, they're not published yet. I've used bits and pieces in a couple of my publications, but I've been putting all my energy into the book *Final Negotiations* [Ellis, 1995]. I'm hoping I can convince you to read my current draft."

"What sort of responses have you received thus far?"

"I've had some encouraging and some not so encouraging feedback, but I'm pushing ahead. I believe in this work, and I'm not going to stop until a good publisher sees it the way I do."

"How do you understand your work? What are trying to do with it?" I ask. Suddenly Ande jumps back on my lap and starts licking my face. Carolyn laughs as Ande's quick tongue flicks near my lips.

"Looks as if she likes you," she says, obviously pleased. "You can let her lick what's left on your cheese plate." I follow her lead, holding out my plate for Ande as she places hers in front of Likker.

"Oh, so that's what she wanted. You must have her trained."

"No, she's trained me," Carolyn corrects, and we laugh together.

"Would you like some ice cream?"

"Sure."

"Oh good. I'm glad you like ice cream," she says, rising from her seat and moving swiftly toward the refrigerator. "I consider ice cream at the end of the day one of the necessities of life."

I clear the dishes and wine glasses from the table and carry them to the sink. "This might be a good point for a quick break if you need to use the bathroom," Carolyn says, pointing to the hallway on the other side of the kitchen. "Meanwhile, I'll make some coffee and gather my thoughts about your question. Nobody has ever asked me what I'm trying to do with my work."

As I walk toward the narrow hall leading to the bathroom, I scan the living space, noticing the unusual round couch in the living room and the maroon, tan, and brown accents that give the house a warm, earthy feel. I wonder if I'm projecting the heightened sensuality I feel in Carolyn's cheerful presence.

When I return to my seat at the table I find a lovely ceramic dish containing several scoops of chocolate almond ice cream. A tiny spoon sits beside the bowl.

"Do you take cream in your coffee?" Carolyn asks, approaching the table with two cups and a small container of half-and-half.

"Black, with no sugar either. By the way, what's the deal with the charming little spoons?"

"Oh, they slow me down. I prefer to savor every mouthful of ice cream, making it last as long as possible." We sit quietly at the table nibbling gently at our treats. The dogs sit patiently by our feet until they hear the spoons scraping the last drops in the bowls. Tails wagging feverishly, the dogs merrily lap up the last licks.

"I've been mulling over your question about how I understand my own work," Carolyn says, returning the conversation to people talk.

"Oh, I hope I didn't ruin your dessert."

"Let me give you some context," she begins, bypassing my tease. "My dissertation research was conducted in two isolated fishing communities. I had been taught to go out and live with the people in the communities I was studying. I talked with them; ate with them; smelled, touched, played, and worked with them; and took notes on everything. I even took photographs. You might say I was learning by doing."

"That's not exactly what the methods books teach, is it?"

"None of the books I read in courses had prepared me for how overwhelmed I felt. I couldn't figure out how to take all the different experiences I was recording and produce a coherent text that answered to the traditions of the field, which was what my professors expected. So I peeled off the chunks I could manage in order to make sense of what I had observed and express what was going on in writing."

"Let me guess this time. I'll bet you had to leave out some of the richest material and make sure you gave the impression of abiding by the rules of scientific method."

"Of course; I wanted to get my degree, and I knew my committee would need to be assured of my neutrality and objectivity. During my time in the field, I often felt torn between remaining involved and keeping my distance as I had been taught to do in methods courses. I forced myself to stop when I felt too emotionally engaged. I thought that was the right thing to do, though even then I had my doubts. But who was I to question everything I had been taught?"

"Wow, so your professors had really gotten into your head. What were they saying?"

"Keep yourself out of the text. Don't write in the first person because that's unprofessional. I thought I had to frame all my observations in the legitimate lexicon of sociological concepts, but that voice didn't come naturally to me."

"I doubt if it comes naturally to anyone," I interrupt.

"And here I thought it was only me," Carolyn replies in an ironic tone. We both chuckle; then she speaks into our laughter. "When I came to USF, I had time to mull over the way I had written my dissertation. I wasn't content with my own presence in the text, or lack of presence, I should say. My emotions and subjectivity had greatly influenced how I understood the Fisher Folk, and it seemed inauthentic to act as if I were substitutable, as if any ethnographer would have seen and interpreted them the same way."

"I recognize that feeling. It can be torturous to write yourself out of the text."

"It was agonizing, but I didn't feel I had a choice. What I did like, however, were the stories I told. I made a concerted effort to bring the Fisher Folk to life on the page. I wanted readers to hear their voices and see them in action, so I wrote these short narrative vignettes that showed what I had told about their cultural practices and attitudes. It was my first attempt at scenic writing, character development, and storytelling and by far the most enjoyable part of writing my dissertation."

"That was nearly ten years ago. What took you so long to come back to the kind of storytelling you love to write?"

"My life was complicated. I was a new faculty member trying to figure out what was expected of me. Then I had to come to grips with the sudden loss of my brother and a serious injury to my knee that left me feeling as if my body were failing me. At the same time I was immersed in the emotional pain my partner, Gene, and I felt as he deteriorated and we entered the late stages of his illness."

"I can understand how that would leave little time for writing," I declare in a wry tone of voice. "But couldn't you have squeezed it in between surgery, rehab, and grief?" I try to make light out of the trauma that had descended on her all at once. *How could one person go through all this and maintain such an optimistic outlook?*

"I guess I lacked time-management skills," Carolyn jests. "At first, I was just trying to hold on—you know, keep myself afloat. But as time passed, I began to see what I was going through as a turning point in how I understood my work as a sociologist. I could use sociology to understand my life, and my life to enlarge my understanding of sociology."

"How did you arrive at that insight?"

"I started keeping notes about how I was reacting to each new plateau of Gene's illness and how we were making sense of it as a couple. Writing the notes was enormously therapeutic and, I thought, sociologically insightful, but I had no notion of what eventually I would do with them. At the time, my emotional life and my sanity were much more important to me than my career. They had to be. Besides, *Fisher Folk* [1986] had gone to press, and I'd published articles in reputable journals, which I'd been told was enough to get me through the tenure process."

"But those publications weren't really breaking new ground like the work you're doing now."

"No, they weren't. I didn't have delusions of grandeur. Like any other young professor, I was trying to fit in and make a home for myself. I wasn't going to throw caution to the wind. I continued writing notes for more than two years and had a private inner excitement that what I was doing could be sociologically important beyond its therapeutic value. Still, I didn't think I was in a position to challenge the boundaries of what counted as legitimate sociological research."

"So you kept it in the closet. What a pity!"

"You know it's not so easy to break free from your socialization as a graduate student."

"Are you kidding? You're talking to an expert on that topic. Someday I may write a book about the good and bad of graduate student indoctrination."

"Graduate education is a little like falling in love," Carolyn declares. She's so comfortable moving from the academic to the personal. "At first you idealize your partner. Later on, you realize the person has flaws like all human beings."

"Yeah, and if you're really lucky, their flaws mesh with yours."

"You haven't seen any of my flaws yet, have you?" she plays along.

"Hmm, flaws? Let me think. Flaws? Flaws? How about your reluctance to tell stories without defending their legitimacy as sociology?"

"You're the first person who has ever told me to drop the defensiveness, so maybe you're the one with the flaw," she challenges.

"Touché! But wait just a second. I'm on your side. I'm saying your stories work without all that defensive jazz, which subtracts from their overall effect."

"But is that enough? Don't I need to fit my work into the ongoing conversation in the field?"

"Only if that's the conversation you want to join, and I don't think it is. Your work doesn't fit within that conversation. That's why you need a different conversation and different conversational partners. I'm talking about a paradigm change, and the way I see it, you can't change an existing paradigm unless you change the conversation."

"How could I possibly be powerful enough to change the minds of scholars who have invested their professional identities in the received view of scientific sociology? We don't even speak the same language, so how in the world could we understand each other?"

"That's precisely the point. 'When you see things from a different point of view, you get tangled up in blue,' to quote Bob Dylan (1975b). Your work centers on existential suffering, which stands outside the boundaries of conventional sociology and its commitment to a stylized, third-person professional voice."

"I can't stand the authoritative tone of the traditional sociological literature," Carolyn replies, turning up her nose. "That voice doesn't come naturally to me." I notice the glow fading from her expression as she talks.

"Then you need to invite people into a new conversation that doesn't follow the rules of the old one," I advise, talking as much to myself as to her. "You show that this new conversation takes you to a different place than the old conversation, a place worth going to, especially for people who have been left out of the old conversation or didn't want to enter it in the first place. Those are the people who you can attract—people like you and me."

"That's a clever strategy. You want to give people a choice of which conversation to join. That's good in theory, but is that a realistic possibility given that the old conversation holds all the power?"

"I think it's a question of the relationship between those holding power and those under their control. What will happen when the powerful people face dissent? If the old conversation resists reasonable attempts to innovate and change the rules, it may very well lose its following or become irrelevant."

"But offering a new conversation doesn't need to be oppositional, does it?" Carolyn asks. "I don't relish an us-against-them mentality."

"That's a good point. The goal is not to replace the scientific perspective with an interpretive one. You don't have to be hostile toward the other conversation. What you need is a space in which to enter into yours and some companions who are willing to listen and converse with you and each other."

"That's what I hope to find."

"You found me, didn't you?" I tease. I love joking with her and watching how her smile lights up the room. "Besides, you're not really in that other conversation anyway."

"I've been operating under the assumption that the conversation I prefer could somehow be joined with a more traditional one."

"I don't see how that possibly would work. For instance, consider the draft of your paper on emotional sociology [Ellis, 1991]. Your focus clearly is not on predicting and controlling emotions. You're trying to move sociologists of emotion away from the one-way, distancing objectifications of mainstream sociology. In fact, you're trying to get away from the whole idea of the rational actor and the necessity of abstracting generalizations. So you're already a marginal participant in the old paradigm—at most—unless you want emotions to become just another variable to put into a structural equation. You don't believe that mainstream sociology is going to give up graphs for stories or facts for meanings, do you?"

"When you put it like that it sounds absurd."

"You'd certainly be swimming against the current, which can be very draining."

"Sometimes I feel as if I'm drowning, and there's no hand reaching out to save me." I reach out my hand, signaling my desire to offer Carolyn a lifeline. She clasps my hand, and continues. "Careful, you might get pulled in with me."

"I can think of a lot worse things," I say as our hands part. "Seriously, I think I know how that feels. No matter how hard you paddle, you're not moving forward, the current keeps pushing you back, and you're sinking. That can be so demoralizing."

"So what you're suggesting is to find a river in which you can swim with the current and where other swimmers are there to keep you safe." We chuckle in unison at the extended metaphor we've fashioned together.

"Don't get me wrong. I understand the desire to win the respect of your colleagues and peers. People like you and me were students for so many years that we lost perspective. We've always wanted to please our teachers and mentors. Then we had to win the approval of our colleagues and senior professors who would judge the significance of our work. Rarely have we been asked who would use our research, though that's the really important question. What difference are we making in the world out there?"

"You and I are on the same page," Carolyn nods.

"We're kindred spirits." I'm stunned by the emotional and intellectual connection I feel with Carolyn.

"We both want social science to be useful, to make a difference in people's lives. I know how much I was helped and changed by writing through my grief and loss, and I believe my stories can help other people cope with their losses and sorrows."

"When I think of the stories you've shown me, the word that comes to mind is audacious. They're daring and brave, even fearless."

"I wasn't trying to be brave. I felt I had to write these stories. In a certain respect the stories were writing me. And I was sure it was the best sociology I'd ever done. But I kept asking myself, 'Is sociology ready for this kind of first-person writing?'"

"Not if you insist on making mainstream sociologists your primary audience. But now I'm repeating myself."

"You're probably right," Carolyn sighs. "But do you think there's an audience for the kind of work I'm doing? I mean, will anyone want to join this conversation?"

"I'm counting on that to make the PhD program in communication take off. No other program is producing interpretive scholars who can do narrative inquiry, critical/cultural research, and performance ethnography. That's going to be our niche."

"Will there be jobs for these students? I doubt that mainstream programs are going to incorporate interpretive social science into their curriculum? I know that hasn't happened in sociology."

"I didn't realize you were such a Doubting Thomas," I joke. "Let's call it a calculated gamble. The demographics are on our side. We're witnessing a rapid increase in the enrollment of women, middle- and working-class people, blacks and Hispanics, and students from Third- and Fourth-world countries. Many of these newcomers have been firsthand witnesses to colonialism and imperialism, so they understand how neutrality, objectivity, and detachment can function as tools of oppression and domination. They're entering graduate school hungry for a research agenda that resonates with their lived experiences, and they're attracted to the idea of a radical democratization of the research process. They resonate with indigenous and narrative ways of knowing. Science is less important to them than living good and meaningful lives and contributing to a society that is committed to social justice."

"So you're banking on a changing population of students to drive the curriculum?" Carolyn replies, and I nod agreement as she continues. "I don't want to rain on your parade, Art, but that sounds naïve to me. I can't imagine the mainstream radically revising the curriculum in deference to the needs of these new populations of students."

"The students won't be the only ones demanding change. There will be other pressures as well."

"What pressures are you talking about?"

"There are so many; I don't know where to start."

"Are you referring to the issues you raised in your handbook chapter [Bochner, 1985]?"

"Oh, you read it?"

"Of course, I did."

"That's a good place to start."

"I've always taken an interest in research ethics," Carolyn says. "So your discussion of the questionable ethics of experimental social psychology really hit home with me. Some of the classical social psychological studies you cite, such as Milgram's studies of obedience [1965, 1974], Asch's conformity experiments [1956], and Rosenthal and Jacobson's *Pygmalion in the Classroom* [1968], are deeply disturbing."

"And we shouldn't delude ourselves into thinking these ethical issues are going to blow over like a summer thunderstorm," I say. "A time may come when social scientists can't justify deceiving subjects the way Milgram [1965] and Asch did because the potential harm to participants is too great. The ends don't necessarily justify the means, especially in cases where the main beneficiary appears to be the career of the researcher."

"Which brings us right back to the question of who benefits from social science research," Carolyn says, "which was uppermost in my mind when I was completing the draft of *Final Negotiations*. I realized I was less concerned about how it might matter to sociologists than about how it could help people immersed in the chaos of loss and grief. I wanted them to realize they could still have a good life on the other side of the pain."

"Maybe that's why reviewers don't get what you're doing," I say. "It's extremely difficult to write a single text aimed at two different audiences. If you reach 'ordinary people,' if they're the ones who identify with, understand, and are moved by your stories, then you run the risk that academics will think the book couldn't possibly be good sociology. I can hear academic reviewers saying, 'Hey, Carolyn Ellis, where's the jargon? Where are the concepts? Where's the theoretical explanation?' One of my professors in graduate school made a big deal out of how academic psychologists vilified Eric Berne's *Games People Play* [1962]. They took this elitist stance that his work was 'too popular,' which meant it wasn't very deep, profound, or theoretical."

"I've also found that academic publishers don't want to mess with trade books, and trade publishers don't believe academics can write well enough to attract a wide public audience," she says. "And who wants to go through the rigmarole of hiring an agent to represent you? Besides, I'm first and foremost a sociologist. It's sociology that I want to change. I want to bring sociology, particularly ethnographic stories, to a wider audience."

"Damn, Carolyn, you're such an intrepid comingler," I rib. "You want to reach a wider audience *as a sociologist*. Fair enough. Saying you're a sociologist shouldn't have to be a disclaimer, though I'll remind you that the esoteric jargon and mind-numbing abstractions of theoretical sociology has little appeal outside the walls of ivy. Other academics have tried this, but only a few have succeeded. Ernest Becker [1973], Margaret Mead [1928, 1935, 1949], Erich Fromm [1941, 1956], Robert Coles [1967, 1989], and David Riesman [1950] come to mind. If that's what you want to do, you should go for it, but you better be prepared to run into roadblocks."

Carolyn tilts her head downward and twists her lips as if pouting. "Maybe I should have another glass of wine," she kids.

"You'll need more than one to take on that challenge," I tease. "Perhaps we should take our lead from your dogs," I add, pointing to Ande and Likker, who have cuddled up on the round coach. Oh, I hope she doesn't take that the wrong way.

"I should warn you," Carolyn says. "Academic shoptalk often puts them right to sleep."

"I see that." Whew. "Unfortunately, we can't help ourselves. I know I can't. Conversations like this one energize me. I wouldn't make a very good dog. I enjoy academic banter too much."

"I want to get back to your point about making social science more accountable to the public. I'm with you on that all the way," Carolyn says, placing her hand briefly on my arm, then withdrawing it. "Too much social science is boring, esoteric, and parochial. People don't pick up academic journals to have a good read. Even graduate students and seasoned professors find a lot of it torturous to read."

"I'm one of those seasoned professors," I say. "I get halfway through an article and start questioning its relevance to how people actually live their lives. What is its social significance? How can people use this knowledge? The research is rigorous and methodologically sophisticated, but is that enough? Too many social scientists insist on addressing trivial questions by means of rigorous methods."

"This is the game we learned in graduate school, isn't it?" Carolyn asks. "We were taught that the goal of the game is to be productive in research, to produce knowledge."

"They didn't call it a game, but that's what it became—a knowledge game governed by rules of how to apply technologies of inquiry."

"You mean research tools and methodologies?"

"Yes, value-free research practices."

"I liked learning methods," Carolyn says, "and I was good at it. But in hindsight I can see the imbalance. Knowing how to do research doesn't mean the research you do will have real human benefits."

"My mentor used the term 'methodological machismo' to refer to the methodology fetish among social scientists. Don't you find it strange that in graduate school our professors talked constantly about knowledge and truth, but rarely mentioned wisdom?"

"Come to think of it, you're right," Carolyn agrees. "Why was that?"

"I guess there's a certain degree of conceit that goes along with talking about wisdom," I continue. "The only academic I ever heard talk about wisdom was Gregory Bateson. He defined wisdom as knowledge of the larger interactive system [1972]. He thought all knowledge had to be grounded in relationality and context, and he had little faith in timeless truths about the social world. 'You can't live without an eraser' was one of his favorite lines." (See Peters, 2010.)

Carolyn laughs. "I like that," she says.

"He also thought science was not just intellectual but also moral and aesthetic," I say into her laughter, realizing how much I'm enjoying the conversation.

"Bateson's views would have sounded the death knell for mainstream social science in the positivist tradition. Why didn't more social scientists follow his lead?"

"In my theory class, I show how the die was cast in the nineteenth century when many of the social science disciplines were formed. They believed they had to ape the methods of the enormously successful natural sciences. Each new discipline developed clusters of specialists and disciplinary journals. But they started without any consensus about the important problems of social life to which their work would be addressed. The focus became research productivity. As a result, they accumulated mountains of data divorced from the most pressing problems of human well-being."

"Geez, when you put it like that, Art, I can't help but feel dejected," Carolyn admits.

"Take heart—the cracks in the foundation of academic social sciences are widening."

"Really, Art, I'm not a pessimistic person. I think as time goes on, you'll find me an upbeat and positive person."

I do hope time will go on. "I could hear that in your lecture."

"Even though I was talking about death and loss?" she smiles.

"The stories were heartbreaking, but the way in which you told them showed how meaningful loss can be. You didn't run away from the pain. You took it in, reflected on it, and drew lessons from it, delving deep into your subjectivity. The vulnerability you exposed made me feel less afraid to face grief and loss, which eventually comes to all of us. The relationality in your stories is akin to Bateson's view of wisdom."

"Wow, I'm flattered. You really do get what I'm trying to do."

"I see your work as a paradigm shift," I say, unable to hold back the excitement bursting out of me. "Your modes of storytelling can provide an alternative to the objectivism of orthodox social science. Instead of detachment, you embrace connection; in the place of separation, you chose engagement; rather than isolating your observer self, you act collaboratively with the people and communities suffering these kind of losses. This kind of vulnerable writing and research may not be for everybody, but surely it's for somebody [Ellis, 1993]. There has to be a place for this work in the social sciences. That's why I consider it imperative to clarify what kind of science social science can be."

"Or whether what we're seeking to produce has to be 'scientific' knowledge. Isn't it possible to do meaningful and useful sociology that isn't, strictly speaking, scientific?"

"These are precisely the kind of distinctions that Richard Rorty's account of inquiry attempts to demystify," I say. "He suggests that we'd all be a lot better off if we understood knowledge as the practices we acquire to cope with reality rather than a product of the procedures we use to get an accurate picture of reality [Rorty, 1979]."

"Coping with reality—I love that idea. That's what *Final Negotiations* [Ellis, 1995] is all about. We couldn't anticipate what reality would throw at Gene and me. All we could do is try to cope with it. That's the kind of reality with which most caregivers are faced. I may only have a sample of one case, and it is a case in which I'm an active participant. But I'm examining myself and the other person and our modes of negotiating our relationship with each other and to Gene's illness. I'm also groping to understand myself and my emotions and looking at other people looking at us. Moreover, the case takes place over nearly a decade. Sociologists have complained about the lack of longitudinal research. They ought to appreciate looking at a detailed case over such a long time period."

"There you go again, defending the legitimacy of your methodology."

"Because that's what my critics bellow about. How is this research? How is what you're doing sociology? How can it be, if it's not adhering to rigorous rules of scientific sociology?"

"Rorty [1985] has an answer for that. He wants critics like those you cite to consider what makes science so special and separate from all other modes of inquiry. Why do the boundaries between science, humanities, and the arts have to be drawn so strictly? Rorty says they shouldn't be. He proposes something akin to fuzzy and fluid boundaries. Consider your situation. You're a member of something called the 'sociological community.' As a member of that community, you've identified a 'subject' or 'experience' of unquestionable sociological merit. If the boundaries of sociology are not sufficiently robust to incorporate your work, then they need to be stretched."

"I'm not criticized for what I'm studying but for how I'm studying it."

"That's because disciplines like sociology want to be considered part of this priestly order called 'science,'" I say. "Rorty is trying to tear down the oppositions and hierarchies in which science is placed above all other modes of inquiry by virtue of its methods. In one of his papers, he says he wants the image of the great scientist to be changed from that of somebody who got it right to that of somebody who made it new [Rorty, 1989]. He wants scholars to talk less about methods and more about ideas, less about rigor and more about originality. That's another thing that impressed me about your lecture—its freshness and originality. You're in the process of making a new sociology."

"I'm getting a headache just thinking about all these distinctions and oppositions. I would like to live in Rorty's world of inquiry, but that's not the one I inhabit right now."

"Right now, indeed. But the tide is turning. Trust me, there's going to be a revolt in the social sciences, and you and I can be a big part of it."

"You've had too much wine."

"No, I'm sober and serious. For the past five years, I've immersed myself in the literature on postmodernism and deconstruction. Their critique of master narratives is compelling [Clifford and Marcus, 1986; Foucault, 1982; Lyotard, 1985; Rorty, 1979]."

"See, I told you. I knew it. You're one of those language people." In an exaggerated French accent, she adds, "Zer is nuting outzide dah text."

"If you mean that language mediates how people interpret and explain the world they live in, including themselves, then, yes, I'm a language person. But my work also focuses on stories, meanings, sense making, and social constructions. I wouldn't call you an 'experience person' just because you repeatedly refer to lived experience. Your work also embodies feelings, subjectivities, and social performances."

"Now look at who's getting defensive!" Carolyn teases. "When I kid you about being a language person, I'm not disputing that discourse is important. I'm saying that lived experience can't be reduced to discourse. It's fuller and more exuberant."

"Actually, when I hear how you talk about lived experience, I realize that you and I are not all that different in our outlook. If we look at language as all the symbolic ways in which lived experience is expressed, then it becomes something we only can understand through its various expressions. Dilthey [1976] wanted the human sciences to focus on giving expression to human experience and understanding these expressions. That's what both of us want to do."

"I presume that Dilthey would have included expressions of all sorts."

"If you take 'all sorts' to mean texts of all sorts, then literature, theater, ritual performances, conversations, and any form of storytelling can count as an expression of experience."

"That's what Clifford Geertz [1986, p. 377] said about the anthropology of experience [Turner and Bruner, 1986]: "[I]n whatever form they come, stories matter, and so do stories about stories."

"While we're name dropping, let me mention Stephen Crites," I say. "He's a professor of religion who wrote one of the classic articles on storytelling, 'The Narrative Quality of Experience' [1971], which examines how stories matter."

"I can understand why you would be taken by that title. It links language to experience, right?"

"Actually, he doesn't talk much about language *per se*. He argues that experience itself is inherently narrative, that stories lie deep in our consciousness. Some stories are so deeply embedded that they form our consciousness. We live in stories, and most of us see our lives as something akin to a moving story, traveling from a past we can recall to a present to which we attend and then extending out to a future we anticipate."

"He's saying that human beings are thoroughly temporal beings?" Carolyn inquires.

"Precisely."

"The notion of life as a temporally 'moving story' strikes me as akin to how we use language. We speak in the present, past, or future tense, at least in English we do."

"You're becoming a language person. How nice," I joke. "Seriously, you've identified a crucial connection. Some philosophers refer to the twentieth century as the century of language because so many of our assumptions about language have been modified. Once viewed simply as a tool for mirroring reality, language is now understood as an ongoing, constitutive part of reality. Language not only designates; it also expresses. Human beings can shape and create language, but language also constitutes and sustains us. The positivists wanted to see language as an instrument of control, but now we understand that language may exert as much control over us as we do over it."

"Okay, I give up. Human beings are language animals. But Crites also seems to be saying that we're time-binding animals. Does he mean that time—past, present, future—is our modality of experience?"

"Yes, that's the narrative quality of experience. Narrative unifies temporal modalities. Only the present exists as lived experience, but, as Augustine [1998] famously observed, there is 'a present of things past, a present of things present, and a present of things future' [Crites, 1971, p. 301]."

"I see those modalities in *Final Negotiations* [Ellis, 1995]. I'm telling the story now, after the events took place. The story is about the past, but it is the present that directs my attention to the past and draws meaning from it."

"And the story is pointed to the future, isn't it?"

"Yes, that's one of the reasons I say it has therapeutic value. My story is not only about where I am but also where I'm headed. Survivors of trauma often want to create a story they can live in with hope and optimism. Or they want to make people aware of injustices they've suffered. Or they want to persuade others to act on their behalf. They want their survival to have meaning into the future."

"That's why Crites [1971, p. 303] says that memory gives storytelling its depth, but anticipation devises its trajectory. The stories that matter most, I think, are those that help us recover a living past and renew our hope in the promise of the future." I pause to take a breath and note a pensive expression on Carolyn's face. "What are you thinking about?" I ask.

"I'm thinking about the affinity between your work and mine. I'm writing stories, and you're reading and theorizing storytelling as a paradigm for the social sciences."

"We do seem to be kindred spirits. Maybe we could take the narrative turn together."

"The narrative turn? Is that a kind of dance?" Carolyn clowns, a big smile covering her face.

"Very funny," I say, curling my nose and twirling a long strand of hair hanging over my right ear.

"All kidding aside, when you turn, don't you move toward something and away from something else? Couldn't we choreograph a dance in which partners slide and spin across the dance floor, moving both away and toward some thing or some feeling? Let's try it," she says, abruptly standing, reaching out her hand and inviting me to join.

"Okay, okay, you have a point," I say, gently resisting her invitation, but briefly squeezing her hand in the process. "I am both moving away and moving toward. Let me see if I can fill in the blanks. Give me a second to collect my thoughts."

"I assume the turn means that you're both using narrative and moving toward it, embracing it like two lovers folding together on the dance floor," she continues.

"You're not going to let go of the dance metaphor, are you?"

"I do love dancing. It's so emotional, expressive, and evocative."

"Ah, now I get it. Dancing embodies the same qualities you're trying to put into your ethnographic writing. That's a nice way to smuggle in your point of view. As for me, I would add that dancing is a form of self-expression. The narrative turn is predicated on what Charles Taylor [1989] calls the study of persons rather than things. The important thing about being a person is that certain issues matter to us. The things that matter to you may not be the same things that matter to me, but something will matter dearly to each of us."

"Like dancing," Carolyn pokes fun again.

"Yes, like dancing, or storytelling, or grieving, loving, acting with compassion, having faith, and so on."

"These sound moral or even spiritual."

"You can't tell stories without moralizing, so I'd say, yes, as storytelling animals, we are moral creatures. We care about the good. The presence of evil in the world is undeniable, but most people point their lives toward the good. I'd guess *Final Negotiations* is decidedly steered toward the good."

"Yes, I am trying to show that we made something good and meaningful out of the difficult and challenging circumstances Gene's chronic illness imposed upon us. But I wasn't thinking of my story as a narrative directed toward the good. Why the good?"

"In *After Virtue,* MacIntyre [1984, p. 216] says that every person is 'a teller of stories that aspire to truth,' which he equates with virtue or the good. All of us find ourselves living in stories of one kind or another. Some of the stories in which we're living are cultural stories passed down to us through the books our parents read to us as children or we absorbed from various media and social institutions. We inherited other stories from our parents in the form of family myths they told us even before we were aware of the part we were supposed to play in carrying the legends and family traditions forward. The values implicit or explicit in these stories start us on our life quest of seeking the good, which is a narrated quest that continues over the course of our lives. For MacIntyre, it is life as a whole that matters most, and narrative is what gives our lives intelligibility and unity."

"The idea of life as a quest for a good story in which to live resonates with me, but the way you expressed it sounds circular: The good life is one spent seeking the good life. Where does one go to find the good?"

"MacIntyre says that the story of a person's life is always embedded in the story of the communities from which the person derives his or her identity. That's why the good life varies from one person to the next. There is a moral particularity to our lives."

"But I rebelled against the values of the community in which I was raised. So did a lot of my friends," Carolyn replies, questioning the importance of her primary socialization.

"That's not unusual. Rebellion is one mode of expressing an identity, but the story you showed me about your brother's death reveals that you didn't cut yourself off completely from your past. Your history is a living history, and the community in which you were raised is the starting point. Everyone begins somewhere, some place. We all have a narrative inheritance." (See Goodall, 2005.)

"But now my identity is situated in an entirely different context."

"Yes, I can see your keen sensitivity to the academic life in which your identity is embedded. You and I were socialized into certain practices that defined the good for us as social scientists. The values we learned to attach to these practices made it difficult for us to break with the past. In my case, I experienced an epiphany—my first wife's breakdown—that weakened the influence of these academic traditions. I saw them in a new light. Kuhn [1970] might have called the whole episode an anomaly." I notice how Carolyn's eyes open wide when I mention the breakdown, but she doesn't ask about it. I better save that story for another day, I think to myself.

"For me it was the crushing blow of my brother's sudden death coupled with dealing nearly every day with Gene's decline and the competing roles of caregiver and loving partner."

"We were seeking for the good and becoming aware through the twists of fate that life threw us that there are better and worse ways to live a life [MacIntyre, 1984, p. 224]. MacIntyre would say that the better or worse is revealed by virtue of the character of a narrative that provides intelligibility and unity to a person's life."

"I like thinking of *Final Negotiations* as a story of my search for the good, though it's a contingent good. It's not an objective good but rather one grounded in the practices and traditions in which my identity is embedded."

"Nicely expressed, and before I forget, I want to tell you how much I admire what you said about how you were offering your story as a point of comparison for other people going through similar experiences. I want to offer one small edit to your statement: your story is more than an offering—it's a gift."

"Am I always going to have to put up with you editing my work?" she jokes.

"If I have my way, you'll have plenty of chances to repay me," I rejoin. "It's been a long time since I enjoyed a conversation as much as this one. It's such a delight to talk about things we really care about."

"You've boosted my spirits. I think we could potentially make a really good team. I do the stories; you do the theory. You know how to make theory accessible and relevant to everyday life. I'm puzzled by one thing, though."

"What's that?"

"You say we need more stories, but theory is where you seem most comfortable."

"Sometimes it's necessary to get out of your comfort zone. I like to theorize, and I'll likely stay immersed in philosophical and theoretical dialogues about narrative truth. But you've shown me how important it is to put flesh on the bones of narrative theory. Your enthusiasm for the first-person voice is contagious. Now I want to write stories that matter too, stories like yours."

"Do you have a particular story in mind?"

"I want to write about my father and the relationship between us. His death had a huge impact on me as a person and as a professor."

"Have you written any of it?"

"It's all in my head except for the text of a eulogy I gave at his funeral, which I want to include in the story. Until I met you I hadn't realized how much I'd suppressed my urge to tell this story."

"Why is it so important to you now?"

"Because of everything we've been talking about tonight—our academic socialization, how the academy can become more personal, that we don't need to hide behind a veneer of professional jargon, and other more personal issues."

"Like what?" Carolyn urges more disclosure.

"When my father died I realized we would never be able to express our grief to each over what we had missed out on as father and son. I didn't ever want to have that feeling again. It was time to become the professor I wanted to be. No more excuses. No more waiting until later. I transferred some of the grief I felt toward my father's loss to the sorrow I felt about not having the courage to express myself more fully and personally in the classroom and in my scholarship. I decided to drop the pretensions of an academic persona and spare no effort to make my work more practical and humane."

"It's fascinating to me how grief works on us and through us. Some of our saddest experiences can lift us to heights we never imagined were possible."

"You can say that again," I acknowledge. We sit in silence for a moment, looking at each other. I meditate on the significance of losses in my life and imagine she is doing the same. I think about how precious this moment is and how rarely I've experienced the kind of kinship and connection I'm feeling with Carolyn. When I look away, I catch a glimpse of my watch. "Oh my gosh, it's after 11."

"I can't believe we've been talking for over three hours."

"And we haven't even gotten to the topic of collaboration between our departments," I grin.

"We'll have to put that one off until our next meeting. That and a lot more. I feel as if we're just getting started."

"Me too. I have many more questions about the work you've been doing and how you do it. I'd also like to tell you more about some of my personal experiences. I think some of them would make good stories."

"Conversations like ours are never finished," Carolyn says. "We merely run out of time. Hopefully, this is just the beginning."

"Yeah, Louis, I think this is the beginning of a beautiful friendship," I mock in my best Humphrey Bogart impersonation, recalling how my friend Barb used to end our phone calls with that line. "Seriously, I've got an early meeting tomorrow, so I better hit the road. Can we set a date to continue our talk?"

"A date?" Carolyn asks tongue in cheek.

"Yes, a date," I say emphatically. "I want you to come to my house and meet my German Shepherd, Martina."

"How about Sunday afternoon at 2?" she asks.

"That would be great," I say as I rise from my chair and start to clear the dessert dishes from the table."

"Oh just leave those," Carolyn insists. "I'll walk you to your car."

We stroll slowly through her living room as the dogs look on from their comfortable resting places on the round couch. "You two stay here," she says as she opens the front door and we exit her house.

As we walk toward the car, a scene from one of my all-time favorite movies, *Annie Hall* (Allen, 1977), flashes through my mind: "We've never kissed before. And I'll never know when to make the right move or anything. So we'll kiss now and get it over with, and then we'll go eat. Okay? We'll digest our food better."

But we've already eaten. Besides, I don't know if she wants to kiss me. Suddenly, I feel Carolyn's hand touching mine. Tightly grasping her hand, I turn toward her, locking my eyes onto hers. She leans toward me and kisses me gently on the lips. Closing my eyes, I breathe in the softness and sweetness of her lips.

I'm so glad we found each other.

CHAPTER TWELVE

Healing a Divided Self

Narrative Means to Academic Ends[1]

> How to encompass in our minds the complexity of some lived
> moments of life? ... You don't do that with theories. You don't
> do that with a system of ideas. You do it with a story.
>
> *Robert Coles (1989, p. 128)*

Several months after a twist of fate brought us together, Carolyn and I traveled to Oxford, England, where I presented a keynote address, "Embracing Contingencies of Lived Experience in the Study of Close Relationships," to a conference of the International Network of Personal Relationships (Bochner, 1990). In the weeks leading up to the conference, Carolyn and I engaged in perpetual conversation about how to bring emotionality, storytelling, and researcher reflexivity into a more prominent position in the human sciences. We wanted to build a bridge between the social sciences and the humanities, and we were convinced this goal could be achieved by offering stories that show the struggles of ordinary people coping with difficult contingencies of lived experience. Replete with characters, scenes, plots, and dialogues, our research stories would have the goal of helping people put themselves in the place of others and consider important aspects of their own lives in the terms offered by the concrete contexts and details of other people's stories (Jackson, 1989).

In the Oxford address, I encouraged social scientists to break away from standard conventions of academic writing in order to bring a closer connection between the research texts we write and the lives they represent. "If we experience our lives as stories, why not represent them as stories?" I asked. At the conclusion of the talk, I put away my manuscript, moved closer to the audience, and ended on this note: "I yearn for a legitimate alternative to the kind of disembodied writing that extols the virtues of objectivity at the expense of making work on close relationships evocative, readable, and closer to the bone of relationship life. We should consider new ways of depicting the ebb and flow of relationship experience in episodic forms that dramatize the motion of connected lives across the curve of time. One way to do this is to make ourselves the objects of research, highlighting our own lived experiences and digging deeply into them." Both feet were now out of the closet.

Coming to Narrative, by Arthur P. Bochner, 276–294. © 2014 Left Coast Press, Inc. All rights reserved.

The audience sat in stunned silence for a few moments, after which several participants raised predictable questions about how reviews of this kind of work could be carried out objectively. During the discussion period I sparred politely with several social psychologists over the differences between narrative truth and historical truth, and between a writer's desire to pull readers into a story and a scientist's determination to pull some*thing* out of a story. When the session ended, several young women approached me. "I'm looking for a graduate school that would encourage and support the kind of work you proposed," one of them said. "Me too," said another. "Where can I apply to learn narrative inquiry? I have stories I want to tell." I looked across at Carolyn. We smiled at each other.

"That was quite a fuss you created at the personal relationships conference," wrote one of my former students in a letter I received when we returned from Oxford. "I guess they'll never invite you there again." A couple of days later, I called Tucker. He had already heard about my splash at the conference—or lack of it. "I guess you've gone completely over to the dark side," he said. When I hung up I let out a sigh of relief. I realized I was now a bit of a disappointment to Tucker, but I was that much closer to becoming the person I took myself to be.

Carolyn and I thought the "fuss" we made was a sign we were onto something. Uplifted by the kinds of feedback we were receiving from students and colleagues at USF as well as our own gut feelings that we could tap into a well of pent-up desire for embodied, evocative storytelling, we collaboratively outlined a joint project to be called "ethnographic alternatives." The project would emphasize subjectivity, self-reflexivity, emotionality, and the goal of connecting social sciences to humanities through first-person, ethnographic storytelling. In 1991, we drafted the first exemplars of the kind of writing we had in mind (Ellis and Bochner, 1991; Bochner and Ellis, 1992), and performed one of stories at an academic conference (Ellis and Bochner, 1991). The following story was my first attempt to merge theory and story into a seamless narrative that could inspire other writers to engage with our project.

I could not fall asleep. I tossed and turned, trying to ignore the anxiety churning through my stomach. Sometimes I have trouble sleeping when I'm away from home or when I'm apprehensive about a presentation. But this was different. It wasn't the hotel room or the upcoming convention that was keeping me awake. Something felt terribly wrong, but I didn't know what. Finally, at about 7:15 a.m., I got out of bed and headed for the shower.

I don't recall how long I had been standing under the water when I heard the phone ring. A few seconds later my roommate, Herb Simons, called to me. "Art, it's your secretary, Sharon. She wants to speak to you. She says it's very important."

My secretary would not call me at a conference unless the roof was caving in. I knew instantly that her call was personal, not departmental. Grabbing a towel, I hurried to the phone, my heart beating rapidly, my mind sorting possibilities.

The voice on the other end was calm and deliberate. "Art, I don't know how to tell you this. Your sister just called. She said your father died last night. He had a sudden heart attack shortly after eating dinner. I thought I should tell you as soon as possible."

I don't remember what I said next. I recall putting the receiver down, standing naked, water dripping down my body, dampening the carpet at my feet, and Herb, rising from his bed, looking pale and puzzled. "My father died last night," I muttered quietly. "I don't know details."

Herb stood in front of me, uncharacteristically silent. His face mirrored the shock that must have shown on mine. Perhaps he sensed the terrible struggle I was having as my mind raced to organize what had to be done next while my body yielded to the emotional reality of death and loss. I felt dazed and confused, like a boxer who is startled by the first powerful blow from a stronger opponent. Stunned by the punch, he hears competing voices, one inside his head whispering, "Ignore the pain, stay with the game plan," the other calling from the site of his body's pain, rejecting the authority of consciousness over bodily experience.

A voice inside my head said, "Get home to Tampa as quickly as possible. Mother will need you. She'll expect you to take control, help arrange the funeral, and keep the family from falling apart." Suddenly the three papers I was to present at the convention held little significance. However, I was too responsible to miss these sessions without forewarning. I should contact the chair of each program, get someone to substitute if possible, and give other participants a chance to prepare for my absence.

But a second, less coherent, voice kept intruding on my thoughts. I felt dizzy and lightheaded, as if I were teetering on the edge of a dangerous cliff. As I wiped away the tears trickling down my face and felt the flood of anxiety swirling through my stomach, I was terrified to realize that I couldn't shut down what I was feeling by an act of will. This voice reminded me that my father's death was not just another event to be organized, experienced, and filed away. It wasn't only my plans for the weekend that had been interrupted, but something much bigger—my self-narrative, the way I recited the story of my life to myself. The plot I had scripted for my life cast my parents and siblings as minor characters. Through this act of imagination, I long ago had re-created myself in order to diminish the significance of a perverse childhood and not be persecuted by it. But now the unspoken life inside me demanded recognition. I tried to make these feelings go away, but my efforts only intensified their grip. While I stood motionless, memories circulated through my head, flashing back a stream of unconnected, incoherent, and frightening family scenes.

As if the jolts produced by waves of unsolicited recollections were not enough, I also had to contend with the void my father's death created. At the moment, it didn't matter that as a child my relationship with my father had been so troubled and destructive or that he had grown old and fragile before I could come to terms with the fierce and violent father of my youth. The chance to rise above our circumstances was gone now. I could never prove any better as a son than he had been as a father. We would never have a final conversation that I could look back on with a sense of resolution or closure. The image I once had of being by his side, of holding or stroking him as he passed—as if a tender, loving touch could magically transform a lifetime of painful experience between a father and his son—had been stolen from me. Our relationship would live on in my mind, but conversation between us had ended. He was gone. We were gone.

I picked up the phone to start informing other people, but as soon as I dialed the first number I began drifting away. Before I could speak I dropped the phone into the cradle and was disconnected. When I picked it up, the phone felt heavy in my hand. How could I make plans when I couldn't even hold on to the phone? Fortunately Herb took control of the situation. He asked me to make a list of people to call and assured me he would contact them. Then he called the airlines and booked an afternoon flight to Tampa for me.

As I sat in the corner and watched Herb organizing my affairs, I recalled the times I had tried to talk to him about my interest in research on death and dying. These conversations never got very far. Herb resisted my invitations to delve deeper, and I usually felt disappointed we couldn't connect on this topic. Now I was beginning to understand why these conversations had been so frustrating and superficial. At the time, Herb's parents were dead and mine were alive. For Herb, death had been personalized; for me, it was academic. Under these circumstances, what did we really have to talk about? How could we possibly speak the same language? As a result of my father's death, I had passed into another dimension, one that was missing when Herb and I had tried previously to converse about death. We still weren't talking about death or loss, but when Herb looked at me from across the room, I felt the kind of communion that can only occur when two people are woven into the same fabric of experience.

On that long plane ride home, I realized as never before that I was a human being. It sounds strange to say that, I know, but I believe it is true. My father's sudden death forced me to grasp the significance of how contingent, limited, and relative human experience can be. Most of us realize that fear of death lingers behind the absorbing details of our everyday lives, but we keep our fear sedated because we sense it could infect us if we let go. When the reality of death interrupts our lives, our immunity weakens. Then, if we allow it, we can drop the canopy of dishonesty covering the brute fact that we don't really control our own lives. One of Freud's greatest contributions was to show how meaning is made out of errors, accidents, and unexpected events (Brill, 1938). Chance changes us (H. Becker, 1994). My father's death made it possible, even necessary for me to see the consequences of splitting the academic self from the personal self in a new light. At my university or at conferences, I normally move in and out of analytical or conceptual frames without experiencing anything akin to an experiential shock or epiphany. But when my father died while I was attending a national communication convention, two worlds within me collided, and I was stunned to learn how tame the academic world is in comparison to the wilderness of lived experience.

As I looked out the window of the plane and saw how small the roads, farms, cars, and houses looked from above, I was reminded of Ernest Becker's (1973) remarks about the puniness of life in the face of the overwhelming majesty of our universe. I felt confusion swelling within me as competing parts of myself struggled for supremacy. A voice inside me questioned the motivation for my drive and dedication as a social scientist: "Admit it, Art, your work sucks energy away so you don't have to face the reality of the human condition." I had no ready response, but I was inspired to scribble some notes on the pad on my lap:

> Academic life is impersonal, not intimate. It provides a web of distractions. The web protects us against the invasion of helplessness, anxiety, and isolation we would feel if we faced the human condition honestly. Stability, order, control—these are the words that social science speaks. Ambiguity, chance, accidents—these are the terms that life echoes. Suppose we achieved the stability, order, and control we seek—what then? No variance—no differences—no chance—no fun—no adventure—no vulnerability—no deniability—no flirtation—no love.

The notes didn't help. They only exaggerated the divisions tugging within me. I felt an obligation to answer back to the first voice, but the only thing I could think of was to reaffirm my commitment to the Deweyan premise that no matter how honest we are about the tragedy of the human condition, we still have to point ourselves toward some hopeful, creative activity. What was it Ernest Becker (1973) said in the final lines of *The Denial of Death*? "Fashion something—an object or ourselves—and drop it into the confusion" (p. 285). But these words begged the question of how to narrow this large gulf between my academic life and my personal life. In the aftermath of my father's death, it seemed obvious to me that life had a different shape and texture than the ways it was sculpted in the classroom and in scholarly journals.

Now the academic man in me stood face-to-face with the ordinary man. What did they have to say to each other? Could they get in touch with each other? Integrate? Harmonize? The sad truth is that the academic self frequently is cut off from the ordinary, experiential self. A life of theory can remove one from experience, make one feel unconnected. All of us inhabit multiple worlds. When we live in the world of theory, we usually assume that we are inhabiting an objective world. There, in the objective world, we are expected to play the role of spectator. It is a hard world for a human being to feel comfortable in, so we try to get rid of the distinctively human characteristics that distort the mythological beauty of objectivity. We are taught to master methods that exclude the capriciousness of immediate experience. When we do, we find ourselves in a world devoid of spirituality, emotion, and poetry—a scientific world in which, as Galileo insisted, there is no place for human feelings, motives, or consciousness. In the objective world, the goal is to speak nature's language without the intrusions of human subjectivity. In some quarters, this kind of world is the only rational world and the only world that can produce knowledge that makes a difference.

I suspect there are as many kind, decent, and loving people inhabiting the objective, scientific world as there are in any other reality. But there is nothing inherent in the scientific method that requires these traits. Findings do not become less scientific if the scientist who reports them has undesirable personality traits or character flaws. Remember the Milgram (1963) experiments on obedience? They were ingenious and elegant exemplars of social scientific research, but they also were spiritually offensive. Laing (1982) warns that "what is scientifically right may be morally wrong" (p. 22). Normally, scientists don't worry about the moral consequences of the knowledge they produce or about what they had to do to get to the truth, but that doesn't mean we (or they) shouldn't thoroughly pursue such issues. Reciting a litany of ruthless indiscretions, Apter (1996) calls psychology "an intrusive and frequently cruel discipline" (p. 22) that contributes significantly to human suffering. In the name of "science," psychologists too often use their warrant of expertise to manipulate not only variables but also people and their lives (Apter, 1996), and psychology has not cornered the market on these dubious practices.

One of the lessons I learned when I first read Kuhn's (1970) *The Structure of Scientific Revolutions* was not to expect too much from science. Kuhn's exemplars taught that the history of science offered no compelling reason to think it is possible to distinguish what is in our minds from what is out there in the world. Kuhn urged scientists to exercise caution, to guard against being smug about pushing the rhetoric of objectivity and value neutrality. Scholars like Joan Huber (Huber, 1995; Huber and Mirowsky, 1997), who proudly display this smugness, often miss the point. The problem is not with science but with a reverent and idealized view of science that positions science above the contingencies of language and outside the circle of historical and cultural interests (Denzin, 1997). Scientific method *per se* does not make it possible for the mind to transcend the skin. Even when science does improve our predictions, it cannot necessarily tell us what to do. When we know how to predict and control behavior, we do not consequently know how to deal with a person justly or empathically (Rorty, 1982b). It's too bad that a century of social and behavioral science has not notably improved our capacity to predict and control (Gergen, 1982; Rorty, 1982b), but even if it had, as Rorty (1982) observes, it would not necessarily help us evaluate the moral or ethical grounding of our actions. Some empiricists may still see social engineering as a moral exemplar of the best that rationality and method can offer, but most of us recognize that the haunting question of how to live a good and ethical life cannot be circumscribed by appeals to hard facts and objective methods.

My personal struggle after my father's death was not a scientific crisis but a moral one, and the moral questions that were raised cast a long shadow over both my personal and my academic life. I needed to take the measure of my own life and of my father's, too. What core values shaped my life as a whole? How was my academic life connected to my personal life? Could my personal life harmonize with my academic life? Remembering the ways I had resisted and rebelled against my family socialization, I questioned whether I had done the same in my academic life. Were the structures of power constitutive of academic socialization even more difficult to resist than those of one's family? Was the academic life I was living one that I had chosen, or was it one chosen for me by my mentors and the orthodox academic practices I had unconsciously internalized and embodied? As the son of working-class parents deprived of high culture, a love of books, or even a university education, I had always felt uneasy and doubtful about whether I really fit in as an academic. I knew it was not coincidental that I had chosen to teach at universities like Cleveland State, Temple, and South Florida, where many of the undergraduates come from working-class backgrounds. It was not difficult for me to feel in touch with my students because the blue-collar kid in me was never removed totally from the ground of my students' world of experience.

I had to admit, however, that my capacity to draw meaningfully from my personal experience in order to touch undergraduate students where they live did not carry over to the rest of my academic world. In the classroom, I thrived on an ability to call on stories that painted my life into their picture. When I was successful, it was largely because of the tacit knowledge we shared that connected their lived experiences to mine. But the world of academic scholarship made different demands on me. As Robert Coles (1989) suggests, graduate education usually teaches us to cover the details of individual experience beneath a blanket of professional jargon. Coles refers to professional, academic socialization as a form of indoctrination into the mindset that theory is the way to get to the core of things. One learns that entering a discipline means stepping into a world that has its own language; if you want to live in that world, you'd better be able to speak that way. We learn to tell our version of the lives we study by translating the terms ordinary people use into the categories and jargon that comprise our field's theoretical language. Looking back on his education, Coles realizes he had learned to force the stories his patients told into the theoretical constructs his discipline embraced. These theories substituted for the concrete details of stories, the teller's representation of the lived life giving way to the social scientist's expertise at abstracting its meaning. Usually the theory is there before the story is heard. Thus, the tale services the theory that explains it.

Moreover, scholarly inquiry is not assumed to start at the site of one's own experience. We learn to "receive knowledge" by focusing outward, relying on the wisdom of our predecessors to preview our own experiences and expectations. "Review the literature. See what others have said. Stand on the shoulders of the giants," we are told. Don't start where you are—start where they have been. That way you can at least avoid being accused of stupidity or ignorance. Fair enough. But how was this helping me now? I had studied, theorized, and taught about loss and attachment for more than two decades, but I had to admit I didn't really begin to know loss until I experienced my father's death. And the more I thought about my own experience of loss, read other people's accounts of loss, and reviewed the theoretical and research literature, the more I began to

282

understand that the academic world was not in touch with the everyday world of experience, the ordinary world. The research literature offered me data, labels, categories, and theoretical explanations, but it didn't express how loss felt and didn't invite engagement with the particularities of the experience. Indeed, the academic world was long on conceptualizations and short on details; long on abstractions, short on concrete events; long on analysis, short on experience; long on theories, short on stories. I had no desire to get rid of concepts, abstractions, analysis, or theory. Like most academics, I know them as the tools of my trade. It was the imbalance that troubled me—how quickly we turn lives and experiences into texts and concepts (Jackson, 1995).

Was it possible to create and inhabit a different world of inquiry, one better suited to integrating the academic and the personal selves, which are so alienated from each other by traditional academic practices? Referring to philosophers, Richard Rorty (1991) says, "We all hanker after essence and share a taste for theory as opposed to narrative. If we did not, we should probably have gone into some other line of work" (p. 71). But in the same essay, Rorty recommends a healthy dose of detailed narrative as an antidote to the essentializing proclivities of social theorists: "Earlier I said that theorists like Heidegger saw narrative as always a second-best, a propaedeutic to a grasp of something deeper than the visible detail. Novelists like Orwell and Dickens are inclined to see theory as always a second-best, never more than a reminder for a particular purpose, the purpose of telling a story better. I suggest that the history of social change in the modern West shows that the latter conception of the relation between narrative and theory is the more fruitful" (p. 80).

Among the definitions for *academic, Webster's New World Dictionary* (1966) includes "too far from immediate reality; not practical enough; too speculative" (p. 7). It's not far-fetched to extrapolate "distanced from reality; remote; impersonal." How about "disinterested" or "neutral"? (I fantasize printing T-shirts that say, "I'm an academic, I'm neutral.") I had been clothed in this image of academic life for twenty-five years, but I was just realizing how poorly it fit me. Knowledge isn't neutral, and it can never be disinterested (Denzin, 1992; Jackson, 1989).

Still, I had to remind myself that the problem is not with the university *per se,* nor is orthodox social science the problem. These are institutions created by other human beings and sustained by our complicity with its membership. We share responsibility by following rules, both tacit and explicit ones, that keep them going. We know we're onto something when we're told, "You mustn't think that way." That's the feeling I got when I read Huber's attacks on interpretive social science and qualitative research (Huber, 1995; Huber and Mirowsky, 1997). I had to wonder why she was telling me I mustn't think these thoughts. Her warnings give me pause to consider whether I've been playing according to rules I didn't know I was following. Laing (1969) declares that "unless we can 'see through' the rules, we only see through them" (p. 105). If we collectively stop complying, we stand a chance of exposing and breaking the rules against seeing the rules.

We can begin thinking thoughts we're not supposed to think. Then who can say what new shape our institution may take?

Explaining My Father

[Lived experience] brings us to a dialectical view of life which emphasizes the interplay rather than the identity of things, which denies any sure steadying to thought by placing it always within the precarious and destabilizing fields of history, biography, and time.... It remains skeptical of all efforts to reduce the diversity of experience to timeless categories and determinate theorems, to force life to be at the disposal of ideas.

Michael Jackson (1989, p. 2)

What I remember best about that weekend in Tampa, right after my father died, was how hard I struggled to explain my father to myself. I didn't want to romanticize our family history—it wasn't pretty—but I didn't want to demonize it either. Strong as his grip had been, it hadn't paralyzed us. His life had been unbearably sad and weary, filled with disappointments, burdens, and betrayals, but ours had not. We got out of prison—he stayed.

I called my mother and told her I wanted to speak at Dad's funeral. Then I locked myself in my office and started to re-create him. It was time to dig up the past. Kierkegaard (1959) says we live forward, but we understand backward. To move forward, I felt I had to look behind. I never understood my father, never really tried to. For a long time I was so ashamed of him that I could scarcely bring myself to admit he was mine. Later on, I had forgiven him, largely because I hated hating him—hated the kind of person it made me. Now that he was dead, I missed him. Looking in the mirror, I saw his face etched onto mine and realized he would always be there looking back at me. I closed my eyes and remembered:

I'm twelve years old. It's a damp, gray, smoggy, afternoon in Pittsburgh. I'm running down Beechwood Boulevard, hurrying to get home. I glance at my watch as I run. It's 6:30. My god, I'm an hour late for dinner—he's going to kill me. What can I tell him? I know, yes, I'll say the newspapers were late, so I couldn't finish delivering them on time. I turn onto Northumberland, picking up the pace. But look at me—there's a hole in the knee of my pants from where I fell, and I'm sweaty and dirty from playing basketball. He's not going to believe me. He'll take one look at me and—Wham! I can already feel it. Maybe he won't be home. I can't remember—was he working away from home today? Oh, please, please, don't be home. I turn the corner onto Severn Street. I'll be home in another minute. I've got to slow down, catch my breath. I don't see our car, what a relief. Then I do—Shit! Fear rumbles through my body! I hate that house! I hate him! I tiptoe up the steps of the front porch, open the front door gently, and close it quietly behind me. I try to scoot swiftly up the stairs to my room to change my pants, but before I can move I hear my mother's voice calling from the kitchen, "Arthur, is that you? Where have you been? I kept your dinner warm in the oven."

Before I can answer he's standing there in front of me, ready to pounce. I already feel his invincible power—hard, relentless, unforgiving. "Don't lie to me, Arthur. You were out playing ball, weren't you?" he asks.

"No, the papers got there late. I just finished delivering them."

"Why, you lazy, no-good liar. Just look at you—you're filthy," he screams in my face, punching me in the stomach.

"Mike, stop. You'll hurt him!" my mother shouts, grabbing at him, but he pulls away and she moves back. Doubled over from the force of his punch, I can't escape. He's too large; I'm too weak. The room is too small and too cluttered. I'm his prey, cornered in his territory, and the fierce, frenzied look on his face shows he won't be denied. Now he moves in for the kill. Unbuckling his belt, he grabs me by the collar with one strong, meaty hand and holds me tightly. Over and over and over again, he belts me with his strap. "I work like a slave while you play! I'll teach you. You no-good little liar. You'll learn."

Later that night, I lay on my bed, licking my wounds and plotting how I could escape this prison. Why hadn't I just kept running, past our house, out of the neighborhood, away from the anger, the fear, the hitting, the hate? What did I do wrong? Okay, I was late for dinner. We always eat at 5:30, except when he's late, then we wait, no matter how late he is or how hungry we are. But all I really did was stop to play, have some fun. Why can't I have fun?

I opened my eyes and reentered the present. Why? I ask myself. Why did he do those things? What made him so violent and impulsive? Where did all that pent-up fury come from? What satisfaction could he possibly have derived from pounding the flesh of a little boy half his size? After all, the fights never really changed anything. I didn't learn any lessons, except perhaps to make promises and tell lies.

Surrounded by hundreds of books lining the shelves of my office, I searched alone for answers. Quietly I culled details from the recesses of my memory, replaying the stories he had told us over and over again when we were children—stories about poverty, abandonment, fear, and anti-Semitism. When I was a child, I thought these stories were boring, irrelevant, and pathetic. I had no sympathy for the man I feared most. Too often, Dad had been a rotten bastard, and if he suffered before I was born, well, that was no reason to take it out on me. Besides, I was too busy learning to read the signs that tipped off an impending fit of rage—so I could get the hell out of the way—to care about whether there was a good explanation for Dad's uncontrollable anger. That I survived the beatings—that all of us did—was remarkable enough.

Hacking (1995) cautions against the impulse to place old actions under new descriptions: "There is no canonical way to think of our own past. In the endless quest for order and structure, we grasp at whatever picture is floating by and put our past into its frame" (p. 89). To say my father "abused" me is to apply a term that was totally outside my interpretive structure as a child. If the folks in my neighborhood were asked to account for such beatings, I can just hear them saying, "Abuse? Who knew abuse? We didn't know from abuse; we knew from discipline." Situating my father's violence within the cultural narrative of child abuse would be an act of "semantic contagion" (Hacking, 1995, p. 256), endowing my story with meanings that weren't available at the time these events were lived. Child abuse was not part of the conceptual space in which we lived. I never placed myself in the child abuse narrative, never thought myself a survivor, never considered my father's brutality a way of accounting for any of the mistakes I made or misfortunes I encountered later. Perhaps I was never sufficiently unhappy to need that story, or perhaps I just couldn't accept the vulnerability it implies. More likely, it never appealed to my appetite for complexity. Yes, I can remember those beatings vividly, but what is it about me that they explain? I don't know.

As adults, when we are in trouble, disturbed, or unhappy, we may feel a need to look to the past to explain why we cope the way we do. Sometimes that can be helpful, and many people testify to the usefulness of such memory work. Yet it is also true that child abuse can be parasitic on this need. It can smooth the rough edges of an indeterminate past, giving a causal structure that fills in the gaps, reconstituting a self by weaving memories of the past into stories that make sense by appropriating the new ways of talking to reveal the lessons of the past. We say, "Me too, I'm one of them. I was abused," as if we've discovered (or recovered) some new, indisputable truth (Hacking, 1995). But if I ask, "Did my father intend to abuse me?" knowing full well that the idea of child abuse was not available to him, then the meaning of his actions becomes considerably less determinate (Hacking, 1995). He operated under a moral code that a father's responsibility was to prepare his son for a harsh, cruel, unforgiving world. Had he known that one day his actions would be called child abuse, would he have acted that way? Where do we draw the line between the terms that describe our ways of thinking about the meanings of one's actions *now* and the intentions that motivated one's actions *then*?

Besides, as I sat there in my office, I wasn't trying to explain myself. I wanted to explain him. Not many of us ever try to explain our parents, think about why they turned out the way they did. We don't think it necessary to explain them. We're too absorbed with ourselves. We may use our parents to explain us, but we don't normally dig much deeper into the past. We don't use ourselves to explain them.

Our family relationships were terribly complicated, and no simple labels can suffice. My father's abusive, hateful, volatile temper wasn't all I remembered. My father was also honest, driven, hard working, and ethical to a fault. He worked too hard—"like a slave," he would say with conviction—and when he finished for the day, seven days a week, he was spent. He had nothing left for us. He was not heroic but rather just an ordinary, fearful, working man—a slave to heavy, demanding, largely unrewarding work. Uneducated, insecure, and raised a poor ghetto Jew, my father was afraid of life. He used to say proudly, "I ask for nothing from nobody," perhaps because, as Jules Henry (1971) said about such men, "The lava of nothingness boils in his gut" (p. 181). He lived beyond the reach of love and may only have felt alive, achieved an intense feeling of selfhood when he was knocking against someone who couldn't hit back. I sometimes think he was only alive physically, his spirit having been crushed by life's contingencies. My father had no functional outlet for the desires buried inside him, and when they were incited, his powers of resistance were not strong enough to contain the flames. And then he exploded. Life's contingencies had submerged the child in him, and when he saw his children expressing the fullness of a child's life, he had to make them suffer the way he must have suffered too. As Alice Miller (1983) observes in reference to masculine, parental cruelty: "Without meaning to and without realizing it, the father treat[s] his child just as cruelly as he treat[s] the child within himself" (p. 95).

Standing in front of the congregation of relatives, neighbors, and friends, I take a deep breath, hoping to stifle the emotion rising to the surface. My voice cracks as I begin to speak:

There is no formula for triumphing over life's limitations. Every person's life is a singular response to the confusion of existence.... There is much in a man's life over which he has no control and for which he is not responsible.... Some men are consumed by blows of fate; others find dignity and self-worth by accepting hardship and suffering as a normal condition of life and doing their best to lessen the burden of others.... My father would be proud to be remembered as a self-made man who stood on his own two feet and planted them firmly on the virtuous ground of duty, hard work, honesty, and integrity. He was a modest man of simple tastes. Only his immediate family—and a friend or two—ever got to know him, and sometimes he was a mystery to us.... My father could not contain the strains of life he felt inside him, the pain and fear and insecurity of his childhood. It was only in his last few years, as I watched his strength and passion fade, that I realized how vulnerable he was and always had been. My father had to be a man before he could finish being a boy. He was given no time for boyish dreams or adventures. The stark reality of poverty and prejudice allowed no opportunity for escape to the distractions of ambitious undertakings.... I wish I could have truly understood and empathized with the massive reality of his boyhood. Then I might have understood why he couldn't relax and experience more of the joy of life and living.

My father was well worth caring about, and many of us did care for him deeply. I only regret that he found our caring so difficult to apprehend as we did his. I can only hope and pray that he knows now that his life was meaningful, that we know he loved us as we love him, in our own fallible way, and that we recognized the good in him.... Now he can rest, secure and in peace.

On Narrative Coherence

David Carr (1986) observes that "Coherence seems to be a need imposed upon us whether we seek it or not" (p. 97). But the sense of coherence that we need does not inhere in events themselves. Coherence is an achievement, not a given. This is the work of self-narration: to make a life that seems to be falling apart come together again, by retelling and "restorying" the events of one's life. At certain junctures in life, this narrative challenge can be a terrible struggle, and we do not always succeed. The unity of life, its apparent wholeness across time, is simply there—sometimes figure, sometimes ground (Carr, 1986). When the flow of time is disrupted unexpectedly, the absence of a sense of coherence can become a grave concern, and we become acutely aware at such times of the unruliness of the orderly, well-planned life we thought we were living. At stake are the very integrity and intelligibility of our selfhood, which rest so tenderly and fallibly on the story we use to link birth to life to death (MacIntyre, 1984).

My father's sudden death disrupted my sense of continuity. Looking back, I saw that one day I had not returned home. Instead, I just kept running and didn't stop until I was too far away to see the past behind me. But now the past was in front of me again. I couldn't change what I remembered taking place. I knew certain things had happened—violent, harmful, unpleasant things—and I could not change that. No matter how I reinterpreted or reframed the meanings of these events, I was constrained by the events themselves. They were fixed in my mind and in my experience, and there was no way to make them vanish. Remaking my father did not mean making him up—interpretations have their limits.

The act of reconstructing the meaning of my father's life was an attempt to reclaim my past. I felt a powerful desire to own up to the experiences that had shaped me—for good or for bad—to revise, reinterpret, and make sense out of my family history from the vantage point of the present. I knew there was no getting to the bottom, no transcendental point of view, no final truth to be rendered. Remaking my father was not a disinterested activity. On the contrary, my self-interest was to be served by casting an image of my father that would free me from his grip, point me toward the future. As Crites (1986) observes, no inquiry aimed at recovering the past is ever conducted in the past: "We appropriate the personal past, in fact, out of the future" (p. 164). In effect, the work of my narrative activity was to restory significant events in my family history into a composition of a continuous life of experience. This is not to say that my life as lived, in fact, is coherent and continuous; only that I would find it impossible to make sense of my life without assuming what MacIntyre (1984) calls the "unity of life," an intelligibility that makes it possible to conceive and evaluate my life as a whole.

The eulogy I delivered at my father's funeral brought a sense of closure, however tentative, to my struggle to make sense of my family history. It marked the end of this phase of my struggle to fit my family story into the larger whole of my life story. I no longer felt I had to hide or deny the validity of the events from which I had run. I also felt I had achieved a deeper understanding of my father's life that broadened my appreciation of the patterns that connected us. But the personal sense of continuity I had achieved by reframing my father did not carry over to my academic life. I still had to deal with my desire to remake my life as a professor. The epiphany of my father's death had been a turning point in the conversation between my academic self and my ordinary self. Something very personal—my father's death—had intruded on my public, professional life. Now

I had to confront the challenge of bringing a sense of unity to the divisions these competing voices expressed. Adam Phillips (1994) says that we all have lives inside us competing to be lived; the accidents that happen to most of us remind us that we are living too few of them. To understand an event in one's life as an accident that was meant to happen, much like a Freudian slip, to see the course of one's life under the influence of coincidence rather than control, and to treat contingency as something not to overcome but to be used is to give oneself the freedom to take chances (Phillips, 1994). This was my opportunity to exercise that freedom, to use this chance to make a different life for myself as a professor. But to do so would mean to review academic life as I knew it and lived it—to question, evaluate, and critique it as honestly as I could. I wanted to identify some of the consequences of omitting the personal self from academic practices—how our teaching and writing and feelings of well-being are affected. What do we fear? Whose interests do our divided selves serve? What would result if we brought these voices into closer contact with each other?

Institutional Depression

> Here at the university, the pain lingers. I cannot clear out. It is hard to heal. Because it is hard to heal I must defend myself: close off, grow scar tissue, thicken my hide. Speech becomes guarded. I give up expressiveness.
>
> *Vivian Gornick (1996, p. 135)*

> I was shocked, almost from the moment I left Columbia, by how little I missed it, how relieved I was not to have to plunge, ever again, into that poisonous atmosphere.
>
> *Carolyn G. Heilbrun (1997, p. 39)*

The university is filled with professors who are depressed (Tompkins, 1996). I've never considered myself one of them, but I've felt on the edge, fighting against depression a number of times. The experience of depression I'm talking about is not the kind we usually think about. What I'm talking about is institutional depression, a pattern of anxiety, hopelessness, demoralization, isolation, and disharmony that circulates through university life. Normally we don't recognize its institutional form because we take for granted the rules under which institutional depression operates, the rules that isolate us from each other while holding us hostage to the satisfactions presumably derived from the model of solitary productivity that governs university life. When we feel pangs of depression, we normally assign the blame for what we are feeling to powerful others—the administration, the chair, the legislature, or some other figure of authority and power over us. It's not that they are undeserving of any of the blame; usually they've earned it. Yet I wonder what we gain when we take ourselves off the hook and act as if our misery is only the result of what they do to us. Then we don't have to look at ourselves, look at our own complicity in sustaining the patterns of relationship that bind us to norms of isolation, absence, and unwillingness to metacommunicate. Gornick (1996) expresses this relational stance pointedly: "First you think, 'It must be them, it can't be me.' Then you think, 'No, it's not them, it is me.' Getting to the third thought, 'It's not them, it's not me; it's the two of us together'—that takes some diving" (p. 122).

Rose (1990) notes that one of the ironic qualities of university life is that we do not see ourselves as embedded in a strange subculture—our department life—within the larger culture of the university, nor do we analyze and talk with each other about either culture in profoundly self-critical ways. During the 1990s five personal accounts that speak to this issue were published (Gornick, 1996; Heilbrun, 1997; Krieger, 1997; Richardson, 1997; Tompkins, 1996), all written by women. These accounts testify to the deep despair, loneliness, and unhappiness experienced in the institutional lives these accomplished women lived. Three of these women retired early; the other two have never held a permanent faculty position. The riskiness of this kind of institutional self-criticism could hardly be more apparent.

The fear of risk and retribution associated with struggles to accommodate difference and change within the existing subcultures of the university goes beyond the local circumstances of these women; it is endemic to the norms of conformity that most of us learn when we are socialized into our discipline (Krieger, 1991; Rose, 1990). As Rose (1990) observes, the way we write is carefully controlled by our disciplines, which have the power to withhold the rewards of publication to nonconforming texts. This is not so much an issue of standards—that is, whether to have standards—but rather a question of which standards to have and whose interests are served by the ones that are accepted and upheld. What is excluded by the rules of conformity that discipline our writing (and the ones that discipline the patterns of interaction among colleagues in a department)?

These questions bring me back to the split between the academic and personal self. After my father's death I began receiving sympathy cards from people in my field who barely knew me, which reminded me that the split between the academic and the personal world often is severed. This gave me pause to question why it is that you rarely hear anyone talk about their personal lives in the papers they give at mainstream conferences and you seldom see the personal self mix with the professional self on the pages of mainstream journals such as *American Journal of Sociology, American Sociological Review, American Educational Research Journal, Communication Monographs, Communication Theory,* or *Human Communication Research.* Obviously, it's because we've been conditioned to separate the personal and professional domains of experience. It's an essential part of our academic socialization. And why is that the case? Because it helps us maintain the illusion that the interests of the ordinary, personal self hasn't prejudiced the academic self. When we insulate the academic from the personal, we imply that the personal voice is, as Jane Tompkins (1989) observes, "soft-minded, self-indulgent, and unprofessional" (p. 122), whereas the academic voice is exalted as the voice of reason, objectivity, and rigor. So we learn to hide our personal self behind a veneer of academic and theoretical detachment, fostering the misconception that it has no influence, no place, no significance in our work. Yet it is rare, indeed, to find a productive scholar whose work is unconnected to his or her personal history. If you are a member of a department long enough, you usually learn the personal story behind each colleague's research interests. Few of us study subjects such as child abuse, addiction, racism, or abortion coincidentally.

We pay a steep price for producing texts that sustain the illusion of disinterest and neutrality by keeping the personal voice out. Our work is under-read; undergraduates find many of our publications boring; graduate students say our scholarship is dry and inaccessible; seasoned scholars confess they don't finish half of what they start reading; and the public hardly knows we exist (Richardson, 1994). Oh, we've learned to rationalize these responses, but we know in our hearts we would like them to be different. We do a good job of protecting our secrets—hiding our embarrassment—but we are troubled by how few of us carry a passion for theory and research into our forties and fifties and sixties, and how many of us have lost the excitement and liveliness we once had. We've seen the casualties of an alienated workforce up close, etched on the blank faces of colleagues who caved in, gave up, stopped caring. This too is a moral crisis, an epidemic of institutional depression. We turn the other cheek, keep quiet, pretend the moral crisis isn't there, but that doesn't make it disappear.

It's about time we wrestled more openly and collectively with these problems. Instead of hiding the pain many of us feel about the ways we are unfulfilled by the life of the mind, we need to muster the courage to speak the truth about "the emotional fallout" of a lifetime of teaching and research (Tompkins, 1996, p. 57). We need to face up to the ways we use orthodox academic practices to discipline, control, and perpetuate ourselves and our traditions, thus stifling innovation, discouraging creativity, inhibiting criticism of our own institutional conventions, making it difficult to take risks, and severing academic life from emotional and spiritual life. No matter how much change may threaten us, we need to consider alternatives—different goals; different styles of research and writing; different ways of bringing the academic and the personal into conversation with each other.

The desire to bring the personal self into conversation with the academic self was the major inspiration for my turn toward a personal narrative approach to inquiry (Bochner, 1994; Bochner, Ellis, and Tillmann-Healy, 1997; Ellis, 1995; Ellis and Bochner, 1996), an alternative to orthodox social science that I have been pursuing since the mid-1980s. Stories ask readers to feel their truth and, thus, to become fully engaged—morally, aesthetically, emotionally, and intellectually (Richardson, 1994). They invite us to enter horizons of the human condition in which lived life is shown as comic, tragic, and absurd, and in which endless opportunities exist to create a reality and live in it (Coles, 1989).

The narrative approach to research in the human sciences that I favor privileges the story. In this work (e.g., Ellis and Bochner, 1996), we try to produce texts that show how people breach canonical conventions and expectations; how they cope with exceptional, difficult, and transformative crises; how they invent new ways of speaking when old ways fail them; and how they turn calamities into gifts. These stories activate subjectivity and compel emotional response (Ellis and Bochner, 1991). They long to be used rather than analyzed, to be told and retold rather than theorized and settled. And they promise the companionship of intimate detail as a substitute for the loneliness of abstracted facts, touching readers where they live and offering details that linger in the mind.

After my father's death, I struggled to bring my academic and personal worlds closer together. I had yearned to do so for a long time; now I felt I had no choice. Twenty years earlier, I had been drawn to communication studies because I thought it could help answer deep and troubling questions about how to live a meaningful, useful, and ethical life. Somewhere along the way these questions gave way to smaller, more precise, more professional questions. But I found when I began listening more closely, students were still coming with many of the same searching questions. They yearn to understand the life in and around them. They want to lead decent and honorable lives, even in the face of the hypocrisy, sham, and betrayal they've already experienced. I know I don't have the answers, but I feel an obligation to help students address the moral contradictions they feel, bring their dilemmas into the realm of public discourse, name the silences, and make them discussable issues. What is education if not an intense, probing scrutiny of moral choices and dilemmas (Coles, 1989)? What does communication studies (or any of the social sciences) have to offer students if we strip away emotional experience; avoid questions of moral contradiction; or act as if duties, obligations, desire, and imagination are outside the scope of what we teach because they can't be grasped as hard data?

Stories as Theories

Shortly after I published an essay titled "Theories and Stories" (Bochner, 1994), I got calls and letters from concerned colleagues in my field who wanted to know whether I really was opposed to theory (and whether I'd lost my mind). I tried to explain that I had not juxtaposed stories against theories; I only wanted to create a space for appreciating the value and uses of stories. This is a good place to revise that explanation.

What I want to say now is that there is nothing as theoretical as a good story. The split between theory and story is false—and it's not false. It's not false when theory is viewed in the terms I used earlier in this chapter—*objective, detached, value-free, beyond human consciousness*. Described in these terms, theory becomes an end in itself, divorced from its consequences, politics, and uses. This is the taken-for-granted sense of theory I heard from a colleague at a tenure-review hearing when she observed, "He's published enough, but his work isn't theoretical." It is also the sense of theory promoted by those who see the purpose of

292

communication research, to take one representative example, as the development of middle-range (Burleson, 1992) or general theories of communication (Berger, 1991) but who do not consider the ways in which describing or explaining reality is different from dealing with it. As Rorty (1979) queries, "What is the point?" "What moral is to be drawn from our knowledge of how we and the rest of nature work?" or "What do we do with ourselves now that we know the laws of our own behavior?" (p. 383). When we don't ask questions like these, we risk forgetting that theorizing is not an activity devoid of context or consequences.

Sometimes the consequences turn out to be wretched. Consider the plight of the families of Europeans killed in the July 1996 crash of TWA Flight 800. Stuck for seven days and nights in uncomfortable hotel rooms in an unfamiliar city, frustrated by the cross-purposes of theory and experience, and bewildered by the insensitivity of officials to their emotional trauma, the families of victims had reached their limits. At a hastily called news conference, a spokesman for the French contingent expressed the feelings many in the group shared: "We don't care about your theories or your examination of the causes of the crash. We want our bodies, and we want to go home" (paraphrased).

But there is no split between theory and story when theorizing is conceived as a social and communicative activity. This is what I mean when I use the term *social theory*. In the world of social theory, we are less concerned about representation and more concerned about communication. We give up the illusions of transcendental observation in favor of the possibilities of dialogue and collaboration. Social theory works the spaces between history and destiny. The social world is understood as a world of connection, contact, and relationship. It also is a world where consequences, values, politics, and moral dilemmas are abundant and central.

As social beings, we live storied lives (Rosenwald and Ochberg, 1992). Our identities—who we are and what we do—originate in the tales passed down to us and the stories we take on as our own. In this sense, stories constitute "our medium of being" (Schafer, 1981a, 1981b). Storytelling is both a method of knowing—a social practice—and a way of telling about our lives (Richardson, 1990). As an academic practice, the approach to narrative inquiry that I take changes the activity of theorizing from a process of thinking about to one of thinking with (Frank, 1995). Theory meets story when we think with a story rather than about it. As Arthur Frank (1995) points out, "To think about a story is to reduce it to content and then analyze the content.... To think with a story is to experience its affecting one's own life and to find in that effect a certain truth of one's life" (p. 23).

Thus, we do not turn stories into data to test theoretical propositions; rather, we link theory to story when we think with a story, trying to stay with the story, letting ourselves resonate with the moral dilemmas it may pose, understanding its ambiguities, examining its contradictions, feeling its nuances, letting ourselves become part of the story (Ellis, 1995). We think with a story from the framework of our own lives. We ask what kind of person we are becoming when we take the story in and consider how we can use it for our own purposes, what ethical directions it points us toward, and what moral commitments it calls out in us (Coles, 1989).

Narrative ethicists like to say that if it's time to end and you're not sure you've made your point, don't try to explain—just tell another story (Frank, 1995). So I end this chapter with one more story, an old tale passed down by Gregory Bateson (1979, p. 13):

> A man wanted to know about mind, not in nature, but in his private large computer. He asked it (no doubt in his best Fortran), "Do you compute that you will ever think like a human being?" The machine then set to work to analyze its own computational habits. Finally, the machine printed its answer on a piece of paper, as such machines do. The man ran to get the answer and found, neatly typed, the words:

THAT REMINDS ME OF A STORY

Note

1. An earlier version of this chapter was published as "It's About Time: Narrative and the Divided Self," *Qualitative Inquiry* 3, (1997), pp. 418–438. DOI: 10.1177/107780049700300404

CHAPTER THIRTEEN

Finishing Touches

A Sense of an Ending

Under history, memory and forgetting
Under memory and forgetting, life
But writing a life is another story
Incompletion

Paul Ricoeur (2004, p. 506)

Keeping Memory Alive

You realize the story you started to write is not the one you end up writing. You find that the longer you extend the period of time about which you write, the more uncertain you become about where you're heading and the meaning of the quest. You don't have a destination in mind. You set out on an unmarked trail in the middle of a vaguely familiar setting, eager to find out where it could lead. You feel most alive when you are trekking along the path. You don't want to come to the end and have to stop. It's the journey that thrills you.

You start without an outline and with no set goal. Plunge in—see what happens, you tell yourself. Trust the process.

Okay, then, there you go. Memories keep flashing by. You try to slow them down. But you can't. You worry about the sketchiness of some of what you recall. You feel as if you're only scratching the surface. You want more than outlines—you want details. Go deeper. Look into the depths of experience and see what's there. But when you do you find what's left are only the shards of the past: traces, signs, clues, strands of thread in webs of meaning. You try to follow the path of the thread from one event, one conflict, one crisis, one feat or triumph to the next, assuming that one thing leads to another, that there is continuity and coherence to your life, only to find that the strings you've woven are loosely bound and tangled. You pull gently at a dropped stitch and end up with a knotted loop. The fabric of continuity and coherence begins to unravel. Still, you can't help yourself—you're driven in the direction of meaning.

Why do you want to make sense of your life? Can't you be content with the idea that life is just one damn thing after another? Is it because there is a flow of time to life, a forward momentum moving toward something? Is it because there are so many empty spaces, so many gaps begging to be filled? Is it because you can't accept the notion that a life just drifts along without shape or purpose, like a log floating down a river? Or because there are things you've tried to forget but couldn't? Maybe this time you can remember them in a new, better, and more forgiving way? You're frightened by the idea that the world of experience is all parts and no whole. Is that it? Or is it because you've been talking to yourself about yourself your entire conscious life? That talk had to amount to something. It had to mean something, didn't it?

Looking back now, you see things that were happening then. You're peeping in on the moments, the epiphanies, the scenes. You're remembering the stories, dwelling in them, feeling their consequences. You're there and not there virtually at the same time. You're seeing yourself seeing yourself. You're a subject and an object, inside and outside. This feels weird—being inside what you're studying.

Stepping away, you ponder the consequences of the episodes that you're re-inhabiting. You can't help judging them as good or bad, right or wrong, just or unjust. It dawns on you how moral these moments were, how they played a part in the making of your soul. You're shocked to realize how little attention you were paying when the most important things in your life were taking place. You weren't unconscious, only absent. This time you can't hide. There's no escape, no closing your eyes. The image is clear. That's you running away—away from home, from family, from relationships, from the things you hated, from the things you were too scared to do. There, in the distance, is what you're running toward. You're trying to get somewhere, but you can't quite make out where.

You think you may be heading toward the lost and found. Suddenly you think you know why you are there and what you have to do. You're hungering to retrieve your past, realizing the nourishment that the stories of the past can provide, how they can feed your understanding of yourself and the meaning of your ties to others. You can't bear the thought of losing the past or allowing it to disappear as it did for your mother (Bochner, 2002a). That's your mission. Keep history alive. But it's not yours alone. It's the calling of all storytellers—to go back and reclaim the past. Pay attention this time. Figure out what you can do with these stories. Keep memory alive. Make it meaningful. There's no reason to relive the past unless it can help you anticipate the future. That's what you're seeking—a life more divine and prophetic; a better life and a more just world in which to live it; a discipline more open, aesthetic, diverse, and appreciative.

Open Ended

In *The End of the Affair*, Graham Greene (2001/1951) calls attention to the impulsive nature of beginnings and endings. "A story has no beginning or end;" his narrator declares, "arbitrarily one chooses that moment of experience from which to look back or from which to look ahead" (Greene, 2001/1951, p. 7). Moving toward a close, I realize that I can't *finish* the stories in this book. I can only strive for "a sense of an ending" while reminding myself that "our need for an ending transforms our lives 'between the *tick* of birth and the *tock* of death,' and stories simulate this transformation but must not do so too simply" (Kermode, 1967, pp. 196–197).

Ending should not be mistaken for finishing. That may be the reason Picasso (Stein, 1946) warned artists never to say they had finished a painting. To claim you are finished, he cautioned, is to imply you're through, you've had enough, which can squeeze the life and soul out of the work. Shutting something down fastens it and, in so doing, deadens it.

When the tale you are telling is a life story, the more you work on it, the more difficult it can become to reach a point of closure. One can always write more chapters, revise or amend existing ones, look at things from different angles.

Eventually, though, time runs out. You must stop this in order to do that.

I end now by looking back at how I put this book together. Positioning myself between the rigor of a scientist and the imagination of a writer, I ventured to produce a text that would transgress the boundaries separating the social sciences and humanities. In this chapter, I review the methodological directives I followed, the ethical obligations I abided by, and the literary strategies I adopted to depict the unfolding of my lived experience.

What This Book Wanted to Be

Initially I thought I wanted to write a pedagogical volume, a book about teaching and learning across the life cycle that could introduce students to the ways and forms of an academic life. But books have a way of taking on a life of their own—if you let them—and I felt as if I was always a step or two behind where the narrative was heading. Now I understand my text as a questioning book that encourages students and scholars in the human sciences to pry into the meaning and importance of the work they do across the course of their professional lives, to examine the functioning of academic conventions as well as the opportunities that arise to break away from received traditions—to innovate, create, and experiment with new or different methods of inquiring into and representing lived experiences. I want my stories to evoke conversation about the activities and relationships that keep people inspired and alive in their academic work as well as those that can dull their motivation (and even their humanity). A life of teaching, writing, and research need not become another form of alienated labor.

Once I understood that this book wanted to blur categories, cross boundaries, rely on observation and imagination, and mix together meditation and argumentation, I began to compose stories aimed at opening a dialogue for reflexive self-criticism of the discipline of communication, the functioning and meaning of the human sciences, and the life we call *academic*. My goal was to touch and reveal some of the deep parts of my experience as a student and professor of communication and as a person whose personal life had been deeply enmeshed with his academic life. As a witness to the development of my field for more than forty years, I endeavored to use what I had learned to open conversations about what we should care about in the human sciences. I wanted to represent my memories of these experiences in genre-bending forms of narration—dialogues, monologues, metalogues, and performative pieces—that would enact these experiences as well as reflect on them. Also, I wanted to layer the stories with the voices of other scholars, teachers, friends, and family members who had given my academic and personal life direction and meaning.

Composing a Life on the Page

Writing this book put me in touch with elusive feelings and perceptions associated with life-changing, paradigm-altering events in my personal and professional life. Most of these events took place a long time ago and, strictly speaking, there is no "reality" against which my account of these happenings, feelings, and relationships can be verified. I imposed on myself a standard of honesty, relying on my memory to tell the stories as truthfully as I could. Applying the benchmark of faithfulness to memory, however, proved complicated. I couldn't simply return to my past and compose a story based on what I found. The events of my past had vanished, and no archive existed from which to retrieve them. Even if such an archive were available, it could not have provided "objective" data. Even if it had, I still would have needed to interpret and draw meaning from the archival material.

I had to rely on my memory, however fallible, to help me step into the shoes of a former self—me at those times—and arrive at interpretations of what the experiences those memories represented could mean. Then I had to carve a story out of those interpretations. Though readers may take the events I remember as a report on my past, my intent was to probe and examine my memories, self-investigating by turning them inside out and upside down. The result is a text that is memoir *and* essay, evocation *and* analysis, story *and* theory (Anderson, 2006; Bochner, 1994; Ellis and Bochner 2000, 2006). I pivot between trying to tell good stories with (and about) real-life, lively characters and making a determined effort to ask difficult questions about the meanings of the events and why they stand out in my memory (Lazar, 2008).

I approached this project systematically, with the mindset of a qualitative researcher, as well as inventively, from the perspective of a writer. First, I attended to incidents I remembered—events, occasions, and episodes happening in the past. Typically we codify and discuss what happens to us as *experiences*. Every person endures a range of experiences, some of which are typical; others that are extraordinary or distinctive (Abrahams, 1986). Though I chose to write about turning points and epiphanies, I do not regard these as uncommon. I expect other people to resonate with some of my experiences by drawing on their own and comparing them to mine. My goal is not so much to have readers see things my way but instead to use my experiences to evoke their own memories and thoughts about them. In this sense, the book is about me but also extends beyond me. What is at stake is the morally complex question of what a good and meaningful professorial life can be.

Second, I relied on typifications to help readers identify with my stories. Experiences depicted in stories embody both *meanings* and *feelings,* and our responses to them "continually gravitate toward typicality, so that afterwards we can find words to talk about what happened" (Abrahams, 1986, pp. 49–50). In short, typifications aid our capacity to recount experiences (Schutz, 1970). We fall back on standardized categories into which our experiences can be assimilated. In this book, for example, I note how the Sixties Experience, the Jewish Experience, the Working-Class Experience, the Academic Experience, the Romantic Experience, and the Death and Dying Experience all influenced my life (see Geertz, 1986). The cultural meanings associated with these typified experiences dwell in and limit me, but they exist in dialogue with meanings and values associated with other evolving experiences and relationships in my life and, thus, should not be taken as deterministic. I use "experience" as a term of relationality and connection. Even the most threatening and/or painful experiences may be beneficially drawn on, revised, reinterpreted, and replayed in some form in the future (Abraham, 1986). This is one of the central ideas about memory and lived experience advanced in this book. We are expected to learn from experiences, and there is no time limit to be imposed on this form of education. When we say, "Live and learn," we mean "Experience and gain knowledge or wisdom from it."

Third, I had to express what happened—to put recollected experiences into words. When we attempt to fit language to experience, we discover a gap between experience and words, between living through and narrating, between the chaos and fragmentation of living a life and the smoothing orderliness we may bring to it when we write, between what we can say about it *now* and what we imagine took place *then,* between how we mourn or celebrate the past and what shape our grieving or reveling gives to our future (Bochner, 2007). As a writer aspiring to truth, I felt obliged to produce a faithful account of the past. But I had to understand and appreciate that I was immersed in a process of re-entering and re-inscribing the past. Thus, what summoned me *now* to remember anchored what I remembered. In other words, what inspired my recollections skewed my memory. Remembering is always an activity under the influence of the present, fusing together what one desires, what one imagines, and what may actually have happened. The reality of my original experiences was transformed into something else, something remembered. For better or for worse, what I remembered became reality. The urge that drove this process was my desire to locate truth, and as Rorty (1989, p. 5) cleverly expressed it, "Where there are no sentences, there is no truth." Thus, the duality of truthfulness rests at the intersection of the demands of discovery and expression.

Fourth, I had to locate the story in my experiences and narrate it—breathe life into it. I wanted to convey meaningful details, but which details would I select? I couldn't remember everything, and I couldn't tell all I could remember. To make a story is to disregard or ignore many details and to accept the inevitable incompleteness of the stories one tells. The stories I composed are based on materials drawn from the flawed process of remembering, where my imagination and memory intersect and collide. These materials had to be transformed into narrative prose that give shape and meaning to the events of my past. But my memories, like anyone else's, are permeated by fissures and discontinuities. Making a story of these events runs the risk of smoothing the bumps and steadying the disorder. In this project, I was preoccupied with delving into the story-truth of emotional dimensions of experiences and the links between personal and academic life, however ragged the edges of truth I could reveal turned out to be (O'Brien, 1990). "The facts of the situation don't matter much," writes David Shields (2010), "so long as the underlying truth resonates.... What happened to the writer isn't what matters; what matters is the larger sense that the writer is able to make of what happened. For that, the power of writing imagination is required" (pp. 41–42).

Fifth, I couldn't write about my life without writing about other people's lives. This is a thorny problem from which I couldn't escape unless I was to write the narratives in collaboration with all the other characters in the stories. Even then, I would run into issues of power and inequality that could disfigure whatever truths I might reach.

I can't speak for the other people whose lives are represented on the pages of this book. I can only make myself accountable to my sentences, to my truth, recognizing that other truths exist as well and that the way I saw things may not be how others perceived them (see Mairs, 2008). Everyone has a somewhat different version of reality, which ultimately depends on who does the telling. I'm not telling anybody else's story, nor am I trying to tie up loose ends. Still, how my stories are read and interpreted implicate and likely affect other people. I did not feel free to disregard the dialectic of expression and protection (Bochner, 1984). Abiding by relational and narrative ethics (Ellis, 2007; Nelson, 2001) I've altered names in some cases; in others I've combined several people into a composite character or reshaped the scene. The goal is compassion toward the other while remaining true to oneself. Not easy. I do not divide the world into heroes and demons. Indeed, I consider all of the people depicted in this book complicated characters immersed in webs of relationships and contingencies of lived experience.

Sixth, I frequently had to call on my imagination in composing these stories. I did not possess tapes of interviews, conversations, phone calls, therapy sessions, or episodes of course meetings. Some critics or readers may, therefore, label my stories "fictions." But as Bonnie Rough (2007, pp. 65–66) explains, "Nonfiction writers imagine. Fiction writers invent. These are fundamentally different acts, performed to different ends." I am asking readers not only to imagine along with me but also to believe. My claim is that "something like this actually happened" (p. 66). I am not free to make up or tell any story or to create a really "good" story. I am bound, instead, by the particular events that I recall actually happening in my life. With the exception of the sessions with my fictional therapist, Dr. Milton, all of the stories I tell represent "real" events. Even Milton is a composite character based on two therapists with whom I interacted across a period of more than a decade. In this book, story-truth is more important than happening truth (O'Brien, 1990). I echo Gornick's (2008, p. 7) sentiment that "what mattered most to me was not the literalness of the situation, but the emotional truth of the story."

Finally, I wrote these stories under the influence of an emotional, moral, and literary urgency that I had rarely experienced in my academic life. Working between the genres of autoethnography and personal essay, I wanted to provide a display of human consciousness—my own—in the process of coping with lived experiences. I also wanted to blur and bend multiple genres of representation—to fuse analytics, poetics, literature reviews, narratives, and fictive and nonfictive modes of expressing lived experiences. I wanted to make modes of communicating lived experience not only *what* we study but also *how* we study it—in forms that can convey the unfolding of lived experience. I experimented with various genres of written texts and poetics—dialogues, stories, layered accounts, reflective essays, and conversations both real and imagined—as ways of expressing emotions, subjective reactions, and my own stream of consciousness. Desiring a healthy and ethical relationship to my past, I hiked down the trails of my memory "not so much a survivor with a harrowing tale to tell as that older sort of traveler, the pilgrim, seeking wondering" (Hampl, 1999, p. 37), ever mindful of life's contingencies, contradictions, and mysteries, my head and heart going hand in hand.

Letting Go

You keep your book under wraps for nearly six years, unsure whether you should ever let it see the light of day. Although you consider it some of the best prose you ever have written, you can't decide whether to make it public. You read the stories again and again, never exhausting your fascination with the events recalled. Some of the stories bring you to tears every time you read them; others make you laugh out loud. You vacillate between sadness and joy, dwelling in the dialectical space of agony and pleasure. These stories must have resonance, you tell yourself. Your partner, Carolyn, assures you they do. If that's the case, you must fulfill your ethical obligation as a teacher and a scholar. You can't keep them to yourself.

Preparing to release the stories from captivity, you anticipate certain questions. The first that comes to mind is, What made you want to tell these stories? You don't have a concise answer. So many reasons existed: because the snapshots were fading; because the scrapbook was yellowing; because old wounds were festering; because there were still things you didn't understand about yourself and your life; because you felt finally old enough to rehash, delve into, and perform your memories; because there were still demons to be banished and both a personal and cultural history of inquiry and pedagogy to be memorialized; because there are things graduate students need to know, lines they need to read between; because there were riddles and contradictions with which to deal, even though you realized you could never get to the bottom of things,

301

never achieve completion or fill all the gaps; because your life as a professor extended over such a diversity of times, places, and cultural history; because you believe the university is an interesting, disturbing, entertaining, bewildering, and valuable place in which to make and spend a life.

Your answer is unsatisfying. It's too vague, too lacking in detail, too ivory tower. You know there was more to it than that. You're going to have to bring it down to earth, express it in language that resonates and communicates feelings.

You decided to tell the story of Brenda's illness to show that we all live on a continuum from madness to sanity and to reveal how blurred the boundaries can be. But who are you trying to kid? That's the polite explanation. The truth is that the story of Brenda's descent into depression never was a story you wanted to tell. In fact, it's a story you were ashamed and embarrassed to tell, a story you kept under lock and key for most of your adult life. That's why you felt you had to write it. You had to try to make yourself live and suffer through it a second time in order to retrieve some of the meaning that had been lost or buried by keeping it secret. You wanted to force yourself to reflect on how markedly the experience had changed, awakened, and emboldened you to become the person you took yourself to be. You were ready, finally, to face who you had been then in order to understand how you got to where you are now.

You've always had the urge to break boundaries. Fitting in was never easy for you. Not in childhood, not in adolescence, not even in the university. No surprise, then, that most of the stories you told in the book revolve around blurred boundaries.

You wanted to tell the story of your relationship to Raymond Tucker to reveal the complications of academic socialization and how easily people can become bound to something they don't want and didn't choose for themselves. How do you know whether you're doing what you want or acting on someone else's instructions? Tucker loved you and you loved him, but he sculpted you into what he wanted you to be. You became a faithful reflection of his infectious desires. You knew for a long time there were other experiences you wanted to have, but you wouldn't let yourself. You were afraid to disrupt the secure identity you had built. Do we ever get over the craving to satisfy our parents? Are we perpetually seeking a spiritual father? What happens to your urge for more life, for exciting experiences, for new challenges when you put another person on a pedestal and act as if he or she possesses special powers? Your sense of reality can become distorted. You may start feeling panicky. You start questioning what could happen to you if you don't get out of this. By what rules should you live your life? Should it be obligation or inspiration? Who do you take yourself to be?

You wanted to tell the story of how Carol Gifford coped with terminal cancer and actively chose how her life would come to an end and how she would be remembered. You've always thought her story pokes holes in the traditional view of life and death as mutually exclusive. The possibilities and limitations of life are intimately connected through our awareness of our own mortality. The shadow of death hovers over every person's life, even in the face of the deadening forces of denial that threaten our capacity to appreciate and absorb all that lived experiences offer. You wanted to express the meaning of the end of Carol's life in a manner that would reveal death and dying as both a first-person and a third-person experience (Heidegger, 1962/2008) and show human finitude's structuring influence over our lives. "(O)f all things that move man," wrote Ernest Becker (1973, p. 11), "one of the principal ones is his [sic] terror of death," which brings into focus the natural contradictions of human existence—a symbolic self and a finite body—a human limitation that can never be resolved or programmed by science. From the first time you read it you've considered Becker's book, The Denial of Death, the greatest achievement in social science in the twentieth century, not so much because of his analysis of what we are to do about death but rather because of its implications for what we are do with life—how, in the face of death, we can meet life with courage (Tillich, 1952).

You wanted to tell the story of your first encounters with Carolyn Ellis. You believe in twists of fate, but you also think one must be prepared when opportunity knocks. You wanted readers to appreciate how much fun the two of you had creating your dance of theory and story that ultimately evolved into the genres of autoethnography and personal narrative inquiry, and how you became immersed in each other's souls. But you also wanted to depict the two of you together plotting a course of transgressing boundaries. You wanted readers to see how difficult it can be to overcome the resistance built into the stories we inherit about what constitutes legitimate research and writing and how the two of you wanted to transgress those rules in order to open a space for emotional and embodied first-person writing in the human sciences. In Carolyn you found a writing buddy, a kindred spirit, a passionate coconspirator, and a life partner with whom you could take this journey of work and play. How lucky can a person be? Oh, how much a person's life turns on relationality.

Boundaries—they're everywhere. You wanted your stories to show that when you become a member of a discipline, you are expected to follow certain rules. Your success depends upon it. You can't contribute to the discipline if you don't know the rules. Academic socialization is a process of clarifying the conventions by which, as a member of a discipline, you must abide. Scholars teach, read, research, write, and publish. To achieve success, you must not only follow conventions; you must also know what is forbidden.

But once you know what's forbidden, then what? You wanted readers to imagine writing with soul. You wanted to get across the point that humans are flawed, messy, and complicated beings who live with contradictions, have ideas and emotions, think and think about thinking, and struggle with vexing questions. You wanted your stories to show that we humans frequently don't know what we're doing; that we sometimes feel vulnerable; bare our souls; keep secrets; feel ashamed, afraid, humiliated, betrayed, and heartbroken. And sometimes we're downright hilarious. We disappoint people, and they frustrate us. You worry that some students are told not to write about these things, that people won't appreciate that kind of writing. It's not scientific. It's not up to community standards. They'll think you're a nonconformist, refusing to adjust, not playing the game, not fitting in. Maybe they'll tell you to take a time-out and that you're starting to sound like a threat to the discipline. What will they do to you? Send you into exile? Deny you tenure? Can writing like that get you sent away?

You wanted your stories to show that research texts are "acts of meaning" (Bochner, 2012; J. Bruner, 1980). They put meanings into motion and, thus, not only represent but also create experiences.

You think your discipline, communication studies, ought to be especially cognizant of the fact that there is no access to the world unmediated by language. The world can't speak for itself. Don't all attempts to represent the world in language involve translating a speechless reality into a form of expression that makes sense—in short, a narrative?

Boundaries. Everywhere boundaries: objectivity/subjectivity, science/art, fiction/nonfiction, facts/meanings, rationality/emotionality. You still don't believe that scholars in the human sciences should privilege data over stories, typologies over concrete details, and graphs over plots of lived experience. You resist the desire among social scientists to replace the concrete details of sensual, emotional, and embodied experience with typologies and abstractions that remove events from their context, distancing readers from the actions and feelings of particular human beings, leaving readers to look through a stained-glass window, to use Edith Turner's apt analogy, seeing only a murky and featureless profile. You think Le Guin (1989, p. 151) got it right when she said, "People crave objectivity because to be subjective is to be a body, vulnerable, violable."

Ending and Beginning

In the academic world, we refer to graduation as a commencement; an ending that is a beginning replete with promises, possibilities, risks, and uncertainty. It may be difficult to know what to make of the past, but it is even more daunting to hazard guesses about the future. Still, I can say with considerable confidence that the paradigm has shifted. The momentum has moved in the direction of far-reaching revisions of what we think the human sciences can become, what they should do, and how.

The world of the human sciences into which I was socialized is not the world I find myself in today—and that's a good thing. Fueled initially by the dual crises of representation and legitimation, the turn toward narrative represented by the "qualitative research revolution" (Denzin, 1996; Gergen and Gergen, 2000) has introduced an astonishing array of new research orientations that reflect radically altered ethical commitments, methodological and writing practices, and conceptions of representation, validity, and objectivity (Bochner, 2000, 2002, 2012; Denzin and Lincoln, 2000, 2011; Holman Jones, Adams, and Ellis, 2013).

The mindset of this new era of research in the human sciences is reflected in the vocabulary, ethical commitments, methodological practices, and research goals of many of those associated with the new paradigms of qualitative inquiry. Where once we saw subjects, now we see participants and cocollaborators. Where once we sought only to predict and control, now we want to learn to talk with, to empower, to transform, and empathize. Where once we were concerned primarily with the accuracy of descriptions, now we ask how useful our descriptions are and what we can do with them. Where once we thought ethics meant debriefing before leaving, now we understand ethics as an obligation to return and give something back. Where once we conceived of our readers or audiences as passive receivers of knowledge, now we construe them as active coconstructors of meaning. Where once we focused on what participants can learn about themselves from us, now we also underscore what we can learn about ourselves from them. Where once we thought it was enough to show that our voice had authority, now we insist that the voices of the people we study be put on a plane equal to our own. Where once we thought we were talking only about *them,* now we sense that we are talking about ourselves as well. Where once we elevated ourselves to the position of confident theorists in command of knowledge, now we can more humbly understand ourselves as vulnerable storytellers with moral imagination.

In the Middle

> Take the tale in your teeth, then, and bite till the blood runs,
> hoping it's not poison; and we will all come to the end together,
> and even to the beginning: living as we do, in the middle.
> *Ursula K. Le Guin (1980, p. 199)*

Moments before he died, Tolstoy remarked, "I don't know what I'm supposed do." Human beings are born not knowing, and we still don't know when we die. But between birth and death we have to choose something to do. I chose the human sciences because I thought they could show me life as it really is lived. But I found that I wanted to do something more than merely receive this knowledge; I wanted to react to it, converse with it, and apply it. But the ruling paradigm encouraged replication, not conversation. Now I know that what I want to do is make people feel stuff; continue my quest to put into circulation self-clarifying and transforming stories; and keep alive the conversation in the human sciences about what can make life good. That may not be what I'm supposed to do, but it does feel like the right thing to do.

EPILOGUE

Story-Truth[1]

> I want you to feel what I felt. I want you to know why story-truth is truer sometimes than happening truth.
>
> *Tim O'Brien (1990, p. 171)*

"I don't know whether my stories are true," I say as I take my customary place on the couch.

"Is that some kind of confession, Art? Are you trying to tell me you've been lying on the couch all this time?" Milton chuckles at his pun.

"N-no," I stutter. "It's no joke."

"Oh, I'm so sorry. For a second I forgot how seriously you take yourself," Milton replies, his mocking tone reminding me how much he's tried to lighten my heaviness.

"This is not about my seriousness. I understand how that can make a person a killjoy. I saw it in my father. He worried about everything, and his angst created a menacing atmosphere of anxiety and apprehension. I was always waiting for the other shoe to drop. I had to be on guard most of the time, which diminished my appreciation for the good things he was trying to teach me, such as the importance of integrity, discipline, and hard work."

"You couldn't act silly?"

"Not in our house. I don't recall any giddiness. Life was serious stuff."

"Don't you think some of your dad's gravitas may have rubbed off on you?" Milton interrupts.

"Of course I do. He passed that on to all of his children. It was an inheritance we didn't want."

"What are you smiling about?" Milton asks, observing my brief hesitation.

"I was remembering a meeting I had with Levine."

"Your philosophy professor?"

"Uh-huh. It came in a flash—must have been triggered by your comment about my seriousness."

"Go on."

"Levine had a vastly different impression of me. He thought I wasn't serious enough. He saw something in me that I didn't see in myself at the time. In class I listened carefully, raised questions, and expressed my desire to get to the bottom of the issues we were discussing, such as freedom, choice, and mortality. But I didn't follow through outside of class. I didn't study and keep up with the reading. One day he took me aside and said, 'I don't think you take yourself seriously. You have

---

Coming to Narrative, by Arthur P. Bochner, 306–317. © 2014 Left Coast Press, Inc. All rights reserved.

to decide what really matters to you.' It was the only time he and I ever talked in private, but those comments changed my whole attitude toward academic work."

"Maybe he recognized that you didn't accept that part of yourself, your intellectual side," Milton observes.

"I guess I'll never know his motive. He wasn't a psychologist, so I doubt he had planned to intervene for the sake of my mental health. He was simply a conscientious teacher who cared about his students. It makes me sad to think he never knew how much he helped me."

"You can't be sure he didn't know. He may have realized that a gentle nudge from someone you admired was all you needed to change course. You don't have to be a psychologist to have that kind of sensitivity."

"You're right. I can't be sure. That's the thing that's driving me nuts. I want to know!" Milton waits for me to continue.

"You see, I get these flashes of memory. They're brief but vivid. In this one, Levine is standing right there in front of me, pipe in hand, tan corduroy sports jacket, the whole works. I recognize the room as his office; I even see myself as the adolescent I was at the time. I'm looking in on myself. I notice how stunned I am by his feedback. He's like a father taking an interest in his son, which my father never did. Dad and I never had this sort of heart-to-heart talk." I start to get choked up and try to catch my breath.

Milton nods. He understands how Levine's caring gesture evokes the sorrow of my frustrated desire for compassionate attention from my father.

Our eyes meet and I continue. "I'm so startled by Levine's statement that I can't say anything. I recall sitting there in silence as he walked away."

"Tell me what bothers you about this episode."

"I don't know if it's true!" I bellow. "We were in his office. I don't think he would have walked out and left me there alone. And it's not characteristic of me to sit still and say nothing."

"So?"

"I can't be certain that this exchange ever happened. The whole incident may be a figment of my imagination."

"Oh, I see. You're worried that your memory may have distorted what actually, literally happened. You want the whole truth, nothing but the truth, is that it?" Milton looks at me, perplexed.

"Yes, I do. Please don't make fun of me."

"You're searching for the Truth with a capital *T*," Milton continues, ignoring my comment. "And you think either you remember accurately or you imagine." Milton pauses, leans forward, and cups his chin with his right hand, pinching his beard. "When did you become such a positivist?" he jokes.

I'm surprised at Milton's determination to make light of this issue. "I'm not a positivist. I just don't trust my memory."

"I don't trust it either, at least not if what you mean is that the events you recall happened exactly as you say."

"Now I'm the one who is confused," I declare. "From the beginning you've encouraged me to dig into my past. I thought what we were doing was unearthing the truth that sits beneath the layers of memories I've shared. Now you tell me that you don't trust my recollections. How can you help me if you don't have valid data on which to base your interpretations?"

"I do have data, rich data," Milton says emphatically. "I have your stories. I consider these stories true but not necessarily accurate. In our work here, we mine these stories for truths, not Truth with a capital *T*."

"But you just said you don't trust my memory. If my memory is untrustworthy, how can it produce anything akin to the truth?"

"It can't as long as you think about memory the way you're talking about it," Milton insists.

"What's wrong with the way I'm talking about it?"

"You say you want a faithful kind of memory, one that produces truth you can trust, right?"

"That sure would make me feel better."

"Then let's think for a minute about the implications of your conception of memory." I nod.

"In your view, if memory is to be trusted, it has to be accurate."

"Agreed."

"In other words, memory has to reproduce experiences exactly as they originally were lived, right?"

"Go on. What's the point?"

"The point is that memory doesn't work this way."

"What do you mean?"

"You seem to think that remembering is a process of searching and retrieving. You talk as if memories are objects you are trying to find, as if events that happened in the past are locked away somewhere in the recesses of your mind. If you can locate them—unlock the box, so to speak—you will recover your experiences in their original form, untouched and unchanged."

"Accurate!"

"Can you see where this leads? Anything short of this idealized perfection of memory is untrustworthy and untrue, which leaves you in the quandary you've been expressing."

"I don't see myself as an objectivist, but I am searching for the key to that box."

"I hate to spoil your fantasy, Art, but memory isn't static. Once something happens to you—an event, experience, or whatever—it's gone. It happened. You may say to yourself at the time, 'Oh, this is important, I want to remember this,' and most of us do this at one time or another. But when we look back on it—recall, recollect, or recount it—what are we doing? We're remembering remembering. Of course, most of the events we experience aren't so immediately notable to us. Not until later, sometimes much later, do we realize they were formidable, shaping experiences. And that's not all..."

308

"You mean it gets worse? I don't know if I want to hear this," I say, a hint of sarcasm in my voice.

"I think you already know it. It's what you teach your students about language all the time."

"Are you referring to the gaps between experience and expression?"

"Yes. Even in the best of circumstances, language is deficient. It can only scratch the surface of an experience. But it's all we have at our disposal. I'm certain this is not news to you. Nor is the importance of time, which you wrote about in that article on the aftermath of your father's death. So you ought to appreciate the fact that the events, experiences, or things we remember do not stay intact. Because we change over time, our memory of the past does as well."

"You're saying there never was any box or any key."

"That's right. Remembering is an active, continuous process. You don't retrieve the past—you engage with it, calling on your memories of it in the present, here and now. There is no little room where each life experience is recorded. You can't locate a tape of your meeting with Levine and play it back. None of us has a tape recorder in our head. We can't press the replay button and relive the experience exactly as it happened."

"Thanks a lot," I say glumly. "You've confirmed my worst fears." Milton raises his eyebrows. "That there's no solid basis for our interpretations of the past."

"Is that what you're worried about?" he asks.

"Damn it, yes. That's what I was trying to say at the start of this session."

"I see." Milton pauses momentarily, a concerned look covering his face. "You're saying something happened between last week and this week that troubles you. I'm surprised. I thought we ended on a good note last week. You seemed quite upbeat."

"I was. I thought we were making progress. Therapy was working. I was no longer resisting my fears, and I felt more able to acknowledge my cravings and hostilities."

"I'm glad to hear that," Milton says. "But why are you using the past tense? What happened?"

"I had one of my introspective moments a couple of nights ago."

"He thinks too much. He could be dangerous," Milton teases.

"Yes, yes, I got to thinking about our sessions. Suddenly it dawned on me that most of the events I've talked about took place a long, long time ago. I realized that a lot of the details were fuzzy. Suddenly a new image entered my mind. I remembered a recent experience I had at a basketball game. I noticed a woman's face in the crowd on the opposite side of the court. I thought I recognized her, but I couldn't be sure. She seemed to be looking right at me, so I waved to her. But she didn't wave back. The guy sitting next to me, a dear friend, looked at me like I was an idiot. I felt silly and embarrassed. What had I done? Why did I think we knew each other? I had filled in details that weren't there. My imagination had taken over."

"Perhaps it was a person you wished to see, an expression of your desire to see her. That could be worth contemplating."

"Maybe, but that's not the point." I stop abruptly, hesitant to express my fears.

"Go on," Milton urges softly.

"A wave of panic swept over me. I thought, What if this is what I've been doing all along? Have I been evading the blurriness of my memories by imagining details that weren't really there? Oh my god, what if I didn't get the stories right? What if my stories about the past are a product of my imagination and not my memory? I got this queasy feeling that the foundation of my self-understanding was crumbling."

"My goodness, Art, you've established an impossible goal. I admire the way you insist on answering to yourself, on holding yourself accountable to a standard of truthfulness. But the way you express your obsession for the truth, you're bound to slide down the slippery slope of reality. You want to know the way things really are, to locate a place of naked truth unimpeded by imagination or belief. You seem to believe that imagination necessarily contaminates memory. Isn't it possible that imagination could actually sharpen memory, make it more useful? Shouldn't you be more respectful of imagination?"

"I'll grant that imagination is important when I'm writing a story or designing a research project, but that's not what we're doing here, is it?"

"I beg your pardon," Milton kids. "That's precisely what we're doing here. We're investigating you—and your life. Therapy is postgraduate research on yourself, and our methodology is conversation and storytelling."

"But shouldn't we insist on true stories?" I continue to resist.

"Now you're sounding like Joe Friday in *Dragnet*—'All we want are the facts, ma'am, nothing but the facts.' But facts don't tell us what they mean. In therapy we're trading on meanings. You say you remember a meeting between you and Levine. You say it with conviction. I believe you. Why do I believe you? Not only because of the sincerity with which you say it but also because of the meanings you attribute to it and the feeling with which you express them. You call the meeting a significant moment in your life—a turning point. Is that true? Was it really a turning point?"

"I've thought of it as a turning point for a long time."

"I'm not surprised, though I meant that as a rhetorical question." Milton smiles. "The point is that your experience of that meeting—your memory of it and the story you tell to represent it—is much more important than the brute fact of the meeting itself, whether it did or did not take place."

"But you've made it clear that I can't retrieve the actual experience itself."

"That's right. You're a good listener. All we have to work with is your current representation of it, the story you've constructed about it."

"Which is not the same as the experience!" I insist.

"That's right, it's not. Think about how we talk about living *through* experiences. People don't say they survived a story; they say they survived an experience. But when you ask them about the experience, what do they do? They tell you a story. Our only access to the past, whether it's something that just happened or something that happened a long time ago, is through the stories we tell after the fact. One tries to arrive at the story in the experience."

"I want something more than access to the past. I want knowledge of it. I want to know that the story isn't just a construction, that it's true. I can verify it."

"Well, you might be able to verify that some events really happened. Either you did or didn't have a meeting with Levine. Maybe he kept his appointment book or you kept yours. Perhaps a photo was taken. Big deal! The factual occurrence of the meeting seems trivial. It's the story of the meeting that is important, and we have nothing to compare it with but another story of the same events. There is no reality against which your memory can be checked."

"Are you saying there's no way to falsify a story?"

"In a manner of speaking, that's right. We can compare one story to another and decide which story is more believable or, if you prefer, trustworthy. That's what they do in courtrooms. Best story—the one that is most convincing—wins. But both stories are constructed. Neither story is a fact. Both sides compose a story that represents what possibly could have happened, how, and why. Anyway, we're not in a courtroom here."

"Possibly could have happened, constructed, made believable, imagined—this sounds to me like what novelists do," I say. "But we're not talking about fiction, Milton. This is about my life. It's nonfiction. Things happened to me—real things! They shaped me. They affect how I perceive things and people, how I talk and think and feel. I can't just make up a story about the way I wished things had been—you know, substitute wish fulfillment for truth. If I can't have faith in the veracity of what I remember, then I have no basis on which to ground my understanding of myself."

"Well, I wouldn't completely discount the possibility that we ourselves—our images and understandings of ourselves—are fictions and that our personal happiness rests on our skill at making a good story for ourselves, one that is useful and believable. Besides, in here honesty is more important than truth. I count on your sincerity, on you believing the story you are telling me and trying to tell it as honestly as possible. Over the time we've been working together I've observed you gradually lowering your guard. It takes courage to express the regrets, confusions, and fears you've disclosed. For example, the day you told me about Brenda's breakdown you were speaking about how painful it felt to talk about how you had acted, and you said, "I wish it were even more painful. I want to feel the sting." When I looked at you I saw the agony written on your face and body. This was not a happening truth; it was a feeling truth. It smarted. Those truths—feeling truths—are more important to the healing process than checks on accuracy."

"What do you mean?"

"I mean you are telling me the truth as you know and remember it. Your body shows it. Your sincerity comes across. You're not purposely inventing things that didn't happen."

"No, I'm not. I tell the stories as I remember them. Sometimes I feel as if I'm reliving them as I'm telling them. But expressing my memories is complicated. I feel as if I'm constantly making things appear smoother than they were. There are gaps, fragments, contingencies—and so much ambiguity. My fears and fantasies mingle with my cravings and desires. And the present gets fused with the past. You mentioned how our images of other people and events change from one point in time to another. My image of my family today is much different from when I was an adolescent or a young man. I don't interpret what was going on between my parents or between my parents and me, or my siblings and me, the same way I did then."

"That's an important observation. You're on to something really crucial. Think of what we do in these sessions. I ask you what happened, and you tell me a story. But we don't stop there. We ask: What does it mean? What does your interpretation say about you? What triggered this memory? How does it feel *now*? You're not so much dwelling in or on the past as you are reflecting on it and using it. I get to observe your consciousness in action. Sure, your flashes of memory appear to take you back in time. For a moment you're reliving the past, something that feels like the past. You're immersed in the felt-past, but you're still here in the now, the present."

"That reminds me of Augustine's famous reflections on time that link past and future to the present. He expresses his awe at how a future that does not yet exist moves into a past that no longer exists through a present that vanishes before it can be noticed."

"Hence, the absurdity of pinning all your hopes on accurate memory of a distant past!"

"That's where you lose me, Milton. I simply can't accept the notion that memory is unimportant."

"No! No! On the contrary, memory is imperative! Without memory we could not bestow coherence and continuity on our experience. Understanding is dependent on recollection, especially our self-understanding."

"There you go again, Milton, adding to my confusion. First, you say memory can't be trusted. Then you say it's crucial. You tell me that my memory couldn't possibly reproduce past experiences in a form akin to the original events. Then you say that my self-understanding is dependent on recollection. You're talking out of both sides of your mouth."

Milton laughs. "I've been known to do that. But I don't think I'm contradicting myself when I say that memories often are incomplete, fragmentary, and shadowy—yet vital to one's self-understanding. Nor do I think it's a mistake to rail against a conception of memory as a thing or object in itself. If memory re-creates, reorganizes, and revises the meanings of past experiences, which I believe it does, then it should be thought of as organic, alive, and active, something I'd call *living memory*. We can't be certain about the past because we're always re-creating it in the present. The difference between your conception of memory and mine is that you want to recover and assess the truth of your memories, whereas I simply want to figure out how you can use them."

"You once referred to therapy as memory work. Is that what you mean by living memory?"

"Yes. We are actively remaking the past. By inhabiting or revisiting the past we can question and reflect on its possible meanings. The work of memory begins with the activity of remembering, a working through and toward the past, making the absences and silences of past experiences come into presence. Memory becomes inquiry."

"I take it that by inquiry you mean research. If that's the case, what do you think of as the raw data of memory work? With what materials does one work?"

"Well, I was never too keen on the rawness of data," Milton teases. "But to answer your question, images and traces of the past—that's what we have to go on. The impressions lodged in memory connect us to our lived history. We traffic in traces of the past."

"That's all? Traces?"

"Oh, there are sometimes harder data—snapshots, diaries, scrapbooks, clippings, old recordings, and that sort of thing. But none of it is terribly firm or illuminating."

"And the methodology to which you referred—conversation—doesn't that add complications as well?"

"You call them 'complications.' I call them opportunities. It depends on your goals, doesn't it?"

"When I think about our sessions, I see how I'm constantly looking back at a past self, an older version of myself. This past self comes into focus momentarily. Then the image fades away. As a research project that would make it corrupted by observer bias, the line between I, the observer, and me, the observed, is crossed. I'm inside what I'm studying. It's like trying to catch your own shadow."

"Oh, I like that image. You're prompted to move when you're chasing your shadow. You don't sit still. And that's true of the past. You can't immobilize or freeze it. It moves as you do."

"That scares me," I admit.

"And it also frees you."

"How?"

"You have an urge to catch up to your shadow or chase your tail, but eventually you realize that this is not something you can achieve. Now you can put your energy into something more useful. Same goes with your search for the truth. We all have an innate desire to seek after truth, but it's not in our nature to achieve it. We don't have the sort of supernatural power it would take to possess ultimate truth."

"Truth beckons but eludes us," I say, slumping into a crouch on the couch.

"Don't act so forlorn. It's not the end of the world."

"If truth has no intrinsic value, I don't know why I'm here. Am I just wasting my time?"

"That's a question you have to answer. On the whole, I'd say clients don't come to me in pursuit of truth; they come in search of happiness. Facts aren't all that important to their search. It's meanings that matter. They want to feel meaningfully alive. Yes sir, I think they want happiness." Milton sits up in his chair. He beams as though he is proud of his insight.

"Isn't there a place for truth in this? What good is happiness based on fiction?"

"The happy person likely doesn't ask that question," Milton says with a grin. "But I don't want to sound disingenuous. I know you're sincerely concerned about truthfulness. I'm only trying to get across the point that what we're trying to do through our dialogues is construct a self to which you can be true. We're seeking a *narrative truth,* a story you can live with that will allow you to move on to the future with hope and optimism."

I start to react but hesitate. I'm momentarily stunned by the narrative notions that Milton has expressed. For a practitioner, he's a damn good theorist. He smiles as we sit in silence.

"I guess, then, you very well might have sat there quietly as Levine took his leave after all," he says. "Our time is almost up," he adds looking over at the clock, "and there's one other thing I wanted to bring up today."

"What's that?" I reply, eager to continue the session.

"It's about your book, the one you've been working on for so long. You haven't finished it, have you?"

"No, I haven't," I acknowledge.

"I don't think you want to finish," he says.

"How can you say that? Of course I want to finish," I insist.

"How many years have you been working on this book?"

"I've worked on it almost exclusively in the summers. I don't think of it as years." *Why is he bringing this up now? Sometimes I doubt whether I see Milton the way he really is.*

"How many summers, then?"

"This is my seventh."

"In some states that would qualify you for a common law marriage. You could marry the book."

"Very funny," I say, annoyed by the direction the conversation is taking. "I'll be done at the end of the summer."

"No, you won't," he challenges. "You'll find some reason you couldn't quite finish it. You're afraid to finish it." Milton shifts to the edge of his seat.

Why is he grilling me like this? "Don't be ridiculous. What could I possibly be afraid of?"

"I can't say."

"You mean you won't say."

"Remember the last time you tried to write a major book?" Milton shifts forward to the edge of his seat.

"I finished everything but the last chapter that time," I defend. Now I'm on the edge of the couch.

"History repeats itself."

I'm getting more and more irritated at Milton's insistence on pushing this topic. "That was thirty-five years ago. I was younger, angrier, and more defensive. I needed approval."

"You told me you let one mediocre review stop you, when all the other reviewers loved it."

"I wanted it to be perfect. I wanted everybody to love and learn from it." I'm defiant.

"So you put it in a drawer and moved on. Nobody got to learn from it."

"That was a foolish and childish decision on my part. I know that now. But this book is different." I hear my voice crack. I take a moment to regain my composure. Then I break the silence. "I'm more mature now. I don't hide behind abstractions and theories. My thoughts and feelings are on practically every page." I can feel my face flush, reminding me how my father looked right before he erupted.

"That's all the more reason not to finish. Someone's bound to call you self-absorbed."

I rise from my seat and begin to pace. "If you're trying to get under my skin, you're doing a good job."

"Part of my job is to peel away your illusions. Didn't you say your life is on every page?"

I pace around Milton's chair, lifting my gaze toward the ceiling and then scanning the whole room before turning my attention back to Milton. Speaking into the silence, I ask, "How many times do I have to explain this to you? When a writer tells personal stories, he separates the stories from himself. In a manner of speaking, he objectifies his experiences in order to delve into their possible meanings. My stories may be about my life, but they're not *only* about my life. The stories feature a kind of life that many other people live—graduate students, instructors, professors, friends, lovers."

"Sit down, Art. Please." Milton remains calm and unflustered as he interrupts my outburst.

I head toward my seat on the couch, but don't miss a beat of my rant. "Look Milton, I don't think you realize how important this book is to me. I'm writing about being enabled and frustrated by the narratives we inherit, the stories we resist, and those we invent; about the significant role that contingency, fate, and chance play in our lives; about growing up while remaining a child; about the cleavage between work and play and the link between the personal and the academic. My book is about stumbling onto things, turning them over, and taking advantage of the lessons they teach; about listening to different voices but trying to express your own; about trying to muster the courage to speak the unspoken even when it terrifies you. It's about acknowledging mistakes you've made and people you've betrayed; about giving yourself permission to write what matters to you, not what others say should matter to you; about the generosity of other people who take an interest in you without asking for anything in return; and about the desire to touch the deep parts of yourself in the quest for a good life. Damn, Milton, I'm not the only one who wants to achieve a healthy relation to the past in order to go forward into the future. Most people do. I tell what I care about and invite readers to consider my consciousness from the perspectives of their own and to challenge themselves to consider the self they want to be."

"I admire your passion, Art. But you haven't given me a reason to believe you're going to finish—quite the opposite, in fact. I'm more convinced than ever that the book is too important to you, too close to your heart to finish. You need this relationship to the unfinished book."

"That's absurd, Milton. It's about the dumbest thing I've ever heard you say. It makes me want to stop therapy. You don't understand me."

"You don't really think you could finish without me?" Milton says.

"Of course, I can."

"We're out of time, Art."

"No Milton! Don't pull that on me. You can't just stop now. No, no, no! No, Milton, not now!"

"Art, Art, wake up! Wake up!" Carolyn pleads, tugging at the back of my arm.

"What? What? What's the matter? Are you all right?"

"I'm fine," she says. "I've been trying to wake you up. You must have been having a nightmare. You kept saying, 'no, no, no' and shaking."

"Whew, I'm glad to be awake. That was an awful dream. I was back in therapy with Milton. Everything I believed in was unraveling. He told me I'd never finish my book. I felt he was abandoning me."

"Milton has been dead for fifteen years. It couldn't have been him. You haven't even mentioned him in, uh, I don't know how long—years."

"I know, but I can't simply ignore the dream. Milton insisted that dreams are a kind of knowing, and I remember how he used to say that in a dream it's possible that all the characters are parts of yourself. Maybe I was in therapy with myself, trying to merge opposing parts of myself. Milton may have been voicing my own fears. I'll have to think about it."

Carolyn embraces me, and we hold each other tight. Our two dogs, Buddha and Zen, jump on the bed, attempting to burrow their way into the hug. Carolyn lifts her head from my pillow and looks directly into my eyes. "It's time to finish the book, sweetheart. It's about time."

Note

1. The following sources were consulted during the preparation of this epilogue: Albright (1994); Augustine (2012); Bochner (2007); Carr (1986); Freeman (2002, 2010); Gornick (2008);

Hammer (2008); Hampl (1999); Kerby (1991); Le Guin (1980); Mairs (2008); N. Miller (2008); Neisser (1994); O'Brien (1990), Ricoeur (1980); Sacks (2008); Schacter (1996); Shields (2008, 2010).

References

Abrahams, R. D. (1986). Ordinary and extraordinary experience. In V. Turner & E. Bruner (Eds.), *The anthropology of experience* (pp. 45–73). Urbana: University of Illinois Press.

Albright, D. (1994). Literary and psychological models of the self. In U. Neisser & R. Fivush (Eds.), *The remembering self: Construction and accuracy in the self-narrative* (pp. 19–40). Cambridge: Cambridge University Press.

Allen, W. [Director]. (1977). *Annie Hall*. [DVD]. Beverly Hills: United Artists.

Allport, G. (1954). *The nature of prejudice*. Reading, MA: Addison-Wesley.

Allport, G. (1955). *Becoming: Basic considerations for a psychology of personality*. New Haven, CT: Yale University Press.

Allport, G. (1960). *Personality and social encounter*. Boston: Beacon.

Anderson, D. (2006). *Watergate: Scandal in the White House*. North Mankato, MN: Compass Point.

Apter, T. (1996). Expert witness: Who controls the psychologist's narrative? In R. Josselson (Ed.), *Ethics and process in the narrative study of lives* (pp. 22–44). Thousand Oaks, CA: Sage Publications.

Asch, S. (1956). Studies of independence and conformity: A minority of one against a unanimous majority. *Psychological Monographs: General and Applied, 70*(9), 1–70. Augustine, St. (2012). *The confessions: Saint Augustine of Hippo*. (M. Boulding, Trans.). San Francisco: Ignatius Press.

Bakhtin, M. (1981). *The dialogic imagination: Four essays.* (C. Emerson & M. Holquist, Trans.). Austin: University of Texas Press.

Barnlund, D. (1968). *Interpersonal communication: Survey and studies*. Boston: Houghton Mifflin.

Barthes, R. (1977). The death of the author. In R. Barthes, *Image-Music-Text* (pp. 142–149). New York: Hill and Wang.

Bateson, G. (1951). Information and codification: A philosophical approach. In J. Ruesch and G. Bateson, *Communication: The Social Matrix of Psychiatry* (pp. 168–227). New York: Norton & Company.

Bateson, G. (1958). *Naven: A survey of the problems suggested by a composite picture of the culture of a New Guinea tribe drawn from three points of view* (2nd ed.). Redwood City, CA: Stanford University Press.

Bateson, G. (1967). Cybernetic explanation. *American Behavioral Scientist, 10*(6), 29–32.

Bateson, G. (1972). *Steps to an ecology of mind: Collected essays in anthropology, psychiatry, evolution, and epistemology*. Chicago: University of Chicago Press.

Bateson, G. (1979). *Mind and nature: A necessary unity*. New York: Hampton Press.

Bateson, G., Jackson, D. D.; Haley, J., & Weakland, J. (1956). Toward a theory of schizophrenia. *Behavioral Science, 1*(4), 251–264.

Baudhuin, E. S. (1970). *Obscene language and persuasive communication: An experimental study*. Unpublished doctoral dissertation, Bowling Green State University, Bowling Green, OH.

Baudhuin, E. S. (1973). Obscene language and evaluative response: An empirical study. *Psychological Reports, 32*, 399–402.

Baum, C., Hyman, P., & Michel, S. (1976). *The Jewish woman in America*. New York: Plume Books.

Baur, M. (2006). American Pie and the self-critique of rock 'n roll. In W. Irwin and J. J. E. Gracia (Eds.), *Philosophy and the interpretation of pop culture* (pp. 255–274). Lanham, MD: Rowan and Littlefield.

Becker, E. (1968). *The structure of evil: An essay on the unification of the science of man*. New York: George Braziller.

Becker, E. (1971). *The birth and death of meaning*. New York: George Braziller.

Becker, E. (1973). *The denial of death*. New York: The Free Press

Becker, G. (1997). *Disrupted lives: How people create meaning in a chaotic world*. Berkeley: University of California Press.

Becker, H. S. (1994). 'FOI POR ACASO': Conceptualizing coincidence. *Sociological Quarterly, 35*, 183–194.

Behar, R. (1996). *The vulnerable observer: Anthropology that breaks your heart*. Boston: Beacon.

Bellah, R. N., Madsen, R., Sullivan, W. M., Swidler, A., & Tipton, S. M. (1985). *Habits of the heart*. Berkeley: University of California Press.

Bellow, G., & Minow, M. (Eds.). (1998). *Law stories*. Ann Arbor: University of Michigan Press.

Bem, D. (1970). *Beliefs, attitudes and human affairs*. Belmont, CA: Brooks/Cole.

Bennis, W. (1964). *Interpersonal dynamics: Ethics and readings of human interaction*. Homewood, IL: Dorsey Press.

Berger, B. (1992). *Authors of their own lives: Intellectual autobiographies by twenty American sociologists*. Berkeley: University of California Press.

Berger, C. (1991). Communication theories and other curios. *Communication Monographs, 58*, 101–113.

Berger, P., & Luckmann, T. (1967). *The social construction of reality: A treatise on the sociology of knowledge*. Garden City, NY: Anchor Books.

Bergman, I. [Producer/Director]. (1960). *The seventh seal* [Motion Picture]. United States: Janus.

Berlo, D. (1960). *The process of communication: An introduction to theory and practice*. New York: Harcourt, Brace, and World.

Berne, E. (1962). *Games people play: The psychology of human relationships*. New York: Grove Press.

Bernstein, C., & Woodward, B. (1974). *All the president's men*. New York: Simon and Schuster.

Bertalanffy, L. V. (1969). *General system theory: Foundations, development, applications*. New York: George Braziller.

Blumer, H. (1969). *Symbolic interactionism: Perspective and method*. Englewood Cliffs, NJ: Prentice-Hall.

Bochin, H. W. (1970). *Richard Nixon: Rhetorical strategist*. New York: Greenwood.

Bochner, A. (1969). *The history of academic debate at Syracuse University*. Master's thesis, Syracuse University, Syracuse, NY.

Bochner, A. (1971). *A multivariate investigation of Machiavellianism and task structure in four-man groups*. Doctoral dissertation, Bowling Green State University, Bowling Green, OH.

Bochner, A. (1978). "On taking ourselves seriously: An analysis of some persistent problems and promising directions in interpersonal research," *Human Communication Research, 4*, 179–191.

Bochner, A. (1981). Forming warm ideas. In C. Wilder-Mott & J. Weakland (Eds.), *Rigor and imagination: Essays from the legacy of Gregory Bateson* (pp. 65–81). Palo Alto, CA: Praeger.

Bochner, A. (1984). The functions of communication in interpersonal bonding. In C. A. Arnold & J. W. Bowers (Eds.), *The handbook of rhetoric and communication* (pp. 544–621). Boston: Allyn and Bacon.

Bochner, A. (1985). Perspectives on inquiry: Representation, conversation, and reflection. In M. Knapp & G. R. Miller (eds.), *Handbook of interpersonal communication* (pp. 27–58). Thousand Oaks, CA: Sage Publications.

Bochner, A. (1990). Embracing contingencies of lived experience in the study of close relationships. Keynote Address, Conference on Personal Relationships, Oxford, England.

Bochner, A. (1994). Perspectives on inquiry II: Theories and stories. In M. L. Knapp & G. R. Miller (Eds.), *Handbook of interpersonal communication* (2nd ed., pp. 21–41). Thousand Oaks, CA: Sage Publications.

Bochner, A. (1997). It's about time: Narrative and the divided self. *Qualitative Inquiry, 3*, 418–438.

Bochner, A. (2000). Criteria against ourselves. *Qualitative Inquiry, 6*, 266–272.

Bochner, A. (2002a). Love survives. *Qualitative Inquiry, 8*(2), 161–170.

Bochner, A. (2002b). Perspectives on inquiry III: The moral of stories. In M. Knapp & J. Daley

(Eds.), *The handbook of interpersonal communication* (pp. 73–101). Thousand Oaks, CA: Sage Publications.

Bochner, A. (2007). Notes toward an ethics of memory in autoethnography. In N. Denzin & M. Giardina (Eds.), *Ethical futures in qualitative research: Decolonizing the politics of knowledge* (pp. 197–208). Walnut Creek, CA: Left Coast Press.

Bochner, A. (2008, April). Resisting institutional depression. *Spectra*. Reprinted in *Women and Language* (2008), *31*, 2–3.

Bochner, A. (2012). On first-person narrative scholarship: Autoethnography as acts of meaning. *Narrative Inquiry, 22*(1), 155–164.

Bochner, A., & Eisenberg, E. (1985). Legitimizing speech communication: An examination of coherence and cohesion in the development of the discipline. In T. Benson (Ed.), *Speech communication in the twentieth century* (pp. 299–321). Carbondale: Southern Illinois University Press.

Bochner, A., & Ellis, C. (1992). Personal narrative as a social approach to interpersonal communication. *Communication Theory, 2*(2), pp. 165–172.

Bochner, A., & Ellis, C. (Eds.). (2002). *Ethnographically speaking: Autoethnography, literature & aesthetics*. Walnut Creek, CA: AltaMira Press.

Bochner, A., Ellis, C., & Tillmann-Healy, L. (1997). Relationships as stories. In S. Duck (Ed.), *Handbook of personal relationships* (pp. 307–324). New York: John Wiley.

Bochner, A., & Fitzpatrick, M. A. (1980). Multivariate analysis of variance: Models, techniques and applications in communication research. In P. Monge and J. Cappella (Eds.), *Multivariate analysis in communication research* (pp. 143–174). New York: Academic Press.

Bochner, A., & Kelly, C. (1974). Interpersonal competence: Rationale, philosophy, and implementation of a conceptual framework. *Speech Teacher, 23*, 279–301.

Bochner, A., & Krueger, D. (1979). On inscrutable epistemologies and muddled concepts. In D. Nimmo (Ed.), *Communication Yearbook 3* (pp. 197–211). New Brunswick, NJ: Transaction Books.

Bochner, A., & Waugh, J. (1995). Talking-with as a model for writing about: Implications of Rortian pragmatism for communication theory. In L. Langsdorf and A. Smith (Eds.), *Recovering pragmatism's voice: The classical tradition and the philosophy of communication* (pp. 211–233). Albany: State University of New York Press.

Boszormenyi-Nagy, I., & Framo J. L. (1965). *Intensive family therapy: Theoretical and practical aspects*. New York: Hoeber Medical Division, Harper & Row.

Bridgman, P. W. (1927). *The logic of modern physics*. New York: Macmillan.

Bridgman, P. W. (1929). The new vision of science. *Harper's, 158*, 443–454.

Bridgman, P. W. (1959). *The way things are*. Cambridge, MA: Harvard University Press.

Brill, A. (Ed.). (1938). *The basic writings of Sigmund Freud*. New York: Random House.

Brink, C. (2000). Secular icons: Looking at photographs from Nazi concentration camps. *History and Memory, 12*(1), 135–150.

Brooks, P., & Gewirtz, P. (Eds.). (1998). *Law's stories: Narrative and rhetoric in the law*. New Haven, CT: Yale University Press.

Broyard, A. (1992). *Intoxicated by my illness, and other writings on life and death*. New York: Fawcett Columbine.

Bruner, E. (1986). Ethnography as narrative. In V. Turner and E. Bruner (Eds.), *The anthropology of experience* (pp. 139–155). Urbana: University of Illinois Press.

Bruner, J. (1986). *Actual minds, possible worlds*. Cambridge, MA: Harvard University Press.

Bruner, J. (1987). Life as narrative. *Social Research, 54*, 11–32.

Bruner, J. (1990). *Acts of meaning*. Cambridge, MA: Harvard University Press.

Bryant, D. C., & Wallace, K. R. (1969). *Fundamentals of public speaking*. Upper Saddle River, NJ: Appleton-Century-Crofts/Prentice Hall.

Burke, K. (1941/1967). Literature as equipment for living. In *The philosophy of literary form: Studies in symbolic action* (pp. 293–304). Berkeley: University of California Press.

Burleson, B. (1992). Taking communication seriously. *Communication Monographs, 59*, 79–86.

Campbell, D. T., & Stanley, J. C. (1963). *Experimental and quasi-experimental designs for research*. Chicago: Rand McNally.

Camus, A. (1946). *The stranger*. New York: Knopf.

Camus, A. (1947). *The plague*. New York: Knopf.

Camus, A. (1955). *The myth of Sisyphus*. New York: Random House.

Caplan, J. (2009). *Concentration camps in Nazi Germany: The new histories*. New York: Routledge.

Carr, D. (1986). *Time, narrative, and history*. Bloomington: Indiana University Press.

Cartwright, D. (1979). Contemporary social psychology in historical perspective. *Social Psychology Quarterly, 42*(1), 82–93.

Cattell, R. B. (1978). *The scientific use of factor analysis in behavioral and life sciences*. New York: Plenum Press.

Charon, R. (2006). *Narrative medicine: Honoring the stories of illness*. New York: Oxford University Press.

Charon, R., & Montello, M. (Eds.). (2002). *Stories matter: The role of narrative in medical ethics*. New York: Routledge.

Chesterton, G. K. (1924). *The illustrated London news*.

Christie, R., & Geis, F. (1970). *Studies in Machiavellianism*. Waltham, MA: Academic Press.

Cicourel, A. (1974). *Cognitive sociology: Language and meaning in social interaction*. New York: Free Press.

Clifford, J., & Marcus, G. (1986). *Writing culture: The poetics and politics of ethnography*. Berkeley: University of California Press.

Cohen, J., & Soyer, D. (2008). *My future is in America: Autobiographies of Eastern European Jewish immigrants*. New York: New York University Press.

Cohen, L. [Musician]. (1967). Hey, that's no way to say goodbye. On *Songs of Leonard Cohen* [Audio CD]. New York: Columbia Records.

Cole, M. (1990). Cognitive development and formal schooling: The evidence from cross-cultural research. In L. C. Moll (Ed.), *Vygotsky and education: Instructional implications and applications of sociohistorical psychology* (pp. 89–110). New York: Cambridge University Press.

Coles, R. (1967). *A study in courage and fear* (Vol. 1, Children of Crisis). Boston: Little, Brown and Company.

Coles, R. (1989). *The call of stories: Teaching and the moral imagination*. Boston: Houghton Mifflin.

Cooley, C. H. (1902). Human nature and the social order. New York: Scribner's.

Coser, L. (1975). Presidential address: Two methods in search of a substance. *American Sociological Review, 40*(6), 691–700.

Cotlin, G. (2005). *Existential America*. Baltimore, MD: Johns Hopkins University Press.

Couser, G. (1997). *Recovering bodies: Illness, disability, and life writing*. Madison: University of Wisconsin Press.

Craig, R. (1999). Communication theory as a field. *Communication Theory, 9*(2), 119–161.

Crites, S. (1971). The narrative quality of experience. *Journal of the American Academy of Religion, 39*, 291–311.

Crites, S. (1986). Storytime: Recollecting the past and projecting the future. In T. Sarbin (Ed.), *Narrative psychology: The storied nature of human conduct* (pp. 152–173). New York: Praeger.

Cronbach, L. (1975). Beyond the two disciplines of scientific psychology. *American Psychologist, 30*(2), 116–127.

Cushman, D. (1977). The rules perspective as a theoretical basis for the study of human communication. *Communication Quarterly, 25*(1), 30–45.

Cushman, D., Valentinsen, B., & Dietrich, D. (1982). A rules theory of interpersonal relationships. *Human Communication Theory*, 90–119.

Cushman, D., & Whiting, G. (1972). An approach to communication theory: Toward consensus on rules. *Communication Quarterly, 22*, 219–238.

Dallmayr, F., & McCarthy, T. (Eds.). (1977). *Understanding and social inquiry.* South Bend, IN: University of Notre Dame Press.

Deetz, S. (1994). The future of the discipline: The challenges, the research, and the social contribution. In S. Deetz (ed.), *Communication yearbook 17* (pp. 565–600). Thousand Oaks, CA: Sage Publications.

Delia, J. (1987). Communication research: A history. In C. Berger and S. Chaffee (Eds.), *Handbook of communication science* (pp. 20–98). Newbury Park, CA: Sage Publications.

Denzin, N. (1992). *Symbolic interactionism and cultural studies.* Cambridge, MA: Blackwell.

Denzin, N. (1996). *Interpretive ethnography: Ethnographic practices for the 21st century.* Thousand Oaks, CA: Sage Publications.

Denzin, N. (1997). Whose sociology is it? Comment on Huber. *American Journal of Sociology, 120,* 1416–1423.

Denzin, N., & Lincoln, Y. S. (Eds.). (2000). *The Sage handbook of qualitative research* (2nd ed.). Thousand Oaks, CA: Sage Publications.

Denzin, N., & Lincoln, Y. S. (Eds.). (2011). *The Sage handbook of qualitative research* (4th ed.). Thousand Oaks, CA: Sage Publications.

Derrida, J. (1976). *Of grammatology.* (G. Spivak, Trans.). Baltimore, MA: Johns Hopkins University Press.

Derrida, J. (1978). *Writing and difference.* (A. Bass, Trans.). London: Routledge.

Dilthey, W. (1976). *Selected writings.* (H. Rickman, Ed., Trans.). Cambridge: Cambridge University Press.

Dylan, B. (1964). The times they are a-changin'. On *The times they are a-changin'* [Vinyl]. New York: Columbia Records.

Dylan, B. (1965). It's alright, Ma (I'm only bleeding). On *Bringing it all back home* [Vinyl]. New York: Columbia Records.

Dylan, B. (1975a). Simple twist of fate. On *Blood on the tracks* [Album]. New York: Columbia Records.

Dylan, B. (1975b). Tangled up in blue. On *Blood on the tracks* [Album]. New York: Columbia Records.

Eadie, W. F. (Ed.). (2009). *21st century communication: A reference handbook.* Thousand Oaks, CA: Sage Publications.

Ellis, C. (1986). *Fisher folk: Two communities on Chesapeake Bay.* Lexington: University Press of Kentucky.

Ellis, C. (1991). Emotional sociology. *Studies in Symbolic Interaction, 12,* 123–145.

Ellis, C. (1993). 'There are survivors': Telling a story of sudden death. *The Sociological Quarterly, 34*(4), 711–730.

Ellis, C. (1995). *Final negotiations: A story of love, loss, and chronic illness.* Philadelphia: Temple University Press.

Ellis, C. (2009). *Revision: Autoethnographic reflections on life and work.* Walnut Creek, CA: Left Coast.

Ellis, C., & Bochner, A. (1991). Telling and performing personal stories: The constraints of choice in abortion. In C. Ellis & M. Flaherty (Eds.), *Investigating subjectivity: Research on lived experience* (pp. 79–101). Newbury Park, CA: Sage Publications.

Ellis, C., & Bochner, A. (Eds.). (1996). *Composing ethnography: Alternative forms of qualitative writing.* Walnut Creek, CA: AltaMira.

Ellis, C., & Bochner, A. (2000). Autoethnography, personal narrative, reflexivity: Researcher as subject. In N. Denzin and Y. Lincoln (Eds.), *The handbook of qualitative research* (2nd ed., pp. 733–768). Thousand Oaks, CA: Sage Publications.

Ellis, C., & Bochner. A. (2006). Analyzing analytic autoethnography: An autopsy. *Journal of Contemporary Ethnography, 35,* 429–449.

Elms, A. C. (1975). The crisis of confidence in social psychology. *American Psychologist, 30,* 967–976.

Erdelyi, M. (1974). A new look at the new look: Perceptual defense and vigilance. *Psychological Review, 81,* 1–25.

Erikson, E. (1968). *Identity, youth, and crisis*. New York: W. W. Norton and Company.

Festinger, L. (1962). Cognitive dissonance. *Scientific American, 207*(4), 93–107.

Feyerabend, P. (1975). *Against method: Outline of an anarchist theory of knowledge*. New York: New Left Books.

Fisher, W. (1984). Narration as a human communication paradigm: The case of public moral argument. *Communication Monographs, 51*, 1–22.

Foucault, M. (1965). *Madness and civilization: A history of insanity in an age of reason*. New York: Random House.

Foucault, M. (1970a). *The archeology of knowledge and the discourse on language*. (A. M. Sheridan Smith, Trans.). New York: Pantheon Books.

Foucault, M. (1970b). *The order of things: An archeology of the human sciences*. New York: Random House.

Foucault, M. (1982). The subject and power. *Critical Inquiry, 8*(4), 777–795.

Frank, A. (1991). *At the will of the body: Reflections on illness*. Boston: Houghton Mifflin.

Frank, A. (1995). *The wounded storyteller: Body, illness, and ethics*. Chicago: University of Chicago Press.

Frankfurt, H. (1988). *The importance of what we care about*. Cambridge: Cambridge University Press.

Frankl, V. (1959). *Man's search for meaning: An introduction to logotherapy*. Boston: Beacon Press.

Freeman, M. (1993). *Rewriting the self: History, memory, narrative*. London: Routledge.

Freeman, M. (1998). Mythical time, historical time, and the narrative fabric of self. *Narrative Inquiry, 8*, 27–50.

Freeman, M. (2002). The burden of truth: Psychoanalytic poiesis and narrative understanding. In W. Patterson (Ed.), *Strategic narrative: New perspectives on the power of personal and cultural stories* (pp. 9–27). Lanham, MD: Lexington Books.

Freeman, M. (2010). *Hindsight: The promise and peril of looking backward*. New York: Oxford University Press.

Frentz, T. (2008). *Trickster in tweed: The quest for quality in a faculty life*. Walnut Creek, CA: Left Coast Press.

Freud, S. (1915). The unconscious. *S.E., 14*, 166–204.

Freud, S. (1961). *Civilization and its discontents*. New York: W. W. Norton and Company.

Freud, S. (1989/1910). *Leonardo da Vinci and a memory of his childhood*. (A. Tyson, Trans.). New York: W. W. Norton.

Fromm, E. (1941). *Escape from freedom*. New York: Henry Holt.

Fromm, E. (1956). *The art of loving*. New York: Harper Collins.

Fromm, E. (1969). *The sane society* (14th ed.). New York: Holt, Rinehart and Winston.

Frum, D. (2000). *How we got here: The 70's, the decade that brought you modern life (for better or worse)*. New York: Basic Books.

Gadamer, H-G. (1975). *Truth and method*. New York: Seabury.

Garfinkel, H. (1967). *Studies in ethnomethodology*. Malden, MA: Blackwell.

Geertz, C. (1973). *The interpretation of cultures*. New York: Basic Books.

Geertz, C. (1980). Blurred genres: The refiguration of social thought. *The American Scholar, 49*(2), 165–179.

Geertz, C. (1986). Experiences, authoring selves. In V. Turner & E. Brunner (Eds.), *The anthropology of experience* (pp. 373–380). Urbana: University of Illinois Press.

Geertz, C. (1995). *After the fact: Two countries, four decades, one anthropologist*. Cambridge, MA: Harvard University Press.

Gerbner, G. (1983). The importance of being critical: In one's own fashion. *Journal of Communication, 33*(3), 355–362.

Gergen, K. (1969). Self theory and the process of self observation. *Journal of Nervous and Mental Disease, 148*, 437–448.

Gergen, K. (1971). *The concept of self*. New York: Holt, Rinehart & Winston.

Gergen, K. (1973). Social psychology as history. *Journal of Personality and Social Psychology, 26*(2), 309–320.

Gergen, K. (1976). Social psychology, science and history. *Personality and Social Psychology Bulletin, 2*, 373–383.

Gergen, K. (1978). Toward generative theory. *Journal of Personality and Social Psychology, 16*(11), 1344–1360.

Gergen, K. (1980). Toward intellectual audacity in social psychology. In R. Gilmour & S. Duck (Eds.), *The development of social psychology*. New York: Academic Press.

Gergen, K. (1982). *Toward transformation in social knowledge*. New York: Springer-Verlag.

Gergen, K., & Gergen, M. (2000). Qualitative inquiry: Tensions and transformations. In N. Denzin and Y. Lincoln (Eds.), *Handbook of qualitative research* (2nd ed., pp. 1025–1046). Newbury Park, CA: Sage Publications.

Giffin, K., & Patton, B. (1971a). *Fundamentals of interpersonal communication*. New York: Harper and Row.

Giffin, K., & Patton, B. (1971b). *Basic readings in interpersonal communication: Theory and application*. New York: Harper and Row.

Gilmour, D., Mason, N., Waters, R., & Wright, R. (1973). Time [Recorded by Pink Floyd]. On *Dark side of the moon* [Vinyl]. London: Harvest, Capitol.

Goffman, E. (1959). *The presentation of self in everyday life*. Garden City, NY: Doubleday.

Goffman, E. (1961). *Asylums: Essays on the social situation of mental patients and other inmates*. New York: Doubleday.

Goffman, E. (1963). *Behavior in public places: Notes on the social organization of gatherings*. New York: Free Press/MacMillan.

Goffman, E. (1966). *Encounters: two studies in the sociology of interaction*. Indianapolis, IN: Bobbs-Merrill Company.

Goffman, E. (1967). *Interaction ritual: Essays on face-to-face behavior*. New York: Anchor.

Goffman, E. (1971). *Relations in public: Microstudies of the public order*. New York: Basic Books.

Goodall, H. L. (2005). Narrative inheritance: A nuclear family with toxic secrets. *Qualitative Inquiry, 11*, 492–513.

Gornick, V. (1996). *Approaching eye level*. Boston: Beacon Press.

Gornick, V. (2008). Truth in personal narrative. In D. Lazar (Ed.), *Truth in nonfiction: Essays* (pp. 7–10). Iowa City: University of Iowa Press.

Greene, G. (2001/1951). *The end of the affair*. New York: Penguin Group.

Greenwald, A. G. (1976). Transhistorical lawfulness of behavior: A comment on two papers. *Personality and Social Psychology Bulletin, 2*, 391.

Grogan, J. (2012). *Encountering America: Sixties psychology, counterculture, and the movement that shaped the modern self*. New York: Harper-Collins.

Grossberg, L. (1979). Language and theorizing in the human sciences. *Studies in Symbolic Interaction, 2*, 189–231.

Hacking, I. (1995). *Rewriting the soul: Multiple personality and the sciences of memory*. Princeton, NJ: Princeton University Press.

Haley, J. (1962). Wither family therapy. *Family Process, 1*, 69–100.

Haley, J. (1963). *Strategies of psychotherapy*. New York: Grune and Stratton.

Haley, J. (1973). *Uncommon therapy: The psychiatric techniques of Milton H. Erickson*. New York: W. W. Norton.

Haley, J. (1976). Development of a theory: A history of a research project. In C. Sluzki, D. Ransom, & G. Bateson (Eds.), *Double bind: The foundation of communicational approach to the family* (pp. 154–165). New York: Grune and Stratton.

Haley, J., & Richeport-Haley, M. (2007). *Directive family therapy*. New York: Haworth.

Hammer, B. (2008). Tender fictions. In D. Lazar (Ed.), *Truth in nonfiction: Essays* (pp. 146–151). Iowa City: University of Iowa Press.

Hampl, P. (1999). *I could tell you stories: Sojourns in the land of memory.* New York: W. W. Norton and Company.

Harding, S. (1986). *The science question in feminism.* Ithaca, NY: Cornell University Press.

Harré, R., & Secord, P. F. (1972). *The explanation of social behavior.* Oxford: Blackwell.

Harris, R. J. (1976). Two factors contributing to the perception of the theoretical intractability of social psychology. *Personality and Social Psychology Bulletin, 2*, 411–417.

Hartsock, N. (1983). The feminist standpoint: Developing the ground for a specifically feminist historical materialism. In S. Harding & M. Hintikka (Eds.), *Discovering reality: Feminist perspectives on epistemology, metaphysics, methodology and philosophy of science.* Dordrecht, Holland: D. Reidel.

Hegel, G. W. (1949). *The phenomenology of mind* (2nd ed.). (J. B. Baillie, Trans.). New York: Macmillan.

Heidegger, M. (1962/2008). *Being and time.* (J. Macquarrie & E. Robinson, Trans.). New York: Harper and Brothers.

Heilbrun, C. (1997). *The last gift of time: Life beyond sixty.* New York: Ballantine Books.

Helmreich, R. (1975). Applied social psychology: The unfulfilled promise. *Personality and Social Psychology Bulletin, 1*, 548–560.

Hempel, C. (1948). Studies in the logic of explanation. *Philosophy of Science, 15*(2), 135–175.

Hempel, C. (1965). *Aspects of scientific explanation: And other essays in the philosophy of science.* New York: Free Press.

Hempel, C. (1966). *Philosophy of natural science.* Englewood Cliffs, NJ: Prentice-Hall.

Henry, J. (1971). *Pathways to madness.* New York: Vintage Books.

Hilty, J. (2010). *Temple University: 125 years of service to Philadelphia, the nation, and the world.* Philadelphia, PA: Temple University Press.

Hollis, M. (1977). *Models of man.* London: Cambridge University Press.

Holman Jones, S., Adams, T., & Ellis, C. (2013). *Handbook of autoethnography.* Walnut Creek, CA: Left Coast Press.

Hovland, C., Janis, I., & Kelley, H. (1953). *Communication and persuasion.* New Haven, CT: Yale University Press.

Howe, I. (1976). *World of our fathers: The journey of East European Jews to America and the life they found and made.* New York: Harcourt Brace Jovanovich.

Huber, J. (1995). Institutional perspectives on sociology. *American Journal of Sociology, 101*, 194–216.

Huber, J., & Mirowsky, J. (1997). Of facts and fables: Reply to Denzin. *American Journal of Sociology, 102*, 1423–1429.

Hugo, V. (1987). *Les misérables.* (L. Fahnestock & N. McAfee, Trans.). New York: Signet Classics.

Ilardo, J. (1972). Why interpersonal communication? *Speech Teacher, 21*(1), 1–6.

Israel, J., & Tajfel, H. (Eds.). (1972). *The context of social psychology.* London: Academic Press.

Jackson, M. (1989). *Paths toward a clearing: Radical empiricism and ethnographic inquiry.* Bloomington: Indiana University Press.

Jackson, M. (1995). *At home in the world.* Durham, NC: Duke University Press.

Jackson, M. (2002). *The politics of storytelling: Violence, transgression, and intersubjectivity.* Copenhagen: Museum Tusculanum Press.

Jourard, S. (1971). *The transparent self: Self-disclosure and well-being.* New York: Van Nostrand Reinhold.

Kaplan, A. (1964). *The conduct of inquiry: Methodology for behavioral science.* San Francisco: Chandler.

Katsiaficas, G. (1987). *The imagination of the new left: A global analysis of 1968.* Boston: South End Press.

Kelman, H. C. (1972). The rights of the subject in social research: An analysis in terms of relative power and legitimacy. *American Psychologist, 27,* 989–1016.

Keltner, J. W. (1970). *Interpersonal speech-communication: Elements and structures.* Belmont, CA: Wadsworth.

Kenyon, G., Clark, P., & De Vries, B. (Eds.). (2001). *Narrative gerontology: Theory, research, and practice.* New York: Springer Publishing.

Kerby, A. (1991). *Narrative and the self.* Bloomington: Indiana University Press.

Kermode, F. (1967). *The sense of an ending: Studies in the theory of fiction.* New York: Oxford University Press.

Kibler, R., & Barker, L. (Eds.). (1969). *Conceptual frontiers in speech communication: Report on the New Orleans Conference on Research and Instructional Development.* New Orleans: Speech Association of America.

Kierkegaard, S. (1959). *Either/or* (Vol. 1). Princeton, NJ: Princeton University Press.

Kleinman, A. (1989). *The illness narratives: Suffering, healing and the human condition.* New York: Basic Books.

Knapp, M., & Miller, G. (Eds.). (1985). *Handbook of interpersonal communication.* Thousand Oaks, CA: Sage Publications.

Krieger, S. (1991). *Social science and the self: Personal essays on an art form.* New Brunswick, NJ: Rutgers University Press.

Krieger, S. (1996). *The family silver: Essays on relations among women.* Berkeley: University of California Press.

Krieger, S. (1997). Lesbian in academe. In B. Laslett & B. Thorne (Eds.), *Feminist sociology: Life histories of a movement* (pp. 194–208). New Brunswick, NJ: Rutgers University Press.

Kuhn, T. (1970). *The structure of scientific revolutions* (2nd ed.). Chicago: University of Chicago Press.

Laing, R. D. (1961). *Self and others.* London: Tavistock.

Laing, R. D. (1965). *The divided self: An existential study in sanity and madness.* London: Pelican Books.

Laing, R. D. (1967). *The politics of experience and the bird of paradise.* London: Tavistock.

Laing, R. D. (1969). *The politics of the family and other essays.* New York: Pantheon Books.

Laing, R. D. (1982). *The voice of experience.* New York: Pantheon.

Laing, R. D., Phillipson, H., & Lee, R. D. (1966). *Interpersonal perception: A theory and a method of research.* London: Tavistock.

Lang, K., & Lang, G. (1953). The unique perspective on television and its effect: A pilot study. *American Sociological Review, 18,* 3–12.

Lasswell, H. D. (1927). *Propaganda technique in the world war* (1st ed.). New York: Knopf.

Lasswell, H. D. (1949). Style in the language of politics. In H. D. Lasswell & N. Leites (Eds.), *Language of politics: Studies in quantitative semantics* (pp. 20–39). New York: George Stewart.

Lawrence, J., & Lee, R. E. (1955). *Inherit the wind.* New York: Random House.

Lazar, D. (Ed.). *Truth in nonfiction: Essays.* Iowa City: University of Iowa Press.

Leary, T. (1967). *Turn on, tune in, drop out* [Audio Cassette]. Chicago: Mercury Records.

Lebo, H. (1992). *Casablanca: Behind the scenes.* New York: Simon and Schuster.

Lee, J. D. (Ed.). (1993). *Life and story: Autobiographies for a narrative psychology.* Westport, CT: Praeger.

Le Guin, U. K. (1980). It was a dark and stormy night; or, why are we huddling about the campfire? *Critical Inquiry, 7*(1), 191–199.

Le Guin, U. K. (1989). *Dancing at the edge of the world: Thoughts on words, women, places.* New York: Grove Press.

Levi, P. (1985). *If not now, when?* New York: Penguin Putnam.

Levi-Strauss, C. (1958). *Structural anthropology.* New York: Doubleday Anchor Books.

Lieblich, A., & Josselson, R. (Eds.). (1997). *The narrative study of lives.* Thousand Oaks, CA: Sage Publications.

Lieblich, A., McAdams, D. P., & Josselson, R. (2004). *Healing plots: The narrative basis of psychotherapy.* Washington, DC: APA Books.

Lindzey, G., & Aronson, E. (Eds.). (1968). *The handbook of social psychology* (Vol. 3). Reading, MA: Addison-Wesley.

Lodge, D. (1975). *Changing places: A tale of two campuses.* London: Secker and Warburg.

Lodge, D. (1984). *Small world: An academic romance.* London: Secker and Warburg.

Lodge, D. (1988). *Nice work.* London: Secker and Warburg.

Loseke, D. (1992). *The battered woman and shelters: The social construction of wife abuse.* Albany: State University of New York Press.

Lyotard, J-F. (1984). *The postmodern condition: A report on knowledge.* (G. Bennington & B. Massumi, Trans.). Minneapolis: University of Minnesota Press.

MacColl, E. (1957). [Songwriter]. The first time I ever saw your face. [Musician] Leona Lewis. Atlantic Records.

MacIntyre, A. (1984). *After virtue: A study in moral theory.* Notre Dame, IN: University of Notre Dame Press.

Maines, D. (1993). Narrative's moment and sociology's phenomena: Toward a narrative sociology. *The Sociological Quarterly, 34*(1), 17–38.

Mairs, N. (2008). Trying truth. In D. Lazar (Ed.), *Truth in nonfiction: Essays* (pp. 89–92). Iowa City: University of Iowa Press.

Manis, M. (1976). Is social psychology really different? *Personality and Social Psychology Bulletin, 2,* 428–437.

Mannheim, K. (1958). *Systematic sociology: An introduction to the study of society.* (I. Ercos & W. Stewart, Eds.). New York: Philosophical Library.

Marlowe, D., & Gergen, K. (1968). Personality and social interaction. In G. Lindsey & E. Aronson (Eds.), *The handbook of social psychology* (Vol. 3). Reading, MA: Addison-Wesley.

Martin, D. (2009, July 17). Walter Cronkite, 92, dies: Trusted voice of TV news. *New York Times,* p. A1. www.nytimes.com/2009/07/18/us/18cronkite.html?pagewanted=all&_r=0.

Maslow, A. (1962). *Toward a psychology of being.* New York: Van Nostrand.

Maslow, A. (1968). *Toward a psychology of being* (2nd ed.). New York: Van Nostrand.

Masur, L. (2009). *Runaway dream:* Born to run *and Bruce Springsteen's American vision.* New York: Bloomsbury Press.

May, R. (1953). *Man's search for himself.* New York: Norton.

May, R. (Ed.). (1961). *Existential psychology.* New York: Random House.

May, R. (1967). *Psychology and the human dilemma.* New York: W. W. Norton.

May, R. (1969). *Love and will.* New York: W. W. Norton.

McAdams, D. P. (1993). *The stories we live by: Personal myths and the making of the self.* New York: Guilford Press.

McAdams, D. P. (1997). The case for unity in the (post)modern self: A modest proposal. In R. Ashmore & L. Jussim (Eds.), *Self and identity: Fundamental issues* (pp. 46–78). New York: Oxford University Press.

McCroskey, J. C., Larson, C. E., & Knapp, M. L. (1971). *An introduction to interpersonal communication.* Englewood Cliffs, NJ: Prentice Hall.

McGinnies, E. (1949). Emotionality and perceptual defense. *Psychological Review, 56,* 244–251.

McGuire, W. J. (1967). Some impending reorientations in social psychology. *Journal of Experimental Social Psychology, 3,* 124–139.

McGuire, W. J. (1973). The yin and yang of progress in social psychology: Seven koan. *Journal of Personality and Social Psychology, 26,* 446–456.

McLean, D. (1971). American pie. On *American pie* [Vinyl]. Los Angeles, CA: Liberty/United Records.

Mead, G. H. (1934). *Mind, self and society from the standpoint of a social behaviorist.* (C. W. Morris, Ed.). Chicago: University of Chicago Press.

Mead, M. (1928). *Coming of age in Samoa: A psychological study of primitive youth for Western civilization.* New York: William Morrow.

Mead, M. (1935). *Sex and temperament: In three primitive societies.* New York: William Morrow.

Mead, M. (1949). *Male and female: A study of the sexes in a changing world.* New York: William Morrow.

Milgram, S. (1963). Behavioral study of obedience. *Journal of Abnormal and Social Psychology, 67,*137–143.

Milgram, S. (1965). Some conditions of obedience and disobedience to authority. *Human Relations, 18,* 57–76.

Milgram, S. (1974). *Obedience to authority.* London: Tavistock.

Miller, A. (1983). *For your own good: Hidden cruelty in child-rearing and the roots of violence.* New York: Farrar, Straus, Giroux.

Miller, G. (1983). Taking stock of a discipline. *Journal of Communication, 33*(3), 31–41.

Miller, J. G. (1978). *Living systems.* New York: McGraw-Hill.

Miller, N. (2008). The ethics of betrayal: Diary of a conundrum. In D. Lazar (Ed.), *Truth in nonfiction: Essays* (pp. 42–58). Iowa City: University of Iowa Press.

Mischel, T. (1969). Scientific and philosophical psychology: A historical introduction. In T. Mischel (Ed.), *Human action: Conceptual and empirical issues* (pp. 1–40). New York: Academic Press.

Moll, L. C. (Ed.). (1992). *Vygotsky and education: Instructional implications and applications of sociohistorical psychology.* New York: Cambridge University Press.

Morrison, J. (1971). *The lords and the new creatures.* New York: Simon and Schuster.

Morse, S., & Gergen, K. (1970). Social comparison, self-consistency, and the presentation of self. *Journal of Personality and Social Psychology, 16,* 148–156.

Myerhoff, B. (1978). *Number our days: A triumph of continuity and culture among Jewish old people in an urban ghetto.* New York: Simon and Schuster.

Nagel, E. (1961). *The structure of science: Problems in the logic of scientific explanation.* New York: Harcourt, Brace and World.

Naisbitt, J. (1984). *Megatrends: Ten new directions transforming our lives.* New York: Warner Books.

Neisser, U. (1994). Self-narratives: True and false. In U. Neisser & R. Fivush (Eds.), *The remembering self: Construction and accuracy in the self-narrative* (pp. 1–18). Cambridge: Cambridge University Press.

O' Brien, T. (1990). *The things they carried.* New York: Houghton Mifflin.

O' Keefe, D. J. (1975). Logical empiricism and the study of human communication. *Speech Monographs, 42,* 169–183.

Pader, E. (2006). Seeing with an ethnographic sensibility: Explorations beneath the surface of public policies. In D. Yanow & P. Schwartz-Shea (Eds.), *Interpretation and method: Empirical research methods and the interpretive turn* (pp. 161–175). Armonk, NY: M. E. Sharpe.

Paine, R. (1969). In search of friendship: An exploratory analysis in middle-class culture. *Man, 4*(4), 505–524.

Parry, A., & Doan, R. E. (1994). *Story re-visions: Narrative therapy in the postmodern world.* New York: Guilford Press.

Pearce, W. B. (1976). The coordinated management of meaning: A rules based theory of interpersonal communication. In G. R. Miller (Ed.), *Explorations in interpersonal communication* (pp. 17–36). Beverly Hills, CA: Sage Publications.

Pearce, W. B., & Cronen, V. (1980). *Communication, action, and meaning: The creation of social realities.* New York: Praeger.

Pelias, R. (2004). *A methodology of the heart: Evoking academic and daily life.* Walnut Creek, CA: AltaMira.

Perret, G. (2001). *Jack: A life like no other.* New York: Random House.

Peters, T. (2010). *The circle of innovation.* New York: Random House.

Phillips, A. (1994). *On flirtation.* Cambridge, MA: Harvard University Press.

Polkinghorne, D. (1988). *Narrative knowing and the human sciences.* Albany: State University of New York Press.

Pompa, L. (1975). *Vico: A study of the new science.* Cambridge: Cambridge University Press.

Popkin, J. (2001). Coordinated lives: Between autobiography and scholarship. *Biography, 24*(4), 781–805.

Popper, K. R. (1972). *The logic of scientific discovery* (3rd ed.). London: Hutchinson.

Rabinow, P., & Sullivan, W. (1979). *Interpretive social science: A second look.* Berkeley: University of California Press.

Radcliffe-Brown, A. R. (1952). *Structure and function in primitive society.* London: Cohen and West.

Radcliffe-Brown, A. R. (1957). *A natural science of society.* New York: Free Press.

Rank, O. (1945). *Will therapy and truth and reality.* New York: Alfred Knopf.

Rank, O. (1958). *Beyond psychology.* New York: Dover Publications.

Rawlins, W. (1983a). Negotiating close friendship: The dialectic of conjunctive freedoms. *Human Communication Research, 9,* 255–266.

Rawlins, W. (1983b). Openness as problematic in ongoing friendships: Two conversational dilemmas. *Communication Monographs, 50,* 1–13.

Reich, C. (1970). *The greening of America.* New York: Bantam/Random House.

Richardson, L. (1990). Narrative and sociology. *Journal of Contemporary Ethnography, 19*(1), 116–135.

Richardson, L. (1994). Writing as a method of inquiry. In N. Denzin & Y. Lincoln (Eds.), *The handbook of qualitative research* (pp. 516–529). Thousand Oaks, CA: Sage Publications.

Richardson, L. (1997). *Fields of play: Constructing an academic life.* New Brunswick, NJ: Rutgers University Press.

Ricoeur, P. (1971). The model of the text: Meaningful action considered as a text. *Social Research, 38*(3), 529–562.

Ricoeur, P. (1980). Narrative time. *Critical Inquiry, 7*(1), 169–190.

Ricoeur, P. (1984–1988). *Time and narrative* (Vols. 1–3). (K. McLaughlin & D. Pellauer, Trans.). Chicago: University of Chicago Press.

Ricoeur, P. (2004). *Memory, history, forgetting.* (K. Blamey & D. Pellauer, Trans.). Chicago: University of Chicago Press.

Rieff, P. (1966). *The triumph of the therapeutic: Uses of faith after Freud.* Chicago: University of Chicago Press.

Riesman, D. (1950). *The lonely crowd: A study of the changing American character.* New Haven, CT: Yale University Press.

Ring, K. (1967). Experimental social psychology: Some sobering questions about some frivolous values. *Journal of Experimental Social Psychology, 3,* 113–123.

Rogers, C. R. (1961). *On becoming a person: A therapist's view of psychotherapy.* Boston: Houghton Mifflin.

Rommetveit, R. (1980). On meanings of acts and what is meant and made known by what is said in a pluralistic social world. In M. Brenner (Ed.), *The structure of action* (pp. 108–149). Oxford: Blackwell.

Rorty, R. (1979). *Philosophy and the mirror of nature.* Princeton, NJ: Princeton University Press.

Rorty, R. (1982a). *Consequences of pragmatism (Essays: 1972–1980).* Minneapolis: University of Minnesota Press.

Rorty, R. (1982b). Method, social science, and social hope. In *Consequences of pragmatism: Essays 1972–1980* (pp. 191–210). Minneapolis: University of Minnesota Press.

Rorty, R. (1985). Solidarity or objectivity. In J. Raijchman and C. West (Eds.), *Post-Analytic Philosophy* (pp. 3–19). New York: Columbia University Press.

Rorty, R. (1989). *Contingency, irony, and solidarity.* Cambridge: Cambridge University Press.

Rorty, R. (1991). *Essays on Heidegger and others: Philosophical papers* (Vol. 2). Cambridge: Cambridge University Press.

Rose, A. M. (1962). *Human behavior and social processes: An interactionist approach*. Boston: Houghton-Mifflin.

Rose, D. (1990). *Living the ethnographic life*. Thousand Oaks, CA: Sage Publications.

Rose, D. (1993). Ethnography as a form of life: The written word and the work of the world. In P. Benson (Ed.), *Anthropology and literature* (pp. 192–224). Urbana: University of Illinois Press.

Rosenthal, R., & Jacobson, L. (1968). Pygmalion in the classroom. *The Urban Review, 3*(1), 16–20.

Rosenwald G., & Ochberg, R. (Eds.). (1992). *Storied lives: The cultural politics of self-understanding*. New Haven, CT: Yale University Press.

Rosnow, R. L. (1978). The prophetic vision of Giambattista Vico: Implications for the state of social psychological theory. *Journal of Personality and Social Psychology, 36*, 1322–1331.

Roszak, T. (1968). Youth and the great refusal. *The Nation*.

Roszak, T. (1969). *The making of a counterculture: Reflections on a technocratic society and its youthful opposition*. New York: Doubleday.

Rough, B. (2007). Writing lost stories: When bones are all we have. *Iron Horse Literary Review, 8.2*, 64–72).

Rummel, R. J. (1967). Understanding factor analysis. *Journal of Conflict Analysis, 11*(4), 444–480.

Russell, B., & Whitehead, A. (1909). *Principia mathematica*. Cambridge: Cambridge University Press.

Sacks, O. (1987). *The man who mistook his wife for a hat and other clinical tales*. New York: Harper and Row.

Sacks, O. (2008). Gowers' memory. In D. Lazar (Ed.), *Truth in nonfiction: Essays* (pp. 59–65). Iowa City: University of Iowa Press.

Sampson, E. (1975). Psychology and the American ideal. *Journal of Personality and Social Psychology, 35*, 767–782.

Sampson, E. (1978). Scientific paradigms and social values: Wanted—A scientific revolution. *Journal of Personality and Social Psychology, 36*, 1332–1343.

Sarbin, T. (Ed.). (1986). *Narrative psychology: The storied nature of human conduct*. New York: Praeger.

Sartre, J. P. (1958). *No exit*. (S. Gilbert, Trans.). New York: Samuel French.

Schacter, D. (1996). *Searching for memory: The brain, the mind, and the past*. New York: Basic Books.

Schafer, R. (1981a). Narration in the psychoanalytic dialogue. In W. Mitchell (Ed.), *On narrative* (p. 31). Chicago: University of Chicago Press.

Schafer, R. (1981b). *Narrative actions in psychoanalysis*. Worcester, MA: Clark University Press.

Schafer, R. (1994). *Retelling a life: Narration and dialogue in psychoanalysis*. New York: Basic Books.

Schlenker, B. R. (1974). Social psychology and science. *Journal of Personality and Social Psychology, 29*, 1–15.

Schlenker, B. R. (1976). Social psychology and science: Another look. *Personality and Social Psychology Bulletin, 2*, 384–390.

Schuck, R. I., & Schuck, R. (Eds.). (2012). *Do you believe in rock and roll? Essays on Don McLean's "American Pie."* Jefferson, NC: McFarland and Company.

Schulman, B. (2001). *The seventies: The great shift in American culture, society, and politics*. Cambridge, MA: Da Capo Press.

Schutz, A. (1967). *The phenomenology of the social world*. Evanston, IL: Northwestern University Press.

Schutz, A. (1970). Some structures of the life-world. In *Collected papers III* (pp. 116–132). The Hague, Netherlands: Springer.

Scott, Sir W. (1819). *Ivanhoe*. London: Constable and Co.

Sexton, A. (1962). *All my pretty ones*. Boston: Houghton Mifflin.

Shannon, C. E., & Weaver, W. (1963). *The mathematical theory of communication*. Champaign: University of Illinois Press.

Shields, D. (2008). Reality, persona. In D. Lazar (Ed.), *Truth in nonfiction: Essays* (pp. 77–88). Iowa City: University of Iowa Press.

Shields, D. (2010). *Reality hunger: A manifesto*. New York: Vintage Books.

Shostrom, E. L. (1968). *Man, the manipulator*. Nashville, TN: Abingdon Press.

Shotter, J. (1975). *Images of man in psychological research*. London: Methuen.

Simon, P. (1968). America [Recorded by Simon and Garfunkel]. On *Bookends*. New York: Columbia Records.

Skinner, B. F. (1953). *Science and human behavior*. New York: Macmillan.

Slater, P. (1970). *The pursuit of loneliness: American culture at the breaking point*. Boston: Beacon.

Sluzki, C. E., & Ransom, D. C. (Eds.). (1977). *The double bind: The foundation of the communicational approach to the family*. New York: Grune and Stratton.

Smith, M. B. (1972). Is experimental social psychology advancing? *Journal of Experimental Social Psychology, 8*, 86–96.

Snow, C. P. (1959). *The two cultures and the scientific revolution*. New York: Cambridge University Press.

Spence, D. (1982). *Narrative truth and historical truth: Meaning and interpretation in psychoanalysis*. New York: W. W. Norton.

Springsteen, B. (1975). *Born to run* [CD]. New York: Columbia Records.

Stein, G. (1946). *Picasso*. New York: Dover Publications.

Stewart, J. (1972). An interpersonal approach to the basic course. *Speech Teacher, 21*, 7–14.

Szasz, T. (1960). The myth of mental illness. *American Psychologist, 15*, 113–118.

Szasz, T. (1961). *The myth of mental illness: Foundations of a theory of personal conduct*. New York: Harper and Row.

Tajfel, H. (1972). Experiments in a vacuum. In J. Israel & H. Tajfel (Eds.), *The context of social psychology* (pp. 69–121). London: Academic Press.

Taylor, C. (1977). Interpretation and the sciences of man. *The Review of Metaphysics, 25*(1), 3–51.

Taylor, C. (1989). *Sources of the self: The making of modern identity*. New York: Cambridge University Press.

Thibaut, J. W., & Kelley, H. H. (1959). *The social psychology of groups*. New York: Wiley.

Tillich, P. (1952). *The courage to be*. New Haven, CT: Yale University Press.

Tilly, C. (1993). Blanding in. *Sociological Forum, 8*(3), 497–504.

Toffler, A. (1970). *Future shock*. New York: Bantam Books.

Toffler, A. (1984). *The third wave*. New York: Bantam Books.

Tompkins, J. (1989). Me and my shadow. In L. Kauffman (Ed.), *Gender and theory: Dialogues on feminist criticism* (pp. 121–139). Cambridge, MA: Blackwell.

Tompkins, J. (1992). *West of everything: The inner life of westerns*. New York: Oxford University Press.

Tompkins, J. (1996). *A life in school: What the teacher learned*. Reading, MA: Addison-Wesley.

Toulmin, S. (1969). *Concepts and the explanation of human behavior*. New York: Academic Press.

Toulmin, S. (1981). The charm of the scout. In C. Wilder-Mott & J. Weakland (Eds.), *Rigor and imagination: Essays from the legacy of Gregory Bateson* (pp. 357–368). Palo Alto, CA: Praeger.

Turner, C. H. (1970). *Radical man*. Rochester, VT: Schenkman.

Turner, V., & Bruner, E. (1986). *The anthropology of experience*. Urbana: University of Illinois Press.

Turner, V., & Schechner, R. (1988). *The anthropology of performance*. New York: Paj Publications.

Van Maanen, J. (1988). *Tales of the field: On writing ethnography*. Chicago: University of Chicago Press.

Waldron, L. (2012). *Watergate:The hidden history: Nixon, the Mafia, and the CIA*. Berkeley, CA: Counterpoint Press.

Waters, R. (1973a). Brain damage [Recorded by Pink Floyd]. On *Dark side of the moon* [Vinyl]. London: Harvest, Capitol.

Waters, R. (1973b). Eclipse [Recorded by Pink Floyd]. On *Dark side of the moon* [Vinyl]. London: Harvest, Capitol.

Watson, J. B. (1913). Psychology as the behaviorist views it. *Psychological Review, 20*(2), 158–177.

Watts, A. (1996/1973). *Myth and religion: The edited transcripts*. Clarendon, VT: Tuttle Publishing.

Watzlawick, P., & Beavin, J. (1967). Some formal aspects of communication. *American Behavioral Scientist, 10*(8), 4–8.

Weber, M. (1947). *The theory of economic and social organization.* (A. M. Henderson & T. Parsons, Trans.). New York: Free Press.

Weber, M. (1958). The three types of legitimate rule. *Berkeley Publications in Society and Institutions, 4*(1), 1–11.

White, H. (1980). The value of narrativity in the representation of reality. *Critical Inquiry, 7,* 5–27.

White, H. (1981). The value of narrativity in the representation of reality. In W. J. T. Mitchell (Ed.), *On narrative* (pp. 1–23). Chicago: University of Chicago Press.

White, H. (1987). *The content of the form: Narrative discourse and historical representation.* Baltimore, MD: John Hopkins University Press.

White, J. B. (1985). Law as rhetoric, rhetoric as law: The arts of cultural and communal life. *University of Chicago Law Review, 52,* 684–702.

White, M., & Epston, D. (1990). *Narrative means to therapeutic ends.* New York: W. W. Norton.

Wiener, N. (1954). *The human use of human beings: Cybernetics and society.* Boston: Houghton Mifflin.

Wilder, C. (1977). A conversation with Colin Cherry. *Human Communication Research, 3*(4), 354–362.

Wilder, C. (1978). From the interactional view: A conversation with Paul Watzlawick. *Journal of Communication, 28*(4), 35–45.

Wilder, C. (1988). A conversation with Heinz von Foerster. In L. Segal (Ed.), *The dream of reality* (pp. 152–166). New York: W. W. Norton.

Wilder-Mott, C., & Weakland, J. (1981). Rigor and imagination. In C. Wilder-Mott & J. Weakland (Eds.), *Rigor and imagination: Essays from the legacy of Gregory Bateson* (pp. 5–42). Palo Alto, CA: Praeger.

Witherell, C., & Noddings, N. (1991). *Stories lives tell: Narrative and dialogue in education.* New York: Teacher College Press.

Wundt, W. (1954). *Volkerpsychologie.* (C. M. Schneider, Trans.). Stuttgart, Germany: Alfred Kroner Verlag.

Index

About the Author

Arthur P. Bochner is Distinguished University Professor of Communication at the University of South Florida and a Distinguished Scholar of the National Communication Association. He is the co-author of *Understanding Family Communication* (Allyn and Bacon); co-editor (with Carolyn Ellis) of *Composing Ethnography* (AltaMira), *Ethnographically Speaking* (AltaMira), and the Left Coast Press book series, *Writing Lives: Ethnographic Narratives*. He has published more than 100 articles and monographs on close relationships, communication theory, narrative inquiry, autoethnography and genre-bending modes of writing in the human sciences. His current research focuses on memory, narrative, and identity. In 2007, he served as president of the National Communication Association.